ARE SAYING ABOUT *SPEAK UP!*

Easy to read, good fluidity, logical order, relatable examples and anecdotes.

—Sarah Le Clair, Student

I found it highly engaging. I wasn't bored or zoning out because the material kept my attention, unlike other textbooks I've used.

—Dana Schmitz, Student

The tone of the book is easygoing, so it helps me feel reassured about my anxiety that's naturally associated with taking Speech.

—Matthew Pactao, Student

The language you're using makes it really easy to understand, even for me as an international student.

—Anna Sandgren, Student

The images really helped me understand what the text was saying—like a visual summary.

—Olivia Baney, Student

Speak Up

AN ILLUSTRATED GUIDE TO PUBLIC SPEAKING

Douglas M. Fraleigh
California State University–Fresno

Joseph S. Tuman
San Francisco State University

With Illustrations by
Peter Arkle

Bedford / St. Martin's
Boston • New York

For Bedford/St. Martin's

Executive Editor for Communication: Erika Gutierrez
Executive Editor: Simon Glick
Editorial Assistants: Mae Klinger and Jamie Weiss
Production Editor: Ryan Sullivan
Senior Production Supervisor: Nancy Myers
Marketing Manager: Adrienne Petsick
Art Director: Lucy Krikorian
Text Design: Jerilyn Bockorick
Copy Editor: Denise Quirk
Indexer: Kirsten Kite
Cover Art: Peter Arkle
Composition: Nesbitt Graphics, Inc.
Printing and Binding: RR Donnelley and Sons

President: Joan E. Feinberg
Editorial Director: Denise B. Wydra
Director of Development: Erica T. Appel
Director of Marketing: Karen R. Soeltz
Director of Editing, Design, and Production: Marcia Cohen
Assistant Director of Editing, Design, and Production: Elise S. Kaiser
Managing Editor: Shuli Traub

Library of Congress Control Number: 2008929031

Manufactured in the United States of America.

3 2 1 0 9 8
f e d c b a

For information, write: Bedford/St. Martin's, 75 Arlington Street,
Boston, MA 02116 (617-399-4000)

ISBN-10: 0-312-44580-6
ISBN-13: 978-0-312-44580-5

Acknowledgments

Acknowledgments and copyrights appear at the back of the book on page C-1, which constitutes an extension of the copyright page.

We dedicate this work to our families.

Joe

To my children, Helen and Nathaniel, who grew magically during the five years in which this project was realized, and to my wife, Kirsten, for all her love and support.

Doug

To my wife, Nancy, who provided excellent feedback plus contributions from her own public speaking students, and my now grown-up kids, Douglas and Whitney, for patiently sharing many an illustration and idea from this book with me. I look forward to all of your future books and articles.

BRIEF CONTENTS

PREFACE

As longtime teachers of public speaking and as former coaches of forensics, we have spent more than forty combined years teaching students the value and power of speech in their own lives and in the shaping of our democracy and society. When we started writing this new introduction to public speaking, we focused on creating a textbook that would distill the best practices that we have developed in our teaching and simultaneously transmit our passionate commitment to the craft and art of public speaking. Our goal has always been to write the kind of book that would grab the attention of students in our own classrooms and to meet the teaching and learning needs of students, colleagues, and friends across the communication discipline.

EFFECTIVE, MID-SIZED, AND TRADITIONALLY ORGANIZED

We recognize that covering the vast field of public speaking—from classical rhetoric and contemporary communication theory to the specific steps of choosing and researching a topic, preparing an outline, and delivering a speech—can be a tremendous challenge given the time constraints of the classroom. In addition, instructors need teaching materials that are comprehensive yet flexible enough to work with a variety of teaching styles.

With these challenges in mind, our goal with *Speak Up* has been to provide the coverage that most books typically offer while getting rid of the excess and including unique coverage and suggestions that we strongly feel will be useful to students. We have focused on offering accessible writing, lively examples, relatively brief chapters, and a traditional organization that will help instructors use *Speak Up* easily, no matter what book or materials they have used in the past.

In addition, we are proud to offer some specific coverage that will be especially useful to any public speaking student:

- **Basics:** Chapter 1 shows today's students why public speaking is right for them, and offers a brief but compelling tour of the history of public speaking that spans the globe, from antiquity to the present.
- **Ethics:** We offer a clear discussion of ethical codes from ethical absolutism to situational ethics, clarify the distinction between legal and ethical speech, and emphasize the requirements for speaking truthfully.
- **Listening:** Unlike other public speaking texts, we provide useful tips for listening from the speaker's perspective.
- **Audience Analysis:** To help students effectively build an audience-centered message, we provide concrete strategies for identifying prior exposure, seeking common ground, and performing situational audience analysis along with demographic analysis of diversity in terms of age, gender, sexual orientation, race and ethnicity, religious orientation, educational background, and political affiliation.
- **Topic Choice:** Because many students find choosing a topic especially challenging, we offer guidelines to help them develop topics that interest and prove useful to listeners, fit the speakers' own knowledge and interests, and factor in the speech context.
- **Research:** A thorough discussion of the research process includes a deep emphasis on the advantages of library and book research, offers suggestions for using library portals and periodical indexes, and provides helpful coverage of the benefits and dangers of Internet research.
- **Language:** Emphasizing the importance of language to speakers, we provide guidelines for choosing clear and concise words and extensive help for incorporating respectful and unbiased language.
- **Delivery:** An in-depth analysis of nonverbal delivery includes eye contact and panning, gestures, and physical movement.

- **Persuasion:** To help students develop their rhetorical skills, we explain the importance of strategic discourse and offer advice for framing arguments based on audience disposition, a section on organizing persuasive speeches (including Monroe's Motivated Sequence), and a full chapter on methods of persuasion organized around ethos, logos, and pathos.

AN ILLUSTRATED BOOK THAT APPEALS TO TODAY'S STUDENTS

Though we were pleased with the text of *Speak Up* during its development, we soon realized that strong coverage, a manageable size, and accessible or even engaging writing might not be enough to truly excite the majority of today's demanding and time-crunched students. In our experience, most students only read a book—if they read it at all—because it is assigned. In response, we wanted to create a book that would offer not only superior coverage of public speaking concepts and skills, but one that students would actually *look forward* to reading. By meeting these goals, we could simultaneously meet the needs of instructors and create a student learning tool that would support significantly better student outcomes.

When we started thinking about the book's visuals, we wanted to create a program that would be useful and even compelling to students, something more than just image after image and page after page of students and professionals standing at podia. So, in conversation with our publisher, we developed an idea: what if we included illustrations depicting all aspects of the public speaking process, from preparation and research to practice and delivery? As opposed to static photographs, illustrations could show the *workings* of each step in the process, from concepts difficult to represent with photographs (such as the thinking behind developing speech topics or the importance of outlining) to action shots showing motion or the passage of time.

The idea snapped into focus when we met Peter Arkle, an illustrator with extensive experience in commercial and nonprofit work. We were pleased that Peter was as excited about the project as we were, and we were thrilled when Peter's illustrations surpassed even our highest hopes—he went far beyond our rough sketch ideas, diving into the material and using his wit, clever writing, and infallible line to truly bring public speaking concepts to life.

Of course, the real test of a book is its effectiveness as a learning tool, and we have been encouraged by the feedback of the many instructors and students who class-tested the book before publication. We were gratified to learn that instructors have enjoyed teaching from the book and have found their students receptive to it. We are even more pleased to learn from students that they have enjoyed using the book and have truly learned from it.

> "I thought it would be a very dry book with little or no material that would be engaging. [*Speak Up*] had the opposite effect: it was engaging, easy to read throughout, and rather entertaining. . . . I would refer to this book in the future because I feel it could be used in everyday life and not just in speech class."
>
> —Michael Mannina, student

FEATURES

- **Comprehensive, mid-sized, and easy to teach.** *Speak Up* gives practical, accessible guidance for all topics typically taught in the public speaking class, backed by the concepts of classical rhetoric and contemporary communication scholarship. With broad coverage and a traditionally organized table of contents, *Speak Up* is still about 25 percent shorter than traditional texts and is easy to teach no matter what sort of materials you have used in the past.
- **A practical, process-oriented approach to public speaking.** *Speak Up* offers the best coverage of the nuts and bolts that students need to give polished, ethical, and effective speeches. We focus on explaining why each theoretical concept is important and then model how students can transform conceptual understanding into better speaking.
- **600 + illustrations that bring concepts to life.** The illustrations exemplify virtually every key concept in the text and

use a fun, engaging approach that encourages students to read and process the material. Inhabited by a vast cast of characters—from traditional and nontraditional speech students to professionals, athletes, and animals of all shapes and sizes—the illustrations pull students in, helping them engage with the text and serving as powerful study aids for review and retention.

- **12 full-text sample speeches.** *Speak Up* offers students the models they need to study and further develop their own personal style. These addresses, from real-life students and professional speakers, offer examples of informative, persuasive, and special-occasion speeches.
- **Useful study tools.** These help students review and understand the most important concepts in the book. Each chapter includes bolded key terms and concludes with a useful chapter summary and a listing of key terms from that chapter. The back of the book offers a full glossary that defines all key terms.
- **A book that students can afford.** *Speak Up*'s manageable, engagingly written chapters are paired with an affordable price, about 40 percent less than traditional speech texts.

RESOURCES FOR STUDENTS AND INSTRUCTORS

Resources for Students

Companion Web Site at bedfordstmartins.com/speakup

This Web site provides quick access to our extensive student aids for *Speak Up*, such as self-assessment quizzes for each chapter, speech topic lists and topic research links, research tools (including tutorials on evaluating sources and avoiding plagiarism), and much more.

Premium Online Materials

These include access to the Bedford Outliner, a powerful online outlining tool; unique video quizzes that pair video clips with content questions, allowing students to see key concepts in action and testing their ability to identify these concepts; the Relaxation Audio Download;

and much more. Premium access is available to be packaged with each new copy of *Speak Up*. To order the book/access code package, use ISBN-10: 0-312-55574-1; ISBN-13: 978-0-312-55574-0.

Video Theater 3.0 CD-ROM

This CD-ROM offers seven full student speeches—informative, persuasive, special-occasion, and demonstration—with analysis and guidance for each speech, plus twenty professional speech clips. These video examples work not just as models but as powerful teaching tools. To order the book/CD-ROM package, use ISBN-10: 0-312-55569-5; ISBN-13: 978-0-312-55569-6.

Outlining and Organizing Your Speech

Merry Buchanan, *University of Central Oklahoma*; ISBN-10: 0-312-45202-0; ISBN-13: 978-0-312-45202-5

This student workbook provides step-by-step guidance for preparing informative, persuasive, and professional presentations and provides students with the opportunity to practice the critical skills of conducting audience analysis, dealing with communication apprehension, selecting a speech topic and purpose, researching support materials, organizing and outlining, developing introductions and conclusions, enhancing language and delivery, and preparing and using presentation aids.

The Essential Guide to Rhetoric

William M. Keith, *University of Wisconsin–Milwaukee*, and Christian O. Lundberg, *University of North Carolina–Chapel Hill*; ISBN-10: 0-312-47239-0; ISBN-13: 978-0-312-47239-9

A perfect complement to the public speaking course, *The Essential Guide to Rhetoric* offers succinct coverage, concrete examples, and jargon-free language to present the core historical and contemporary rhetorical theories and their practical applications. Part I provides an overview of the ways in which the history of rhetoric has framed big issues: publics, the rhetorical situation, and persuasion, among many. Part II shows how the rhetorical concepts come to life through invention and in thinking through traditions of trope, argument, and speech.

The Essential Guides to Interpersonal and Small Group Communication

Dan O'Hair, *University of Oklahoma*, and Mary O. Wiemann, *Santa Barbara City College*; *Interpersonal Communication* ISBN-10: 0-312-

45195-4; ISBN-13: 978-0-312-45195-0; *Small Group Communication* ISBN-10: 0-312-45194-6; ISBN-13: 978-0-312-45194-3

These brief guides have been designed to give instructors flexibility in designing their basic courses. Each booklet begins with a useful introduction to communication theory and then addresses the essential concepts and skills that students need. They can be used to supplement *Speak Up* in the public speaking course or in combination to create an innovative teaching package for the introduction to communication course.

Media Career Guide: Preparing for Jobs in the 21st Century, Sixth Edition

James Seguin, *Robert Morris University*; ISBN-10: 0-312-46914-4; ISBN-13: 978-0-312-46914-6

Practical and student-friendly, this revised guide includes a comprehensive directory of media jobs, practical tips, and career guidance for students considering a major in communication studies and mass media.

Research and Documentation in the Electronic Age, Fourth Edition

Diana Hacker, *Prince George's Community College*, and Barbara Fister, *Gustavus Adolphus College*; ISBN-10: 0-312-44339-0; ISBN-13: 978-0-312-44339-9

This handy booklet covers everything students need for college research assignments at the library and on the Internet, including advice for finding and evaluating Internet sources.

Resources for Instructors

Instructor's Resource Manual

Steve Vrooman, *Texas Lutheran University*; ISBN-10: 0-312-53601-1; ISBN-13: 978-0-312-53601-5

This comprehensive manual is a valuable resource for new and experienced instructors alike. It offers extensive advice on topics such as setting and achieving student learning goals; managing the classroom; facilitating group discussion; understanding culture and gender considerations; working with ESL students; evaluating speeches (for both instructors and students); and evaluating Internet resources. A special section in Part I gives instructors advice for using an illustrated text in their classrooms. In addition, each chapter of the main text is broken down into detailed outlines, in-class activities and exercises, worksheets, take-home projects, and recommended supplementary resources.

Print and Electronic Test Bank

Steve Vrooman, *Texas Lutheran University*; Print ISBN-10: 0-312-53602-X; ISBN-13: 978-0-312-53602-2; Electronic ISBN-10: 0-312-54208-9; ISBN-13: 978-0-312-54208-5

Speak Up offers a complete testing program, available in print and for Windows and Macintosh environments. Each chapter includes multiple-choice, true/false, and fill-in-the-blank exercises, as well as essay questions.

Instructor's Materials at bedfordstmartins.com/speakup

The companion Web site to *Speak Up* offers rich teaching resources for new and experienced instructors, including a downloadable version of the *Instructor's Resource Manual*, PowerPoint slides for each chapter in the text, speech assignment suggestions, discussion questions for sample speeches, an electronic gradebook for online quizzing, and links to course management software, including WebCT, Blackboard, and Angel.

Microsoft PowerPoint Slides

Each PowerPoint overview—one for each of the nineteen chapters in the text—provides support for the key concepts in each chapter for use in the classroom. All illustrations from the print text are included in these PowerPoint slides. Instructors can customize these slides to fit their own needs. The overviews are available for download from the instructor's section of the book's companion site at www.bedfordstmartins.com/speakup.

ESL Students in the Public Speaking Classroom: A Guide for Teachers

Robbin Crabtree and Robert Weissberg, *New Mexico State University*; ISBN-10: 0-312-45197-0; ISBN-13: 978-0-312-45197-4

As the United States increasingly becomes a nation of non-native speakers, instructors must find new pedagogical tools to aid students for whom English is a second language. This guide specifically addresses the needs of ESL students in the public speaking course and offers instructors valuable advice for helping students deal successfully with the challenges they face.

Video Resources

Professional Speeches

Bedford/St. Martin's is proud to provide a wide range of professional speeches to adopters in DVD and VHS formats, including more than twenty volumes of the esteemed *Great Speeches* series along with other collections of professional speeches such as *Greatest Speeches of All Time*, Volumes 1 and 2; *Great Speeches: Today's Women*; *Kennedy and King: Promises and Dreams*; and many more. For more information, please contact your local publisher's representative.

Student Speeches

Volume 1 ISBN-10: 0-312-19223-1; ISBN-13: 978-0-312-19223-5; Volume 2 ISBN-10: 0-312-25610-8; ISBN-13: 978-0-312-25610-4; Volume 3 ISBN-10: 0-312-39300-8; ISBN-13: 978-0-312-39300-7

Three videotapes of student speeches provide students with attainable models for study, analysis, and inspiration. Included are a variety of speeches that fulfill the most common assignments in public speaking—informative and persuasive speeches—by students of varying ability from Texas Tech and the University of Oklahoma.

The Bedford/St. Martin's Video Library

A wide selection of contemporary and historical videos focuses on public speeches and media-related issues. Qualified instructors are eligible to select videos from the resource library upon adoption of the text.

ACKNOWLEDGMENTS

We would like to provide special thanks to Bedford/St. Martin's President Joan Feinberg and Editorial Director Denise Wydra for convening the first meeting to discuss this project at the 2003 NCA convention and for seeing it through to completion. Executive Editor for Communication Erika Gutierrez joined this project in 2004 and did an outstanding job working with us and sharing ideas for *Speak Up*, while

Director of Development Erica Appel did an excellent job keeping the project on track. Shepherding any textbook from manuscript to production is a daunting task, even more so when working with a brand-new idea that creates new challenges. We appreciate Erika and Erica's enthusiasm and their professionalism, which enabled us to complete the project on time.

We owe a particular debt of gratitude to Executive Editor Simon Glick, who has been with us on this project from conception to completion. Simon served as a well-informed sounding board and a conduit to our artist, fostering an environment where we not only refined our manuscript, but through weekly sessions also created suggestions for literally hundreds of possible illustrations. For once (at least in our experience of writing a textbook), we worked with both the left and right sides of our brains.

It was a pleasure to collaborate with professional artist Peter Arkle on this project. It has been exciting to work on a new concept in higher-education textbook publishing—regular use of illustrations to help teach course concepts. Peter's ability to depict our ideas in pictures was simply amazing.

Bedford/St. Martin's editorial assistants also deserve a huge round of thanks. Jamie Weiss and Mae Klinger both did excellent work handling tasks both massive and mundane while we were working with the art and developing our message.

Designer Jerilyn Bockorick did a wonderful job with the design and layout of our book, consistently using her visual and bookmaking skills to blend illustrations and text and achieve truly inspired results. Art Director Lucy Krikorian's work with the original design of the book was much appreciated, as she played a major role in our efforts to launch an *illustrated* speech text.

Marcia Cohen, Director of Editing, Design, and Production, gave a virtuoso performance running the show in New York and overseeing the skilled professionals who guided the book from manuscript to bound book, while Managing Editor Shuli Traub made sure that all the diverse efforts needed to create this book were completed on time. Project Editor Ryan Sullivan expertly guided the process from manuscript through pages; he got us page proofs with great efficiency and displayed incredible patience as we worked hard to review each chapter. Picking up where Ryan left off, Senior Production Supervisor Nancy Myers put in the hard and careful work needed to turn hundreds of manuscript pages with more than six hundred illustrations into the finished product, as did Sandy Schechter, lining up permissions for the book's many sample speeches and speech excerpts.

Beyond producing the book itself, we have been fortunate to work with a crackerjack marketing team. We look forward to working with Marketing Manager Adrienne Petsick as the book hits campus. We also thank Marketing Assistant Kelly Thompson for a great job managing the class-testing of this book; Richard Cadman, Rachel Falk, and Casey Carroll for helping to conceptualize early versions of the project; Sally Constable for helping develop our marketing and sales message; and Dennis Adams for his brilliant work overseeing Bedford/St. Martin's Humanities Specialists.

We also want to thank Professor Steve Vrooman from Texas Lutheran University for his hard work in developing the *Instructor's Resource Manual* and Test Bank for this book. We were privileged to have such an experienced teacher and author working on our ancillary materials.

We are also grateful to the many reviewers and class-testers who gave us feedback on *Speak Up* and helped us make it even better: Matt Abrahams, *DeAnza College*; Diane Auten, *Allan Hancock College*; Kevin Backstrom, *University of Wisconsin–Oshkosh*; Kathleen Beauchene, *Community College of Rhode Island*; Sandra J. Berkowitz, *University of Maine*; Laurie Brady, *University of Arkansas*; Catherine Brewer, *Diablo Valley College*; Judy Carter, *Amarillo College*; Michelle Coleman, *Clark State Community College*; Deborah Adams Edwards, *DeVry University–Tinley Park Campus*; Karen Erlandson, *Albion College*; Beth Freeburg, *Southern Illinois University–Carbondale*; Chris B. Geyerman, *Georgia Southern University*; Cristina Gilstrap, *Drury University*; Deric M. Greene, *Villa Julie College*; Zachary Hall, *Allan Hancock College*; Kathleen L. Henning, *Gateway Technical College*; Lawrence A. Hosman, *University of Southern Mississippi*; Mary Anne Keefer, *Lord Fairfax Community College–Fauquier Campus*; Rona Leber, *Bossier Parish Community College*; Sandra B. Mongillo, *South Suburban College*; Barry Morris, *Pace University*; Mary Haselrud Opp, *University of North Dakota*; Holly J. Payne, *Western Kentucky University*; B. Hannah Rockwell, *Loyola*

University Chicago; Fritz Scherz, *Morrisville State College–Norwich Campus*; B. Christine Shea, *California Polytechnic State University*; Greggory Simerly, *Middle Tennessee State University*; Judith A. Vogel, *Des Moines Area Community College*; and Steve Vrooman, *Texas Lutheran University*.

We would like to thank our own speech teachers and forensics coaches for their contributions to our development as public speakers and teachers. We thank our faculty colleagues for their support and understanding as we balance teaching, writing, and other academic responsibilities. We are grateful for the many students and forensics team members who have worked with us to develop and present speeches over the past quarter century, and we hope that our book will help a new generation of students gain public speaking skills and confidence.

The authors' friendship began at the 1977 Governor's Cup Speech and Debate tournament in Sacramento, California. This is our third major book project, and it continues to be a privilege and pleasure to write together. Our families have been exceptional at supporting our work and serving as sounding boards for ideas. After many years watching our respective families (Nancy, Douglas, and Whitney for Doug; Kirsten, Helen, and Nate for Joe) grow and mature in the same way our writing has developed, we both appreciate the opportunity to continue to share ideas and write with one another—something we will do long after *Speak Up* is (hopefully) in its tenth edition.

CONTENTS

OK
GET THE BUTTERFLIES
FLYING IN FORMATION

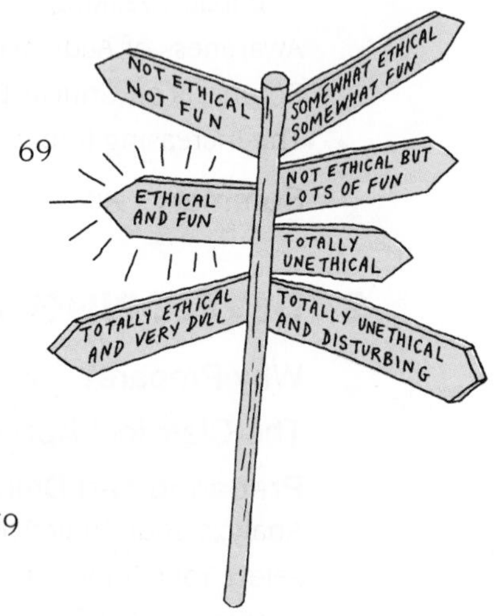
NOT ETHICAL NOT FUN
SOMEWHAT ETHICAL SOMEWHAT FUN
NOT ETHICAL BUT LOTS OF FUN
ETHICAL AND FUN
TOTALLY UNETHICAL
TOTALLY ETHICAL AND VERY DULL
TOTALLY UNETHICAL AND DISTURBING

Oh, I get it now. All I need to do is to LISTEN.
At last!

WORD ASSOCIATION
ANIMAL RIGHTS
FAKE FUR
COUNTERFEIT MONEY
COUNTERFEIT SOFTWARE
IDENTITY THEFT

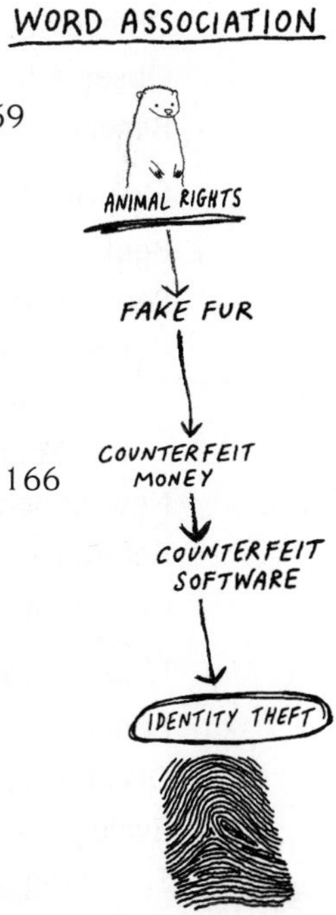

My argument is solidly supported.

The unemployment rate is 4.7%.
Unemployment is down.
STATISTIC
NOT A STATISTIC

MAIN IDEA
SUPPORTING IDEA
SUPPORTING IDEA
SUPPORTING IDEA
SUPPORTING...
SUPPORTING FURNITURE

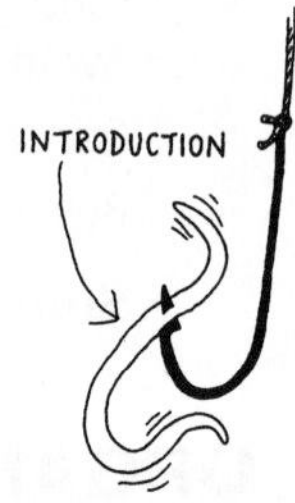
INTRODUCTION

This is an outline of my speech about dog ownership.

LANGUAGE AND DELIVERY

12 LANGUAGE AND STYLE 333

This is the only part that really matters.

Good afternoon, sir. I'm calling today to tell you all about the wonderful benefits you'll receive when you choose to switch...

What a lovely couple. Just look at them...

Speak Up

As I was saying...

1

INTRODUCING PUBLIC SPEAKING

"Public speaking is right for you."

Back when Lance Armstrong was winning the Tour de France year after year, bike-racing fans around the world revered him as a ferocious competitor and an inspiration. All those hours devoted to training. All that strategizing and suffering as he pedaled through perilous mountain stages against hundreds of world-class cyclists hungry to beat him. And all that force of will to ultimately win seven Tours while ignoring relentless accusations that he was using performance-enhancing drugs.

Yet some would argue that Armstrong didn't exert his *biggest* impact until he began writing and speaking on behalf of cancer survivors. Having recovered from cancer himself, Armstrong paired his fame as an athlete with his talents as a public speaker to persuade millions to support his new foundation devoted to caring for people affected by cancer. He wielded so much influence as a public advocator of cancer care that, today, people around the world proudly wear the yellow "Live Strong" wristbands indicating their support of the Lance Armstrong Foundation.

Armstrong's story—and many others like it—help explain why public speaking is a required course in so many colleges and universities. As his story proves, public speaking is a vital skill for anyone seeking to inform, influence, or persuade others. And most professions require abilities in all three areas. For example, as the leader of a team developing a new video game controller, you may have to deliver a presentation to a group of managers updating them on the group's progress. As a leader in a not-for-profit environmental organization, you may need to give a talk during a major fundraising dinner to influence potential donors to open their wallets. As an account manager for a company that offers strategy consulting services, you may be called on to deliver a persuasive presentation on a new methodology to an important potential customer.

Yet many college graduates enter the work world without any experience in public speaking. As Marilyn Mackes, executive director of the National Association of Colleges and Employers, noted: "For more

than ten years, we've asked employers about key skills, and they have consistently named communication skills as critical, yet have also said that this is something many candidates lack."[1] A public speaking course helps you master skills that will enable you not only to advance in your career but also to excel in other courses (especially your major) *and* make valuable contributions in other areas of your life—such as community service and local politics.

Of course, you may find the thought of giving a speech terrifying. If so, you're not alone. A survey by Whitworth and Cochran[2] found that public speaking is Americans' number-one fear, while another researcher noted that many people find it "even scarier than rattlesnakes."[3] But there's good news: you *can* learn to master public speaking—just as most people learn to read, ride a bicycle, or use the Internet. In our fifty-plus years of teaching public speaking, we've seen students gain confidence and lose their fear of public speaking as they acquire experience with it.

This book walks you through the steps you need to follow in order to create and deliver an effective speech—one that gets a favorable response from your listeners. In the chapters that follow, we explain each step in clear terms and show you how to make smart choices at each stage of the speech preparation process. And we supplement these explanations throughout with illustrations that depict key points and major concepts. These images are not only interesting and fun, they also will help you grasp and remember the most important concepts in the book.

But before we jump into the process of preparing and delivering an effective speech, we first take a few moments to explore the field of public speaking itself. In this chapter, we take a closer look at the benefits of studying public speaking. We also survey the rich tradition of public speaking and consider highlights of contemporary trends in the study of public speaking.

WHAT IS PUBLIC SPEAKING?

What is public speaking, exactly? This activity has several characteristics that distinguish it from other types of speech.

YOU ARE A PUBLIC SPEAKER WHEN

Public speaking features communication between a speaker and an audience. In public speaking, the speaker does most of the talking, while the audience primarily listens. However, that does not mean audience members don't respond to what they're hearing. Audience members may smile, frown, or look puzzled. Talented speakers recognize these signals and modify their message if needed—for example, clarifying a point when they notice confused expressions on their listeners' faces. Audience members might even respond with more than just silent facial expressions. For instance, they may applaud the speaker or shout out words of encouragement and appreciation if they're pleased with or excited by the speaker's message. Or they may boo or heckle the speaker if they disagree with or disapprove of the message. However, in public speaking, even the most energetic interjections are usually brief. For the majority of the speech, the speaker "has the floor."

Public speaking is audience centered. In public speaking, the presenter chooses his or her message with the audience's interests and needs in mind. Good speakers consider what topic would be appropriate for their audience on a particular occasion. They also

develop their message in a way that their audience will find interesting and understandable.

For example, suppose you recently got a job as a product developer at a furniture company. You've asked to meet with members of your company's management team to discuss a new line of dorm furniture that you'd like to launch. At the meeting, you want to persuade your listeners to approve funding for a proposed line. In preparing your speech, you think about what members of the management team care about most: the company's profitability, its ability to increase revenues while reducing costs. So, you develop explanations for how the proposed campaign will enhance profitability ("This new line will increase sales 10 percent over the next two quarters while cutting our expenses 5 percent—leading to a 6 percent increase in profitability"). You make sure to avoid sales-style language, such as "This new design is bold and provocative," because you know that such language will hold little interest for your business-oriented listeners.

Public speaking emphasizes the spoken word. Any speaker can supplement his or her speech with pictures, charts, videotapes, handouts, objects, or even a live demonstration. However, public speakers devote most of their time to *speaking* to their audience. The spoken word plays the central role in their delivery, though speakers use gestures, posture, voice intonation, eye contact, other types of body language, and even audiovisual aids to heighten the impact of their words.

Public speaking is usually a prepared presentation. Few public speakers simply walk up to the lectern or podium and make up their talk as they go. The best speakers choose their topic in advance, carefully consider what they might say about that topic, and then select the best ideas for the audience they will be addressing. They organize those ideas, choose their words carefully, and practice delivering the speech before the big day. Even people who suspect that they may be called on to deliver an impromptu speech—for example, at a community-service awards dinner—know how to quickly piece together a few comments as they step to the front of the room.

WHY STUDY PUBLIC SPEAKING?

As you make your way through life—completing degrees, advancing in your career, establishing yourself in a neighborhood or community—you'll encounter many times when you will need to speak in

public. As a student, you may have to deliver an oral report in class. As a parent, you might want to address the school board to express a concern about the programs offered at your local high school. As an employee, you may be called to explain a new product to the sales team. As a citizen, you could decide to speak out in favor of a mayoral candidate or persuade a judge that a parking ticket recently left on your windshield should be voided.

By studying public speaking, you can deliver effective presentations in all these settings: in the classroom, on the job, and in your community. The more skilled you are at public speaking, the more you can participate in the public discourse that shapes every dimension of life—and the more you can influence others to take the actions you believe should be taken. Talented public speakers thus have the power to bring about needed change in the world around them.

Using Public Speaking as a Student

Of course, you'll need to start practicing your public speaking skills to get through this class. But the skills you acquire by working your way through this book will also help you as you complete your degree and participate in additional educational opportunities throughout your life. Those later opportunities may include adult-education workshops, other higher-education degrees, or professional development courses. Instructors in all types of courses often ask students to stand up on the first day of class and introduce themselves as well as explain what they hope to get from the class.

Many instructors also require students to deliver oral presentations on research projects and other coursework. Students with strong public speaking skills can share their findings more effectively than those with a limited background in presenting speeches.

Think about other students you know who have given oral presentations in your classes: most likely, you've noticed that those who give thoughtfully crafted and skillfully delivered presentations make a better impression on the instructor *and* the rest of the class. Equally important, the information they offer is probably more useful to listeners than information delivered by less skilled speakers.

Public speaking skills also enhance your ability to participate in campus activities. If you belong to an organization or a club, team, sorority, or fraternity, you may want to speak out at a group meeting or represent your group before the student senate or other campus organizations. When you present an effective speech to these audiences, you boost your chances of achieving your goal—whether it's persuading your sorority to take up a new social cause or convincing the student senate to fund a job fair in the area of your major on campus.

National Association of Colleges and Employers. *Job Outlook 2006—Student Version* (NACE Research 2005), 5.

Using Public Speaking in Your Career

A knack for public speaking is one of the most important assets you can possess in the workplace. Jean Gatz, a professional speaker and workplace consultant, notes that verbal skills "are essential in every work environment" and that knowing how to listen (another skill taught in public speaking courses) is "equally important."[4] In the National Association of Colleges and Employers 2006 Job Outlook Survey, communication skills were tied with honesty and integrity as the most important quality or skill for job candidates to possess.[5] Employees themselves agree that communication skills are important. In the survey "Making the Grade? What American Workers Think Should Be Done to Improve Education," 87 percent of the 1,014 U.S. adult workers surveyed rated communication skills as very important for performing their jobs.[6]

No matter which career path you choose, you'll almost certainly need public speaking skills. Consider these examples:

- A police officer faces an angry crowd on the verge of violence. The officer talks calmly and rationally to the group, diffusing the tension and preventing a brawl.
- A nurse wants to explain to her hospital's management team why high patient loads and long working hours justify the nurses' union strike threat. By making her case persuasively, she builds support for the union's position, and the two parties forge a contract agreement without a strike.
- An accountant has the opportunity to explain recent changes in tax law to a group of investors. Impressed by the speech's clarity and the accountant's expertise, several audience members decide to become clients.
- An elementary schoolteacher faces a roomful of parents who are skeptical about a new math curriculum, which differs markedly from how they learned math in "the good old days." The teacher clearly and energetically presents research results defending the curriculum, and the parents happily accept the new methods.

Using Public Speaking in Your Community

Beyond work or school, you may wear many different hats in your community. For example, you might be active in service organizations, athletic leagues, clubs, religious groups, or political committees. If you're a parent, you may find yourself taking on leadership roles in your children's schools, sports, clubs, or other activities. You may also decide to get involved in a social cause that you feel passionate about. In each of these endeavors, public speaking skills can help you.

For example, Tammy Duckworth, a veteran wounded in Iraq, returned home from combat and decided to run for Congress. She and ten other post–September 11 veterans ran for the House in 2006. They needed to deliver campaign speeches not only discussing the Iraq war but also explaining their stances on health care, gas prices, and the economy.[7]

To participate in and contribute to your community, at times you will need to speak out. You may actively seek out opportunities to lead, or you may be encouraged to take leadership roles. Or, as a group member, you may simply have a point you want to share. However you decide to get involved in your community, the skills you learn in a public speaking class will help you ensure that others hear and respect your views.

PUBLIC SPEAKING: A GREAT TRADITION

For centuries, people around the world have studied the art and practice of public speaking and used public address to inform, influence, and persuade others.

As far back as the fifth century B.C.E., all adult male citizens in the Greek city-state of Athens had a right to speak out in the assembly and vote on proposals relating to civic matters. Sometimes as many as six thousand citizens attended these meetings.[8] Indeed, the ancient Greeks were the first people to think formally about rhetoric as well as teach it as a subject. A century later, the Greek scholar Aristotle wrote *Rhetoric*, a systematic analysis of the art and practice of public speaking. Many of Aristotle's ideas influence the study of public speaking even today. Later, in first-century B.C.E. Rome, senators vehemently debated the issues of the day. Cicero, a Roman politician, was a renowned orator and a prolific writer on rhetoric, the craft of public speaking. Another noteworthy Roman rhetorician, Quintilian, emphasized the ideal of an ethical orator—the good person speaking well.

Yet the tradition of public speaking was not limited to Greece and Rome. From the time of Confucius in the fifth century B.C.E. until the end of the third century B.C.E., China enjoyed an intellectual climate whose energy rivaled that of ancient Greece.[9] Scholars traveling throughout China passionately advocated a variety of systems of political and economic philosophy. In fifteenth-century western Africa, traveling storytellers recited parables and humorous stories, while in northeastern Africa, Islamic scholars embarked on lecture tours attended by large crowds.[10] On feast days in one African kingdom (near present-day Mali), it was traditional for a bard to dress in a bird's-head mask and deliver a speech encouraging the king to live up to his predecessors' high standards.[11] Native Americans prized oratory, too; indeed, many of them deemed oratorical ability a more important leadership quality than even bravery in battle.[12]

Háu khola
əni tlé
أهلا وسهلا
你好

The tradition of public speaking flourished in colonial America as well. During the Great Awakening of the 1730s and 1740s, preachers sought to revive religious zeal, which had been waning in the colonies. George Whitefield traveled through the colonies and drew large crowds with his dynamic open-air sermons.[13] He preached in fields because churches weren't large enough to accommodate his listeners.[14] Jonathan Edwards's well-known 1741 sermon "Sinners in the Hands of an Angry God" impelled worshippers in Enfield, Massachusetts, to shriek and moan as Edwards described "the God that holds you over the pit of hell, much as one holds a spider."[15] Fervent preaching was not limited to men: more than one hundred evangelical women preached from the time of the Great Awakening to the early nineteenth century.[16]

Of course, the American Revolution presented numerous opportunities to demonstrate the power of oratory. Colonists took to the

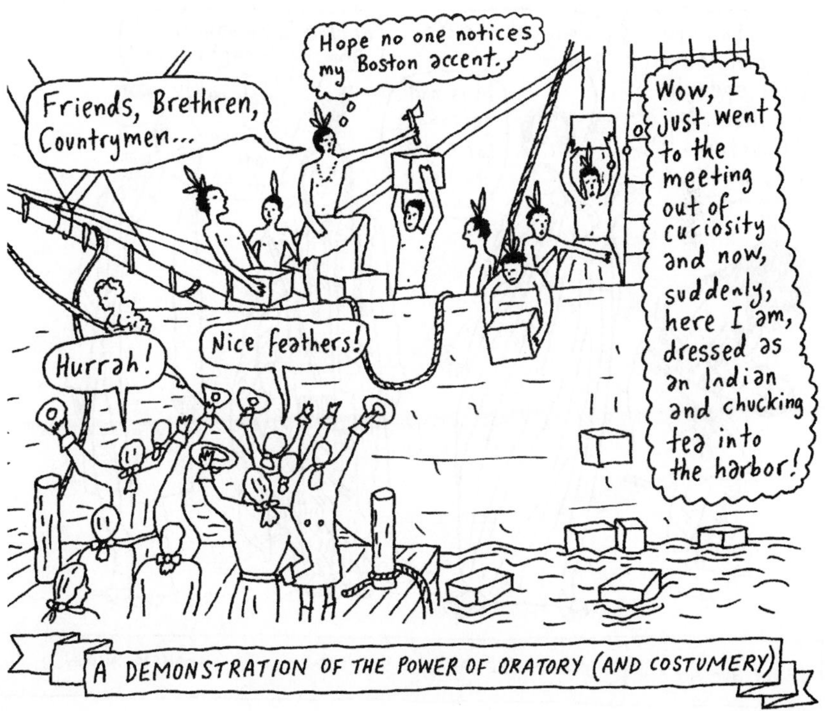

streets to passionately decry new taxes. Then they launched the famous Boston Tea Party, in which they dressed as Mohawk Indians, boarded three ships in Boston Harbor, and hurled the vessels' cargoes of tea overboard.

Later, political leaders in each of the states energetically debated the merits of ratifying the U.S. Constitution and the Bill of Rights. In the nineteenth century, public speaking became a hallmark of American society. Through public address, Americans freely debated political issues, expanded their knowledge, and even entertained one another. Political debates drew particularly large and enthusiastic crowds. Take the debates between Abraham Lincoln and Stephen Douglas, opponents for a U.S. Senate seat from Illinois in 1858. More

than fifteen thousand people gathered to hear the contenders in Freeport, Illinois—a town with just five thousand residents.[17]

The antislavery movement spurred additional use of public speaking to drive major social change. Frederick Douglass, a former slave who moved audiences with his discussion of life under slavery, counted among the most compelling antislavery speakers. Women also actively participated in the American Anti-Slavery Society, holding offices and delivering public lectures. Consider Angelina Grimké—an eloquent orator who won audience members' commitment to the antislavery cause with graphic descriptions of slave abuse she had witnessed while growing up in South Carolina. Other women—such as Elizabeth Cady Stanton, Susan B. Anthony, and Lucy Stone—took leadership roles in the women's suffrage movement that also arose around this time. These able orators used fiery speeches to convince

Americans that women deserved the right to cast a ballot at the polls—a radical notion at the time.[18]

During the twentieth century, public address continued to define the American landscape. After World War I, President Woodrow Wilson traveled through the United States advocating the League of Nations, while Republican leaders rushed to the same tour stops and presented the opposite viewpoint.[19] In 1963, a whopping 250,000 people gathered near the Lincoln Memorial in Washington, D.C., to hear Martin Luther King Jr. deliver his "I Have a Dream" speech,[20] an address that instantly excited the imaginations of people around the world. In a similar vein, the Million Man (Washington, D.C., 1995) and the Million Woman (Philadelphia, 1997) marches culminated in public speeches by activists on the issues closest to their hearts—including job creation, human rights, and respect for African Americans.[21] And in the past few years, tens of thousands of "Promise Keepers" have crowded into football stadiums to hear speakers address issues of family and religion.

Today, people seem to communicate more through e-mail, blogs, videoconferences, BlackBerries, and cell phones than they do through public address. Nevertheless, public speaking still counts among the most potent leadership tools around. After the terrorist attacks of September 11, 2001, for example, U.S. president George Bush didn't merely post a message of condolence and resolve on the White House Web site. Instead, he stood before crowds of New Yorkers, acknowledged their bravery and loss, and vowed to take action. He also addressed a joint session of Congress at the U.S. Capitol—a speech that millions of Americans watched on their TVs or listened to on their radios. Through his address, Bush demonstrated the shared resolve that can arise when members of a democracy connect through public address.

PUBLIC SPEAKING: A DYNAMIC DISCIPLINE

Clearly, public speaking has a long history, and many of the principles taught by ancient scholars such as Aristotle are still relevant today.

However, it's also a dynamic discipline that has evolved to reflect changes in society. In this section, we highlight several of these major changes: new ways of depicting the public speaking process, greater awareness of audiences' cultural diversity, new emphasis on the importance of critical thinking in preparing a speech, and increasing attention to ethics in public address.

From Linear to Transactional: Evolving Views of the Public Speaking Process

At the dawn of the modern communication disciplines, scholars viewed all forms of communication—including public speaking—as a linear process. In their view, a speech was a one-way flow of ideas from speaker to audience. That is, the speaker "injected" listeners

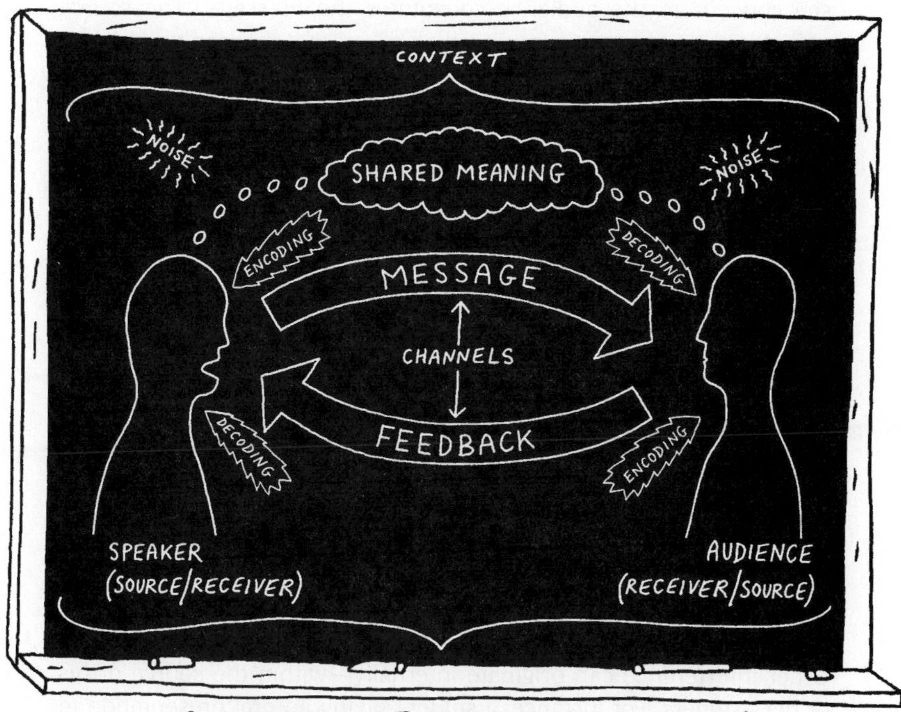

A MODEL OF COMMUNICATION

WE ARE ALL CHANNELS

with his or her ideas, much as a doctor injects a patient with a vaccine or antibiotic.

This linear process involves several key elements. Specifically, a person with an idea to express is the **source**, and the ideas that he or she conveys to the audience constitutes the **message**. The source **encodes** the message, meaning that he or she chooses **verbal** and **nonverbal symbols** to express the ideas. Verbal symbols are the words that the source uses to convey an idea; nonverbal symbols are the means of making a point without the use of words, such as hand gestures, movement, and facial expressions.

The source communicates the encoded message through a **channel**, the medium of delivery. For example, to deliver their message, speakers could simply use their voices to address a small group, rely on a microphone or the broadcast airwaves to give a speech to a huge crowd, or even post a speech online for later viewing from faraway places.

In the linear model, sources communicate their messages to one or more **receivers**, who try to make sense of the messages by **decoding**. To decode, receivers process the source's verbal and nonverbal symbols and form their own perception of the message's meaning.

Noise (also called **interference**) could impede the communication of messages. Some interference comes from external sources. For example, a political candidate delivering a speech to a crowd could be drowned out if a fleet of military jets roared by overhead. Other interference can originate internally—within the source or his or her listeners. For instance, a student giving an oral presentation in

class might have forgotten key elements in her speech when she started thinking about a recent argument with a coworker. Meanwhile, several members of her audience had difficulty focusing on her message because they, too, were distracted by other thoughts.

Scholars today no longer view communication as a one-way transmission of messages from source to receiver. Instead, they consider communication—including public speaking—a **transaction**, an exchange in which all the participants continuously send *and* receive messages.[22] For example, suppose you're about to deliver a speech. As you organize your notes at the lectern, you notice a man in the front row of your audience yawning. In this case, the man is both a receiver of your message and a sender of his own message: "I hope you're not planning to talk for two hours."

Participants in a public speaking transaction can also send and receive messages by providing **feedback**. An audience member who shouts "That's right!" in response to a compelling point in a speech is giving feedback. People listening to a speech can also convey feedback in nonverbal ways. For example, an audience member leans forward to express interest, nods vigorously to show agreement, folds her arms to signal disagreement, or adopts a puzzled look to convey her confusion.

In the transactional model of communication, the participants in a public speaking exchange seek to create **shared meaning**—a common understanding with little confusion and few misinterpretations.[23] Good public speakers don't merely try to get their point of view across to their audience. Instead, they strive to improve their

own knowledge, seek understanding, and develop agreements when they communicate with others.[24]

For example, suppose an audience member nods when the speaker says, "Our nation faces an identity theft crisis." The speaker must assume the role of *receiver* and decode the message behind that nod. The nod may mean "I agree," or it could mean "Well, duh, we all know that. Move on!" To better decode the message, a speaker may look for additional cues, such as signs of understanding or boredom on the faces of other audience members. Suppose the speaker determines that the nod conveyed agreement that identity theft is a serious problem. He or she might respond by saying, "Since we agree that identity theft has reached epidemic proportions, let's take a look at how we can prevent it." This speaker and his or her audience have created shared meaning.

Awareness of Audiences' Cultural Diversity

Most effective and ethical public speakers today take into account the cultural backgrounds of their listeners. By **culture**, we mean the values, traditions, and rules for living that are passed from generation to generation.[25] Culture is learned, and it influences all aspects of a person's life, including religious practices, use of language, food choices, dress, and ways of communicating with others.

In the United States, public speakers have increasingly needed to consider the range of cultures represented by their audience members as American society has grown more culturally diverse. In the words of Arnoldo Ramos, who was born in Costa Rica and now is executive director of the Council of Latino Agencies, the United States is a nation where everyone comes from somewhere else.[26] In 2001, as much as 19 percent of all children in the United States were living with at least one foreign-born parent.[27] And increasingly, the birthplace of U.S. residents born abroad is a nation in Asia or Latin America, such as Mexico, the Philippines, China, or India.[28] This trend is exemplified by a list of the most common surnames of home buyers: Rodriguez, Garcia, and Hernandez have joined Smith and Johnson in the top ten, and Nguyen is number fourteen.[29]

Communication scholars have recognized the importance of understanding and relating to persons from diverse cultures. Myron Lustig and Jolene Koester note that it is no longer likely that your clients, customers, coworkers, or neighbors have the same values,

customs, or first language as you do. Your career success and personal satisfaction will increasingly depend on how well you can communicate with persons from other cultures.[30]

The most effective public speakers are sensitive to their audience members' cultural backgrounds. For example, they avoid biased language and ethnic jokes. They also adapt their delivery to acknowledge their awareness of different cultural norms regarding communication. For example, audience members from one particular culture might interpret extensive eye contact as rude or disrespectful, while individuals from another culture might welcome it. Savvy speakers take pains to identify the cultural norms of their audience and customize their presentation accordingly.

An audience member's culture not only influences how he or she perceives a speaker's behavior; it also affects the person's **worldview**—the "lens" through which he or she sees and interprets

CONFLICTING WORLDVIEW PROBLEM #2

reality. And worldview in turn influences how listeners respond to a speaker's message. For example, suppose your audience members' culture maintains a worldview that says, "It's not polite to challenge a speaker's claims." In this case, your listeners may decline to ask questions during or after your speech, since (to their thinking) asking questions may come across as challenging and therefore disrespectful to you. But without questions, you don't have the feedback you need to assess whether your listeners have understood you.

Listeners' worldviews can also affect how they respond to a speaker's words during a presentation. For instance, the debate over United States immigration policy in 2006 aptly revealed how a person's worldview can influence his or her interpretation of—and therefore response to—a speaker's message. In 2006, the U.S. House of Representatives passed a bill intended to make illegal residence and assisting such efforts felony offenses, and to provide stiff fines for employers who hired illegal immigrants.[31] The Senate Judiciary Committee countered with a proposal to bolster security at the U.S./Mexico border, create a "guest worker" program for immigrants, and allow immigrants already in the United States to pay a fine and earn eventual citizenship.[32]

Americans were deeply divided over which policy was better, owing to their vastly different worldviews on who should be entitled to work and to obtain citizenship in the United States. To some people, the fact that immigrants were in the United States illegally was all the justification needed for stiffer criminal penalties and a denial of the opportunity to earn citizenship. As one proponent of that viewpoint stated, "Giving amnesty to illegal aliens would be similar to catching a man driving a stolen car and then allowing him to keep the car and providing him with a lifetime supply of gas."[33] To other people, immigrants' work ethic and family values warranted a less restrictive approach. An advocate of this viewpoint stated, "They work, they pay taxes, they live here, they get married and have children here, they shop here, and they worship in local churches and are an asset to local economies."[34]

Where do you stand on the immigration policy debate? It depends on your worldview. More important, where does your *audience* stand on the topic that you're discussing in your speech? By understanding your listeners' worldviews, you can more easily gauge their likely reaction to your speech—and craft an appropriate and effective message.

Emphasis on Critical Thinking

In addition to encouraging greater attention to cultural awareness, scholars of public speaking have begun emphasizing the importance of critical thinking skills for speakers who are preparing presentations. Through **critical thinking**, you decide "what to believe and how to act after a careful evaluation of the evidence and reasoning in a communication."[35] You also analyze your own assumptions, and the ideas of others, examining the reliability, truth, and accuracy of ideas before making a judgment about an issue or question.[36]

Before you present ideas to an audience, you should feel confident that those ideas are reasonable. Rather than assuming that your beliefs are true, suspend judgment and consider other perspectives. For example, suppose you drive a car to campus and often have trouble finding a parking spot. You decide to propose a solution to the campus authorities: demolish an old building on campus and replace it with a parking structure. Historical preservation advocates, environmentalists, and campus parking officials may well have alternative viewpoints. To use your critical thinking skills in preparing to present your proposal, you would carefully consider the perspective of each of these groups, and then modify your opinions if other ideas made sense.

In exercising your critical thinking skills, you would also evaluate the probable truth of a claim you're making. Anybody can make a claim, but not all claims are based on careful analysis. For example, let's say you're researching the environmental impact of building a

THIS IS CRITICAL THINKING

* CONSIDER DIVERSE PERSPECTIVES (SOME PEOPLE ENJOY MARCHING)
* RESEARCH (LOOK FOR SURPRISES)
* EVALUATE EACH POSSIBILITY (DON'T JUST OBSESS ABOUT HAVING TO CUT YOUR HAIR)
* KEEP AN OPEN MIND (THE MORE IDEAS YOU LET IN, THE STRONGER YOUR OWN IDEAS WILL BE WHEN THEY COME OUT)

new parking garage on campus. In this case, the views of a scientist who has studied the issue are more likely to be accurate than are unsupported opinions presented by an ill-informed person in an angry letter to the editor of the local newspaper.

The Increasing Importance of Ethics

Ethics, a set of beliefs shared by a group about what behaviors are correct or incorrect, are not a new consideration in public speaking. In the first century C.E., the Roman rhetorician Quintilian argued that parents and teachers should strive to produce "the good person speaking well." That is, communicators should be virtuous, moral, and public spirited, in addition to being effective orators.[37] Today, as unethical communication has increased in the United States, people have stepped up their demands for ethical public speaking. Americans are tired of politicians, lawyers, and multimillionaire chief executive officers who have lied

blatantly to the public. And they have had their fill of journalists who have fabricated news stories in the hopes of winning awards. According to one-third of adults responding to a 2005 Gallup Poll, people don't even consider doctors and members of the clergy as having high credibility.[38]

Consequently, ethics have begun playing an increasingly prominent role in the study of communication, to say nothing of other disciplines as well. As it turns out, there's far more to public speaking than just presenting your message in a way that induces your audience to agree with you and to take the actions you have advocated. You must also treat your listeners ethically. That means telling the truth, helping your audience make a well-informed decision about your topic, avoiding manipulative reasoning, and incorporating research materials properly in your speech. We say more about ethical public speaking in Chapter 3.

SUMMARY

"Public speaking is right for you."

In this chapter, we introduced the field of public speaking. Key elements of public speaking are communication between speaker and audience, a focus on the audience by the speaker, an emphasis on the spoken word, and a prepared presentation. We also examined the benefits of mastering public speaking—on the job, in the classroom, and in your community.

Next, we turned to the rich tradition of public speaking, citing examples from across time (including antiquity) and from around the world (such as ancient Greece and Rome, China, Africa, and the United States).

We also examined the ways in which public speaking has evolved as a discipline to reflect changes in society. We provided examples of several contemporary developments in the field: new ways of viewing the public speaking process, an emphasis on understanding your audience's cultural background, the usefulness of critical thinking when you're planning your speech, and the increased attention to ethics in public speaking.

Key Terms

PUBLIC SPEAKING: A DYNAMIC DISCIPLINE

source
message
encode
verbal symbols
nonverbal symbols
channel
receivers
decode
noise (interference)
transaction
feedback
shared meaning
culture
worldview
critical thinking
ethics

2

DEVELOPING YOUR FIRST SPEECH

"Preparation and perseverance are the keys to a successful speech."

On August 28, 1963, tens of thousands of Americans traveled huge distances to join the March on Washington for Jobs and Freedom. Gathering at the Lincoln Memorial, they sang civil rights songs and hymns and listened to speeches advocating support of civil rights.[1] After nearly three hours, the final orator stood at the lectern, with the Lincoln Memorial in the background, and addressed an audience that had expanded to about 250,000 people.[2]

The speaker, Martin Luther King Jr., told the audience "I have a dream . . . a dream big enough to include all Americans."[3] The dream that King shared—one in which people would "not be judged by the color of their skin but by the content of their character"—had his listeners cheering and weeping with emotion as he concluded his address. Covered by major television networks and newspapers, the speech captured the imaginations of people around the world. And in the aftermath of the March on Washington, Congress passed civil rights legislation that banned discrimination in public facilities, in laws or practices pertaining to voting rights, and by employers.

King's "I Have a Dream" speech has won renown among speech scholars as the greatest oral presentation of the twentieth century. A gifted public speaker, King won his first oratorical contest at the age of only fifteen.[4] Yet he still diligently prepared for the March on Washington speech, putting more care into it than any of his previous public addresses.[5] Indeed, he typically invested much time in speech preparation, writing multiple drafts of his Nobel Peace Prize acceptance speech and spending as many as fifteen hours preparing a typical Sunday sermon.[6]

The careful attention that King gave to preparing his addresses illustrates an important lesson that can benefit all public speakers, whether they have experience or are new to public speaking: *preparation and perseverance are the keys to a successful speech.* We have found that students who have a well-organized plan for speech preparation, and who devote enough time to following that plan, become more effective speakers than those who rely solely on natural talent and confidence.

In this chapter, we provide a preview of the speech preparation process. We begin by discussing the importance of preparation. Next, we cover the five major issues you should keep in mind while prepar-

YOU ARE NOT PREPARED WHEN...

You waited until the last minute.

You focused on length, not quality.

ing a public address. Finally, we lay out steps you can follow to deliver a successful speech early in the term and offer tips for minimizing speech anxiety. In Chapters 15–19, we offer additional guidance for preparing major speech assignments, including informative or persuasive speeches, talks for special occasions, and group presentations.

WHY PREPARE?

For beginning speakers, preparation is crucial. The more rigorously you prepare your speech, the more likely you'll avoid three common problems that inexperienced public speakers typically encounter:

- *Leaving too little time for planning and practicing.* Students who wait until the last minute to develop their speeches usually deliver weaker addresses than their better-prepared classmates. Why? If you put off your assignment until just before the due date, you can't plan or practice your presentation. And without a plan or sufficient practice, you risk losing track of your thoughts while delivering your speech.
- *Focusing on length rather than quality.* Beginners sometimes focus more on meeting time requirements than on developing their ideas. They write down the first thoughts that come to mind, or simply insert chunks of researched material. They don't consider what information might be most interesting, useful, or convincing to their listeners, nor do they try to organize their ideas in a way that their audience can easily follow. And the result? A disjointed, lackluster presentation.
- *Failing to follow the assignment.* A speech may impress a classroom full of beginning speakers if it's delivered well and includes interesting details.

You did not follow the assignment.

> Yet it will not succeed if it fails to meet your instructor's assignment about matters such as which topics are acceptable, how the speech should be organized, or number of sources required. Make sure to clarify such expectations before preparing your speech.

Fortunately, you don't have to succumb to these challenges. This chapter introduces steps of the speechmaking process that will help you avoid these stumbling blocks and deliver a successful speech.

THE CLASSICAL APPROACH TO SPEECH PREPARATION

The speech preparation process that we outline in this book is based on principles of rhetoric that ancient Greeks conceptualized. Cicero (106–43 B.C.E.), a Roman lawyer and politician who is one of history's most famed orators, elaborated on these concepts. Public speakers have been learning about these ideas for the past 2,400 years.

In his treatise *De inventione*, Cicero maintained that effective speakers attend to five key matters while preparing a speech: invention, arrangement, style, memory, and delivery. These "classical

canons of rhetoric" form the basis of speech preparation to this day. Here, we take a closer look at the canons.

- 
  Invention is the generation of ideas for use in a speech, including the speaker's own thoughts on the topic and ideas from other sources. Speakers generate a large number of ideas for their speeches and then choose those that will best serve their purpose in an ethical manner. Talented speakers select the best ideas for a particular speech based on their analysis of their audience, their choice of topic and purpose, and the research they conduct and evidence they gather.
- 
  Arrangement refers to structuring ideas to convey them effectively to an audience; today, we refer to this as *organization*. Most speeches have three main parts: an introduction, a body, and a conclusion, with the body serving as the core of a speech. Effective speakers arrange the ideas in the speech body based on the goals they hope to accomplish by delivering the speech. For example, in a persuasive speech, the three main points might explain a problem, analyze the cause of the problem, and offer the solution.
- **Style** is the choice of language that will best express a speaker's ideas to the audience. Through effective style, speakers state their ideas clearly, make their ideas memorable, and avoid bias.
- 
  Memory (preparation) is somewhat analogous to practice and refers to the work that speakers do to remain in command of their material when they present a speech.[7] This canon originally emphasized techniques for learning speeches by heart and for creating mental stockpiles of words and phrases that speakers could inject into presentations where appropriate.[8] In contemporary settings, most experienced speakers don't recite speeches by rote

memory; instead, they prepare notes, practice with them, and weave extemporaneous comments into their rehearsed speeches.

- **Delivery** refers to the speaker's use of his or her voice and body during the actual presentation of a speech. A strong delivery—one in which the speaker's voice, gestures, eye contact, and movements are appropriate for the audience and the setting—can make a powerful impression. Chapter 13 covers delivery skills in detail.

The five canons—invention, arrangement, style, memory, and delivery—inform the steps you will follow to prepare and deliver an effective speech.

PREPARING AND DELIVERING YOUR FIRST SPEECH

It's happened: you've just begun this course, and already your instructor has assigned your first speech. The remainder of this chapter offers a quick guide to the steps for preparing and delivering your first assigned speech. By following each of these steps, you should be able to pull together a workable speech and deliver it on the appointed day. If you want to know more about any of these steps, use the following table to find the corresponding chapter where each step is discussed in more detail.

If you want to know more about	Go to
analyzing your audience	Ch. 5
selecting a topic for your speech	Ch. 6, pp. 164–69
determining your speech's purpose	Ch. 6, pp. 169–77
creating a thesis statement	Ch. 6, pp. 178–79
generating supporting materials	Ch. 8

(continued)

If you want to know more about	Go to
selecting main and supporting points	Ch. 9, pp. 252–61
organizing the body of your speech	Ch. 9, pp. 261–70
outlining the body of your speech	Ch. 11
organizing and outlining the introduction and conclusion	Ch. 10
incorporating transitions	Ch. 9, pp. 271–72; Ch. 11, pp. 325
considering word choice	Ch. 12
incorporating audiovisual aids	Ch. 14
practicing your speech	Ch. 13, pp. 367–72
delivering your speech	Ch. 13

Analyze Your Audience

To make your speech worthwhile for your listeners, start with **audience analysis**. Learn about the audience members (or make educated guesses) before you select a topic and choose the ideas you will use to develop your topic. What should you focus on while analyzing your audience? We recommend sizing up listeners' interests and backgrounds. By understanding your audience members, you can boost your chances of selecting a speech topic that will appeal to them.

At this early point in the course, you may not have had the opportunity to conduct a detailed, formal analysis of your audience. However, you probably have spoken with classmates and learned about their interests and backgrounds. You may also have heard them share information about themselves, particularly if your instructor had the students in the course introduce themselves to the entire class or to another classmate on the first day. In addition, you and the other students will likely have shared experiences in class and at your college or university. Use your knowledge of these shared experiences to anticipate your listeners' attitudes and interests.

If you feel you need to do more to analyze your audience, here are some questions you could ask several classmates.

- Are there popular sports teams, activities, and traditions on campus? Unpopular experiences such as scarce parking or difficulty in signing up for required classes?
- Are the students in our class interested in politics? Do they share any common viewpoints on political issues?
- Are many of our classmates first-year students? Seniors? Do most of them live on campus or commute? Are most working to finance their education?
- What are the cultural backgrounds of the people taking this class?

Jot down responses to these questions as well as your own thoughts about topics that may interest your classmates.

Select Your Topic

Your **topic** is the subject you will address in your speech. The topic for your first speech will depend on the assignment your instructor has given you. Typical assignments include informing the class about an interesting issue you studied in another course, telling the class about a pet peeve, or sharing a cultural tradition with your audience.

To choose a topic, list as many possibilities as you can and then use your audience analysis to select one that you think would appeal most to your listeners. Your topic should also interest you. When you personally care about the topic, you'll be more willing to invest energy in preparing and practicing the speech. And, you'll convey your

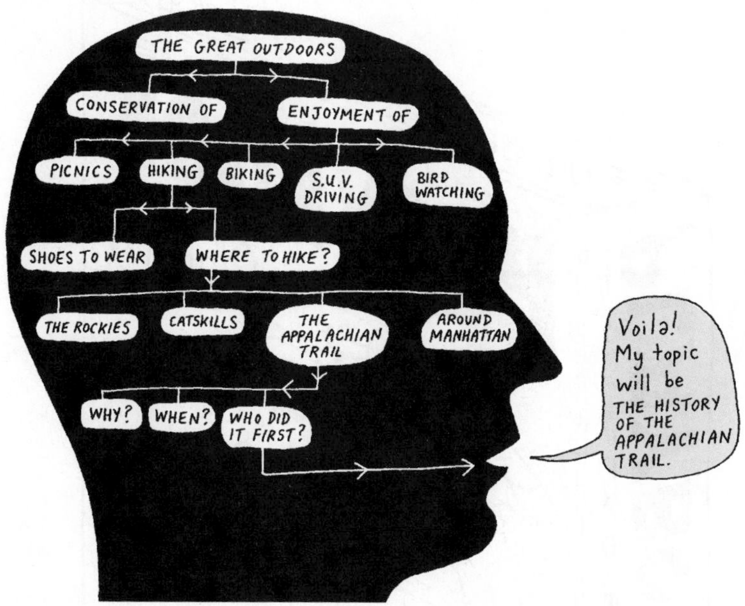

interest in the topic while delivering your speech, which in turn will further engage your audience.

Finally, make sure to avoid overused topics—such as how bad the cafeteria food is, whether steroids should be used in sports, or how to make a peanut butter and jelly sandwich or a pizza. Every instructor has a list of "reruns" that he or she would prefer not to watch again. If you choose a topic that is often presented in student speeches—for example, abortion or legalization of marijuana—you must make sure to take a fresh perspective or approach. If you have any doubts whatsoever whether your topic is appropriate, be sure to check with your instructor.

Finally, consider ways to narrow your topic. Most topics are too broad to cover in a five- or ten-minute presentation. For example, it would be impossible to tell your audience everything there is to know about your major, your culture, or your favorite sport in a single speech. Select one or more *aspects* of your topic that you think will most interest your audience and that you can also cover in the

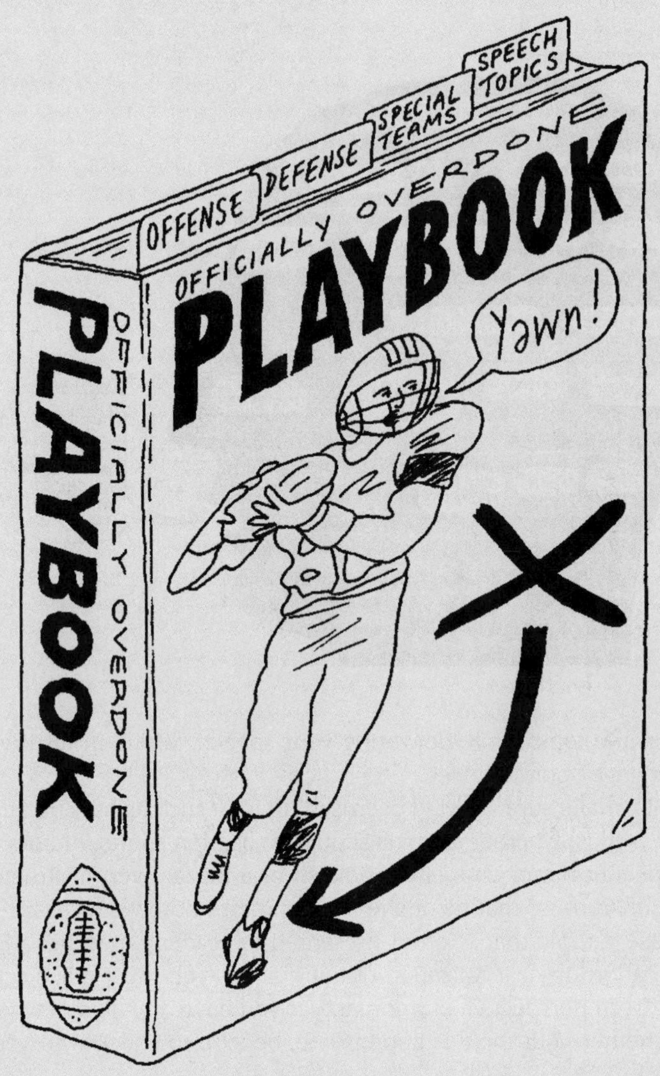

AVOID OVERUSED TOPICS

available time for your speech. For example, instead of trying to describe your entire culture, you might focus your topic on how your family or neighborhood celebrates a particular holiday.

Determine Your Speech's Rhetorical Purpose

Your speech's **rhetorical purpose** refers to the primary goal of your presentation. For example, do you want to help listeners understand a process or become more aware of a problem? Persuade your audience to support a cause? Mark a special occasion, such as a graduation, memorial service, or wedding? Inspire audience members and move them emotionally? Provide a lighthearted and entertaining—yet worthwhile—look at your topic? Speeches typically have one of the following objectives:

- *Informing*: increasing your audience's understanding or awareness of your subject.
- *Persuading*: trying to influence your audience's beliefs or actions with respect to your subject.
- *Marking a special occasion*: speaking at events such as graduations, memorial services, weddings, awards ceremonies, and holiday commemorations.

Clarifying your rhetorical purpose helps you shape the content of your speech. The ideas you ultimately develop and the information you present must support the purpose you've defined. For many classroom speeches, your instructor may specify a rhetorical purpose. If he or she has not, determine the purpose yourself. How? Decide whether you want your audience members to understand, believe, feel, or do something in particular about your topic after they listen to your speech. For instance, if you're giving a speech about an accomplished leader and you want your listeners to feel reverence and awe for what this person has accomplished, your rhetorical purpose would be to mark a special occasion related to the person and thus inspire and move audience members.

Create a Thesis Statement

Once you've selected your topic and identified your rhetorical purpose, draft a **thesis statement** for your speech. The thesis statement sums up your speech's main message about your topic in one sentence and reflects your narrowed topic and rhetorical purpose. Basically, the thesis statement should convey your speech's bottom line, enabling audience members to understand the essence of your overall speech message. Here are some examples of thesis statements:

- "Today I will inform you about how the New Year is celebrated in my culture."

- "Today I will describe a vegan diet and explain its health benefits."
- "Today it is my great pleasure to introduce an honored speaker at graduation."
- "We gather on this wonderful day to celebrate the life of an important scientific pioneer."
- "Tonight, I hope to entertain you with a humorous look at online shopping."

Develop Your Main Points

Main points are the major ideas that you will emphasize in your presentation. By calling attention to these points, you help your audience understand and remember the most important ideas from your speech. When speakers fail to do so, their listeners have difficulty following and retaining the speech's message.

As you select and narrow your topic, you may already begin getting ideas for main points. Researching your topic can generate additional possibilities. To identify your main points, think about which ideas would be most interesting to your audience and would best help listeners understand your thinking about the topic you've chosen.

Each main point you select must also support your thesis statement. Otherwise, your audience may conclude that you're straying off course. Or they may lose interest or become confused.

Generate Supporting Materials

Once you've selected your main points, generate **supporting materials**—information that bolsters and fleshes out the claims made in each of those points. There are several types of supporting materials, including examples, definitions, testimony, statistics, and narratives.

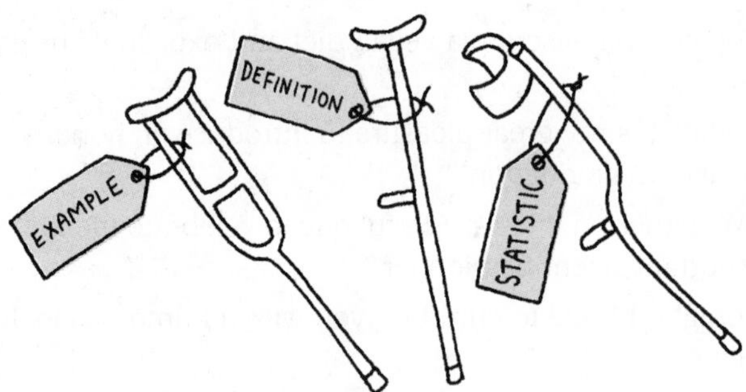

GENERATE SUPPORTING MATERIALS

You can generate some of these materials internally by **brainstorming** and externally by conducting research.

To brainstorm potential supporting materials, ask yourself questions such as "What do I know about my topic?" "What do I think is most important or interesting about this topic?" List all the responses to these questions that come to mind. Your goal is to create a diverse list of many possible ideas, not to make a final decision about which ones you will use. Therefore, write down all ideas that come to mind.

Through **research**, you can gather information from experts that will enhance your understanding of the topic and strengthen your speech's credibility. Even if your instructor requires less research for your first speech than for later assignments, you should still do a little research to answer any questions you have about your topic area.

How do you conduct research on your topic? Consider visiting a library, searching the Internet, and interviewing authorities on the subject. As you research, be sure to record, copy, or print any useful information you unearth. Write down what the source of the information says word-for-word, so you can accurately quote it if you decide to use the information in your speech.

For each research source you consult, be sure to write down the **bibliographic information**, noting the following items so you can incorporate them into your outline and your speech:

- The author—the writer or sponsoring organization of a book, an article, or an electronic database entry.
- The author's qualifications to write or speak on the subject—his or her job title; relevant education or job experience; or academic or institutional affiliation.
- The name of the source—the title of a book; the title of an article and the name of the periodical or newspaper it ran in; or the name of a person you interviewed.
- Publication date—the copyright date for a book you used; publication date of a periodical or newspaper you researched; date you accessed a Web site; or date you conducted an interview.
- The page(s) on which you found relevant information in a printed source or the URL of an online source.

SELECTING THE BEST IDEAS

After brainstorming and researching supporting materials for your main points, select the *best* materials from all the ideas you've collected. Again, choose supporting materials that would most interest your listeners and help them grasp what you're saying about your topic.

Organize and Outline the Body of Your Speech

A speech should be well organized, meaning that your ideas are structured in a way that enables the audience to follow your message easily. To organize your speech, draft an **outline**. Your outline contains the text of your speech in complete sentences or briefer phrases (depending on what your instructor prefers).

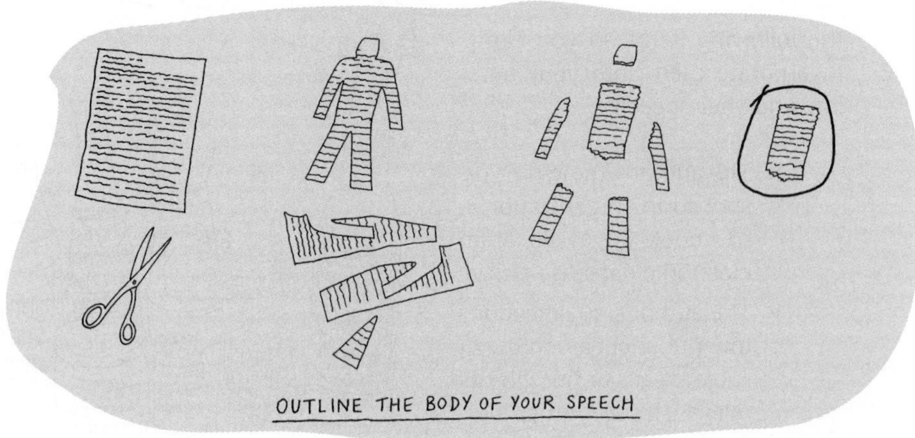

A speech outline has three major parts: the introduction, the body, and the conclusion. The **body** is the core of your speech and is where you present your main message about your topic. For this reason, we recommend outlining the body of your speech before outlining the introduction, even though the body follows the introduction when you actually deliver the speech.

To create a full-sentence outline for the body of your speech, first express each of the main points you've selected as a single sentence that states a key idea you're planning to emphasize. Then number each main point with a roman numeral. It is common to have between two and five main points, although your instructor may ask you to develop a single main point in your first speech.

Next create subpoints from the supporting materials you have gathered through brainstorming and research. **Subpoints** explain, prove, or expand on your main points. In your outline, indicate each subpoint with a capital letter, and indent each under its corresponding main point.

An important principle of outlining is **subordination**. Each main point must relate to your specific purpose, and each subpoint must relate to the main point that it supports. If you include additional supporting material under any subpoint, it must relate to that subpoint. Note also that you must use at least two subpoints for each point, if you have subdivisions at all. Here's a generic example of how subordination might look in a typical outline:

I. Main Point 1
   A. Subpoint
   B. Subpoint
      1. Sub-subpoint
      2. Sub-subpoint
II. Main Point 2

Outline Your Introduction and Conclusion

The **introduction** to your speech serves several vital purposes. Each purpose is the basis for one major section of the introduction, as shown in the list below (your instructor may require a specific combination or order of these elements):

I. *Attention-getter*. Start your speech with a brief story, quotation, striking fact or statistic, or humorous incident that grabs listeners' attention while also hinting at what your speech will cover.
II. *Thesis statement*. In a single sentence, convey the topic and purpose of your speech.
III. *Show the audience "what's in it for them."* In one or two sentences, summarize why audience members should listen to your speech. Will you provide information they need to know? Information they will want to share with friends and family?
IV. *Establish your credibility*. To show that you are a believable source of information on your topic, indicate any relevant expertise, experience, or education that you have.

V. *Preview your main points.* To help the audience understand where you will be going in your speech, list each main point using no more than one sentence per point.

The **conclusion** of your speech summarizes what you have said and leaves the audience with a memorable impression of your presentation. There are two main parts to a conclusion:

I. *Summary of your main points*—a brief recap of the major points you made during your speech.
II. *Clincher*—a closing sentence or paragraph that leaves your audience with a vivid memory of your speech. A clincher may be related to the introduction (for example, supplying a happy ending to a story you began in the attention-getter). Or it may consist of a statement or quotation that characterizes the content of your speech.

Incorporate Transitions

Once you've outlined the body, introduction, and conclusion, you will want to create transitions to connect the parts of your speech. A **transition** is a sentence that tells the audience that you are moving from one major idea to another. Transitions are especially helpful in the following places:

- between the introduction and your first main point
- between each main point
- between the final main point and the conclusion

Here are some examples of transitions:

- "First, let's talk about . . ." (*transition from introduction to first main point*).
- "Now that we've considered . . . , let's move on to . . ." (*transition between two main points*).
- "This completes our discussion of . . ." (*transition from final main point to conclusion*).

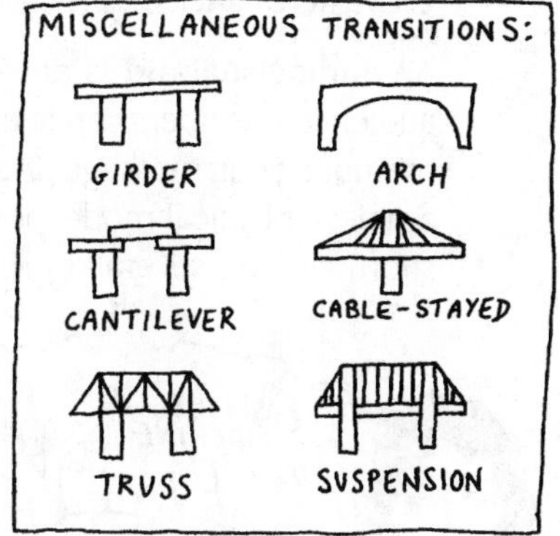

Consider Your Word Choice

Reread your entire outline, this time looking for opportunities to revise your word choice with appropriate style in mind. **Style**, or effective word choice, can help make your speech much more memorable and engaging for listeners. When revising for style, select words that your audience will understand, use precise terms to express your ideas, and choose language that makes your speech come alive. Focus on simplifying your sentences because audiences cannot reread parts of your speech if they become confused, and make sure to avoid biased language that may hurt others and damage your credibility.

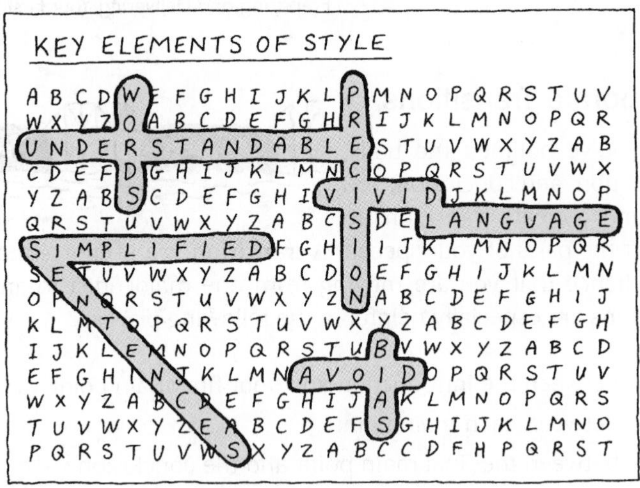

Consider Audiovisual Aids

An **audiovisual aid** is anything (in addition to your speech) that your audience members can see or hear that helps them understand and remember your message. Traditional aids include actual objects (for example, a physical model of DNA), video and audio recordings (such as a short clip of several birds and their calls), drawings, photographs, charts, maps, and graphs. PowerPoint presentations or other electronic slideshows are also common aids. Some instructors may allow or even require aids in the first speech.

To get the most from your audiovisual aids, make sure each one supports your point. For example, if you want your audience to appreciate the differences between bird calls, an audio recording that clearly demonstrates those differences would be entirely relevant. Also take care that audio aids are loud and clear and that visual aids are uncluttered and large enough for your audience to see them from all points in the room. The key point to remember is that audiovisual aids should support your spoken presentation, not overshadow it.

Practice Your Speech

After outlining your speech, revising for style, and creating any audiovisual aids, make sure to practice your speech. With practice, you'll feel more confident about your presentation—and more comfortable talking in front of your classmates. Becoming more comfortable through practice will allow you to work on the **extemporaneous delivery** of your speech; that is, your ability to deliver your speech smoothly and confidently from your outline without reading from it. To do this, practice delivering your speech from your outline at least four or five times, until the content starts to feel familiar. Then condense your outline into a set of briefer notes. Using these notes, try delivering the speech in a more conversational way, explaining the main points and subpoints in your own words, without reading word-for-word. If you have time, condense your outline even further to a list of your main points and the titles of summaries of the subpoints supporting each main point. This will be the outline you use when actually presenting your speech. Consider documenting your speaking outline on a series of index cards, recording one main point and the

title or a summary of each subpoint on each card. Or, you could write the speaking outline on a small number of 8.5 x 11-inch pieces of paper, in large type.

Deliver Your Speech

The moment has come: you're watching a classmate wrap up her speech, and you're next in line. As you approach the lectern and start delivering your speech, keep the following guidelines in mind:

- *Project your voice.* Speak loudly and slowly enough that your audience can easily hear what you are saying.
- *Maintain an even rate of speaking.* Many speakers tend to rush through a speech, particularly if they are nervous. Speak at a rate that enables you to pronounce the words clearly and allows the audience to follow your speech.
- *Convey interest in your topic.* Maintain energy and variety in your speaking voice, so that you build audience enthusiasm for your speech.
- *Maintain eye contact.* Try to make eye contact with people in each section of the room during the course of your presentation.

Each speech you deliver is a learning experience. Your instructor (and perhaps your classmates) will offer feedback after your presentations. Use these suggestions to prepare future speeches; you'll soon see your public speaking skills improve.

OVERCOMING SPEECH ANXIETY

As you follow the steps for preparing your first speech, you may begin experiencing some nervousness about delivering your talk. If so,

you're not alone. Many people feel nervous (at the very least) before they speak in public, even professionals who know their subject well.[9] The symptoms of **speech anxiety**—the worry or fear that some people experience before giving a talk (also called **stage fright**)—can take a wide variety of forms. Some people experience the stereotypical sensation of "butterflies in the stomach," as well as sweaty palms and a dry mouth. Others endure nausea, hyperventilation, and downright panic.

A little nervousness can actually be a good thing when you're giving a speech: it helps focus your attention. But in its extreme forms, speech anxiety can prevent you from speaking clearly or keeping your train of thought while delivering your presentation. Though speech anxiety is quite common, you *can* learn to manage it. As one seasoned public speaker put it, "You may not be able to get rid of the butterflies, but you can at least get them flying in formation." The following strategies can help you combat speech anxiety.

Select a Topic You Know and Enjoy

If you know your subject well, you'll find researching and planning your speech relatively easy, which leaves you more time to practice your delivery. And with more practice, you'll be better prepared and more relaxed in front of your audience. When you're familiar with your topic, you'll also notice that it's easier to explain the topic naturally, as you would in a conversation with a friend. And when you select a subject that you also enjoy, your interest adds enthusiasm to your speaking voice, which engages your audience even more.

Start Preparing Early

Resist any temptation to procrastinate in preparing your speech. Select a topic as soon as possible after receiving an assignment. Also complete an outline of your speech well before the day you're scheduled to present it. Drafting an outline mitigates anxiety because it shows you that you've at least established the basics for your presentation. It also

Er...um...
This isn't really my area but...er...
Let me start by saying that HEDGE FUNDS are private instrument investments... Er...
I mean private investment instruments...
ACME WORM Co.
10TH ANNUAL HEDGE FUND MANAGERS CONFERENCE
Mmm? Well I suppose I have to say something about WORM FARMING.
Yawn! Excuse me.
You must never overfeed your worms. Yawn!!
Overfeeding can lead to odor problems...
BIG BANK
10TH ANNUAL WORM FARMERS GALA

	8	9	10	11	12	13
	PICK TOPIC ✓ ~~DOGS CATS~~ PETS✓	RESEARCH Who keeps records?	RESEARCH Survey? Visit vet?✓ online?	RESEARCH Rules✓ Library✓	READ ✓	Buy onions / Make outline
14	15	16	17	18	19	20
STOP PROCRAST-INATING!	Lilly's birthday PRACTICE	REVISE✓ MORE ✓ PRACTICE	YET MORE PRACTICE + GET HAIRCUT	REST + RELAXATION	THE BIG DAY	Ha ha ha! You did it!!!

EARLY PREPARATION IS KEY

gives you time to develop the full speech and "test drive" it with trusted friends, family members, or teachers to get their ideas for fine-tuning it.

Take Care of Yourself

Get a good night's sleep before a speech. And avoid excessive sugar and caffeinated beverages the morning of your presentation—these will only get you hyped up even more. If you don't feel much like eating on the day of your speech, consume a light meal before you deliver your presentation. Then reward yourself with a favorite feast when it's all over.

Also budget your time in the days leading up to your speech. It's hard to get sufficient sleep, prepare nutritious meals, and practice your presentation if you have to work six hours, study for a test, and write a ten-page paper the day before you deliver your talk. Having too much to do in too little time intensifies anyone's anxiety. To avoid this scenario, look at the syllabi for all your courses early in the semester to see when major assignments are due. Consider other commitments as well, such as job, family, and community responsibilities. Then plan your time so that the days leading up to your speech are as relaxed as possible.

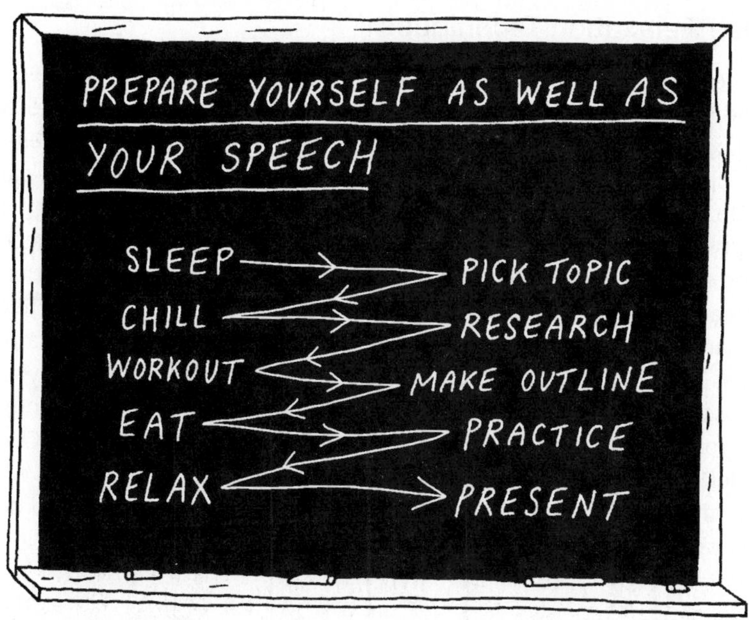

Visualize Success

Researchers have found that visualizing success reduces public speaking students' anxiety.[10] With **visualization**, you imagine yourself scoring a resounding success, such as presenting your speech without a hitch and winning enthusiastic applause from an appreciative audience. Make your visualization as specific as possible. For example, imagine yourself striding confidently to the front of the room. Watch as you present your speech to the audience in the same way you would converse with a friend—natural and relaxed. Visualize the audience nodding in agreement with a key point, smiling when an idea hits home, and laughing at your jokes. Listen to the thundering applause as you wrap up your speech. The power of positive thinking is no mere cliché. When you visualize success, you can ease your anxiety—if not eradicate it entirely.

Use Relaxation Techniques

When you're suffering from speech anxiety, your muscles tense up, and your mind swarms with negative thoughts. You know you should relax. But who can chill out on command? **Relaxation strategies**—techniques that reduce muscle tension and negative thoughts—can help. For many people, exercise is a powerful relaxation strategy. It helps you expend energy before you tackle preparing your speech, and it leaves you relaxed and limber on the day of your presentation. It's also renowned for clearing your mind. But exercising doesn't necessarily mean heading for the nearest gym to lift weights or take a pilates class. All you have to do is practice tightening and releasing your muscles—wherever you are at the moment. Breathe in as you tighten a group of muscles, and then exhale as you release the tension. Consider progressing from your neck muscles down to your feet. You can use this and other relaxation techniques even as you're waiting to deliver your speech.

Here's another relaxation strategy: budget some time for an activity that you enjoy—reading, watching a movie (comedies are great for relaxation), listening to music, gardening—before the day of your speech. If you simply don't have time for such activities, imagine yourself in a situation or setting that you find peaceful and serene—whether it's sitting silently atop a mountain, strolling along a beach during a gorgeous sunset, or enjoying some other scene that you find restful.

Volunteer to Speak First

Many public speakers experience more anxiety shortly before their presentation than during the speech itself.[11] If this describes you and you're going to be one of several speakers in a class or program, ask to speak first—or as early as possible in the lineup. That way, you'll present your speech early, and you'll have less time to work up a debilitating level of worry.

SUMMARY

"Preparation and perseverance are the keys to a successful speech."

The most successful presentations in history, such as Martin Luther King's "I Have a Dream" speech, usually derive from careful thought, planning, and preparation. Both beginning and more experienced speakers should remember this lesson—even a first-time speaker can give a much improved presentation by taking a bit of extra time and effort.

In this chapter, we emphasized the importance of preparing for public speaking. First, we introduced the five classical canons of rhetoric, a set of guidelines that continue to inform the way many speech instructors teach speech preparation today.

Next, we presented a step-by-step process for preparing your first speech. It's important to note that preparing a speech is a craft comprising a set of specific skills that you can master. The main steps are: analyzing the audience; selecting a topic; determining the rhetorical purpose; creating a thesis statement; developing main and supporting points; organizing and outlining the body, introduction, conclusion, and transitions; considering word choice and audiovisual aids; and practicing and delivering the speech. By making good choices at each step of the speech preparation process, you improve your chances of delivering a successful presentation.

In this chapter, we also outlined some basic techniques to help you overcome your speech anxiety by emphasizing the idea that you can channel your nervousness to help you become a better speaker. To help you "get the butterflies flying in formation," we suggest that you select a topic that you know and enjoy, and that you give yourself adequate time to prepare and practice your speech. Also strive to take care of yourself by balancing responsibilities with personal needs such as getting enough rest, relaxation, and exercise. To keep a positive outlook, try visualizing success and practicing relaxation techniques. Finally, ease your nervousness on the day of the speech by volunteering to go first.

Key Terms

THE CLASSICAL APPROACH TO SPEECH PREPARATION

invention
arrangement
style
memory (preparation)
delivery

PREPARING AND DELIVERING YOUR FIRST SPEECH

audience analysis
topic
rhetorical purpose
thesis statement
main points
supporting materials
brainstorming
research
bibliographic information
outline
body
subpoints
subordination
introduction
conclusion
transition
style
audiovisual aid
extemporaneous delivery

OVERCOMING SPEECH ANXIETY

speech anxiety (stage fright)
visualization
relaxation strategies

NOT ETHICAL NOT FUN
SOMEWHAT ETHICAL SOMEWHAT FUN
NOT ETHICAL BUT LOTS OF FUN
ETHICAL AND FUN
TOTALLY UNETHICAL
TOTALLY ETHICAL AND VERY DULL
TOTALLY UNETHICAL AND DISTURBING

3

SPEECH ETHICS

"Strive to be an ethical public speaker."

All of us face difficult choices throughout our lives. For example, imagine that your romantic partner recently modeled a new, expensive sweater, saying, "I just love this fabric. What do you think? Do I look good in this?" You find the sweater downright ugly, but you know (from experience) that if you answer honestly, you will hurt your loved-one's feelings and perhaps even start a fight. Yet you also feel uncomfortable telling a lie. So you hesitate, wondering what exactly to say.

Some of these difficult decisions may have much more significant consequences. Consider Joe, a college student on a scholarship with solid grades and a reputation for integrity. Joe is preparing a speech that he'll need to deliver in his public speaking class at the end of the week. The speech is important because he cares about public speaking but also because he needs to maintain a B + average to keep his scholarship. He's done some research on his topic already, and has found some excellent supporting materials, which he has documented diligently. But he still needs to do more work, and he plans to wrap up his research the night before his speech. That evening, his car breaks down on the way to the library. By the time he gets the car towed to a garage and returns home, he has run out of time to do the rest of the research he needs to finish developing his speech. Panicked, he jumps on the Internet and soon finds the text for a great speech related to his topic. He really likes the language in the speech and doesn't think he could get the information across as well in his own words, so he considers cutting and pasting a few paragraphs from the speech into his own outline. He knows this would amount to plagiarism, but he tells himself, "It would just be this once, I don't have time to put the text into my own words, and if I don't do it my scholarship could be on the line." The scenario with your romantic partner's sweater and the story about Joe demonstrate the difficulty posed by ethical dilemmas—situations in which the right decision isn't immediately clear.

In public speaking, **ethics**—rules and values that a group defines to guide conduct and distinguish between right and wrong—can

come into play during every stage of the process. For example, as you research and write your speech, you must make decisions about what information you'll include in your presentation and how that information will influence your audience. As you deliver your speech, you have to make choices about the language and tone of voice you use, and how those aspects of your presentation will affect your listeners.

How do people make ethical choices? Some adopt a code of behavior they commit to using consistently. These individuals are demonstrating **ethical absolutism**—the belief that people should exhibit the same behavior in all situations. For instance, you would be using ethical absolutism if you decided to tell your romantic partner how you really felt about the sweater. In this case, your code of ethics might contain a principle saying, "People should always tell the truth, even if doing so hurts loved ones."

Other people use **situational ethics**—which hold that correct behavior can vary depending on the situation at hand. Joe, for example, would be (inappropriately) using situational ethics if he decided that, under the extenuating circumstances, it would be okay for him to plagiarize "just this one time."

Whether you tend to see ethical decisions in absolute or situational terms, there are some generalizations that apply in most situations. For example, most societies believe that it's more ethical to tell the truth than to lie. In the context of public speaking, most people believe that lying is wrong. They see it as an ethical violation, not to mention (in some circumstances) a possible violation of the law.

Yet some of these same individuals might think little or nothing of intentionally exaggerating their qualifications during a job interview—especially if they believe that "everybody does it and gets away with it." Thus, many people use a blend of approaches to making ethics-related choices. In truth, most people are not strictly absolutists—even those who generally follow a strict ethical code may sometimes face dilemmas that compel them to engage in situational ethics, and all of us face such situations at some point in our lives.

In this book, we do not presume to tell you what your ethical system must be; we do insist, however, that you always strive to make the most ethical choice. To help you with such choices, in this chapter we expose you to the kinds of communication-related ethical dilemmas

that speakers and audience members sometimes face, and we explore behaviors most people consider unethical. As you'll discover, one guiding principle that can help you make ethical choices is that of respect for other people—treating others in ways you would like to be treated, as well as avoiding treating them in ways you would *not* want to be treated. For instance, if you would resent a public speaker who had withheld important information in order to persuade you to take a particular action, you shouldn't exhibit that same behavior in your own speeches.

Ethics can also vary across societies, making them **culturally relative**. For example, in some cultures, people consider knowledge as something that is owned collectively rather than by individuals. In cultures with strong oral and narrative traditions, for example, stories are passed from one generation to another, and are shared as general cultural knowledge. In such cultures, people don't consider working together or paraphrasing without attribution as cheating or any other form of unethical behavior. When discussing ethics in this book, we reflect a Western cultural perspective, which holds that individuals do own the knowledge they create. This perspective informs the academic guidelines and honor codes that are stated explicitly by most colleges and universities in the United States—indeed, you will often find these guidelines cited in your instructors' syllabi. Thus, we require proper citation and attribution of sources for all speeches.

As you approach the following sections about ethics and public speaking, consider your own approach to making ethical decisions while developing and delivering presentations. What are your beliefs regarding proper behavior in general and in public speaking in particular? Do you always honor these beliefs strictly—or only in certain situations? To help you answer these questions, let's consider some of the ethical issues you may confront in public speaking. These include communicating truthfully, crediting others' work, using sound reasoning, and behaving ethically when you're listening to someone else give a speech. Though making ethical choices in public speaking situations can sometimes be difficult, this chapter will help you develop a responsible system for doing so. The key word here is *responsibility*: whenever you give a speech, you wield power—over what your listeners think, how they feel, and what actions they end up taking. You're thus responsible for your audience's well-being. And making sound ethical decisions as you develop and deliver your speech constitutes one important way to shoulder that responsibility. The following sections offer guidelines for exhibiting ethically responsible behavior in public speaking.

LEGAL SPEECH, ETHICAL SPEECH

As we connect ethics and public speaking, it is worth observing that many people in the United States often confuse (sometimes intentionally) **ethical speech** with **legally protected speech**. While these two concepts sometimes overlap—that is, what you say is both legal and ethically responsible to your audience—they are most definitely *not* the same. Ethical speech refers to incorporating ethical decision making into how you engage the public speaking process *and* ultimately what you say. It means that you follow guidelines for telling the truth and avoid misleading an audience—because such actions are ethical, and *the right thing to do*.

Focusing on legally protected speech, by contrast, refers to using the law as your boundary for what you may say *and* how you say it. Thus, with this approach you would use legal guidelines in making decisions about telling the truth or withholding information based upon whether there is a legal requirement to make a certain action or a legal consequence for violating the rules. When you rely on legal guidelines for acceptable speech, your decision-making calculus has nothing to do with ethics; it is only driven by what is technically within legal rules. If you (unethically) use legal protection as your guiding principle for speaking, you can technically stay within the bounds of what is lawful but still speak unethically.

It's vital to note that far more types of speech are technically legal than are strictly ethical. In the United States, the First Amendment to the Constitution mandates "freedom of speech," and this freedom allows for a vast range of legally protected statements. In fact, there are relatively few exceptions, and these are typically handled in narrow terms (such as slander—intentional falsehood about another person), fighting words (words meant to provoke a violent response), and obscenity (hard-core, sexually explicit expression). Political speech—expression that relates to political discourse—is the most legally protected and privileged form of expression under the First Amendment. However, just because something is political speech (or any form of legally protected speech), doesn't mean that it is ethically responsible. For example, in a speech at the Conservative Political Action Conference in March 2007, columnist Ann Coulter referred to Democratic presidential candidate John Edwards with a homophobic sexual epithet. As political speech, her comments were fully protected by the law, but that does not make her speech ethically responsible.

Be certain you understand the distinction between ethical and legal speech when crafting your own presentations—and remember that when you consider ethics here, you are doing more than just what is legally required—you are doing what is morally correct for your situation.

COMMUNICATING TRUTHFULLY

The most basic ethical guideline for public speaking is: *tell your audience the truth.* How do you feel when someone has lied to you? If you're like most people, you resent it and feel manipulated by it. Audience members who discover that a speaker has deceived them seldom believe that person—and they rarely do what he or she asks of them. They also remember being lied to. A known liar will have trouble ever convincing future listeners of his or her credibility or trustworthiness.

That being said, the words *truth* and *truthfully* are fairly subjective and elude precise definition. It is easier to describe truth in public speaking by examining what is *not* truth.

Lying

Public speakers who lie are intentionally seeking to deceive their audience. Why do people lie when giving a presentation? Some fear what their listeners would do if they knew the truth; they don't trust their audience to react in a supportive or understanding way. For example, an older student once fabricated his identity as a military veteran for a speech he gave in which he demonstrated gun-safety tips. He suggested that he had gone into the army straight out of high school and had received training in the usage of many firearms. He told this lie because he believed that it would give him more credibility in his audience's eyes. Yet the audience might have accepted his suggestions anyway; after all, a safety certification course is a worthy credential in itself. By lying about his background, he risked losing his listeners' trust if they ever learned of his deception.

Half-Truths

When a speaker reveals only part of the truth—and then mixes it with a lie—he or she is telling a **half-truth**. In practice, a half-truth has the same damaging impact as a lie: it deceives the audience. Consider the example of a corporate manager who is required to explain to the board of directors why her company has lost so many top executives in recent months. In her presentation, she says that many departing executives had simply elected to take early retirement or had accepted positions at other companies—normal occurrences in business. The part of her answer regarding accepting positions at other firms was true. But the part of her answer regarding early retirement was a half-truth. As it turned out, two of the executives who chose to retire early did so as part of a legal settlement related to accusations of accounting malpractice.

False Inference

When a speaker presents information that leads listeners to an incorrect conclusion, that speaker has caused a **false inference**. Speakers who commit this ethical breach intentionally drop hints designed to make their audience believe something that isn't true. For example, in a presentation titled "UFOs, Extraterrestrials, and the Supernatural," a student described a series of events that occurred in a Midwestern town: an increase in the number of babies with birth defects, a rise in the rate of kidnapping, and a jump in the amount of farmland seized by the federal government. This student did not say outright that there was a government conspiracy to conceal the presence of aliens and UFOs, or a plot to cross-breed aliens and humans. However, he clearly intended his audience to draw this inference from his presentation. In reality, the increase in birth defects amounted to exactly one—from six to seven. The increase in kidnapping was actually a statewide statistic, caused by a change in laws about divorce and child custody. And the government seizure of land had happened—but

only for the construction of a highway overpass. The speaker had arranged his facts specifically so that his audience would conclude that the government was trying to conceal the presence of aliens.

False inferences can also occur accidentally; for example, if a speaker gathers insufficient data and therefore unknowingly presents an incomplete understanding of the speech topic to the audience. Accidental false inference isn't unethical, but it prevents you from conveying accurate information to your audience. Thus, it damages the effectiveness of your speech. To avoid an accidental *or* a deliberate false inference, avoid overgeneralized claims based on statistical findings. And always explain to your audience what the statistics mean and how they were derived.

Taking evidence out of context is another form of false inference. Here the speaker shares a source's data or statements without explaining how they relate to the original situation. The speaker uses these facts or words *selectively* to support an argument. For example, in a speech about the propensity of pit bulls to attack people, a student once quoted an animal behavior expert out of context to imply a genetic predisposition towards attack: "[T]here is an observable tendency in the genetic makeup of pit bulls to viciously attack humans. . . . " The student did *not* explain to her audience that the quotation came from this longer statement:

> Some have argued that there is an observable tendency in the genetic makeup of pit bulls to viciously attack humans. But surely this is not the case. While it is true that *some* pit bulls have attacked *some* humans, there is no research to definitively prove a genetic tendency to attack humans. More study of this is needed.

Philosophers—and cheating romantic partners—have long argued about whether keeping silent about something is the same thing as lying about it. Thus, **omission** is another source of false inference—here, presenters mislead the audience not by what they say but by what is left unsaid. For example, in a presentation about on-campus drug use, a student government representative was asked about the extent of drug use and abuse in her campus dormitory. In response, she merely smiled and moved on to another question.

OUT-OF-CONTEXT EVIDENCE

"... ~~Some have argued that~~ there is an observable tendency in the genetic makeup of pit bulls to viciously attack humans. ~~But surely this is not the case. While it is true that some pit bulls have attacked some humans, there is no research to definitively prove a genetic tendency to attack humans. More study of this is needed~~..."

"... Some have argued that there is an observable tendency in the genetic makeup of pit bulls to viciously attack humans. But surely this is not the case. While it is true that *some* pit bulls have attacked *some* humans, there is no research to definitively prove a genetic tendency to attack humans. More study of this is needed..."

Her silence implied that there was no drug problem in her dormitory. But in fact, her dorm had the worst record for on-campus substance abuse. If silence about a topic will mislead your audience, and if you are aware of this likelihood but withhold information anyway, you have acted unethically through omission. Such actions suggest that you view your listeners as consumers of information and take an unethical and cynical *caveat emptor* ("let the buyer beware") approach to public speaking.

To communicate truthfully—and therefore ethically—never lie, never tell half-truths, and never cause false inferences—whether by taking evidence out of context or omitting pertinent information. There are always alternatives to these behaviors. For example, if you fear that the truth may weaken your argument, then you need to do further research and think about your topic. There are at least two sides to every issue, as well as multiple solutions and perspectives to consider. If you fear what the audience might think if they knew the truth, consider the opposite: how will they react if they learn you have deceived them? In most situations, listeners will react to a lie much more negatively than to an unwelcome truth.

ACKNOWLEDGING THE WORK OF OTHERS

Researching a speech topic exposes you to a wealth of interesting facts, information, and ideas—many of which you will want to include in your presentation. But finding these materials also raises some questions: Should you include a particular piece of information in your presentation? If so, how should you use it? And how will you acknowledge its source?

Listeners—and especially speech instructors—want speakers to demonstrate their own ideas and thinking during a presentation. At the same time, all of us recognize that most speeches can be enhanced by research and examples from outside sources. The question is, how should you reconcile these objectives? To do so, you must use a blend of materials that demonstrates your own ideas and also ethically incorporates and acknowledges the original ideas of others. This approach is honest for you and fair to your listeners and sources.

Imagine coming across an article or published essay addressing the same topic as your speech—as Joe did when he was rushing to complete his speech preparation. Maybe you admire the way the authors have worded their prose. Would there be a problem if you incorporated a few lines from the article word-for-word into the text of your speech without citing the quotations? What about taking a preponderance of the ideas from the publication and making them your own by rewording them but not attributing them to the author? Would that be unethical? The answer to both questions is an unequivocal "Yes!"

Presenting another person's words or ideas as if they were your own is called **plagiarism**, and it is always unethical. If you plagiarize, you mislead your audience by misrepresenting the source of the material you've used. Equally important, when you plagiarize, you are stealing the ideas and words of another person.

Though plagiarism is wrong, people sometimes have difficulty discerning the line between plagiarism and appropriate use of researched material. To illustrate why, let's consider plagiarism in two contexts: quoting from a source and paraphrasing the work of others.

Quoting from a Source

Suppose a student named Larissa gave a speech informing her audience about the history of drive-in movie theaters. She had drawn her inspiration from a magazine article she saw in an airport, while traveling home from school for the holidays. She thought the topic was unusual enough to make an interesting presentation, and she later shared the idea with her instructor, who approved the choice of topic.

When trying to research the topic, however, Larissa could find little or no material beyond the magazine article she had found in the airport. Panic set in as the day for her in-class speech approached. In desperation, Larissa decided that no one in her class could have known about the article because it was published in a magazine called *Nevada Horizons*, sold only in the greater Las Vegas area, and because Larissa attended college at the University of Michigan—in Ann Arbor. Rationalizing her actions, she took the article and used nearly all of it verbatim as her speech.

It turned out that the magazine article had appeared simultaneously in several different publications, including a large national newspaper. As fate would have it, Larissa's instructor had read the article in the newspaper. Larissa earned an F in the class and was suspended from school.

Clearly, what Larissa did constituted plagiarism. But suppose that she had taken only one-third, one-half, or even just a few lines from the story and represented the material as her own. Would any of these scenarios still constitute plagiarism? Yes. Whether she lifted five pages or one page or only a single sentence, she would still be stealing the original author's words and ideas. By analogy, whether you steal one or two eggs—or an entire dozen—will matter little to a shop owner. Either way, you stole the eggs.

Plagiarism is particularly common among students who research their speech topics online. The temptation to lift and use text from a Web site can be overwhelming, but doing so without attribution is stealing. Students also face the danger of unintentional plagiarism when they copy a quotation from a source and paste it into a notes document without writing down the citation information; when they return to their notes later, they may not remember that they had copied and pasted the material as opposed to writing it themselves.

Most of the direct quotations you use in a speech will be short—a line or two, or at most, a paragraph. To avoid plagiarism, you must attribute the quote to its source. How should you cite the source? If Larissa had used just several quotes from the magazine article, she might have attributed this material in the following way:

> As Roberta Gonzales wrote in the June 19 issue of *Nevada Horizons* (p. D4), "The growth and popularity of drive-in theaters tracked with the affordability of automobiles for a larger and younger population of drivers."

The first part of this sentence is the attribution. Note that the page number is mentioned. In delivering your speech, it's okay not to cite the page numbers of all your sources. However, we strongly suggest that you document a complete citation on your speech outline or text. That way, anyone (including your instructor) who wants to check your facts can easily do so. Before preparing your speech, make sure to check with your instructor to find out if he or she has additional expectations for proper attribution.

Paraphrasing the Work of Others

Suppose Larissa never lifted the text from the magazine article verbatim. Instead, she used **paraphrasing**—restating the original author's ideas in her own words. Would this constitute plagiarism?

This is where the rules defining plagiarism are a bit less clear. Is it stealing if you use your own words but not necessarily your own ideas? Your teachers will not expect you to be an authority on every speech topic you address; you *will* have to research your subject matter. This may cause you to wonder: "How could it be plagiarism if I'm paraphrasing someone else's words or ideas? After all, these are *my* words!"

Students at the college level regularly struggle with this challenge. To resolve the dilemma, consider this simple rule of thumb: if you're using most or all of the original material, simply rearranged and restated in your own words, you're still taking another person's ideas and presenting them as your own. This isn't the same as directly copying without attribution, but it is wrong on several fronts. For one thing, you're not generating your own ideas and opinions about your topic—so you're not meeting your instructor's expectations. For another, you're being unfair to the person whose ideas you're presenting as your own.

The safest bet is always to acknowledge the original source of any material you use in your speech, whether you are directly quoting or paraphrasing. And avoid paraphrasing large portions of an original source or another work in its entirety. For example, if Larissa had paraphrased some ideas from the magazine article, she could have mentioned the author and source of her material in this way:

> According to Roberta Gonzales, writing in the June 19 issue of *Nevada Horizons* on p. D4, drive-in theaters tended to grow in popularity with Americans who were increasingly able to afford and enjoy the freedom of automobiles. This was especially true of younger drivers, who yearned for freedom of mobility and a common place to meet and socialize outside the scrutiny of mom and dad.

In this case, Larissa would have appropriately paraphrased the material and given proper credit to the original source.

Common Knowledge

There are limited situations—known as **common knowledge**—where you can use information from a source without giving a direct citation. Common knowledge information is widely known and disseminated in many sources. For example, you may not need to cite the fact that France presented the Statue of Liberty to the United States in 1886 but you might need to cite a source if you wanted to give statistics such as the statue's total weight (125 tons), the weight of the statue's concrete foundation (27,000 tons), or the distance the statue's torch sways in the wind (5 inches).[1] Be sure to check with your instructor on guidelines for common knowledge. But most importantly, remember the following: if you are in any doubt, include the citation.

USING SOUND REASONING

When public speakers intentionally misuse logic to deceive their audience, they are acting unethically. In this section, we discuss four ways in which a speaker might misuse logic: hasty generalization, post hoc fallacy, personal attacks, and bandwagoning.

Hasty Generalization

A speaker who intentionally generalizes about all members of a group from information based on a limited part of the group is making a **hasty generalization**.

For example, a student once suggested in his speech that all fruits and vegetables grown in California should be taken off the market because of a number of reported cases of E. coli infection. Although he generalized about all fruits and vegetables grown in the Golden State, the information on which he based his statement applied only to a

type of broccoli that had been grown in Monterey County, in the central part of the state.

The speaker was correct about the need to take broccoli grown in that particular area off the market, but he intentionally overgeneralized about all fruits and vegetables produced in California. Before making such a claim, this student should have researched other types of vegetables (and other types of broccoli) grown in Monterey and across the state. And he should have avoided mentioning fruit entirely—there was no indication that the E. coli problem affected it.

Post Hoc (After the Fact) Fallacy

A **post hoc fallacy** occurs when a speaker wrongly identifies the cause of one event as the event that immediately preceded it. (The Latin phrase *post hoc* literally means "after this.") Here the speaker's line of reasoning goes something like this: "Event B happened after event A; therefore, event B was caused by event A."

For instance, in a speech about notorious murders, a student described the killing of a famous man by one of his children. The student reported that the man had recently remarried, after divorcing his wife of twenty-five years. The student then suggested that "the divorce caused the man's son to commit the murder—because a child's anger over divorce is known to be a cause of aberrant behavior." If the student had used this reasoning along with other evidence (such as findings from a psychiatrist's examination of the son), he would *not* have

committed this fallacy. But because he offered no other evidence, he misled his audience, especially given that the "child" in question—the son—was an adult at the time of the murder. This speaker could not credibly claim that the divorce, in itself, caused the murder.

Personal Attacks

Some speakers try to compensate for weak arguments by making **personal attacks**—also known as *ad hominem attacks*—on their opponents. (In Latin, *ad hominem* means "to the man.") In a campaign speech, for example, one candidate for student body president referred to her rival as a "tree-hugging environmental whack job." Her goal? To stir up listeners' bias against outspoken environmentalists on campus. The speaker used these words to persuade the audience to reject the other candidate as an extremist. This tactic was unethical, because she supplied no evidence to support her claims, and those claims were not relevant to her opponent's qualifications for serving as student body president.

Bandwagoning

As an additional consideration, avoid using reasoning that implies an argument must be true because most people believe it is. Originally labeled as the **ad populum fallacy**, today it is more commonly know as **bandwagoning**—because it implies that the sheer number of people behind a point makes the point more persuasive and invites the audience to rhetorically "jump on the bandwagon" and go along with the conclusion. Bandwagoning is especially common in advertising and marketing. When a fast-food restaurant proclaims "billions served," it is implying that because so many people eat the same fast food, the food must be worth consuming, *and* that the audience for this message should do the same! Likewise, when a newspaper ad for a new movie trumpets: "Last week more people watched this movie than any other movie in America!" it suggests that the film must be worth paying for because so many other people have paid for it.

Yet it is important to note that some arguments may be both true *and* commonly believed or followed. Although many people buying into an argument does not make that argument true, the fact that many people believe it does not prove that the argument is *false* either. Bandwagoning only creates an unethical fallacy when the speaker relies on the effect as the primary means of proving the point, instead of using other objective forms of evidence or logical explanations to convince an audience.

BEING AN ETHICAL LISTENER

So far, we've focused our discussion of ethics on speakers' responsibilities. But audience members also have a responsibility to demonstrate ethical behavior. The qualities that characterize what we call an **ethical audience** include courtesy, open-mindedness, and a willingness to hold a speaker accountable for his or her statements. When you're listening to someone who's giving a speech, consider the following guidelines for exhibiting ethical behavior.

Show Courtesy

The old adage about treating others as you expect to be treated applies just as much in public speaking as in all other areas of life. When someone else is delivering a presentation, extend to him or her the courtesy you would appreciate if you were speaking. Courteous behavior includes focusing your attention on the speaker as soon as he or she begins the presentation. Stop any activities that may distract you or the speaker, such as reading a newspaper, working on a class assignment, texting your friends, or chatting with the person sitting next to you. Let the speaker see that you are paying attention.

Demonstrate an Open Mind

Avoid prejudging the speech or speaker. Even if you have a strongly held belief on the topic or you dislike the speaker, look for parts of the message—or aspects of the speaker—that signal common ground. And consider the fact that you might hear something that changes your mind—or that broadens your perspective on the speech topic.

Hold the Speaker Accountable

Prejudging a speech or speaker is clearly unethical. But mindlessly swallowing what the other person says in his or her presentation can be equally damaging. To avoid this damage, you need to hold the presenter accountable for his or her claims. How can you do so? If time is available at the end of the speech, ask questions that prompt the speaker to explain or defend statements that you think require additional evidence. If your instructor allows time for a longer exchange, don't hesitate to honestly (and respectfully) express your response to the speech. Convey questions and opinions politely, focus on the content of the speech itself, and scrupulously avoid attacking the speaker's character. For example, say, "Can you tell us more about how you arrived at those figures?" not "You obviously didn't care enough to do a thorough job in your research." In offering feedback to the speaker on his or her presentation, frame your comments or suggestions constructively—that is, in ways that can help the person build his or her public speaking skills. Avoid destructive feedback, which only diminishes the presenter and denigrates his or her speech.

SUMMARY

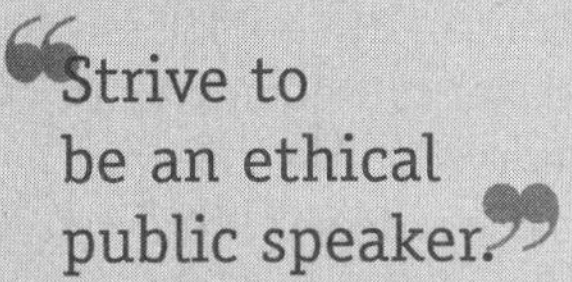

As you saw in Joe's story at the beginning of this chapter, public speaking can present numerous ethical challenges—dilemmas that make it difficult to determine what constitutes right and wrong behavior. This chapter has focused on those challenges—from speakers' as well as listeners' perspectives. Whether you strive to communicate truthfully, use and acknowledge others' work, employ sound reasoning, or be an ethical listener, there's one theme that crosses all these ethical concerns: how can you best show respect for others? People have different ways of deciding what constitutes ethical behavior in public speaking. But by asking yourself if an action you're considering taking would demonstrate respect for others, you can more easily make the right—and ethical—choices. When you demonstrate respect for your audience by exhibiting ethical behavior, you win listeners' trust and boost your chances of getting your message across. And when you show respect for speakers as an audience member, you help them deliver more effective presentations. Everyone benefits when presenters *and* listeners attend to speech ethics.

Key Terms

ethics
ethical absolutism
situational ethics
culturally relative

LEGAL SPEECH, ETHICAL SPEECH

ethical speech
legally protected speech

COMMUNICATING TRUTHFULLY

half-truth
false inference
taking evidence out of context
omission

ACKNOWLEDGING THE WORK OF OTHERS

plagiarism
paraphrasing
common knowledge

USING SOUND REASONING

hasty generalization
post hoc fallacy
personal attacks
ad-populum fallacy (bandwagoning)

BEING AN ETHICAL LISTENER

ethical audience

I agree, but...
She agrees!

Wow, they all look so excited, they must all totally agree with me.
No way!
WRONG!!

Hey, what happened?
I disagree...
I object...
I dispute...
I contradict...
I reject...
I quibble...

SUDDEN REALIZATION
CLUNK!
OUCH!

Oh, I get it now. All I need to do is to LISTEN.
At last!

4 LISTENING SKILLS

"Listening is a vital skill in public speaking and beyond."

Jason was psyched. While preparing an informative speech on the ways young people use the Internet, he focused on the popularity of MySpace.com. An active MySpace user, Jason found the topic fascinating and looked forward to developing the speech. To learn more about the habits of other students using MySpace, he conducted six face-to-face interviews with classmates from his speech course. He felt pleased with the amount of information his classmates were sharing during the interviews. But when Jason later reviewed his interview notes, he realized they were a bit sparse.

With time running out, Jason finished developing the presentation using the few insights he could pull from his notes. On the day of his speech, Jason proudly presented his claims about young people's use of MySpace and their opinions about the site. As he spoke, he felt confident and comfortable talking in front of his class. All that

changed, however, during the question-and-answer period after the speech. Judging from the questions his classmates were throwing at him, few—if any—of his fellow students agreed with his observations about student MySpace users. Feeling confused and blindsided, Jason wondered how things could have gone so wrong.

Jason's unpleasant experience reveals the importance of listening in public speaking. Unfortunately for him, he missed two opportunities to listen. When he was interviewing his classmates, he failed to pay enough attention to take detailed notes. Later, when he reviewed his notes and saw that they were sparse, he couldn't remember many details from the actual interviews—further suggesting that he hadn't listened carefully during the conversations. Jason also failed to listen to his audience as he was delivering his speech. If he had paid careful attention to his classmates while he was talking, he may have detected both auditory and visual signs that they disagreed with his claims: one or two of his listeners may have muttered sarcastic comments such as "Yeah, right" or "Is he kidding?" And several of them may have been shaking their heads or rolling their eyes. By failing to listen carefully while researching *and* delivering his speech, Jason never connected with his audience members and lost credibility with them.

As Jason's story reveals, listening is a vital skill for public speakers at all stages of the speech preparation process. Yet many novice speakers find this idea surprising. After all, it's the *audience* who has to listen, right? To be sure, audiences can be good listeners by respectfully and carefully attending to the speaker's message. But speakers have many opportunities to practice good listening skills while preparing and delivering a presentation. Think about it: You interview people to research your speech. You practice your presentation in front of trusted friends or family members and listen to their feedback. And you deliver your speech, paying attention to your audience's responses to decide whether you need to adjust your voice, volume, pacing, or some other aspect of your delivery. Fail to listen at any of these stages, and you risk ignoring important information that you need to present the most effective speech possible.

Who needs to demonstrate good listening here?

A: THE AUDIENCE? B: THE SPEAKER? C: BOTH?

Research further affirms the importance of listening—versus merely hearing—for both public speakers and their audiences, because listening and hearing are two different activities. For example, several studies have suggested that people can miss virtually all the content of oral messages when they only hear, rather than listen (imagine the droning teacher's voice in Charles Schulz's *Peanuts* cartoons).[1] **Hearing** means merely receiving messages in a passive way. **Listening** means actively paying attention to what you're hearing, processing the message to decide on its meaning, and remembering what you've heard and understood.

For example, suppose you're interviewing Mel, a pet owner, for an informative speech about health insurance for pets. When you ask for his opinion on this type of insurance, Mel says, "Don't get me wrong; I think people should do what's best for their pets." After a pause, his voice gets a bit louder, his eyes widen, and he says, "But that insurance is expensive!" If you only *heard* Mel's response (but didn't really listen), you would probably conclude that *Mel thinks the insurance is expensive*. But if you actually *listened* to Mel by paying attention to his words *and* other delivery cues, such as an agitated facial expression and a loud voice, you would have noticed that Mel had especially strong feelings about the high cost of pet health insurance. You might even conclude that Mel is unwilling to purchase it even if he thinks it beneficial for his beloved pet. Your listening might then lead you to ask further questions to learn more about Mel's views on the subject.

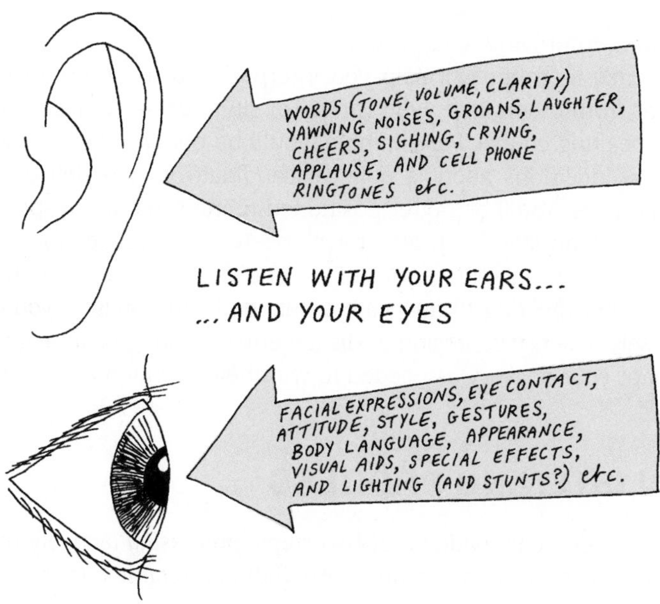

If you're less skilled at listening than at hearing, you're not alone—many people have similar difficulty. Yet you *can* learn how to strengthen your listening skills, and this chapter offers helpful guidelines. In the pages that follow, we explore the importance of listening in public speaking, examine the process of listening, and then consider the causes behind ineffective listening behaviors. We then offer suggestions for listening effectively that you can put into practice as both a speaker *and* an audience member.

WHY LISTEN?

As we've seen, listening is a crucial skill for both speakers and audience members. How you listen as a speaker—while preparing and delivering a speech—can have a powerful impact on the quality of your presentations and your ability to connect with your audience. How you listen as an audience member can strongly affect your ability to absorb the information the speaker is imparting to you. Equally important, improving your listening skills as both a speaker and an audience member will help you interpret and use more of what you hear from others in a wide variety of situations—not just in your public-speaking course. For example, you'll be better able to evaluate and make decisions about a political candidate who is delivering a public address. You'll be better positioned to interpret and respond to a neighbor who stands up at a town meeting and argues for an increase in the special-education budget. And if *you're* the one standing up at a town meeting to advocate a change in the budget, you'll be more likely to sense confusion or disagreement among your neighbors and adapt your delivery as needed to win their attention and support.

THE LISTENING PROCESS

Effective listening is made up of two steps: *processing* (actively thinking about what you've heard and observed) and *retaining* (remembering what you have heard).

Processing What You've Heard

When you engage in **processing**, you actively think about a message you're receiving from someone else—not only the words but also the nonverbal cues. For example, suppose you're a small-business owner who's meeting with Jeff, a salesperson for eLogic, a business-software

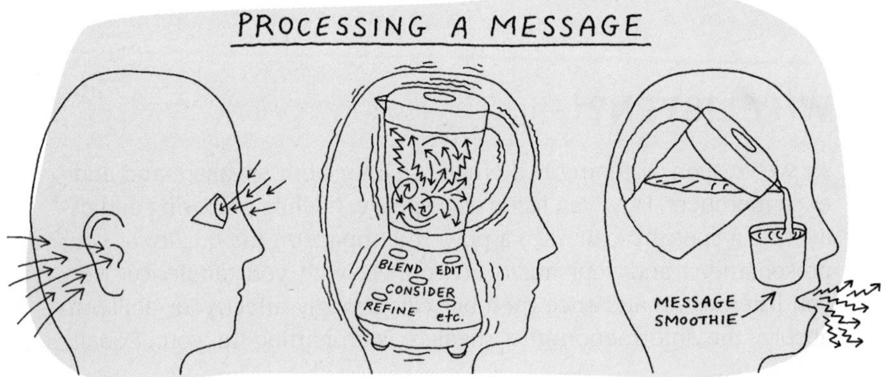

developer. You want to decide whether eLogic's software for tracking and fulfilling orders is right for your business. As Jeff describes the product, you do more than just listen to his words. You also consider the implications of what he is saying, how using the software will affect your bottom line, and whether Jeff represents a reputable company. You then mull over questions such as: "Can my business afford this investment? Will I need to provide extensive training to help my workers learn the new software? Are there other programs that would deliver similar advantages but are easier and cheaper to use?" By weighing these matters—that is, by processing the information in your mind and possibly through jotting down notes—you stand a better chance of making a smart decision for your business.

Retaining What You've Processed

The more carefully you process what you're hearing, the more you will engage your powers of **retention**—your ability to remember what you've heard. In fact, in a ten-year study of listening patterns, one of the authors of this textbook found that poor retention of a speech was directly related to audience attentiveness during the presentation.[2] This study also found that individuals with poor attention habits remembered only a fraction (25 percent or less) of what was said in a speech. Worse, what they *could* recall was often inaccurate or confused with something else they had in mind at the time of the presentation. Among people who fail to process what they're hearing, the ability to accurately recall what they hear decays over just three to six hours after the original communication.

The study also revealed a recurring pattern of attentiveness in people who did not listen well. At the beginning of a presentation, poor listeners tended to pay little attention. Their attention quickly improved as a presentation continued, but then just as quickly fell to a very low level, only to rebound near the end of the speech. Clearly, the sporadic levels of attention made it much harder for these listeners to process messages; no wonder, then, that they retained very little.

To further see the connection between processing and retention, consider your own listening behavior as a student. How much do you retain if you pay little attention to your instructors in class? If you take

notes during lectures, how accurate are they? How much do you remember from lectures in which you did not process what you were hearing? There's no doubt about it: the more you process messages, the more likely you'll remember what you heard—and retain it accurately.

THE CULPRITS BEHIND POOR LISTENING

What causes ineffective listening—especially in public speaking situations? The culprits include specific behaviors: unprocessed note taking, nonlistening, interruptive listening, agenda-driven listening, argumentative listening, and nervous listening. Later in this chapter we will also be discussing defeated listening and superficial listening.

Unprocessed Note Taking

While researching your speech, you may decide to take notes during interviews. And while listening to a speech, you might take notes based on what you're hearing. People who engage in **unprocessed note taking** in these sorts of situations take word-for-word notes without thinking about what they're writing down. That is, they listen *only* to take notes—not to process what they're hearing and writing. The words they hear enter their consciousness and just as quickly

exit, deposited on their notebooks or in their laptops. Unprocessed note takers usually have trouble remembering what was said in an interview, a lecture, or a speech. And they miss opportunities to ask clarifying questions or to comment in informed, thoughtful ways. Not surprisingly, unprocessed note taking greatly hampers retention, since it skips the processing stage of listening.

Nonlistening

People who engage in **nonlistening** simply do not pay attention to what they're hearing. For example, if you're overly interested in your own questions during an interview, you won't be attuned to what the interviewee has to say in response. In a lecture, you are likely to engage in nonlistening if you are more focused on your own thoughts about the subject than on what the speaker has to say. Not surprisingly, nonlistening prevents you from processing another person's message—and therefore keeps you from retaining it.

Interruptive Listening

With **interruptive listening**, one person consistently interrupts another. You've probably seen or heard instances of interruptive audi-

ence members, shouting things like "yeah right!" or blurting out questions before the speaker is ready to entertain them. Speakers can also be interruptive listeners. For example, a speaker might see an audience member raise her hand; instead of recognizing her and listening to her question, the speaker rudely cuts her off mid-sentence and finishes the question for her. In either capacity, speakers who do this are likely to miss certain aspects of the question or comment. Worse, they often come across as rude and arrogant, thus losing the respect of audience members.

Agenda-Driven Listening

Public speakers who focus solely on the mechanics of their presentation may demonstrate **agenda-driven listening**. This listening challenge applies primarily to a speaker giving a presentation who also has to accommodate questions and comments from audience members. For example, as audience members raise questions and offer comments during the speech, you think only about your next point. Perhaps you scan your notes while a listener asks a question or you provide monosyllabic and overly brief responses—revealing that you're not really listening to your audience. Not surprisingly, this behavior can annoy audience members and damage your credibility.

Argumentative Listening

People who feel in conflict with individuals they are listening to may display **argumentative listening**—listening to only as much as they need to fuel their own arguments. Argumentative listening can also afflict speakers who feel personally attacked by audience members during question-and-answer sessions. Because they hear only part of what a questioner has asked, they can't respond to the question in a thoughtful, informed way. And that hurts their credibility.

You can also fall victim to argumentative listening during an interview if you disagree with the interviewee's opinions or ideas. Here, you may focus more on your own views and miss out on everything the other person has to say.

Nervous Listening

People who fall victim to **nervous listening** feel compelled to talk through silences because they're uncomfortable with a lapse in the conversation. This occurs often in interpersonal situations. For example, imagine that you've just met an attractive new person and you've tried to strike up a conversation with him. When he takes a long moment to respond to a question, you start filling in the silence with nervous chatter—making it even more difficult for him to respond.

In the realm of public speaking, nervous listening can cause just as much havoc. If an interview subject takes a long time to answer a question, a nervous listener might ask more questions or blurt out a string of comments; the interviewee would never have any opportunity to answer, and the interviewer would end up with incomplete research. Or imagine giving a speech introduction in which you ask a provocative question in an attempt to engage the audience. If no one in the room responds to your question, you might get thrown off and feel compelled to say something—anything—to get the speech moving again. You might fill in the silence with a random joke or comment, only to see your listeners look confused or annoyed.

Nervous listening—in any context—can damage your ability to gather and interpret information from others that you need to deliver an effective speech. If you feel twinges of nervousness, collect yourself and wait a few beats before continuing.

BECOMING A BETTER LISTENER

Despite the many different behaviors constituting ineffective listening, you *can* overcome the challenges through practice and attention to a few details. In this section, we offer suggestions for improving your listening skills through **interactive listening**. In interactive listening, you filter out distractions, focus on what the other person or people have said, and communicate that you've paid attention.

Filter Out Distractions

There are potentially countless distractions in any speaking situation, both external and internal. External distractions could be anything from street noise, a flashy visual aid left up during an entire presentation, or chattering audience members. Internal distractions, often referred to as **internal noise**, are any thoughts that make it hard for you to concentrate—for example worrying about how well you're doing in class or about other pressing assignments, thinking about a

ONE LISTENER EXPERIENCING INTERNAL NOISE

movie from the night before, or pondering aspects of your personal life. If you are an audience member, filtering out distractions means focusing on the speaker and the message while avoiding other elements or activities that could draw your attention, such as gazing around the room, studying for another class, or surfing online. As a speaker, filtering distractions during presentations or question-and-answer sessions means focusing on reactions or questions from audience members—rather than looking ahead to your next point. While conducting interview research, filtering distractions means focusing on the question that you've just asked and the interviewee's response, rather than looking ahead to your next questions or thinking about unrelated topics.

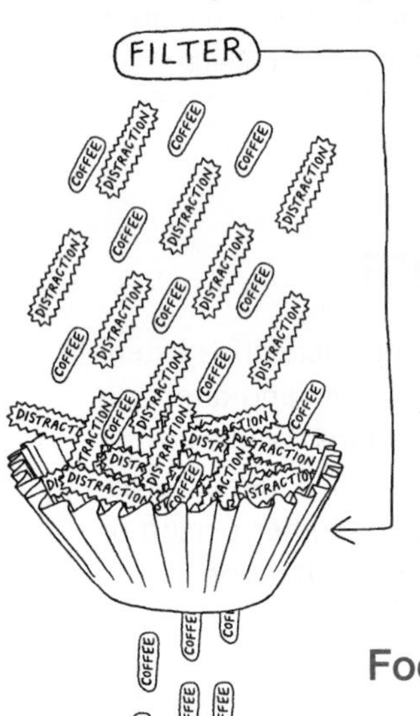

Focus on the Speaker

In any listening situation, keep your mind on what the speaker is saying, not on what you may be about to hear or what you're going to say next. Ask yourself, "What does this statement that I've just heard mean? Do I agree or disagree with it? Do I have questions or comments of my own about it—or even a different point of view? How might other people think or feel about this comment or issue?"

Show That You Are Listening

As a responsible listener, you should show the speaker that you are listening. How? Use a combination of nonverbal and verbal cues. Look at the other person while he or she is speaking *and* as you are responding. Indicate nonverbally—perhaps with alert posture and a smile or nod of your head—that you are paying attention.

When the opportunity presents itself, you can also verbally communicate that you are listening. As an audience member, you can ask thoughtful questions during a question-and-answer session or even applaud appropriately at a rousing portion of the speech. As a speaker, paraphrase questions asked by audience members to show that you understand and to allow them to correct any misinterpretation. And in interview situations, maintain eye contact and be ready to move into new lines of questioning based on your interviewee's responses.

MAXIMIZING YOUR AUDIENCE'S LISTENING

Despite your best efforts, you may occasionally find yourself delivering a speech to audience members who do not listen well. For example, doing audience surveillance, you may notice listeners engaged in **defeated listening** if they feel that your presentation is too difficult to follow or **superficial listening** if audience members *act* as if they are listening but are actually distracted by external elements such as a conversation with a neighbor or their own newspapers, cell phones, or homework.

Just as you can benefit from strengthening your own listening skills, as a speaker you can also help your audience members overcome their own listening challenges. The good news is that you can take steps to help your audience members listen more effectively as you're delivering your speech.

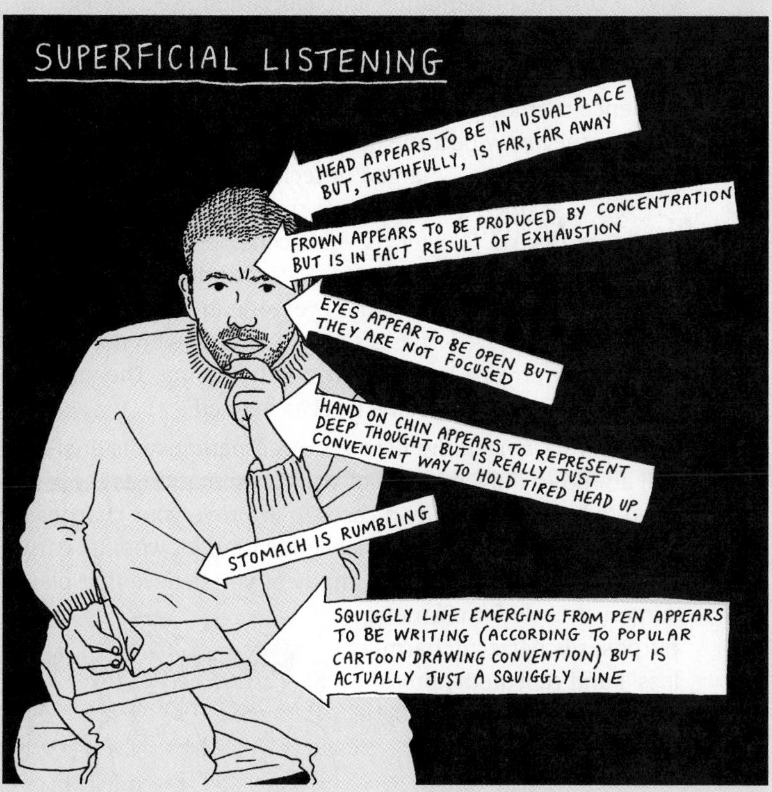

SUPERFICIAL LISTENING

HEAD APPEARS TO BE IN USUAL PLACE BUT, TRUTHFULLY, IS FAR, FAR AWAY

FROWN APPEARS TO BE PRODUCED BY CONCENTRATION BUT IS IN FACT RESULT OF EXHAUSTION

EYES APPEAR TO BE OPEN BUT THEY ARE NOT FOCUSED

HAND ON CHIN APPEARS TO REPRESENT DEEP THOUGHT BUT IS REALLY JUST CONVENIENT WAY TO HOLD TIRED HEAD UP.

STOMACH IS RUMBLING

SQUIGGLY LINE EMERGING FROM PEN APPEARS TO BE WRITING (ACCORDING TO POPULAR CARTOON DRAWING CONVENTION) BUT IS ACTUALLY JUST A SQUIGGLY LINE

Anticipate Ineffective Listening

Just as you analyze your audience when choosing a topic appropriate for your listeners, you can also use it to reduce ineffective listening by your audience:

- *Consider your listeners' attention and energy levels.* For example, people listening to a speech at 8:30 on a Monday morning will likely have a limited attention span. Many may be tired from the weekend and may not have adjusted to the new week. Therefore, avoid delivering a long speech with no audience interaction during such times. Instead, give a concise presentation and allot time for active listener participation.
- *Assess your audience's knowledge and abilities.* If your audience members know little about the subject of your speech, they may become defeated listeners if you include jargon or technical details. To avoid that, explain concepts and define key terms. Also, consider any barriers to audience understanding, such as whether everyone in your audience has a similar capacity with the English language or anyone has problems with hearing. Then adjust your word choice or volume level as needed.

- *Watch for argumentative listeners.* Argumentative listeners will attend to only as much of your presentation as they need to build up their own case. To improve your chances of keeping their attention, acknowledge their viewpoints early in your speech ("I know that many of you believe that plastic surgery merely for cosmetic purposes is perfectly harmless") and repeatedly press your main message throughout the presentation.

Tailor Your Delivery

As you deliver your speech, pay attention to factors that affect your audience's ability to listen: voice, volume, fluency, projection, rate, and pausing. Speaking too quietly can inhibit listening, as may poor fluency, fast delivery, or excessive pausing. Be sure to maintain eye contact with your audience and avoid obtrusive gestures or turning your back on the group while adjusting a visual aid.

Use Audiovisual Aids Strategically

Audiovisual aids can help you capture audience attention and thereby encourage listening. Therefore, consider spacing these aids throughout your speech to maintain interest. Also, don't present an audiovisual aid until you want your audience to see or hear it. When you are finished with it, put it away, outside your listeners' view or hearing range.

Front- and Back-Load Your Main Message

Listeners tend to pay the most attention just after the beginning of the speech and then near the end. For this reason, front-load your main message—that is, present it early in your speech. Then use your conclusion to give listeners another opportunity to process and retain your message.

LISTENING WHEN YOU ARE IN THE AUDIENCE

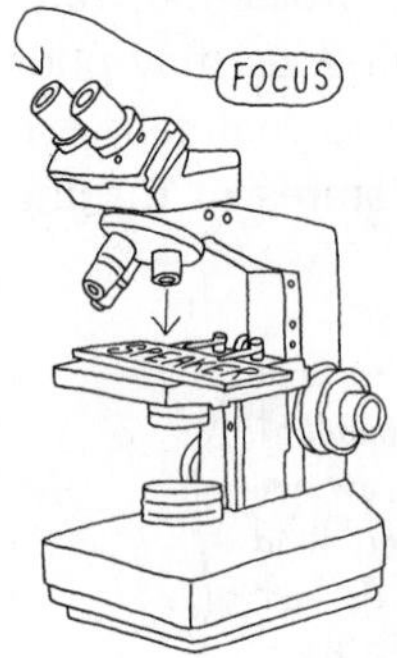

When you're an audience member, listening not only helps you retain the speaker's message, it also enables you to provide the speaker with an informed **speech critique**—written or oral feedback offered after a presentation. Critiquing is an essential component of public speaking classes because it helps speakers learn from their experiences. Your instructor will likely specify what you should cover in a critique. The guidelines below can also give you additional guidance.

- *Take notes.* While listening to a presentation, jot down your thoughts about the speaker's delivery and message. By recording your impressions as you form them, you'll be able to access your thoughts when it comes time to offer your critique.
- *Identify main points.* As you take notes, begin to distinguish what you think are the speaker's main points—these are the two or three most important ideas that the speaker wants you to remember (speechwriters sometimes call these "takeaways" or the "take-home message"). You can identify main points by listening carefully to the introduction; most speakers will preview main points during that part of the speech. You can also listen for signaling language in the transitions of the speech. Finally, speakers often restate their main points during the speech's conclusion.
- *Consider the speech's objectives.* To provide **constructive criticism**—feedback a speaker can use to improve his or her skills—strive to understand what the presenter is trying to accomplish. Identify the speech's general rhetorical purpose—to inform, persuade, or mark a special occasion—as well as the specific speech purpose. Next, evaluate how well the speaker achieves his or her goal.

- *Support your feedback with examples.* Offering an overly general comment such as "good eye contact" or "work on your organization" is not particularly useful to a speaker. Support generalizations like these with specific examples, such as "You made eye contact with people on every side of the room," or "You had a good preview, but I found the organization of your main points difficult to follow." Specific comments help speakers know which behaviors to do more of during their next speeches, and which to avoid.
- *Be ethical.* Be courteous in your critiques and treat the speaker the same way you hope and expect to be treated when it's your turn to receive feedback. During the speech, avoid prejudging the speaker or a topic. Think critically about the message you're hearing. And make sure that you hold the speaker accountable for his or her words. If you are offended by or disagree with something in the speech, tell the person while providing your critique. But do so courteously, and avoid making your comment sound like a personal attack. Explain why you disagree, and offer examples.

SUMMARY

"Listening is a vital skill in public speaking and beyond."

Because most humans come into this world with the capacity to hear, too often we take this particular sense for granted—assuming (falsely) that merely possessing the ability to receive audio stimuli makes us capable of understanding the sounds and words we encounter. In truth, hearing noises, sounds, and words is not the same thing as listening to them. *Hearing* refers to passively receiving this stimuli; *listening* refers to how one processes and understands them. This is particularly relevant where public speaking is concerned—because both speakers and audience members must develop good listening skills. It is important to note that listening is not limited to words only or even sound—tone of voice, rate of speech, and visual cues such as body language and gestures also convey a tremendous amount of information that you as a listener can use to understand a message.

To make the transition from hearing to listening, it is important to understand that true listening takes place when a person pays attention to a message and then processes that message, coming to his or her own conclusions and thereby also engaging the capacity for retention—remembering the message. Research has shown that inattentive listeners typically follow a consistent pattern of attention: they pay little attention at the beginning of a presentation; then their attention improves quickly and falls again, only to rise once more at the speech's conclusion.

There are a host of culprits that lead to unsuccessful listening, including unprocessed note taking, nonlistening, interruptive listening, argumentative listening, agenda-driven listening, and nervous listening. In this chapter, we have explored how the listening process works, what causes ineffective listening, and how to improve your listening skills both as a speaker and an audience member. Listening is vital not only for developing and delivering a successful speech but also for observing and critiquing a presentation, and happily it is a skill that can be learned. These skills include filtering out distractions, focusing on the speaker, and showing that you're listening.

As a speaker you can also take steps to improve audience listening by anticipating defeated, superficial, or other forms of ineffective listening; tailoring your delivery to audience needs; using audiovisual aids; and front- and back-loading your message.

As an audience member, make sure to take notes and identify the speaker's main points. And when giving feedback, make sure to offer constructive criticism by considering the speech's objectives, supporting your feedback with examples, and always keeping appropriate ethical guidelines in mind.

Key Terms

hearing
listening

THE LISTENING PROCESS

processing
retention

THE CULPRITS BEHIND POOR LISTENING

unprocessed note taking
nonlistening
interruptive listening
agenda-driven listening
argumentative listening
nervous listening

BECOMING A BETTER LISTENER

interactive listening
internal noise

MAXIMIZING YOUR AUDIENCE'S LISTENING

defeated listening
superficial listening

LISTENING WHEN YOU ARE IN THE AUDIENCE

speech critique
constructive criticism

Today I'll be addressing CENSORSHIP and TECHNOLOGY...

Wow, they're really not into this. I need to get their attention.
BEEP!
CLICK!
CLICK!
BEEP!
CLICK! CLICK! CLICK!

I see a lot of you have TECHNOLOGY...
Well, how would you feel if the government controlled everything you saw, listened to, and wrote?
I should have been doing this all along.

5 AUDIENCE ANALYSIS

"Let the audience drive your message."

You're standing with a crowd on the street, waiting for a speech from a woman who has decided to run for a seat in Congress. You heard her speak last week at your college, where she tried to rally student support for her candidacy. And you found her presentation quite convincing; you're now excited to vote for her because she seems to care, she appears quite well informed, and as someone who cares about education she would do much to benefit students like you.

Today, this candidate is addressing a larger group of voters, many of whom are students from your campus. Soon after she begins her speech, however, you find yourself feeling annoyed and restless. She seems to be covering the exact same topics she addressed during last week's speech, and she's even using some of the same gestures. You exchange glances with several of your dormmates who were at the speech the previous week. They roll their eyes, and a few of them wander off. But even as members of the crowd walk away or shift

AAAAGH! I didn't mean to look bored!

their weight restlessly, the speaker plows forward with her talk without making any adjustments to her delivery style or content. She seems oblivious to the fact that she has lost much of her audience's attention. Apparently, she failed to analyze her audience while developing her speech, and failed to do so while delivering it.

Perhaps you have experienced generic speeches—canned presentations delivered in exactly the same way each time, no matter the audience or setting. When a speaker just "phones in" a speech, listeners react usually with boredom, irritation, and lack of attention. The audience members lose—because they stop listening and miss out on any valuable information the speaker is sharing. The presenter loses—because he or she gets a reputation for being insensitive or dull.

By contrast, speakers who tailor their message to their listeners create enormous value for their audience *and* themselves.

- First, listeners become much more interested in and attentive to the speech.
- Second, listeners experience positive feelings toward the speaker when he or she has made an effort to understand listener concerns.
- Third, listeners open their minds to the speech message because it targets their specific needs, interests, and values.

The skills of analyzing your audience are also used far beyond the realm of public speaking. Most of us intuitively practice these skills during our daily interactions with others. For example, suppose

you want to ask your instructor for an extension on an assignment that you know you can't finish by the deadline. You might develop a casual and straightforward approach if your professor interacts comfortably with students and has granted extensions to other students in a previous semester. On the other hand, you'd probably take a very different and more careful approach if your professor tends be formal and distant or is known to be unsympathetic to excuses.

Even in everyday conversation, we continually shape our messages as we focus awareness on the people we're talking to; therefore, it's not surprising that this skill is highly important in the context of public speaking. To learn about your audience before developing your speech, you will need to gather various kinds of information about your listeners.

In this chapter, we organize the types of information you will need to gather into the following categories: situational characteristics, demographics, common ground, prior exposure, and audience disposition. We also provide some tips for gathering these details, as well as suggestions for what to do if you discover halfway through a speech that you've misread your audience.

SIZE MATTERS

UNDERSTANDING SITUATIONAL CHARACTERISTICS

Situational characteristics are factors in a specific speech setting that you can observe or discover *before* you give the speech. They include audience size, time, location (forum), and audience mobility.

Size

Audience size is simply the number of people who will be present for your speech. In a classroom setting, the size of your audience will be obvious. But in the world beyond school, this information may not be so apparent. For example, if the leader of a charitable organization asks you to give a speech at an awards dinner, you would need to ask how many people will be attending: Seven to ten people? Twenty-five to thirty? Three hundred? A thousand?

When it comes to speech presentations and audience, *size matters*. That is, the number of audience members affects how you'll craft *and* deliver your message. The smaller the group, the greater the

opportunity for you to interact with your audience—for example, through question-and-answer sessions. With small audiences, you can also communicate a more detailed and specific message, because you're tailoring it to the needs of just a few people. Conversely, the larger the audience, the less opportunity you have for interaction. Therefore, you'll have to work harder to anticipate your listeners' questions and craft a more generally accessible message.

Consider the example of Jeanine, a marketing representative for a software company. Jeanine's boss asked her to visit several cities and deliver big sales presentations—what the boss described as "dog and pony shows"—for a revolutionary new software product designed to create striking visual presentations. Up to that point, Jeanine had only presented the product to small groups of five to seven people in intimate boardroom settings. In contrast, the dog and pony shows would be in large hotel ballrooms, and her audiences would range from three to five hundred prospective customers.

As she prepared for the first presentation, Jeanine realized that unlike her previous experiences, she simply would not be able to answer every audience member's question as it cropped up; if she did, she'd never get through the presentation. Nor would she have time for a lengthy question-and-answer period. With this in mind, she decided to incorporate some of the more likely audience questions into her presentation.

Jeanine also realized that among audience members there would be great variety in knowledge about computers. So she decided to cover technical issues by "teaching to the middle": rather than pitching her speech to the few listeners who would be extremely computer savvy, or slowing things down for the few who knew very little about technology, she focused her content for the large group in the middle. That way, she could feel confident that her talk would be accessible to the largest portion of her audience.

Time

Time is an important aspect of any presentation you will deliver, both in terms of the time alloted for the speech and your listeners' own time rhythms in the day. Thus, you will want to consider two aspects of timing: presentation time and body clock.

Presentation time is the length of time you have to deliver your presentation. Is it one minute? Five minutes? Twenty minutes? As long as you wish? The answer should shape how you prepare and deliver your speech.

For example, when your presentation time is short, you have to make tough choices about what to include and what to leave out. Remember, though, that some of the most powerful, persuasive messages—television ads—are just fifteen to thirty seconds long. Yet they convey extensive information and can strongly influence an audience's behavior. To exert the most impact in a very short speech, carefully reduce your message to something your audience can quickly digest.

NOT CONSIDERING BODY CLOCK

If your presentation time is relatively long, you'll have more opportunity to develop your main points. But you'll also be more at risk of digressing—or veering away from your central message. With long speeches, concentrate on sticking closely to your main message. That way, you'll keep your audience members—and yourself—focused.

Body clock—also known as **chronemics**—refers to the time of day or the day of the week when your audience members will be listening to your presentation. If you have a choice about when to give your presentation, which days and times would you select—and which would you avoid?

If you sought to avoid 8:30 on a Monday morning, you'd be making a wise choice. Many students are still mentally rooted in the weekend and will have difficulty focusing on your speech. Similar distractions abound for people close to lunchtime, at the end of the day, or at the end of a week.

Nevertheless, you can still deliver an effective speech at such times. For example, you might include more humor or anecdotal references to engage your audience. Or with your teacher's approval, you might open by asking direct questions of some audience members, which

heightens their attentiveness. Finally, you could simply shorten your speech to match your audience's attention span.

One of the authors of this book was once invited to give a presentation to a group of lawyers at 3:00 P.M. on a Tuesday. The twenty-five minute speech—about effective negotiating strategies—was part of an all-day conference. Unfortunately, the conference schedule lagged, and the presenter realized that he would have to speak much later, at 4:30 that afternoon. Since his listeners' attention span would be minimal at that time, he quickly reframed the speech: five minutes of simple tips plus a quick question-and-answer period. Invigorated by the concise and lively presentation, the lawyers were fully engaged and asked spirited questions at the conclusion of the speech.

Location

Location, also known as **forum**, is the setting where your audience will listen to your speech. Speech locations vary widely—from classrooms and auditoriums to conference rooms and outdoor venues. And each type strongly influences how you deliver your speech.

Consider the following true story. Joe, a high school junior, was running for student-body president. Each candidate had to deliver a campaign speech at an afternoon rally. The location of the rally was the recently completed high school quad, a sunken plaza built about eight feet below the foundations of four surrounding brick buildings. This design produced some rather spectacular acoustics when sound within the plaza was projected against the brick buildings.

Joe spoke first at the rally. Concerned that huge crowd would not be able to hear him, he had decided to speak with a microphone. But he didn't realize that the plaza design would amplify his voice anyway. When he spoke into the microphone, the sound was so loud that his listeners grimaced and groaned. Because of his inattention to location, Joe's speech was literally too painful to hear!

Joe failed to consider the acoustics of his speech location. In addition to acoustical problems, locations can present other challenges, such as availability of audiovisual equipment (are there electrical outlets for your audiovisual aids, or should you bring handheld visual aids?), lines of sight (will your listeners be able to see your visual aids?), and lighting (is it adequate?).

How to anticipate and address location challenges? Go to the place where you'll deliver your speech. Stand there, and imagine yourself giving the presentation. Now position yourself where the audience will be and imagine listening to the speech. Will all your listeners be able to see and hear you?

If Joe had taken stock of the forum for his speech ahead of time, he might not have elected to use a microphone. Given the size of the forum, he might also have decided to walk from behind the podium

NOT TAKING FORUM INTO ACCOUNT

and make himself more accessible to his audience so listeners could hear *and* see him better.

Mobility

Different speech settings may have different implications for your audience's mobility—the degree to which listeners move around during a speech. For example, if you're giving a presentation in a classroom, lecture hall, or conference room, your audience will likely be **stationary**—listeners will be relatively motionless (sitting or standing) as you're talking. If you are delivering a presentation at an exhibitor's booth at a sales conference, on a town common, or on a city sidewalk, your audience members will probably be **mobile**—strolling by, stopping for a moment to listen to you, or drifting off to get on with their day.

If you're making a presentation in a college classroom, you know that you will have a captive audience because your listeners' grades depend in part on their class attendance and

participation. Don't fall into the trap, though, of taking a captive audience for granted. Surely you have experienced lecturers who do exactly that; knowing that their audience must remain present sometimes misleads teachers into assuming that they don't have to work as hard to capture the audience's attention. Veteran teachers know they should work just as hard to keep the attention of a captive audience.

Capturing the attention of a mobile audience is clearly more challenging than that of a stationary one. To do so, take a hint from the salespeople who make their livings at conventions and county fairs selling everything from rugs and hot tubs to produce and kitchenware. These vendors contend with an entirely mobile audience, so they must draw an audience's attention quickly and magnetically. For example, a seasoned vendor might try to sell a fruit and vegetable knife by arranging colorful, pre-cut fruit in pleasing shapes such as a flower or windmill. She might also make the speech interactive—stopping passersby and encouraging them to "test drive the knife, have some fruit, watch a little slice and dice!" You can adapt these effective techniques to your own presentations by offering fun (and maybe edible!)

visual aids and making your presentation interactive by inviting audience members to come over or by asking invitational questions that fit with your overall message (just make sure that the questions are appropriate to the speech setting and aren't invasive or personal).

INCORPORATING DEMOGRAPHICS

In addition to considering situational characteristics, you also need to take demographics into account. **Demographics** refers to certain characteristics of your listeners—for example, age, gender, sexual orientation, race, ethnicity, religious orientation, educational background, and political affiliation. By assessing your audience members' demographics, you can better anticipate their beliefs about your topic, their willingness to listen to your message, and their likely responses.

Each of us is the target of demographic research every day by marketers and advertisers. Remember watching Saturday-morning cartoons when you were younger? The shows were full of ads for sugary cereals, sweet desserts, fast food, and toys—all products that marketers believe will appeal especially to a young audience. And companies target their selling to adults in similar ways. You will usually see beer and car commercials broadcast during televised football games

111
EY-DAVID

because those advertisers believe that football audiences—often males, certainly people who enjoy tailgating—will be interested. Or you may notice that financial companies often advertise during televised golf or tennis competitions—sports that are thought to have more affluent participants and viewers.

In this section, we examine demographic characteristics you should consider while developing and delivering your speeches.

Age

Age can affect how audience members respond to your message. For example, a presentation on safe snowboarding would not likely interest most retired persons. But it may hold great appeal for athletic students in their late teens and early twenties.

Naturally, when you're speaking to a large group of diverse listeners, their ages may vary considerably. How can you consider age when targeting these varied listeners? Try tailoring your supporting materials (such as examples and quotations) to the needs of different age groups within your audience. For instance, older listeners may not understand references to popular musical groups or late-night comedy shows that younger people tend to appreciate. And younger

listeners might not get references to classic film stars like Greta Garbo or Cary Grant or perhaps even some less recent rock stars such as Elvis Presley. For younger listeners, you might also try to avoid referring to events that took place before they were born unless you place the events in context for them.

Gender Composition

The **gender composition** of your audience—*mixed* (male and female) or *single gender* (all female or all male)—affects how your listeners will respond to your speech. Some stories, illustrations, or examples might resonate better with one gender grouping than another.

Car sellers, for example, pay close attention to differences in buying patterns between genders. In recent years, marketers in the automotive industry observed that more women have been buying cars, and that sales pitches aimed at men did not work so effectively with female customers. Minh, a former student of ours and an automotive salesperson, told a story that shed light on this development. In Minh's experience, effectively selling Volvo station wagons to men and women required two very different approaches.[1] To appeal to men, Minh emphasized the cars' turbocharged engines, high-performance tires, and special detailing. To capture women's interests, he stressed features related to safety, reliability, and fuel economy. While Minh aimed the same broad message at all shoppers: "You'll want to buy this wonderful car," he tailored the specifics of the message to each gender.

Minh's example shows that you should consider messages that will be most effective for your audience members based on their gender. Yet it is essential to remember that you must never assume you know about an individual audience member's views based on gender—the views of countless men and women cut against the grain of traditional ideas of **gender stereotypes**, oversimplified and often distorted views of what it means to be male or female. Likewise, ethical speakers never resort to **sexist language** or language with a bias for or against a given gender.

Sexual Orientation

Another demographic characteristic that has become increasingly important to consider and acknowledge is the **sexual orientation** of your audience members. This can include straight men and women as well as gay men, lesbians, bisexuals, and transgendered individuals—or GLBT for short. Amid the controversy surrounding questions of status and equal protection for GLBT citizens (such as whether their unions should be accorded legal marital status or whether they should be allowed to serve openly in the military), it is obvious that not everyone in the United States feels comfortable with or accepting of people based on differences in sexual orientation.

Given this environment, some might quibble with or object to acknowledging the GLBT demographic, but we believe strongly that acknowledging members of the GLBT community is not only a smart and strategic move for a speaker, it is also an ethical responsibility. Statistics vary, but estimates have often suggested that gay or lesbian people (only two parts of the GLBT designation) account for between five and ten percent of our population.[2] Since speakers have a responsibility to all members of their audiences—not simply those in the dominant majority—ignoring GLBT listeners means excluding a substantial portion of an audience from the discussion, and potentially alienating that portion.

Acknowledging a difference in sexual orientation can be accomplished both overtly and passively, depending upon what is appropriate for your speech and your situation. Open and overt acknowledgment of these differences might be accomplished by including examples or illustrations that reference GLBTs as well as straight people. So, for example, a speech on conflict in relationships might include examples of gay or lesbian couples in the same breath with examples of heterosexual couples. Likewise, a speech that deals with

parenting could include the story of two fathers raising a child, along with examples featuring a mother and father, or a single parent.

You can offer passive acknowledgment of the GLBTs (and do so sensitively) through inclusive word choice when referencing sexual or relational orientation. For example, instead of only speaking of "married couples" or a "wife searching for a husband" (or vice versa), you might refer to "loving partners" or "individuals looking for a long-term commitment." Inclusive word choice invites everyone in the audience to share in the speech, while avoiding language that privileges one form of sexual orientation over another.

Race and Ethnicity

In the United States today, the population is far more racially and ethnically diverse than in previous eras. With this increased diversity, your audience members are likely to come from a wide variety of racial and ethnic origins. In preparing and delivering your speeches, you need to be sensitive to your listeners' diverse backgrounds and speak to their varied interests. But at the same time, you must not generalize about particular races or ethnicities. For example, Americans of white European descent don't all necessarily feel the same way about affirmative action. Neither do all Americans of African descent.

Still, **race**—common heritage based on genetically shared physical characteristics of people in a group—*can* affect how listeners respond to a speaker's message. This is especially true where racial issues are sensitive, affecting people throughout their lives.

Ethnicity—cultural background that is usually associated with shared religion, national origin, and language—is another important demographic aspect to consider as it can shape beliefs, attitudes, and values of audience members. A student named Gunther learned this lesson the hard way. Gunther gave a presentation to members of his campus's student-run Middle Eastern Society and spoke to an audience he had been informed consisted of students who had fled from Iraq shortly after the U.S. invasion in 2003. Attempting to show courtesy, Gunther addressed his listeners as "Iraqis."

Only later did Gunther learn that his audience had been made up of Assyrians who had been living in Iraq. Although Assyria no longer exists as an independent nation, there are millions of people who continue to identify themselves as Assyrian. They speak a common language, share religious beliefs, and have their own distinctive traditions and customs. While many of the Assyrians in Gunther's audience realized his mislabeling of them as Iraqis was unintentional, they still took offense at being categorized with an ethnic group with whom they did not identify. They (rightly) concluded that Gunther hadn't cared enough to find out about their actual backgrounds. Offended and annoyed, many of Gunther's listeners didn't bother to listen to much of his presentation.

Religious Orientation

Religious orientation—a person's set of religious beliefs—is another demographic characteristic that can influence how people respond to your speech. In the United States alone, there are as many as twenty-three hundred different religious identifications—including Baha'is, Buddhists, Christians, Confucians, Hindus, Jews, Muslims, and Zoroastrians—to name just a few.

For some people, religious orientation strongly shapes their views on a wide range of issues—including but not limited to gay marriage, abortion, and men's and women's roles in family life and society. Moreover, some of the larger religions have numerous subdivisions whose adherents possess conflicting beliefs about specific issues. For example, Anglicans and Roman Catholics share common elements in the celebration of the Eucharist, but they are widely divided over issues such as allegiance to the papacy or the admission of women to the priesthood. Likewise, Muslims don't all necessarily agree about every issue, and Reform and Orthodox Jews certainly part ways over several issues. Thus, like any other demographic characteristic, religious orientation does not preordain (pardon the pun) an audience's reaction to a given message, yet it can still exert great influence. Presenters who craft their speeches accordingly stand a better chance of connecting with their listeners.

Consider the example of the late Pope John Paul II's address to the state of Israel at the Yad Vashem Holocaust Memorial in March 2000. The pontiff knew that many Jews thought that his predecessors had been indifferent to Jewish suffering during the Holocaust. Demonstrating his sensitivity to their feelings, the pope repeatedly used Old Testament passages to describe suffering and awareness of human evil. In addition, he firmly condemned any act of hatred, any persecution, and all displays of anti-Semitism directed at Jews by Christians, at any time and in any place.

Why did the pope make this last point about Christian anti-Semitism when speaking about the Holocaust? For some Jews, the roots of anti-Semitism extend back to a period called the Inquisition, in which Jews suffered at the hands of the Catholic church. In addition, since World War II, there has arisen much controversy about the role of the Catholic church and particularly Pope Pius XII (pope from 1939–58) in the Holocaust; some supporters claim that Pius's actions led to the saving of the lives of thousands of European Jews, while critics claim that the church (with Pius as its leader) was either too silent about the Holocaust or possibly aided the Nazis.[3] Pope John Paul understood that these concerns might shape Jewish listeners' perceptions of his qualifications to speak at Yad Vashem. By analyzing his audience's religious orientation, the pope gained valuable insight into how best to construct his speech. At the ceremony itself, he was visibly moved as he laid a wreath at a granite slab that covered the remains of unidentified Jewish vicitims of the death camps and then ceremoniously lit an eternal flame. The pope then gave a heartfelt speech sharing some of his own memories of the fate of his Jewish friends in Poland during the war and decrying the Nazi atrocities. Because John Paul II was aware of the situation and especially his audience members' likely religious concerns, he gave an effective speech that connected with and moved his audience members, including several Holocaust survivors.

Educational Background

Your audience's **educational (and informational) background** can also influence their reaction to your speech. For example, suppose many of your listeners are already familiar—through formal education or life experiences—with the facts you plan to present in your speech. If you're aware of this familiarity beforehand, you'll know that you won't have to provide extensive background information and explanations in your speech. But if your audience is unlikely to have exposure to your topic through formal schooling or life experience, you'll need to provide more explanation and examples to help them understand your presentation.

Consider the story of Roy, a civil engineer responsible for civic projects such as building new bridges and highways. To get approval for his projects, Roy often made presentations about zoning issues to a civilian commission. When doing careful analysis of his audience's educational backgrounds, Roy realized that the panel members actually knew very little about the necessary zoning issues. The commission members lacked formal training in zoning, and because they served brief two-year terms, none served on the commission long enough to acquire extensive knowledge about the relevant issues. Roy therefore kept his speeches simple, explaining or avoiding technical terms. To help his listeners decide how to vote, he explained how issues currently before them compared with issues on which they had voted in the past.

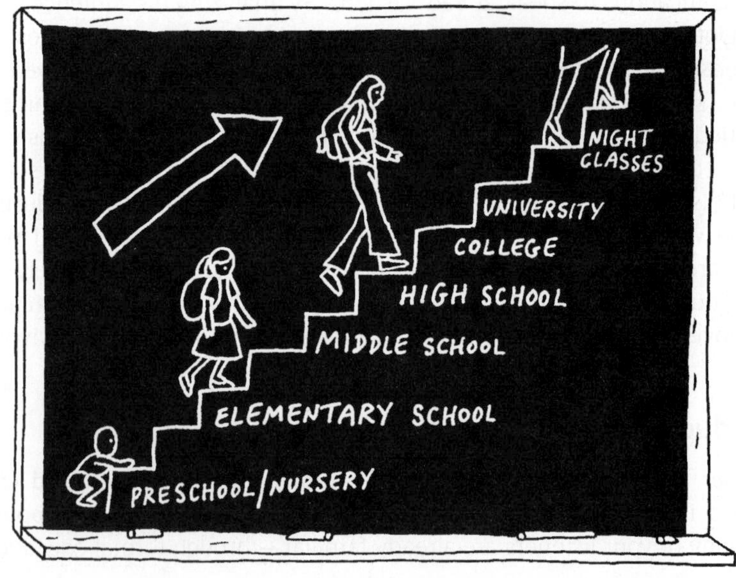

Listeners who lack background in your subject might also benefit from audiovisual aids that clarify the points you're making. Carefully repeating your main points can also help your audience members understand your presentation by giving them time to absorb and process the information.

Political Affiliation

In some respects, **political affiliation**—a person's political beliefs and positions—is the most difficult of the demographic characteristics to pin down. Traditional labels like "liberal" or "conservative" and "Republican" or "Democrat" elude specific meaning and are so broad as to be relatively useless in predicting a person's views on every issue. "Conservative," for example, may refer to *fiscal conservatism* (belief in balanced budgets and reduced taxes), *law and order conservatism* (belief in the need for a stronger criminal justice system), *defense conservatism* (belief in the necessity for a strong defense and military preparedness), or *social conservatism* (positions on controversial social issues like

abortion or the right to die, often informed by religious perspectives). Members of your audience who identify themselves as conservative won't all necessarily hold the same beliefs about each of these dimensions of conservatism. Likewise, membership in a political party does not guarantee that someone will vote for a specific candidate or respond to a speaker's message in a predictable manner.

Nevertheless, knowing your listeners' political orientation—as well as their views on specific political issues—can you help determine how to craft your speech. In a highly polarized political climate, attention to your listeners' political orientation becomes especially crucial to making a successful presentation.

Putting the Demographic Pieces Together

Great public speakers use their knowledge of their listeners' demographic characteristics to understand the people they are addressing—and to make their messages more effective. Every audience is unique; by identifying characteristics that many of your listeners share, you gain insight into how they might respond to your message. You can then incorporate these insights as you develop your speech and frame your message for the audience.

For example, Jackie, a fifty-two-year-old medical doctor, was asked to give a speech about safe-sex practices. Her goal? To convince her listeners that safe-sex practices decrease the likelihood of unwanted pregnancy and sexually transmitted disease. Her audiences? A group of teenagers in a facility for runaways, and a group of middle-income, working-class parents at a school meeting.

Jackie knew she would need to craft her message differently for each audience. The teenagers, all runaways, were suspicious of authority figures, especially older individuals who wanted to lecture them on their behavior. In her speech to the teens, Jackie avoided calling attention to the age difference between herself and her listeners. She also took care not to lecture them. Instead, she invited them to share their experiences, which made them feel understood. And just as importantly, Jackie avoided scare tactics because she wisely realized that her young listeners had already been exposed to threats and intimidation that had prompted some of them to run away in the first place.

By contrast, in Jackie's speech to the middle-income parents, she worked hard to build trust immediately. She wanted them to see her not only as a doctor, but also as an adult woman and a mother. She made pointed references to raising her own daughter and talked about the difficulties of parenthood. She also knew that some of the parents in her audience didn't want to acknowledge that their children were sexually active. So, she avoided saying things that would make her listeners intensely uncomfortable, such as "You need to make sure that your child does not become pregnant or come down with a sexually transmitted disease." Instead, she cited recent statistics detailing the transmission rate of deadly diseases among youths who did not follow safe-sex practices.

SEEKING COMMON GROUND

Another way to analyze your audience is to look for **common ground**—beliefs, values, and experiences that you share with your listeners. Consider Jay, a student at a commuter school who gave a persuasive presentation to convince his listeners to use mass transit

instead of driving to school. Like many of his listeners, Jay had spent his first year of college driving to school every day—getting caught in traffic, having trouble finding parking, and arriving late for classes. As he presented his arguments, Jay shared his own experiences with driving because he knew that many of his listeners faced these same challenges. And he knew that by establishing this common ground, he would gain credibility with his listeners.

In some cases, you can communicate your perception of common ground nonverbally. For example, a candidate for national political office dons a cowboy hat while delivering a speech to voters in Texas or a sports cap from a local team. Of course, merely putting on a hat doesn't necessarily mean that you share actual common ground with your audience. Use this technique only if you feel a genuine sense of shared identity with your listeners. And then reinforce that authenticity by referring to the common ground verbally during your speech.

IDENTIFYING PRIOR EXPOSURE

Do you remember hearing your parents or teachers giving you a lecture you had heard before—and finding yourself completely unconvinced because their points were not even persuasive the first time?

Or perhaps you've heard a sales pitch or an ad slogan that seemed lame the first time you heard it, and only more so every subsequent time? This can be a problem for public speakers too—as a student named Henry discovered when giving the fourth of five speeches required of him in an advanced speech class. His fourth speech was a prepared, persuasive presentation that critiqued the existence of "global warming." In making this speech, Henry picked up where he had left off with his second speech (given earlier in the semester), an informative speech explaining how people uncritically accepted what they learned from television news media. In the second speech, Henry had used "global warming" as one of the examples of "stories that television media pushes on people." In that same speech, he offered explanations of things the "media ignored" about global warming, and how audiences "just accepted them." At the time, his class audience was impressed by his speaking ability, but fairly critical of his points about global warming. When he revisited the issue in the fourth speech, he repeated the same criticisms of global warming—and was later surprised to learn that the audience was not in agreement with anything he said. The mistake he made was *not* in taking an unpopular position about global warming, it was instead in ignoring the audience's reaction to what he had said the first time and simply repeating the same arguments for the same audience a second time.

Analyzing your audience also includes gauging listeners' **prior exposure**—the extent to which they have already heard your message. The degree of this prior exposure should guide you either to include particular points in your speech or craft something entirely new. How can you determine whether your audience has had prior exposure to your topic—and use that information to shape your presentation? Ask yourself the following questions:

Has my audience heard this message before? If your answer is "No," your listeners have had zero prior exposure and will have no preconceived notions about or positions on your message. You can craft your message as you want, but you may have to explain all relevant issues and concepts in basic terms. If your answer is "Yes," then your audience has had prior exposure. Move on to the second question.

Has my audience responded positively to the message? If the goal of an earlier speech on your same topic was persuasion, consider whether the audience members actually took the actions or adopted the beliefs that the speaker advocated. If the purpose of that earlier speech was to inform, determine whether the audience members became interested in the subject and understood the information the speaker presented.

If you answer "Yes"—your audience responded positively to the message in the past—then use the new speech to reinforce the previous message, add any pertinent new information, and motivate your audience to take action (if you are giving a persuasive speech).

If you answer "No"—your audience did not respond positively to the message in the past—then avoid the approach used in the previous presentation. Now, proceed to the third question.

Why did the previous message fail? Assess what went wrong the last time your audience heard the message. Then use the resulting insights to tailor a more successful approach. In the case of Henry's speech, it would have benefited him to ask his classmates why they disagreed with his position in his first speech. Perhaps he would have discovered that some of them questioned his knowledge of science, some of them only knew about climate change from what they had heard on television, and some may have even found Henry a bit arrogant. Knowing the answers to this question would have given Henry other options for his fourth speech.

If your audience has had a major change in perspective since the previous presentation, consider whether you need to adjust your message to accommodate listeners' new viewpoints. George W. Bush's 2004 reelection campaign and the 2006 midterm elections reveal what can happen to speakers who fail to alter their message after their listeners' perspectives have shifted. In 2004, Bush based his campaign communication strategy on acknowledging the difficulty of the war in Iraq—while extolling the leadership qualities of commitment and consistency. In every campaign speech he gave, Bush reiterated his commitment to winning the conflict in Iraq and establishing democracy there as an alternative to terrorism. While stressing the consistency of his position on Iraq, he painted Democratic challenger John Kerry as a "flip-flopper," and the presidency, Bush implied, was no place for a flip-flopper. Many voters found Bush's message persuasive—and cast their ballots for him at the polls in November.

Two years later, Bush urged House and Senate Republicans to run with the same message during the midterm elections of 2006. Initially, GOP members reluctantly went along with him—

even asking him to be their spokesman in a series of addresses to the nation. But the president and his advisors wrongly assumed that because voters had responded positively to his message in 2004, they would do so again in 2006.

Their mistake? They didn't ask themselves whether anything had changed for voters since their prior exposure to the message. As a result, they underestimated the shift in public sentiment about Iraq, which had turned from support for the war to opposition. Voters who in 2004 believed that democracy in Iraq was possible—or that a decisive military victory was attainable—had grown decidedly skeptical about those same possibilities by 2006. The election outcome, in which Democrats swept into the House and Senate, was more a resounding rejection of Bush's message than an endorsement of the Democratic platform. And it cost the president and his party control of both chambers of Congress.

IDENTIFYING AUDIENCE DISPOSITION

Finally, complete your audience analysis by assessing listeners' **disposition**—their likely attitude toward your message. In most situations, audiences can be divided into one of three groups: hostile, sympathetic, and neutral.

A **hostile audience** opposes your message or you personally and therefore will resist listening to your speech. In contrast, a **sympathetic audience** already holds you in high personal esteem or agrees with your message and will respond favorably to your speech.

A **neutral audience** has neither negative nor positive opinions about you or your message. Listeners may be neutral for several possible reasons. Some are apathetic and simply not interested in you or your ideas. Others may be very interested in hearing you talk but lack strong feelings about your topic. The key thing to remember about neutral audiences is that—depending on how you deliver your speech—they can tip toward supporting your message or opposing you.

As with the other elements of audience analysis, gauging your listeners' disposition can help you figure out how to craft your speech. For example, suppose you'll be facing a uniformly hostile audience. In this case, you probably should define realistic goals for your speech. Though you may not be able to persuade your listeners to follow a course of action you recommend, you might succeed in getting them to reevaluate their opposition to your message or to you personally. Thus, seek incremental or small changes, as opposed to a complete turnaround in attitudes.

An excellent example of this is when Senator Edward (Ted) Kennedy was invited to speak in October 1983 at Liberty Baptist College, a conservative Christian school established by the Reverend Jerry Falwell. Kennedy, a well-known liberal lawmaker, agreed to speak at the school though he knew that he would face a hostile audience. For his speech, Kennedy addressed the emotionally charged subject of separating church and state. His speech, entitled *Truth and Tolerance in America,* focused on the appropriate place for religion in discourse about politics. In a speech that at times found common ground with Baptists and Reverend Falwell himself, Kennedy carefully but clearly celebrated and encouraged religious groups to enter political discourse where moral and ethical questions were concerned, while encouraging them to avoid name-calling or disparaging those who disagreed. It is unlikely Kennedy convinced many in the audience to change their minds about contentious issues like abortion—but he did make incremental gains with the audience on a personal level as audience members respected his courage for addressing them and appreciated the lengths to which he had gone to find some commonality with the audience.[4]

If you're addressing a sympathetic audience, you don't need to bother investing a lot of time and energy in trying to convince listeners that your ideas have merit or that you're a credible speaker. Instead, push for more commitment from them: rather than simply asking your audience members to agree with you, urge them to act on your message.

If you'll be facing a neutral audience, determine whether your listeners' neutrality stems from apathy, disinterest, or a lack of firm conviction about you or the issue you are addressing. Then, figure out how to overcome these forces of neutrality and get your listeners to support you—not oppose you.

Note, though, that many audiences don't fit neatly into just one dispositional group. In most cases, some listeners in a particular audience will be hostile, others sympathetic, and still others neutral. You'll need to tread carefully to deliver the most effective speech possible. If most of the people in your audience are neutral, a small percentage is sympathetic, and the remaining few are hostile and very vocal, what should you do? Expend just enough effort to silence the hostile listeners. Make an equally modest effort to motivate your sympathetic listeners to act on your message. And devote the lion's share of your energy to reaching your neutral listeners—and persuading them to take your side.

GATHERING INFORMATION ABOUT YOUR AUDIENCE

Thus far, this chapter has reviewed the types of information you will need to analyze your audience. Here we will examine three techniques you can use to obtain that information: surveying, interviewing, and observing.

Surveying Your Audience

A **survey** is a set of written questions that you ask your audience to answer in advance of your speech. Surveys allow you to ask your future audience members direct questions about topics related to your speech. If the audience is small—let's say thirty or less—try to survey all of them. If it is larger, you may want to survey a smaller, representative sample.

There are three general types of questions you may want to ask in a survey: fixed-response, scaled, and open-ended questions.

Fixed-response questions—such as true/false, multiple-choice, or select-all-that-apply questions—give your respondents a set of specific answers to choose from.

Fixed-response questions are useful to gain concrete insights into an audience's experience with or views of a topic. For example, if Megan, a student, wanted to give an informative speech on why visiting the dentist is a good idea (because she herself has always been afraid of the dentist!) she could ask fixed-response questions to find out if audience members have experience with dental care or even to learn about potential for common ground—maybe other audience members are also nervous about dentist visits.

Scaled questions measure the intensity of feelings on a given issue by offering a range of fixed responses. The ranges vary; sometimes they take the form of a numerical scale—for example from one (lowest) to ten (highest)—or a list of options including "strongly agree," "agree," "neutral," "disagree," or "strongly disagree."

Determining the intensity of your audience's feelings about a topic can help you determine their prior exposure and disposition. For her speech on visiting the dentist, Megan sought to discover the extent to which pain influenced people's attitudes about visiting the dentist. If her classmates were very frightened by the prospect of any pain, she could focus her points on advances in dental anesthesia and new teeth-cleaning technologies that lessened uncomfortable scraping.

Open-ended questions invite respondents to write an answer of their choosing, rather than offering a limited set of responses. For such a question, Megan might ask respondents to describe any problems they have had with dentists.

Open-ended questions can help you identify issues that you might otherwise not have considered or covered

Megan Dambrowski's DENTAL SURVEY

1. Have you ever been a patient at a dentist's office?
YES ☐ NO ☐

2. In the past, why have you gone to the dentist?
(CIRCLE AS MANY AS NECESSARY)
A: REGULAR CHECK-UP B: SPECIFIC PROCEDURE (e.g., cleaning)
C: SPECIFIC PROBLEM (e.g., cracked filling)

3. Have you ever been given an anesthetic at a dentist's office? YES ☐ NO ☐

4. Please respond to the following statement by circling the answer that best reflects your feelings:
"I am nervous about visiting the dentist."
STRONGLY AGREE ———— I am terrified of the dentist.
AGREE ———— I get nervous when I visit the dentist.
NEUTRAL ———— I am neither nervous nor excited.
DISAGREE ———— I don't mind going to the dentist.
STRONGLY DISAGREE – Whoopee, it's time to go to the dentist!

5. When you are going to have dental treatment, how important is it to you that you experience no pain? PLEASE ANSWER ON A SCALE OF 1 TO 10, WITH "1" REPRESENTING "NOT IMPORTANT AT ALL" AND "10" REPRESENTING "VERY IMPORTANT".
1 2 3 4 5 6 7 8 9 10

6. Describe any problems you may have had during recent visits to the dentist (e.g., pain, discomfort, etc.).

THANKS Megan

in your other questions. So if Megan wanted to know the range of dental problems her audience members had experienced, she could best find out through an open-ended question.

Open-ended questions also allow respondents to communicate in their own words. In fixed-response questions, perhaps none of the options accurately describes the views of a specific audience member; open-ended questions allow each person to state an individual, nuanced answer.

Interviewing Your Audience

In addition to distributing surveys, you may want to **interview** audience members; ideally you will do so in person, but you can also conduct interviews over the phone or even via e-mail or IM. Interviews allow you to interact through (hopefully face-to-face) conversation, learning facts and hearing stories you can't get through a survey. Interviews also allow you to get to know members of your audience before you speak; this can serve as a great ice breaker, especially effective if you don't know the people you will be addressing. Finally, you may find it more practical to interview a few audience members than distributing a survey to a large group.

If you use interviews, carefully consider to whom you talk. It would be easiest to talk to any audience members you already know, and if the group has a leader, it would be logical to interview him or her. But your audience may have diverse backgrounds and interests, in which case you should try to interview a range of audience members.

When conducting interviews, ask the same sorts of fixed-response, scaled, and open-ended questions that are used in surveys. It is often a good idea to use fixed-response or scaled questions to get an overall impression of your interviewee's views on a topic, and then ask open-ended questions to gain more insight. During your

interview, make sure to put into practice your listening skills, by paying attention and always being respectful. Make sure to prepare your questions ahead of time, show up at the interview location as scheduled, observe appropriate grooming habits, be friendly, and make sure to thank your subject after the interview is over; after all, he or she is helping you out with your presentation!

Interviews and surveys are two effective methods of obtaining information about your audience. But you may not always have the chance to communicate with any audience member before you speak. If this is the case, you will also need to rely on less direct methods to learn about your audience.

Considering and Observing Your Audience

Along with surveys and interviews, you can always learn about your audience by considering or observing its members. Ask yourself why your audience will be attending the speech. If your talk will occur during a class, you have a captive audience, your status as students provides you with obvious common ground, and you share some background in the academic discipline of the course. If you are a member of the College Republicans asked to participate in a debate at the College Democrats club, you would likely find a hostile audience. Those attending would be there voluntarily, and free to leave at any time. Politics would be a major interest to your audience, and the fact that both you and your audience participate in political clubs on campus would give you some common ground.

Finally, consider seeking out literature about your audience members. If they belong to an organization, they may have pamphlets or brochures that they distribute. Or, there may be newspaper or magazine articles or even books written about them.

SITUATIONAL AUDIENCE ANALYSIS

Occasionally in your speaking experience you may find that you have done everything you are supposed to do regarding audience analysis by tailoring a presentation to an expected audience—only to arrive at your speech opportunity to discover that the audience you are facing is not quite the audience you expected. At other times, you may notice that the audience does not seem to be following along while you are delivering a message, or that listeners seem to disagree strongly with your main points. The following suggestions will help you analyze the audience *in the moment*—a skill known as **situational audience analysis**.

If the audience ends up being different than the one you expected, avoid communicating your surprise—audience members will likely interpret your comments to suggest that you are not prepared. Next, take a quick look at your outline and check whether the examples you have chosen make sense with this new audience. If the audience is smaller than you expected, consider jettisoning a portion of your outline and making time for questions and answers. Also, quickly consider whether your assumptions about common ground,

prior exposure, or disposition of audience still apply. Finally, consider your audiovisual aids. Do they make sense for the new audience configuration? Since it will be difficult to create new visual aids at this point, decide if there are some you can or should get rid of since the new audience may already be informed about the topic. Or, you may want to provide more explanation for certain aids because the new audience is less informed.

And because communication is a transaction between you and your audience, during your delivery your audience will be sending you messages as well. What if you are delivering your speech and your audience seems confused, lost, or hostile? Try to read the mood of your audience members and adjust your delivery appropriately. If listeners seem confused, slow down, leave out some of the specifics or technical concepts, and instead explain a few of your points in more detail; humor might also lighten the mood and get listeners on your side. Or if listeners seem bored or unengaged, consider inviting audience questions or spice up your delivery by adding enthusiasm to your delivery and varying your tone of voice—either approach will allow you to increase audience interest.

You may notice from your listeners' body language, gestures, or even their voices that they are opposed to your position. In this situation, you can always flash a sincere smile or use a comforting tone of voice. You may want to reconsider common ground with the audience and your audience's prior exposure to your message. If you can see another element of common ground you share with audience members, you may wish to incorporate that into your speech. Likewise, if the new audience seems to have less prior exposure to your message than you anticipated, you may want to discard some of the points from your outline. If there is more prior exposure—coupled with a slightly more hostile disposition—emphasize points of common ground even more strongly.

SUMMARY

"Let the audience drive your message."

In this chapter, you discovered five ways to analyze your audience: assess situational characteristics, consider demographics, identify common ground, gauge prior exposure, and anticipate your audience's disposition. You also found suggestions for gathering information on these elements of audience analysis. Finally, you learned that exceptional speakers analyze their audience while they're preparing a speech *and* while they're delivering it if necessary to retain their audience's attention and support.

Given the fact that audience-driven presentations are consistently the most effective, we strongly encourage you to analyze your audience in advance of your presentation, and then to use that analysis as a tool to shape your main points, your supporting material, and even your delivery and the ways you use your time and visual aids. Yet it is important to recognize that audience analysis is an ongoing process—a process worth reexamining as you develop the topic and speech message and hone the final product into a speech. It may even be the case that the audience slightly changes on the day of your delivery. Don't be afraid to alter things in your speech if assumptions you made about the audience are no longer accurate. Being flexible and open to that possibility will help you to craft and deliver a speech message that is targeted for the specific audience you address.

Key Terms

UNDERSTANDING SITUATIONAL CHARACTERISTICS

situational characteristics
audience size
presentation time
body clock (chronemics)
location (forum)
stationary
mobile

INCORPORATING DEMOGRAPHICS

demographics
age
gender composition
gender stereotypes
sexist language
sexual orientation
race
ethnicity
religious orientation
educational (and informational) background
political affiliation

SEEKING COMMON GROUND

common ground

IDENTIFYING PRIOR EXPOSURE

prior exposure

IDENTIFYING AUDIENCE DISPOSITION

disposition
hostile audience
sympathetic audience
neutral audience

GATHERING INFORMATION ABOUT YOUR AUDIENCE

survey
fixed-response questions
scaled questions
open-ended questions
interview

SITUATIONAL AUDIENCE ANALYSIS

situational audience analysis

Let's talk about WINTER CAMPING.
Brrr!
I'd rather talk about SUMMER SUNBATHING!
OK. Let's chat about ABORTION.
Oh no...
No way you'll change MY mind!
Well then, let's have a nice little discussion about REINSTATING THE MILITARY DRAFT.
Wow...
... that's just what we were thinking about.
AMAZING, you really can find a topic that is of interest to yourself and your audience.

6 SELECTING YOUR TOPIC

"Use your topic to focus the message."

The first major assignment in Maria's public speaking class was to "prepare a speech on a topic of interest to you and your audience." Immediately, she thought, "How do I know which topic to pick?" She had many different interests, but how to decide which one would make the best choice? The course had barely started, and already she felt overwhelmed.

But when Maria thought more about her situation, she realized that, in a sense, she chose topics many times every day. When she wanted to start a conversation with a friend, family member, or the student standing behind her in the long line at the bookstore, she needed to figure out what to talk about. In these situations, she tried to select subjects that interested herself *and* the other person. And usually these topics led to satisfying conversations.

With this in mind, Maria considered several topics for her speech. Winter camping? It was one of *her* favorite activities, but probably not one that the average student could be persuaded to enjoy. Abortion? She had strong beliefs on the subject but wondered if it had already been covered adequately in the news media or if she could even change anyone's mind on the subject. How about reinstating the draft—for men *and* women? Maria came from a military family and had enjoyed her parents' and siblings' energetic debates on both sides of that issue. With calls for sending more troops to Iraq, she decided that the students in her class—most of whom were draft-eligible—would find this subject relevant. Now Maria had selected a topic that was interesting to her and relevant to her audience.

As Maria's experience shows, you can find a good topic for your speech if you put your mind to it, even if you are initially unsure about which topic to choose. In this chapter, we present a process for selecting and refining your topic—including developing a list of possibilities, choosing the most promising one from the list, and narrowing that topic so that it meets your speech's objectives and can be covered in the time available for your presentation.

DEVELOPING A SET OF POTENTIAL TOPICS

Possible speech topics are as varied as human experience. For example, your topic could be lighthearted or serious, address ancient history or current events, or relate to professional interests or a recreational activity—and that's just the beginning. Here are some topics we've seen students select over the past several years:

airplane "black boxes"
black holes
Cleopatra
cloning
gasoline prices
genetically modified foods
Great Wall of China
health insurance reform
high-stakes testing
hot new careers
history of toilets
Hmong weddings
hurricane recovery
Iditarod dogsled race
immigration reform
Mary Magdalene
my dog Max
organic foods
outsourcing of jobs
Peruvian civilizations
port safety
religious themes for school assignments
Venus
zebras

Generally, it is the speaker's responsibility to select a topic, though in some instances you may be assigned a topic by your instructor, employer, or those who have invited you to speak. When you are called on to choose your own topic, there is a process you should follow to select the best topic for your speech. The first step is to develop a diverse set of possibilities using these strategies: brainstorming, word association, mind mapping, and research.

Brainstorming

Through **brainstorming**, you list every idea that comes to mind, without evaluating its merits. Your goal is to develop a sizeable list of topics quickly; later you will consider which one would be best. Do not censor any idea at this point in time—just let your thoughts flow.

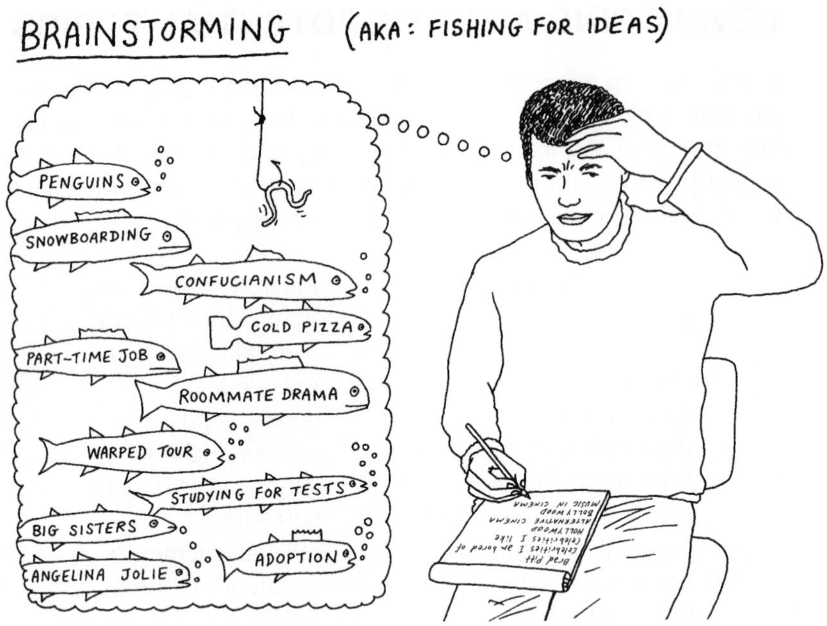

To brainstorm, consider your interests and experiences, issues that you care about, organizations you belong to, people you admire, events you find significant, places you have been, and lessons about life you have found important. Think about favorites in each of these categories. For example, what is your favorite use of spare time? The most interesting course you have ever taken? The best organization you've ever belonged to? By focusing on questions like these, you will soon build up a good list of potential topics.

Word Association

To use **word association**, start by listing one potential topic (as you do when brainstorming). Then write whatever comes to mind when you think about that idea. The second idea may suggest yet a third one, and so on. Write each new thought to the right of the previous idea. If you use word association for every topic idea that you generated while brainstorming, your set of options will grow.

WORD ASSOCIATION

With this technique, even a topic that would not be a good choice may lead you to an appropriate one. Consider what Mike, a public speaking student, experienced. His assignment was to deliver a speech on "a tip for college success." One of Mike's ideas was "my football coach," an unlikely topic for this assignment. But he associated his coach's name with the coach's favorite saying: "Success comes when preparation meets opportunity." That quotation formed the basis for Mike's excellent speech on study habits.

Mind Mapping

To use **mind mapping**, write down a word or phrase in the middle of a large piece of blank paper and then surround it with words and images representing other ideas that come to you.

Here are some tips for mind mapping:

- Use images—sketches, doodles, symbols—in addition to words.
- Start from the center of the page and work outward.
- Print rather than write in script.
- Use colors to indicate associations and make ideas stand out.
- Use arrows or other visual devices to illustrate links between different ideas.
- Don't get stuck on one concept. If you run out of ideas, move on to a new theme.
- Jot ideas down anywhere on the paper, as they occur, wherever they fit.
- Be creative and have fun with the experience![1]

By using colors, pictures, and symbols to create a mind map, you use both sides of your brain.[2] Thus, you generate more—and more creative—topic ideas.

DECIDING THAT YOU NEED TO START OVER AFTER DRINKING A NICE CUP OF COFFEE...
7
DECIDING WHAT IS FUNNY 6
DECIDING WHAT IS CLEVER 5
DECIDING WHAT IS IMPORTANT 4
DECIDING WHAT IS INTERESTING 3
JUST START AND YOU WILL END UP SOMEWHERE —BETTER THAN NOWHERE
DRAGGING IT OUT INTO THE LIGHT SO YOU CAN LOOK AT IT 2
VISUAL AIDS
BRAIN PHOTO
PHRENOLOGICAL CHART
MIND MAPS OF FAMOUS PEOPLE
SOMETHING FUNNY?
Mind map of a cartoon cha-ra-ct-er
IDEAS FOR SPEECH ABOUT MIND MAPPING
1 Include this actual mind map: THE MIND
The phone rings.
It'S my editor. He sounds happy. (HE ALWAYS DOES)
DISTRACTIONS CAN BE USEFUL.
THEY? WHAT?
THEY MAKE YOU LOOK AT WHAT YOU'RE DOING WITH FRESH EYES
IDEAS POURING OUT OF A HAT INSTEAD OF A RABBIT
Show mind.
POSSIBLE TO MIND MAP LIVE IN FRONT OF THE AUDIENCE?? —LIKE BEING AN IDEA MAGICIAN!!
FRESH EYES ARE HARD TO KEEP
It's hard to keep seeing that way... NOTHING TO DO WITH SPECTACLES. IT'S ABOUT PAYING ATTENTION
A BIG PIECE OF PAPER IS USEFUL
MUSIC?
WHAT WOULD MAKE A GOOD SOUND-TRACK?
SPARKLE
YUCK!
FRESH EYES $1.00 per lb
MAP OF MY KITCHEN
TOO BORING!
THE FRIDGE
THE STOVE
THE CAT
THE CAT'S BOWL
THE SINK
AIR
YOGURT
DISCOVERING WHAT IS IN YOUR HEAD 1
ALMOST LUNCHTIME
POINT: If you think about anything long enough (and explore/research it) you will find out INTERESTING THINGS
BUT in order to find the INTEREST you have to be INTERESTED.
NO YAWNING
LOOK AT OTHER TYPES OF MAPS
CLARITY
AS LONG AS IT MAKES SENSE TO YOU IT DOESN'T MATTER WHAT IT LOOKS LIKE
IF SOMETHING ISN'T WORKING JUST STOP
MIND MAPPING
(YES THIS IS THE MIDDLE OF THE PAGE)
WHO INVENTED MIND MAPPING?
WHO INVENTED PAPER AND PENS?
WHO INVENTED INVENTION?
OTHER QUESTIONS:
ACTUALLY I CAN'T THINK OF ANY MORE QUESTIONS AT THE MOMENT. I MIGHT COME BACK TO THIS...
MAPS = SPAM BACKWARDS
1. IS IT POSSIBLE TO MIND MAP ON A COMPUTER?
Sort of but it's just not the same.
Paper and pen work best
WHO INVENTED THE QUESTION MARK?
THE MORE YOU PUT DOWN ON THE PAGE THE MORE LIKELY YOU WILL COME UP WITH AN ORIGINAL IDEA OR WAY OF LOOKING AT SOMETHING
?
MY OPTOMETRIST ALWAYS TELLS ME TO REMEMBER TO STOP WORKING AND LOOK OUT THE WINDOW AS OFTEN AS POSSIBLE
IT LOOKS A BIT DULL OUT
A MIND
A MAP
NO!
WHAT ARE THOSE BUMPY BRAIN BITS CALLED? ?????
CONVOLUTIONS
(NOT CRENELATIONS → THOSE ARE ON CASTLES)
ANOTHER MAP
MONTANA
NORTH DAKOTA
SOUTH DAKOTA
IDAHO
WYOMING
NEBRASKA
UTAH
COLORADO
WHAT IF ALL THE STATES WERE SQUARE?
WOW! WHAT WOULD AN EDWARD MUNCH MIND MAP LOOK LIKE?
YAWNING if not drawn carefully can look like SCREAMING, or, for that matter, the other way round.
MY DICTIONARY IS OLD... SO OLD THAT I WAS WORRIED THAT "PIXEL" WOULDN'T BE IN IT.
PIXEL USA
100W
THIS BRAIN LOOKS UNHEALTHY
CEREBRUM
FRONTAL LOBLE
PONS
MEDULLA OBLONGATA
SPINAL CORD
MESENCEPHALON
LOOKS SORT OF BIRD-SHAPED
DO BIRD'S BRAINS CONTAIN THIS BIRD-SHAPED BIT
THE SCREAM PERSON'S HEAD IS SHAPED LIKE A LIGHT-BULB
IS THIS PERSON BORED, TIRED, SCARED OR ANGRY, OR JUST A BAD DRAWING
I LIKE THESE RANDOM POTATO-SHAPED BLOBS FILLED WITH WORDS
BLAH BLAH BLAH BLAH BLAH BLAH BLAH BLAH BLAH BLAH BLAH BLAH
PAUL KLEE HAD A LOT TO SAY ABOUT ARROWS
DON'T WORRY ABOUT ERRORS —JUST SCRIBBLE THEM OUT!
DRAW BETTER ARROWS
IN MIND MAPPING THINGS END UP TOGETHER ON THE SAME PAGE IN UNUSUAL AND INSPIRING COMBINATIONS. FOR EXAMPLE: LOOK AT THE WAY THE SPINAL CORD NOW LEADS INTO A POTATO!
I AM A BIRD BRAIN!
Birdus brainus truncata
{THE SHORT-TAILED BRAIN BIRD}
THIS IS NOT WHAT I AM MEANT TO BE THINKING ABOUT.
EDWARD MUNCH "The Yawn"
So..?

Research

Through **research**, you consult print or online publications to help you find topic ideas. General newsmagazines or newspapers are good sources for topics because they include articles on current events, science, famous people, and the arts. Many libraries keep recent periodicals and newspapers in easily accessible locations. You can also find potential topics by searching subject-based indexes on the Internet.

SELECTING THE BEST TOPIC

You've generated a list of topics through one or more of the techniques described so far. Now you need to select the best one. To make your choice, consider your audience's needs, your own interests and knowledge, and the setting in which you'll deliver your speech. Also, weed out topics that crop up every semester in public speaking classes, such as capital punishment, the legalization of marijuana, and steroids in sports. Your instructor may have a list of such overused topics. Finally, be careful with highly inflammatory topics. You should not select any position that you cannot support with ethical ideas, and it is almost certainly counterproductive to take a position that has no chance of persuading the audience. The following guidelines can help you pick the one best topic from the list of possibilities you've generated.

Consider Your Audience

Your audience members will devote valuable time to listen to your speech. In return, you owe them a presentation that they will find interesting and important.

Based on your preliminary audience analysis (see Chapter 5), determine your listeners' priorities and background. The topic you select should meet one or more of these criteria:

- It will interest your audience.
- It's something your listeners need to know about—for their own or society's benefit.
- It will likely inspire, entertain, or emotionally move your audience.

CHOOSE A TOPIC THAT APPEALS TO AS MANY AUDIENCE MEMBERS AS POSSIBLE

Consider Your Own Knowledge and Interests

Among all the potential topics you've accumulated, which ones are you most interested in and knowledgeable about? When you choose a topic you're familiar with and passionate about, you'll give a more fluent and enthusiastic presentation. One of our students captivated his audience with a speech on Legos (though his classmates had not played with toys for years) because his enthusiasm for the subject was so infectious. Conversely, a student who appeared totally uninterested

in her topic of job interviews failed to connect with her listeners, even though this subject was highly relevant to them.

Your listeners are also more likely to believe your claims if they know you have experience with the subject area. One student discovered firsthand the perils of selecting a topic she knew little about. Although she had no children or child-care experience, she chose to talk about why day-care centers are better than in-home day-care providers. Because of her inexperience, she made some assumptions that didn't line up with the experience of some parents in the class: she based her cost figures on national averages, which differed markedly from the local community's, and maintained (without providing proof) that in-home day-care providers typically have no background in child development. Since these claims were inconsistent with the experiences of class members who had children, she had to defer to more knowledgeable classmates during a question-and-answer session. By the time she sat down, she had lost most of her credibility on this topic.

Finally, by selecting a topic you're familiar with, you streamline the research process. You can focus on researching information that supplements the facts you already know, rather than gathering general background information.

Consider the Speech Context

The **context** of your speech is the occasion, surrounding environment, and situation in which you will deliver your presentation. These factors often make one topic choice better than another.

For example, if you are asked to speak at an awards banquet for a campus organization to which you belong, the audience will expect an upbeat speech on a topic related to that organization. A speech on more serious ideas, such as the need for changes in higher education, would be better saved for a more formal occasion.

Situational characteristics such as audience size and mobility, as well as the time of day and physical setting of your speech, should also influence your topic choice. For instance, suppose you need to play an audio snippet to present a certain topic effectively. In this case, you would not choose that topic if you will be making your

speech in a large, noisy location where listeners would have difficulty hearing the clip.

Finally, some circumstances may dictate a topic or type of topic. In a history class, your instructor may assign you an oral report on ancient China. On the job, your manager may ask you to prepare a sales presentation on a new product. The nature of the assignment may also influence your topic choice. In most classroom assignments, your teacher will expect you to include references to research; thus, you will need to choose a researchable topic. A humorous speech about your experiences as a food server, horror stories about your ex-roommates, or a demonstration of how you make your favorite fruit salad will not fit this type of assignment.

Choose a Topic and Stick to It

Once you've selected an appropriate topic from your list of possibilities, stick with it. In our experience, students who agonize over their topic selection for days or waver back and forth among several different possibilities lose valuable speech preparation time.

To support this suggestion, an analysis of more than one thousand speech diaries maintained by public speaking students revealed a consistent difference between strong speeches and weaker ones: the topic selection process. The more successful speakers carefully considered their topic choice but chose a topic promptly and then stayed with it, investing the bulk of their time in preparation. Less successful speakers spent days trying to settle on an acceptable topic.[3]

REFINING YOUR TOPIC

Once you have selected a topic, you must refine it. That is, you decide how you want your speech to affect your audience (your rhetorical purpose). Then you narrow your topic to achieve that effect.

Decide Your Rhetorical Purpose

Your intended effect on the audience constitutes your **rhetorical purpose**. In a public speaking class, your purpose will often be assigned for each speech. Outside the classroom, your purpose may be assigned (for example, by your employer) or dictated by the context of a special occasion (such as a wedding, memorial service, or roast). For other speeches, the choice of purpose will be left to you. The scenario that follows shows how one public speaking student might go about deciding her rhetorical purpose.

Amber's instructor allowed students in her class to select their own topic and purpose for their first speech. Amber chose her major, theatre arts, as her topic. She then considered a variety of purposes:

- *Informing*. When your purpose is **informative**, the message is educational, and your objective is to increase the audience's understanding or awareness of your subject. For example, Amber could tell her audience about the courses taken by theatre arts majors.

- *Persuading.* When your purpose is **persuasive**, you seek to convince audience members to consider or adopt a new position or belief, strengthen an existing position or belief, or take a particular action. For instance, Amber might try to persuade her audience to attend a play put on by the theatre arts department.

- *Marking a special occasion.* When your purpose is to **mark a special occasion**, you seek to honor an occasion by entertaining, inspiring, or emotionally moving your audience. To illustrate, Amber could amuse her audience by roasting her favorite director or move listeners by providing a tribute to a drama professor at a retirement dinner.

Each of these options would result in a speech that related to theatre arts on campus in some way. However, the rhetorical purpose of each would be different—to inform, to persuade, or to mark a special occasion. Therefore, each would have a different effect on Amber's audience.

Narrow Your Topic

Once you've determined your rhetorical purpose, think about which aspects of your topic you want to cover in your speech. That is, how will you narrow your topic so that you fulfill your rhetorical purpose? You can't cover all aspects of the topic in a single speech, so you need to decide which aspects to focus on.

DON'T BITE OFF MORE TOPIC THAN YOUR AUDIENCE CAN CHEW

Narrowing your topic is vital for several reasons. First, it allows you to fit your speech into the available time. Whether you are speaking in a classroom or in your community, it is inconsiderate to take more than the time allocated for your presentation, and audiences may stop listening if you exceed the time limit. And resist any urge to speak fast, or to cover each idea sketchily, in order to say everything you had planned. Audiences don't respond well to those tactics, either.

Second, narrowing your topic helps you focus your speech. This is an especially important step for new speakers who often select overly broad topics. When giving a speech on a specific sport such as cricket, a novice speaker might try to cover the equipment required, the rules, techniques for playing well, and maybe even the sport's history—way too much for the speaker to cover or the listeners to remember.

Conversely, one of the best sports speeches we have heard succeeded because the speaker effectively narrowed the topic of tennis. She focused on four interesting professional tennis personalities. And the points she covered—such as the classic 1973 "Battle of the Sexes" match between Billie Jean King and Bobby Riggs—captivated her audience. Even listeners who were not tennis fans or had not yet been born when that match took place enjoyed and remembered the speech.

How should you narrow your topic? Many of the same techniques you used to select your topic can also help you narrow that topic.

BROAD TOPIC:

NARROWER TOPIC:

NARROWED TOPIC:

Remember Your Audience. Ask yourself whether the aspects of your topic will be interesting or important to your listeners. Kendra, a student who wanted to deliver a speech about figure skating, surveyed her classmates and found that few were interested in a speech about how to skate. However, most of the class planned to watch the Winter Olympics on television. Kendra then narrowed her topic with the Olympics viewers in mind and chose to explain how her classmates could score the skating events while watching at home.

Draw on Your Interests and Expertise. Your special expertise or unique perspective on an aspect of your subject area can help you narrow the topic. Consider Caesar, a student who had attended school in both Mexico and the United States. He selected high-stakes testing (tests where failure has serious consequences, such as the inability to graduate or be promoted) as his speech topic, and narrowed that topic based on his own educational experiences. He compared the tests that U.S. students take with the tests students needed to take in

Mexico. His listeners were interested to learn that some of the same controversies that have swirled around testing in the United States have also emerged in Mexico.

Review Your Rhetorical Purpose. Try to narrow your topic to an aspect appropriate for your rhetorical purpose. For example, suppose you wanted to do a speech on climate change.

USING YOUR RHETORICAL PURPOSE TO NARROW THE TOPIC

INFORMATIVE TOPIC: "How Global Warming Works"

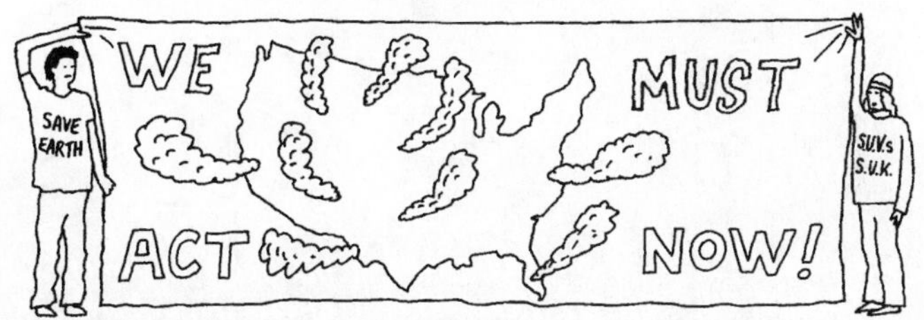

PERSUASIVE TOPIC: "The U.S. Should Institute a Carbon Tax"

SPECIAL-OCCASION TOPIC: "Commemorating the Melting of the Polar Ice Caps"

Explaining why the earth's average temperature is increasing would be a good way to narrow your topic if your rhetorical purpose was to give an informative speech. Alternatively, if your purpose was to persuade, you might advocate a tax on carbon emissions. If your purpose was to deliver a speech to entertain, you might present a highly exaggerated look at the effects of global warming.

Evaluate the Situation. You can also use situational characteristics to help narrow your topic. For example, one student, Michelle, was interested in entomology (the study of insects), so she chose bugs as her topic. Initially, she considered narrowing her topic to the use of insects to determine the time of death of a murder victim. But she rejected that idea when she remembered that she would be delivering her speech shortly after lunch—when listeners might be especially squeamish. Ultimately, she (wisely) narrowed her topic to interesting facts about bees, including how they make honey, a perfect after-lunch focus.

DRAFTING YOUR SPECIFIC PURPOSE STATEMENT

After you've identified your rhetorical purpose and narrowed your topic, your next step is to determine your **specific purpose**—the objective of your speech—and express it in a concise phrase.

To write your specific purpose, start with a phrase expressing your rhetorical purpose ("to inform," "to persuade," or "to mark a special occasion"). Then follow those words with language indicating what you want to accomplish in your speech. For example:

- "To inform my listeners how home-schooled students can still participate in dances, parties, sports, and extracurricular activities during their high school years."
- "To persuade my audience members to pay careful attention to the flight attendant's safety presentation when traveling by air."
- "To mark a special occasion by delivering a moving tribute to Elvis Presley on the anniversary of his death."

THE SPECIFIC PURPOSE FOCUSES SPEECH DEVELOPMENT

You can use your specific purpose to guide which ideas you should develop in your speech. When selecting ideas, choose those that help you accomplish your specific purpose and exclude those ideas that are not relevant. Thus, like the sideline on a football field, your specific purpose indicates which ideas are "out of bounds," given your speech's objective.

DRAFTING YOUR THESIS STATEMENT

Once you have determined your specific purpose, create your **thesis statement**—a single sentence that captures the overall message you want to convey in your speech. This statement conveys the "bottom line" of your speech, the ultimate message that all the facts and ideas in your speech support. As long as your audience members can remember your thesis statement, they should be able to recall the essence of your speech.

YOUR THESIS STATEMENT MUST BE ONE SENTENCE

WRONG

The dog ate my homework, then my special fella broke up with me, then my grandmother died and I had to go to the funeral. After that my computer crashed and my car broke down on the way here and then the doctor called and said I had iron-poor blood. For all these reasons I should not be penalized for turning in this assignment late.

Due to unforeseen and serious circumstances, I should not be penalized for turning in this assignment late.

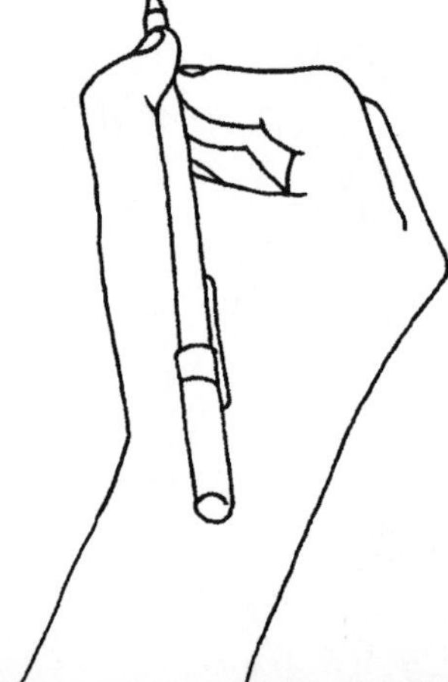

In this book, we use the term *thesis* to mean the main position of any type of speech. Some speech instructors may prefer using the term *thesis statement* when a speaker is advocating a position in a persuasive speech and the term *topic statement* when a speaker intends to inform or mark a special occasion. Your instructor will inform you if he or she prefers this alternate usage.

Here are some examples of thesis statements:

- "The Hmong New Year includes many culturally distinctive features."
- "Here is how our college makes accommodations for students who are called into military service."
- "A week-long meatless diet can show you the path to a healthier lifestyle."
- "You should sign up for a service-learning course."
- "The Duke University women's basketball team has much to celebrate at this year's awards banquet."

Here are some guidelines for ensuring that your thesis statement conveys your purpose and topic to the audience efficiently and accurately:

- *Keep it to one sentence.* Make sure your thesis consists of a single sentence that states the bottom line of your speech.
- *Express your intentions.* Ensure that your thesis or topic sentence clearly conveys what you hope your audience will know, do, or feel after listening to your speech. Listeners can better follow your message if they know what to expect.
- *Be consistent with your specific purpose.* Since your specific purpose guides how you research and prepare your speech, make sure that your thesis statement communicates the same idea as your specific purpose statement. That way, you'll avoid the all-too-common problem of presenting a thesis in your speech introduction that differs from the content of the body of your speech.

YOUR SPECIFIC PURPOSE AND THESIS STATEMENTS SHOULD AGREE (OR AT LEAST GET ALONG WELL TOGETHER)

SUMMARY

> Use your topic to focus the message.

As Maria's story revealed, selecting a topic for your speech can seem overwhelming at first. But the systematic approach described in this chapter can help you move past any feelings of frustration or confusion. In this chapter, we focused on the importance of carefully considering the topic for your speech, emphasizing that your topic should fit with your own interests as well as those of your audience members. We explained how to develop a set of potential topics and then pick the best one based on your understanding of your audience, your own interests and knowledge, and the context of the speech. We then explained how to refine your topic by determining your rhetorical purpose and narrowing your topic to the most relevant aspects, given the time available for your speech.

Next you discovered how to write your specific purpose statement, a phrase starting with your rhetorical purpose and indicating what you hope to accomplish in your speech. You also saw how to create a thesis or topic statement, one sentence indicating what your speech is about. These two statements help you develop your speech as well as communicate the essence of your topic to your audience.

Key Terms

DEVELOPING A SET OF POTENTIAL TOPICS

brainstorming
word association
mind mapping
research

SELECTING THE BEST TOPIC

context

REFINING YOUR TOPIC

rhetorical purpose
informative purpose
persuasive purpose
marking a special occasion

DRAFTING YOUR SPECIFIC PURPOSE STATEMENT

specific purpose

DRAFTING YOUR THESIS STATEMENT

thesis statement

KAW!
KAW!
KAW!
KAW!
COUNTY COURTHOUSE
We shoot the crows because they're ANNOYING.
CHIEF
We are APPALLED!
There must be a nonlethal alternative.
Let's call the Audubon Society.
OK, so crows are remarkably nervous birds and they are particularly scared of owls. Interesting. Thank you.
BIRDS
PLASTIC
EEK!
COUNTY COURTH
AMAZING!! Research works.

7 RESEARCHING YOUR SPEECH

"It is not a fact until you prove it to the audience."

When Katie, Mandeep, and Sherri learned that the police in their town were shooting crows that gathered atop the local courthouse, they were appalled. When the students called the police department to complain, the police chief explained that the practice was unavoidable because the crows were annoying, they left droppings that posed a health risk, and other solutions were too expensive.

Unconvinced by the police chief's explanations, these three students decided to actively oppose the shooting. After gathering signatures on petitions and presenting them to city officials, they were invited to speak about the subject at a city council meeting. The police chief would also attend to present her side of the issue.

Katie and her friends knew that the city council meeting was a make-or-break opportunity and that they must be prepared to respond to the police chief's claims. So they decided to find out

whether the crows indeed constituted a health hazard, whether other towns had found alternatives to shooting, and how effective and costly these alternatives were.

In other words, these three students set out to *research* their presentation so that they could convince the city council to stop the practice of shooting crows.

WHY RESEARCH?

Researching materials for your speech offers you several important benefits. For one thing, research helps you learn more about your topic before you select and develop your main points. Equally important, it enables you to gather **evidence**—information from credible research sources that you can use to support your claims. If audience members are uncertain about a point you are making (or if they disagree with you), evidence may convince them to accept that point.[1] If they accept that the source of your evidence is trustworthy and better informed than they are, they are more likely to agree with your claim, even if they would not accept your opinion alone.

When you are informed about your topic and provide compelling evidence, you also gain **credibility** as a speaker—the perception on the part of your audience that you're qualified to speak on the topic in question.[2] Audience members will see that you are well prepared and more likely to know what you are talking about because you have taken the time to research.

In this chapter, you'll discover valuable guidelines for researching your speech—including how to approach the research process, as well as how to find, evaluate, and use evidence in your speeches.

CREDIBLE EVIDENCE CONVINCES AUDIENCES

CREATING A RESEARCH PLAN

Good researchers develop a strategy for finding and keeping track of the information they need. Gaining experience, they improve on that strategy throughout their lifetime, particularly as new technologies change the nature of research. What follows are steps to help you formulate your **research plan**.

Inventory Your Research Needs

Begin by deciding your research objectives. If you have limited knowledge of your topic, you may want to do some general research to learn more about the basics. On the other hand, if you know your topic well—for example, you already have a good idea of your thesis and even some of your main points—you might want to use research to learn more about specific aspects of your topic. When determining which aspects of your topic to research further, also consider your rhetorical purpose and your instructor's research requirements. Finally, before moving ahead with your research, make a list of the subject matter you need to research and the questions you need to answer.

Find the Sources You Need

Once you have created a research inventory, consider where you can find the information you need.

First, remember that finding specific sources is not always an exact science. Although there are many tools to help you find excellent support materials, it can be helpful to think of the process as a mystery or a treasure hunt: there's great stuff out there on your topic just waiting for you, and it's your job to find it.

Your school or community libraries are two great places to start your search. If you have access to people with expertise on your topic,

WHEN YOU HAVE A PLAN

you may also want to set up an interview or two. Although the Internet can be a useful source of information, remember that there are greater risks in using Web sites than other types of sources. And it's always advisable to mix Internet research with research from other sources.

We recommend strongly that you consult with a research librarian at your school or local library. Such librarians are experts at tracking down hard-to-find information and thus can be amazingly helpful and knowledgeable about the resources available on your topic. More often than not, they will point you in the best direction for finding the most useful and credible sources.

You will also need to consider what types of sources will best meet your research needs:

- *Books* tend to provide extended and broad analysis of the topics they cover. They are one of the best sources to consult to access *synthetic* thinking on your topic because book authors often combine information from diverse sources along with their own analysis or critical judgments.
- *Journal articles*, by contrast, are often peer reviewed, and typically provide expert analysis of a subject designed for insiders.
- *Newspapers* can provide you with a "first draft of history"; that is, what people said about events just as those events were happening.

- *Recent newspapers* and *quality online sources* can provide you with up-to-the-minute information.
- An *interview* can be a great idea if an on-campus or local person is an expert on your topic.

Develop a list of potential research sources by researching library indexes (often available online), searching on the Internet, and considering credible people to interview. When searching library indexes, make a list of **keywords**—words or terms related to your topic and also synonyms of those words. If you do not find what you are looking for under the keywords you have chosen, be persistent; try using broader, narrower, or related terms until you come upon useful sources.

TYPES OF KEYWORDS FOR SEARCHES

Keep Track of Your Sources

As you research, keep a hard-copy list or create a file on your computer where you record the bibliographic information (or citation) for each of the sources you find. This is vital so that you can appropriately cite your sources when referring to them in your speech, and also so that you can relocate those sources at a later time.

For each source, keep track of the following information:

- name of author or organization
- title of the work
- title of the publication if the work is in a newspaper, a magazine, or an anthology
- date and volume number of the publication
- publisher, city, and year of publication if the work is in a book
- page number where the reference appears
- URL and date accessed for Internet sources

EVALUATING A SOURCE'S CREDIBILITY

No matter where you gather evidence for your speech (library, Internet, or interviews), you must select the most credible sources possible. Why? When you use credible sources, you can be most confident that the facts you present are accurate, and you increase the likelihood that the audience will accept your claims.[3]

To evaluate the credibility of a given source, examine four distinguishing characteristics: expertise, objectivity, observational capacity, and recency.

Expertise

Expertise is the possession of knowledge necessary to offer reliable facts or opinions about the topic in question. An expert source has education, experience, and a solid reputation in his or her field. For example, a nutrition professor would likely have expertise on the question of whether eating red meat is healthy, while a seasoned backpacker would have expertise on how to prepare for a long hiking trip. Likewise, you can look for expertise in printed or online sources by evaluating whether the authors or sponsoring organizations are well established and well informed in the areas about which they are writing.

Objectivity

Sources who demonstrate **objectivity** have no bias—prejudice or partisanship—that would prevent them from making an impartial judgment on your speech's topic. People can be biased for several reasons. Some have economic self-interest, or the desire to make money, so they may slant facts or explanations to make certain alternatives seem more attractive. Other biased people may need to please superiors; for example, a government worker who defends poorly conceived government policies. Still others have what's called ego investment: they're so wrapped up in a pet theory or cause that they lose their ability to evaluate it with an open mind.

Needless to say, you should avoid evidence from biased sources. If you use biased evidence, audience members are unlikely to accept

the point you are trying to prove.[4] Furthermore, if you use biased information, you cannot be confident that you have met your ethical duty to present truthful facts to the audience.

Observational Capacity

A person who has **observational capacity** is able to witness a situation for him- or herself. For example, a person who spends a week watching the reconstruction efforts in New Orleans after Hurricane Katrina would have more credibility on the subject than someone who gets his or her information on the reconstruction from watching the news on national TV. Sources with training and experience also make more credible observers. Thus, a person with expertise in child development would learn more by watching children respond to a violent video game than would a member of the general public.

Recency

Credible sources are also characterized by **recency**, or timeliness. Generally, newer evidence is more reliable than older evidence, because many aspects of life change constantly. For instance, in the late 1980s, HIV/AIDS was considered a death sentence, but now drug therapy is prolonging the lives of many HIV-positive people.

Because ongoing change is a reality, recent evidence is likely more accurate than older evidence. If you have a choice between pieces of evidence from two equally credible sources—one from three months ago, the other from several years ago—you should generally select the more recent evidence.

Of course, some evidence is classic and endures to this day. For example, though the teachings of Confucius are ancient, they command more respect today than the precepts of many contemporary philosophers. And the ideas of Machiavelli are still pertinent to the subject of international relations, even though they are almost five hundred years old. To decide whether evidence is outdated, ask yourself: "Has the claim made by my source become doubtful or false because of changing circumstances since the claim was made?"

With these criteria for source credibility in mind, let's now look closely at three major strategies for researching your speech: using a library, searching the Internet, and interviewing experts in your topic.

CONDUCTING LIBRARY RESEARCH

Libraries remain one of the best resources for researching your speech. Despite the Internet's increasing popularity as a research tool, the library still offers you convenient access to the broadest

range of *credible* sources. In addition, libraries allow you access to strong evidence and credible sources that are not available on Web sites. And last but not least, no search engine has been able to match the experience and expertise of professional librarians in guiding you to the best material on your topic.

Local and school libraries house a wealth of information sources, including books, periodicals, newspapers, reference works, and government documents.

Books

Books are one of the best systems that humans have ever developed for storing and conveying information; they have important advantages as information sources and are often the best place to start your research. Books have been the primary tools for sharing and storing ideas throughout human

history (for example, a surviving part of the Egyptian *Book of the Dead*, written on papyrus, dates from the sixteenth century B.C.E.), and many of today's books contain thousands of years of accumulated human knowledge. Most books are easily portable, and you don't have to plug books in or log on to use them. Books never crash, seize up, or shut down because of a low battery or power outage. And it's easier to read a book on a plane, in a park, or in the bath than any other information source.

In addition, many books are written by people with extensive expertise in their subject—though of course you should always check each author's credentials using the four criteria described earlier.

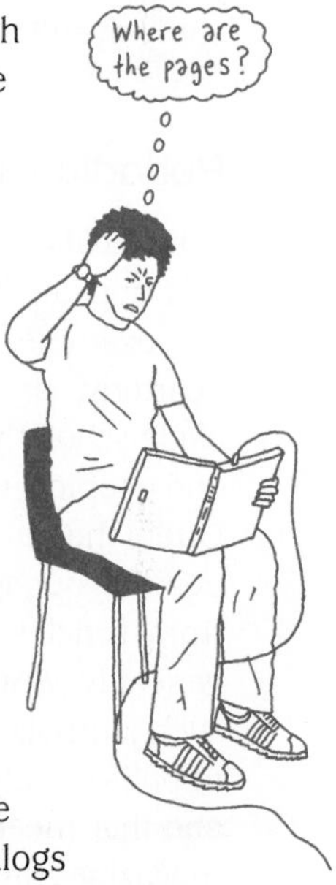

Typically, books are longer than most other information resources, and thus they are likely to provide more in-depth information on your topic, along with more analysis and consideration of a wide range of ideas on the topic. Additionally, most books are reviewed and edited before they are published, a process that improves the accuracy of the information in them.

To find books related to your topic, start by searching your library's electronic catalog by subject (such catalogs are usually available online, allowing remote access, and you can also search online catalogs by author name and book title). After entering your search terms, you'll see a list of links specifying relevant book titles. By clicking on these links, you can find bibliographic information as well as details on where in the library the books are located and whether certain titles have been checked out or are available in the stacks.

Finally, here's a tip followed by some expert library users. After you find some books on your topic in a

library's catalog, go into the library stacks and locate the books you have identified. But don't just pull the books you found and leave; instead, browse through some of the books *nearby* on the shelves. Because libraries organize nonfiction books by topic—usually using the Library of Congress or Dewey Decimal systems—the nearby books are likely to have similar coverage but also touch on some different but related areas. These nearby books might point you to aspects of your topic you haven't yet considered.

Periodicals

Periodicals are publications that appear at regular intervals; for example, weekly, monthly, quarterly, or annually. They include scholarly journals and news and topical-interest magazines. Often the most credible information on your speech topic will come from articles in scholarly journals generally written by people with expertise on a subject. Articles in such journals are subjected to **peer review**. That is, an editor decides to publish only articles that are approved by other experts in the field and that meet the publication's other requirements. In contrast, news magazines are particularly helpful for speeches on current events.

The following strategies will help you locate appropriate periodicals.

Consult General Periodical Indexes.

General periodical indexes list articles on a wide variety of topics. You can find these indexes in traditional bound volumes as well as online. Most university libraries, as well as more and more public libraries,

ONLINE INDEXES OFFER THE BEST OF BOTH WORLDS: THE QUALITY OF LIBRARY MATERIALS AND THE SPEED OF THE INTERNET.

have subscriptions to such indexes, and an increasing number are available electronically.

Online indexes are particularly helpful because they include **full text sources**—links to the complete texts of the articles in question. When they do not provide the full text, indexes often supply an **abstract**, or a summary of the article's contents. The abstract can help you assess whether the article would be useful for your speech.

The *Readers' Guide to Periodical Literature* is a general index familiar to many people. It includes numerous magazines popular with the general public. However, other general indexes contain more useful references for college speeches. Typically, these indexes are online, offer access to several thousand journals (many of which are peer reviewed), and cover a wide spectrum of academic disciplines.

GENERAL PERIODICAL INDEXES ONLINE

Academic Search Premier	Includes approximately 4,700 full-text journals, including 3,600 peer-reviewed journals on a wide range of subjects.
Expanded Academic ASAP	Updated weekly and includes indexes, abstracts, and full texts for 3,500+ journals, of which 2,100 are peer reviewed, on a wide range of subjects.
InfoTrac OneFile	More than 11,000 titles (with coverage dating from 1980), including journals related to popular, business, and professional topics.
JSTOR (Journal Storage)	Archive of over 1,000 scholarly journals in arts, humanities, social sciences, and science. Allows full text searches and provides scanned articles.
LexisNexis Academic	Full-text documents from more than 6,000 news, business, legal, medical, and reference publications, plus primary sources from a variety of periods in history.

Use Specialized Periodical Indexes. Specialized periodical indexes focus on specific subject areas and are increasingly available online.

SPECIALIZED PERIODICAL INDEXES

AGRICOLA (Agriculture)
Art Full Text
Biological Abstracts (also known as *BIOSIS*)
Communication Abstracts
Criminal Justice Abstracts
Cumulative Index to Nursing/Allied Health (CINAHL)
Education Full Text/Abstracts/Index
Humanities Full Text/Abstracts/Index
Index to Legal Periodicals
MEDLINE (medical journals)
Music Index
Philosopher's Index
PsycINFO
Science Direct
Social Sciences Full Text/Abstracts/Index
Social Work Abstracts

Ask Your Reference Librarian for Help. If you've found a citation in a general or specialized periodical index for an article that looks promising, but you can't find the periodical, ask the reference librarian to assist you. If the library doesn't have the periodical in question, the librarian can probably get the article that you need through interlibrary loan. He or she can also help you navigate the Internet to find articles listed in indexes.

Newspapers

Newspapers are another useful source, especially when you need very current information. Newspapers are sometimes said to provide a "first draft of history" because their articles represent journalists' views of current events as those events are unfolding. Many college libraries have indexes for articles published in major national newspapers, such as the *New York Times, Washington Post, Christian Science Monitor,* and *Wall Street Journal.* Your library may also have indexes for your local newspaper or papers from large cities in your region. *Editorials on File* reprints editorials from newspapers across the United States and Canada—the selected editorials take diverse perspectives on current issues.

General newspaper indexes include *ProQuest Newspapers*, the *Gale Group National Newspaper Index*, *NewsBank*, and *LexisNexis Academic*; many such indexes provide links to full-text articles. More specialized indexes such as *Ethnic NewsWatch* and the *Alternative Press Index* also cover a wide number of newspapers.

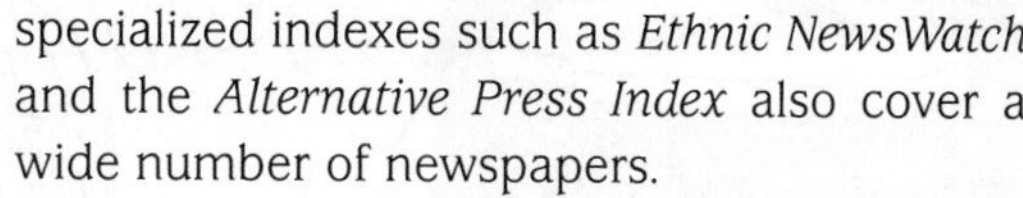

Reference Works

Reference works are compilations of background information on major topic areas. They are helpful for exploring introductory research on your subject area or discovering a specific fact (such as the number of people with Internet access worldwide or the capital of Kazakhstan). However, other sources such as books and scholarly journals provide more in-depth information about your topic. Reference works are increasingly available in both printed and online form in your library.

There are several major categories of reference works. Most include general works that cover a comprehensive range of topics and also include specialized works that focus on a single subject (for example, philosophy or art) in more detail. **Encyclopedias** offer relatively brief entries providing background information on a wide range of alphabetized topics. **Dictionaries** offer definitions, pronunciation guides, and sometimes etymologies for words, while **quotation books** offer famous notable quotations on a variety of subjects. **Atlases** provide maps, charts, and tables relating to different geographic regions. Finally, **yearbooks** such as the *Statistical Abstract of the United States* are updated annually and contain statistics and other facts about social, political, and economic topics.

Government Documents

If your topic relates to government activities, laws, or regulations, government documents can provide useful information for your speech. Document authors may be experts, but beware of documents motivated by political objectives. To find such documents, use the following resources:

- *Monthly Catalog of Government Publications* (also known as *GPO Monthly Catalog*) provides citations to federal publications, congressional hearings, and committee reports. Hearings are generally held before major federal legislation is adopted, and experts on both sides of the topic typically testify.
- *GPO Access* (www.gpoaccess.gov) contains links to congressional hearings and reports plus the *Congressional Record*, which covers all debates in the House and Senate. Legislators often add news articles, reports, and other documentation to the *Record*. *GPO Access* also includes links to Supreme Court opinions, oral arguments before the Court, and opinions of lower federal courts, as well as information issued by the executive branch of the federal government.
- *CQ Electronic Library*. *CQ Weekly* provides information about bills pending in Congress and articles about major issues confronting the federal government, while *CQ Researcher Online* provides extended reports on major news issues.

USING THE INTERNET

The **Internet** has become the "go-to" research option for many college students. The Pew Research Center's survey "The Internet Goes to College" found that 73 percent of college students said that they use the Internet

more than the library, whereas only 9 percent reported using the library more when searching for information.[5]

But searching the Web can be a bit like sending an untrained dog out to retrieve the morning newspaper. He might come back with the paper, but he could just as easily end up digging in your flower bed or eating a neighbor's chicken. Put another way, you can't always be certain that your search will generate the information you need. By understanding the benefits *and* limitations of Internet research, you can get the most from this tool.

Benefits of Internet Research

Internet research allows you convenient access to information on nearly any topic without leaving your desk. Even better, many libraries offer you access to full-text periodical and newspaper indexes from remote locations—such indexes are among the most useful available online, and we recommend that you focus on them when the convenience of researching from your own computer is important. In terms of reliable information online, we also recommend researching the "invisible Web" (covered later in this chapter), which is more likely than the standard Internet to offer credible sources.

The Internet also offers speed—enabling you to track down a news report or a research finding almost instantly, from anywhere in the world. Finally, this research tool puts an immense volume of information at your fingertips. Peter Lyman and Hal Varian of the University of California, Berkeley, School of Information estimate that the **World Wide Web** contains about 170 *trillion* bytes of information on its surface, which is seventeen times the size of the print collections in the Library of Congress.[6] With careful searching online, you may be able to find quality information that simply does not exist in your own library.

Disadvantages of Internet Research

Despite the Web's vastness, most of the world's knowledge is still contained in printed works. Authorities in many fields publish their works primarily in books and scholarly journals. And many of these works are copyrighted, so they won't likely be available on Web sites that a typical online search engine will lead you to. If they are available, you may need to pay a fee to access them.

INFORMATION DOESN'T REALLY JUST FALL FROM THE SKY.

Moreover, you can't assume that information you find online is credible, since most of it is not vetted in the same way books and periodicals are. There are literally millions of **Web sites** created by individuals, advocacy groups, clubs, and businesses that may contain incorrect or biased information.[7] And as anyone with a free blog, MySpace page, or ISP knows, in the online world it's a snap for anyone to publish as much and as often as desired.

Some students have been taught to evaluate the quality of a Web site by assessing its URL's (or Web address's) **top-level domain** (for instance, .com designating a company, .org designating an organization, or .edu designating an educational institution). However, Web sites may opt

BE CAREFUL WITH INTERNET RESEARCH: YOU NEVER KNOW WHAT YOU'LL GET.

to register as .com, .net, or .org without restriction.[8] Furthermore, the name of a Web site does not necessarily indicate that source's credibility. For example, a site such as "tobaccotruths.org" may look like it was created by research scientists with impeccable credentials—but it could actually have been created by public relations specialists funded by the tobacco industry; similarly, a professional, polished design provides no guarantee of a site's credibility. Of course many .com sites include nonobjective information as companies try to promote their products or services, but even sites with .gov or .edu might not be fully credible: for example, government agencies are unlikely to criticize their own programs, and some .edu URLs offer students' personal sites.

Evaluating the Credibility of Online Sources

Evaluating the credibility of Web sites can be particularly difficult. Many sites fail to identify authors or the dates of publication, and even sites that indicate authorship may provide no information on authors' credentials. And of course, many articles are posted online without expert reviewing or editing.

Thus, it's essential that you develop guidelines for evaluating the credibility of all sites you're considering using. For example, if a Web site provides the name but not the qualifications of an author, research that author further either online or in periodical indexes such as the *Expanded Academic ASAP* to see if he or she has published in scholarly journals. For online documents that don't indicate an author, try to determine what organization sponsored the site, and then assess that organization's credibility through further research.

How can you learn about a sponsoring organization? Robert Berkman, a faculty member of the graduate media-studies program at the New School University, suggests reviewing the organization's stated purpose to gain insight into its objectivity or bias. Also research the credentials of any listed directors or board members of the organization. Consider whether they may have any political or economic interest that compromises their objectivity.[9]

The Virtual Chase, a Web site established to teach legal professionals about online research, offers the following additional guidelines for assessing the credibility of Internet information.[10]

- *Analyze links to and from other Web sites.* If the linked sites are credible, the site in question is more likely to be credible.
- *Does another credible source provide information similar to that found on the site you're evaluating?* If so, that's a good sign of credibility.
- *Does the site weigh arguments for both sides of an issue?* If so, this suggests objectivity—a key criteria for credibility.
- *Is there advertising on the site?* If so, evaluate whether the site's creator(s) may have an economic incentive to offer content that pleases the advertiser.

- *Consider the site's word choice.* A source is more likely to be suspect when it uses biased language (see Chapter 12) or denigrates those with opposing viewpoints.

Searching the World Wide Web

How do you conduct an effective search for information online? Two tools—search engines and Web directories—can help.

Search engines are specialized programs (sometimes called "spiders" or "crawlers") that continually visit Web pages and index what they find. To use one, you enter specific search terms, and the engine searches millions of Web pages to find the best matches for the terms you have entered.[11] The program then displays the results

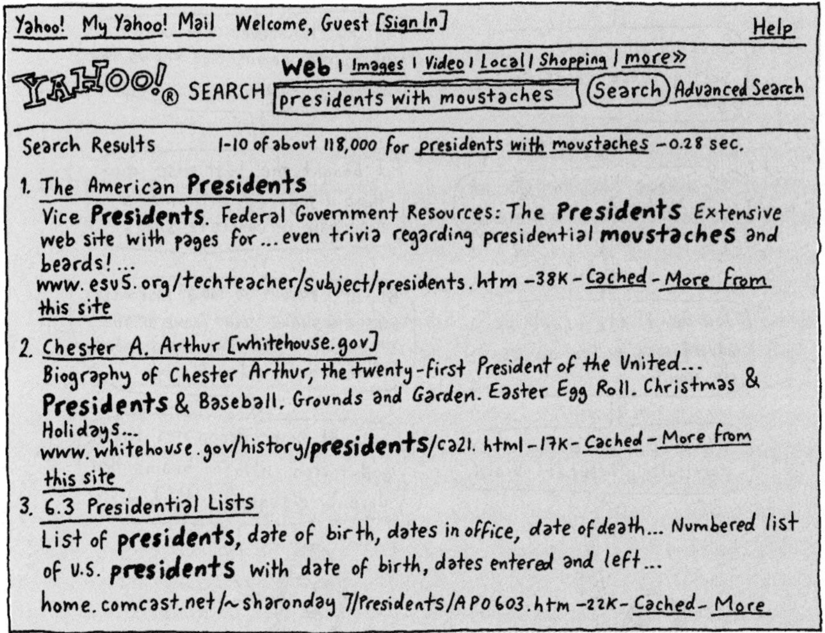

RESULTS FROM A SEARCH ENGINE

of your search as a list of Web pages. These pages are represented as live links accompanied by brief information about each site's contents.

All search engines sort results in an effort to make them more useful. Some engines organize the results by listing them according to specific criteria—such as how frequently your keywords are used, whether keywords occur near each other, or whether keywords appear in the title or near the top of a page.[12] Other engines list sites based on how many other sites link to them. But beware—a search engine may prioritize sponsored sites. If so, carefully consider the sponsor's credibility. Regardless of which search engine you use, start with the first ten or twenty sites listed in your results: they are more likely to contain useful information. Still, you may find other useful sites on subsequent results pages.

ADVANCED SEARCH OPTIONS FROM A SEARCH ENGINE

Another type of search engine is a **metasearch engine**, which searches several different search engines at once. A metasearch engine may find more of the available Internet resources than any single engine, but it requires simple search requests that all the search engines involved can understand. Also, according to librarians at the University of California, Berkeley, metasearch engines tend to look through smaller search engines and highly commercial ones—suggesting that you may end up with information that's not only limited but also biased.[13] In fact, some critics note that advertisers or media outlets may pay metasearch engines to prioritize their links in the results for certain searches. Thus, be extra careful when evaluating metasearch results.

Which search engine is best for you? Try several and compare their features and functionality. You can also check online for reviews of engines that highlight key features and provide updates as more features become available.

POPULAR SEARCH ENGINES

Search Engine	Features
Google (www.google.com)	Probably indexes more Web pages than any other engine. Prioritizes sites linked by popular sites and considers relevance.
Yahoo! (www.search.yahoo.com)	Indexes a huge number of Web pages and combines results with sites from Yahoo! directory.
MSN (www.msn.com)	Includes links to news, images, local databases, and the *Encarta* encyclopedia. "Search Builder" allows user to prioritize factors.
Ask (www.ask.com)	Results ranked by subject-specific popularity. Ask attempts to determine which sites are linked by experts; it also suggests narrower topics.

POPULAR METASEARCH ENGINES

Metasearch Engine	Features
Clusty (www.clusty.com)	Queries directories and search engines, including Ask, MSN, and Open Directory. "Clusters" search results into categories.
Dogpile (www.dogpile.com)	Queries Google, Yahoo!, MSN, Ask, and also directories. "Best of Breed" icon lists each search engine's top-ranked sites.
Info (www.info.com)	Queries Google, Yahoo!, MSN, Ask, LookSmart, and Open Directory. Offers results from single search engines.
Surfwax (www.surfwax.com)	Queries Yahoo!, LookSmart, MSN, and CNN. "Focus" feature suggests broader, narrower, and similar terms.

Many search engines also offer **advanced search**, which provides commands for making searches more precise. For example, you can search for Web sites containing all your search terms, a particular phrase, or those *not* including certain words (this last function can help you narrow your results considerably). Advanced search also allows you to limit your search by date of posting, language, country, file format, or domain. It also allows you to conduct a "safe" search that eliminates sites with pornographic or explicit content.

Web directories are compiled by human editors who review Web sites and index them into subject categories and subcategories. Depending on the directory, you can locate links to Web sites by selecting categories and subcategories, by entering search terms as you would with a search engine, or both.

Popular Web directories include the *Librarians' Internet Index* (lii.org), which is built by university librarians and focuses on sites with credible authors, thorough coverage, and contrasting viewpoints on major issues; *Academic Info* (academicinfo.net/table.html), which emphasizes scholarly oriented sites, including library and museum collections; and *Infomine* (infomine.ucr.edu), which is built by university librarians and targets resources for college faculty and students. Yahoo! (dir.yahoo.com) and Google (directory.google.com) also offer directories in addition to their search engine tools.

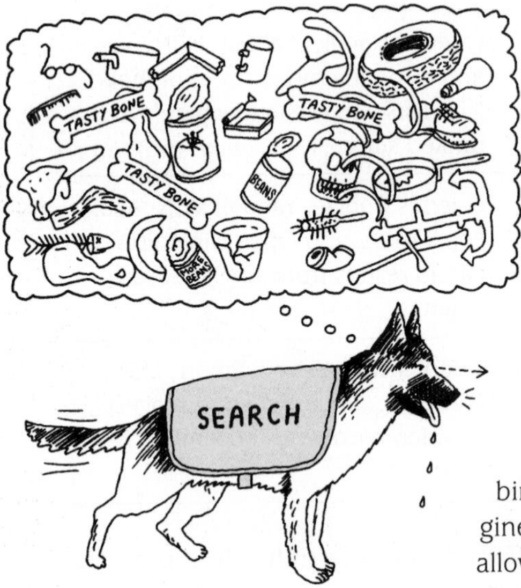

Directories can be advantageous because human editors read each page, judge its quality, and place it in appropriate categories. Search engines, on the other hand, can cover more Web sites than a human being could possibly cover in the same time.[14] Because search engines and directories have different strengths, it is helpful to use both in your research.

Hybrid search engines combine directories and search engines in one. For example, Yahoo! allows you to search its directory of sites that have been visited and evaluated by editors. Alternatively, Yahoo! lets you search the Web and obtain links to sites that have not been evaluated (along with sites included in the directory).

The Invisible Web

The **invisible Web** consists of information that is available online but that can't be accessed by standard search engines. This invisible (or

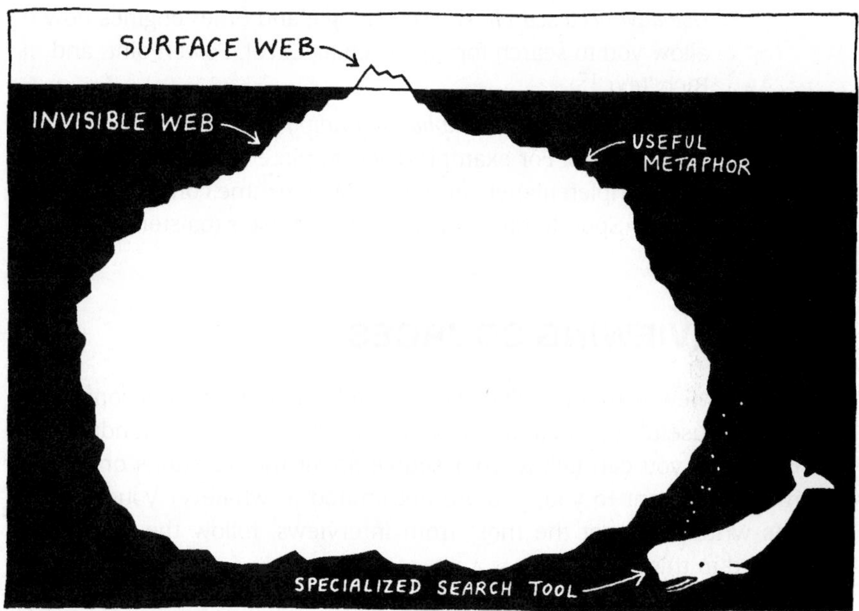

"deep") Web contains 400 to 550 times the information found on the surface Web.[15] Some of this information is stored in databases that can only be reached with specialized search tools. For example, to search a college or university's library resources online, users must often first enter a login or password to gain access; this password procedure makes it impossible for traditional engines or directories to search these resources.

Other examples of online information considered part of the invisible Web are breaking news reports, exchanges posted in an Internet chat group, or data generated by scientific monitoring equipment, along with streamed audio or video content.[16]

But how do you locate this information? These tips can help:

- *Include "database" as one of your keywords when using a search engine.* If you use the search words "global warming" and "database," your results will likely include databases where you can find quality information.

- *Use advanced search features.* Google and other engines now allow you to search formats such as Excel, PowerPoint, and Rich Text.[17]
- *Use search tools that emphasize finding resources on the invisible Web.* For example, try Complete Planet (aip.completeplanet.com), GoshMe (goshme.com), Library Spot (libraryspot.com), and OAIster (oaister.org).

INTERVIEWING SOURCES

An interview with a credible source of information on your topic can provide useful information for your speech. When you conduct an interview, you can talk to your source about the questions or issues most important to you; you are not limited to whatever your source has written. To get the most from interviews, follow the steps discussed in this section.

Prepare for Your Interview

First, determine what you want to find out through an interview. Are there any questions you are having difficulty answering through library and Internet research? Are there any individuals who, if interviewed, would add credibility to your speech?

Next, decide whom to interview. The person you talk with should be an expert on the subject; on most topics, a roommate or relative would not be the best source of evidence. If your school has a department focused on your subject, ask the chair or another knowledgeable person to recommend faculty who would make good interview subjects for your speech.

Off-campus sources such as high-ranking members of political organizations, government agencies, businesses, nonprofit entities, and community groups or clubs can also prove useful. Many of these individuals are "people-persons" who will appreciate the opportunity to talk about their areas of expertise. If the person whom you would like to interview is too busy, he or she may give you a lead about another potential subject.

Set Up Your Interview

If possible, contact in person those people you would like to interview. (It's far easier for busy people to say "No" to an interview request via e-mail or over the telephone than face-to-face.) Identify yourself, explain that you're preparing a speech, and describe what you hope to learn from the interview. Be prepared to answer any questions the interviewer may have, such as wanting to know more specific information about you or about the speech you're researching. Finally, be willing to accommodate the person's schedule.

Plan Your Interview Questions

Once you have set up your interview, decide what you want to ask the person you will interview. Prepare focused questions that he or she is in a unique position to answer, rather than general questions you could easily address through your own research.

If you want the interviewee to elaborate or provide examples, formulate open-ended questions that require more than a "yes" or "no" response. For example, instead of saying, "Do you approve of the latest ruling in this case?" ask "What are your thoughts about the latest ruling in this case?"

You might also plan to ask the interviewee a candid question, one that you think he or she would prefer to avoid. But be sure to phrase such a question professionally. Coming across as needlessly confrontational will only put your interviewee on the defensive and may cause him or her to clam up.

For more information on types of questions to ask during an interview, see Chapter 5, "Audience Analysis."

Conduct the Interview

Arrive on time for your interview, and dress professionally unless the occasion warrants different attire (for example, an interview on a farm). When you arrive, greet your interviewee and introduce yourself if you have not already met.

Keep these considerations in mind during the interview:

- *Start with friendly, easy-to-answer questions.* Straightforward questions allow you to establish rapport before you pose more difficult questions. If the interviewee has a limited amount of time, however, move on to your most important questions quickly.
- *Stay focused.* If the interviewee digresses, politely steer the discussion back to the topic.

- *Maintain eye contact.* Though you may occasionally need to look down at your questions or to take notes, keep the interview conversational and relaxed through frequent eye contact.
- *Be open to new information.* If new and valuable ideas come up, don't feel forced to stick to your planned questions. Feel free to deviate from them to explore the new information.

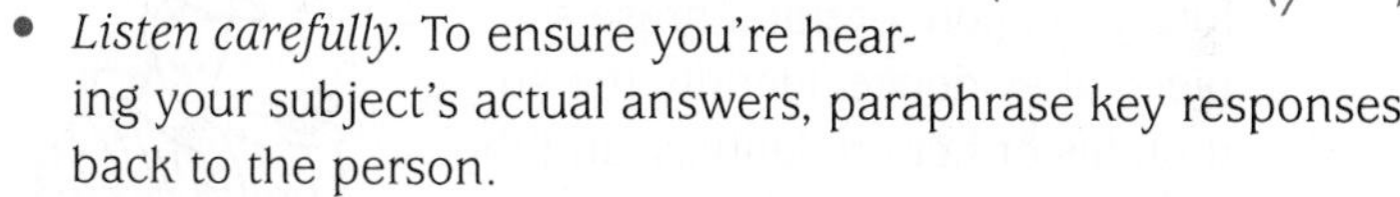

- *Listen carefully.* To ensure you're hearing your subject's actual answers, paraphrase key responses back to the person.
- *Tape the interview if your subject gives permission.* Recording an interview secretly is a serious breach of ethics.

Evaluate Your Notes

Immediately after the interview, check your notes to see whether you wrote down all the responses you may want to use in your speech. If you did not get everything in your notes, write down the person's answers while the interview is still fresh in your mind. If you cannot remember an answer accurately, contact the interviewee again to clarify his or her response, rather than guessing. For any answers you want to use in your speech, run them by the interviewee to make sure you're quoting or paraphrasing him or her accurately. And no matter what, send a thank-you note to the person.

PRESENTING EVIDENCE IN YOUR SPEECHES

You've gathered credible evidence for your speech from library and Internet research as well as interviewing. Now, how do you actually present that evidence during your speech? Here are several important considerations:

- *Document all your sources,* and provide a complete citation for each one in your speech outline.
- *Cite each source in your speech at the time you present evidence.* Before you quote or paraphrase a piece of evidence, identify the author, his or her credentials, and the publication if applicable. For example, "In an interview, Janna Wirch, a longtime ornithologist, maintained that crow droppings do not constitute a health hazard." Here's another example: "In an article published last Thursday on the Concerned Citizens' Web site, author Paul Dunn, the group's director, wrote that violent crime has decreased 3 percent over the past year." In citing Internet sources, specify the date of the source's publication if available. Otherwise, cite the date you visited the Web site.
- *Paraphrase responsibly.* If you are **paraphrasing** evidence (stating it in your own words rather than word-for-word from your source), be sure to accurately represent the author's intent. It is unethical to present evidence using **power wording**—that is, to reword evidence in a way that better supports your claim but that misrepresents the source's point of view.

SUMMARY

"It is not a fact until you prove it to the audience."

Katie, Mandeep, and Sherri, whom we met at the beginning of this chapter, have numerous possible strategies for researching their presentation on crow-shooting that they will deliver at an upcoming city council meeting. You can use these same strategies for researching your own speeches. In this chapter, you learned that providing evidence for the claims in your speech can help make your presentation more convincing and can make you more credible as a speaker. To gather evidence, you were advised to research your speech topic, first by creating a search strategy.

Next, you were encouraged to focus on credible sources, especially those found at the library and those that have undergone peer review, and learned that it is imperative that you carefully assess the credibility of Web sites because they can be created without any checks on content.

You discovered tips for collecting evidence from libraries, the Internet, and interviews, as well as for evaluating the credibility of each source based on four key criteria: expertise, objectivity, observational capacity, and recency. These criteria mean that credible sources should be knowledgeable on the topic, able to analyze the topic in an unbiased manner, and be in a position to observe or study the topic. Generally speaking, more recent evidence is more credible than older evidence.

You also learned how to present evidence during your speech. When you do so, you begin by citing the source (author, qualifications, title of information resource, and date), and then you present a word-for-word quotation or accurate paraphrase.

Key Terms

WHY RESEARCH?

evidence
credibility

CREATING A RESEARCH PLAN

research plan
keywords

EVALUATING A SOURCE'S CREDIBILITY

expertise
objectivity
observational capacity
recency

CONDUCTING LIBRARY RESEARCH

periodicals
peer review
full text sources
abstract
reference works
encyclopedias
dictionaries
quotation books
atlases
yearbooks

USING THE INTERNET

Internet
World Wide Web
Web sites
top-level domain
search engine
metasearch engine
advanced search
Web directories
hybrid search engines
invisible Web

PRESENTING EVIDENCE IN YOUR SPEECHES

paraphrasing
power wording

Nice point. You deserved to win...
Thanks... but thanks to our school's continved belief in Title IX, we both win.
You're right. That's another nice point.

8

USING SUPPORTING MATERIALS FOR YOUR SPEECH

"The sum of the parts determines the success of the whole speech."

Graciela was a member of her college's varsity tennis team, so for her informative speech topic she chose to focus on Title IX, the federal law prohibiting sex discrimination by educational institutions that receive federal aid. As she began her research, one of the first things Graciela discovered is that there are three ways a school can demonstrate compliance with Title IX. Graciela's first feeling was relief: the assignment called for an eight-to-ten-minute speech and it would take at least six to explain the ways a college could comply. She was more than halfway done!

Then Graciela reconsidered. Of all the points that she could make about this important and sometimes controversial law, would the details about compliance be the most important and interesting aspects to share with her audience? She decided to do more research about how Title IX issues were handled at *her* school. And she found a tremendous amount of material: articles in the school newspaper about the impact of Title IX when it was first applied on campus, stories from athletes about their experiences on the college's first women's teams, and even a copy of the program from the first women's tennis tournament ever held on campus.

Now Graciela had ideas and evidence that would be much more relevant and interesting to her classmates. By going the extra mile to find engaging support, she had the materials she needed to create sound support for her main points.

As we note in Chapter 2 and throughout the book, every speech offers a limited number of main points. **Supporting materials** are the different types of information that you use to develop and support your main points. You discover these materials as you research your speech. They then become the building blocks that you put together to construct a successful speech.

Selecting the best supporting materials for your main points is a key step in the speech preparation process. It's like choosing the right mix of ingredients for a special meal you'll be preparing. In an excellent speech, the supporting materials fit together to help your listeners better understand your message, capture their interest, and convince them that you've done your research and are informed about your topic.

Consider a class period in which you learned a lot about a subject, a political argument you found persuasive, or a movie that kept

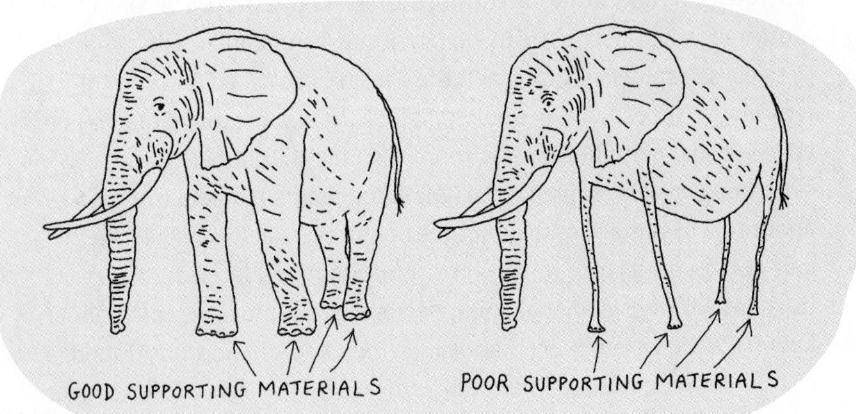

you glued to your seat for hours. Chances are good that the teacher used understandable language and examples that clarified the concepts and made the subject seem relevant. The person making the political argument likely offered convincing proof of his or her claims and touched your emotions in a way that you remembered at the voting booth. And the movie probably combined an interesting story with memorable characters and an exciting plot. With the right supporting materials, you can craft a speech that has an equally strong impact on your audience.

In this chapter, we show you why supporting materials are important, what supporting materials you can use, and how to present supporting materials more effectively.

WHY USE SUPPORTING MATERIALS?

Supporting materials strengthen your speech in many ways. They build audience interest in your topic and help the audience under-

SUPPORT IS IMPORTANT

stand your ideas. In addition, they convince the audience that your points have merit, and they breathe life into your speech.

Building Audience Interest

If you want audience members to actively listen to your speech—and ignore everything else in the meantime—you must motivate them to focus on what you're saying. By selecting supporting materials that appeal to your listeners' interests, you sweeten the odds that they will pay attention to you. For example, suppose your school is located in the Midwest region of the United States and you're developing a speech on emergency preparedness. In this case, you might put together supporting materials that focus on preparing for tornadoes—common events in the Midwest—rather than hurricanes or earthquakes.

And by including supporting materials that surprise audience members, make them laugh, or touch their emotions, you increase the chances that they will listen to what you are saying.

SELECT SUPPORTING MATERIALS THAT RELATE TO THE AUDIENCE

Enhancing Audience Understanding

If you're presenting information that's new to your listeners, they may have difficulty understanding your topic. For instance, let's say you're preparing a speech on string theory that you'll present to an audience comprising mostly liberal-arts students. In this case, supporting materials such as definitions could help your audience members understand the meaning of technical terms such as *superstrings*. And brief, accessible examples could help them grasp the basic concepts behind your topic and help them form mental images of a superstring.

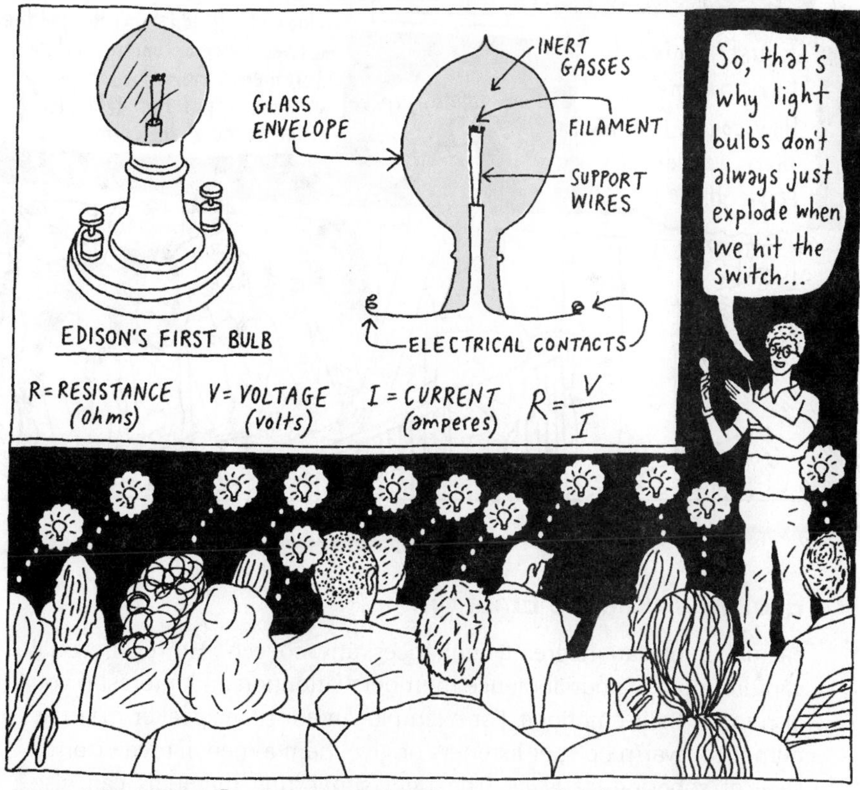

ENHANCING AUDIENCE UNDERSTANDING

Winning Audience Agreement

You can't expect your listeners to unthinkingly embrace all the claims you make in your speech. Rather, audience members may be skeptical of a point if they've never heard it before, if it strikes them as counterintuitive, or if it contradicts their worldview. Supporting materials help convince your audience that your claims merit their consideration. If you quote an expert, present a demonstration, or provide examples to illustrate your point, you give your audience reasons to agree with you.

Evoking Audience Emotion

Factual information greatly enhances any speech. However, you'll capture more of your audience members' attention and interest if you also touch their emotions. For example, an effective speaker may use humor to "warm up" her listeners or give them a mental break from a slew of sobering statistics. The right supporting materials can also stimulate listeners' empathy, anger, or commitment.

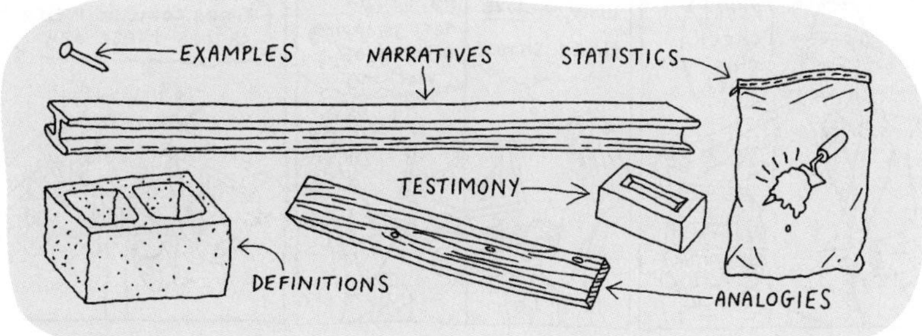

TYPES OF SUPPORTING MATERIALS

There are many types of supporting materials you can choose from to develop your main points. Below, we take a closer look at some of the more common types: examples, definitions, testimony, statistics, narratives, and analogies.

Examples

Examples are samples or instances that support or illustrate a general claim. In everyday conversation, you probably use examples frequently. To illustrate, suppose you tell a friend that parking is difficult on your campus, then you point out that you couldn't find a spot three times last week and your roommate had to drive around for thirty minutes to find a space. In this case, you are using examples to support your claim that parking is difficult.

To illustrate a point in your speech, you might use several **brief examples**—as shown in the following excerpt from a speech arguing that Americans' privacy is at risk:

> Eunice Moscoso and Rebecca Carr noted the following examples of loss of privacy in the *Atlanta Journal-Constitution*, April 20, 2004:
>
> - Data brokers can sell records of your marriages or divorces, lawsuits, old addresses, and the names, addresses, and phone numbers of your relatives and neighbors.

EXAMPLES OF THREATS TO PRIVACY

- More than one-third of all American workers were monitored on desktop computers by their bosses in 2001.
- In the nation's capital and in other metropolitan areas, cameras watch people at numerous corners and public gathering spots.

You can also use **extended examples** to illustrate a point. An extended example provides details about the instance being used, giving your audience a deeper and richer picture of your point. In a speech on the influence of drug-industry sales representatives on physicians' prescribing practices, the following extended example provided details about how far some sales reps will go to gain influence:

> In the *Atlantic* magazine, April 2006, Carl Elliott, an instructor at the University of Minnesota's Center for Bioethics, provided an example of a drug-company representative who arranged for a $50,000 consultant to advise a medical clinic that was struggling to make a profit:
>
>> [The consultant] spent eleven or twelve hours a day at the clinic for months. He talked to every employee, from the secretaries to the nurses to the doctors. He thought carefully about every aspect of the practice, from the most mundane administrative details to big-picture matters such as bill collection and financial strategy. He turned the practice into a profitable, smoothly running financial machine. And prescriptions for [the representative's company's] drugs soared.

Definitions

When you introduce new information to audience members, you may well use terms unfamiliar to them. If you don't take time to define these terms, your listeners may have difficulty understanding your message—which can leave them frustrated.

For example, suppose you're preparing an informative speech on the Persian Empire, and you want to explain that the Persians practiced a religion called Zoroastrianism. This term will likely be new to

your audience, so you'll need to define it. There are several different types of definitions you could use:

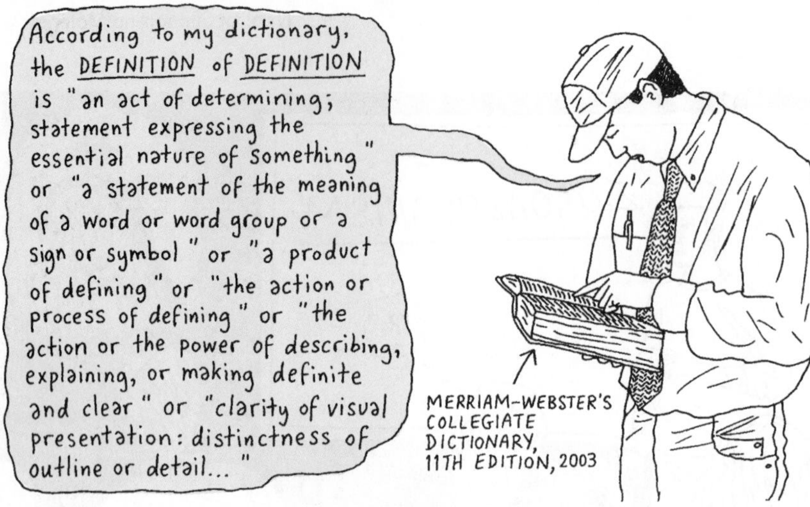

A **dictionary definition** provides the meaning of a term as presented in a dictionary. You might use a general dictionary or, if available, a more specialized one for your topic. For example, according to *Cambridge Dictionaries Online*, Zoroastrianism is "a religion which developed in ancient Iran, and is based on the idea that there is a continuous fight between a god who represents good and one who represents evil."[1]

An **expert definition** comes from a person who is a credible source of information on your topic. For example:

> According to Mary Boyce, Professor of Iranian Studies at the University of London, in *Zoroastrians: Their Religious Beliefs and Practices*, 1979, Zoroastrians believe that "there is a supreme God who is the creator; that an evil power exists which is opposed to him, and not under his control," [that this god] "created this world for a purpose," [and that the world in its present state will have an end that] "will be heralded by the coming of a cosmic Saviour, who will help to bring it about."[2]

An **etymological definition** explains the linguistic origin of the term. This type of definition is appropriate when the origin is interesting or will help the audience understand the term. For example: "Zoroastrianism has been so named in the West because its prophet, Zarathustra, was known to the ancient Greeks as Zoroaster.[3] Zoroastrians believe that Ahura Mazda (God) revealed the truth through Zarathustra."

A **functional definition** explains how something is used or what it does. For instance, a speaker might define Zoroastrianism in terms of how it is practiced by its followers:

> According to the Ontario Consultants on Religious Tolerance, March 24, 2005, Zoroastrian worship includes prayers and symbolic ceremonies. The rituals are conducted before a sacred fire. [Practitioners] regard fire as a symbol of their God. Members are dedicated to a three-fold practice, as shown in their motto: Good Thoughts, Good Works, Good Deeds.[4]

Testimony

Testimony consists of information provided by other people. Typically, you will find testimony from the sources you research at the library, online, or through interviews.

EXPERT TESTIMONY

Expert testimony consists of statements made by credible sources who have professional or other in-depth knowledge of a topic. As with any source, you must carefully assess any expert testimony and be sure that expert sources have specialized knowledge of the topic, objectivity, and observational capacity. Testimony from expert sources is likely to increase audience members' acceptance of your claims. Thus, you should try to use expert testimony when you are asserting claims that the audience may not accept.

A second type of testimony is **lay testimony**, which consists of statements made by persons with no special expertise in the subject they are discussing. Because they lack expertise, lay sources should generally not be used to prove factual claims in a speech. For example, testimony from lay persons would not credibly prove that a low-carbohydrate diet improves people's health or that the U.S. economy has been helped or hurt by the outsourcing of jobs. However, lay testimony can help you show how a typical person has been affected by your topic. Thus, you could quote lay sources to explain their own experiences with a low-carbohydrate diet or to discuss how they were affected when their own jobs were moved overseas.

Statistics

Statistics are information (or data) presented in numerical form. They can help you quantify points you're making in your speech and help your audience understand how often certain types of situations occur. While other supporting materials such as examples or anecdotes help the audience understand a single instance, statis-

tics can help you show the big picture regarding multiple instances or instances over time of the situation you are discussing.

For example, in a speech on the rising costs of a college education, you might present an example of a single student who struggled to afford $850 for books and supplies in 2005. Then you could use statistics to argue that this cost is typical:

> The College Board has reported that the cost of books and supplies for the 2005–06 academic year ranged from $801 to $904 depending on the type of institution a student attended.[5]

Though useful, statistics also have disadvantages. Specifically, as your use of statistics increases, so does the chance that your audience members will perceive your topic as overly complicated.[6] A long string of statistics may also bore or confuse your listeners if they're struggling to figure out what "all those numbers" mean. To present statistics in a way that helps your audience understand the information *and* remain interested in your speech, apply these guidelines:

- *Limit the number of statistics you present.* Of all the possible statistics you could offer your audience, select the best few.
- *Use visual aids to explain your statistics.* For example, you could use a bar graph to illustrate increases in textbook costs, tuition, and overall cost of living over the past eighteen years.

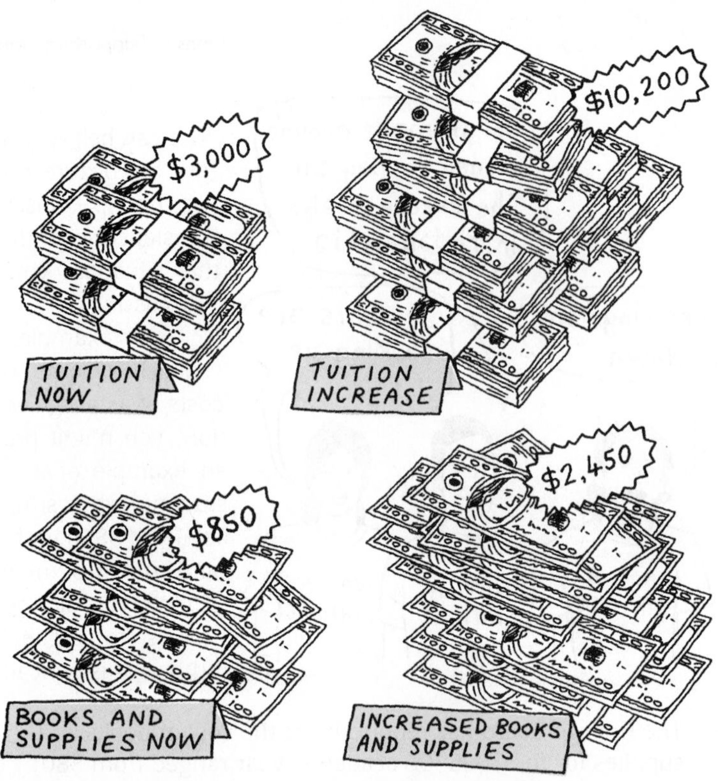

- *Establish context.* Explain what the statistics imply for your listeners. For instance, "thanks to these yearly increases in school-related costs, the average price for books and supplies is now $850 and tuition is $3,000. At the rates of increase I've just presented to you, books and supplies will cost nearly $1,600 more, and tuition will rise by $7,200, in just three years."

Narratives

Narratives are anecdotes (brief stories) or somewhat longer accounts that can be used to support your main points. Narratives stimulate your listeners' interest because we humans (by our very nature) love a good story.[7]

Here is a medium-length anecdote offered by a student in his speech about how the city of Los Angeles improved water quality in the Los Angeles River:

> On March 6, a writer for the *Los Angeles Times* filled an aquarium with water taken from the Los Angeles River. Two goldfish, Little Ed and Little Antonia, were plopped into the tank, to see if they could survive in the river water. One month later, the fish were still going strong. You can follow the fish's progress on a Web cam on the newspaper's Web site, and the fish even have their own page on MySpace.[8]

In a speech on healthier living, a presenter used the following somewhat longer anecdote to show how it is possible to improve your health through lifestyle changes:

> Arkansas governor Mike Huckabee knew he had a problem when he sat down at a staff meeting and his chair collapsed. Soon after this, he was diagnosed with type-2 diabetes and was told by his doctor that unless he changed his lifestyle, he had ten years to live. So the governor began what he called a "twelve-stop program" to stop unhealthy habits. First he walked. Then he ran, working his way up to the Little Rock Marathon. He exchanged junk food for a healthy diet. He dropped 110 pounds and no longer needs diabetes medication. He also spearheaded a Healthy Arkansas Initiative in his home state and joined with former President Clinton and the American Heart Association in a campaign against childhood obesity.[9]

Anecdotes like these are great for capturing audience attention or for illustrating a point. Consider incorporating such anecdotes as

THIS IS A NARRATIVE

attention-getters or when you want to show how concepts play out in the real world. And you can always use a quick anecdote—lasting no more than five or ten seconds—to reenergize an audience after tackling complex or technical material.

It can be more challenging to use longer narratives to develop supporting points because each one should only take fifteen to thirty seconds to present. But you can use longer narratives to provide touchstones or organizational elements that also support your main points. For example, in a speech about life lessons learned from a chance bear encounter in Yellowstone National Park, a student could include the following narrative points:

- *Studying dangerous wildlife before the Yellowstone trip*, to underline the importance of preparation in life.
- *First sighting the bear*, to underline the necessity of paying attention in all situations.
- *Walking carefully away from the bear*, to emphasize the value of calmness and self-control.
- *Being grateful that the bear didn't tear her head off*, to remind audience members that there are things larger than ourselves in this world.

USING A NARRATIVE TO STRUCTURE MAIN POINTS

Analogies

An **analogy** is a comparison based on similarities between two phenomena, one that's familiar to the audience and one that is less familiar. This type of comparison helps listeners use their existing knowledge to absorb new information.[10]

Here's how one speaker cited an analogy to help his listeners understand how a jellyfish-like sea creature known as a siphonophore emits a red glow to lure its prey:

> According to Steven Haddock of the Monterey Bay Aquarium Research Institute, in a July 7, 2005, article on the CNN.com *Science & Space* Web site:
>
> > The tiny lure mechanism [is] something like a Tootsie Pop. In the core of the lure, the blue green light is emitted. It is covered by a red material, so when the light is triggered, it passes through this red surface. The wavelength of the light is converted, and looks orangey-red on the outside.[11]

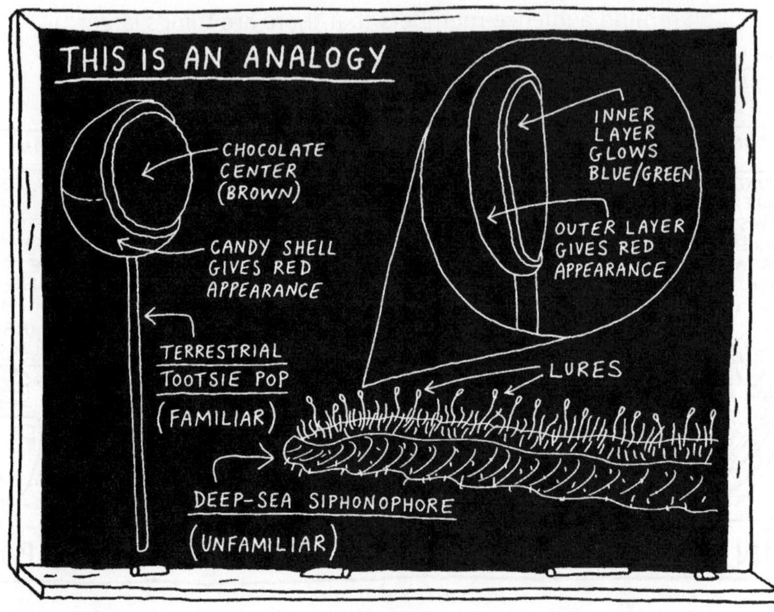

When you are preparing a speech, one effective approach is to provide analogies that draw on concepts you heard in speeches your classmates have delivered. That way, you'll know that your audience members already understand those concepts, and you'll demonstrate goodwill to show that you have learned from your classmates' speeches. Additional good sources of analogies are familiar sights and traditions on your campus, or aspects of college life that your listeners can all relate to.

GUIDELINES FOR USING SUPPORTING MATERIALS

How can you exert the strongest impact with your supporting materials? The following guidelines can help.

Use a Variety of Supporting Materials

In the previous section, you learned about a number of different types of supporting materials. But to get the best results, you should use a variety of these types to support your main points. If, on the other hand, you use the same type of supporting material over and over, your effectiveness will be reduced as fatigue sets in with your audience.

For instance, one funny personal example might pull listeners into your speech, a well-chosen analogy can help your audience understand

a key point, and a startling statistic can convince audience members that a problem you're describing is serious. By contrast, a speech that uses mainly one type of support—say, mostly analogies, personal examples, or statistics—will quickly lose your listeners' interest.

Appeal to Different Learning Styles

Select supporting materials that appeal to different audience members' learning styles. *Active learners* learn best by "doing something active" with the material being presented, while *reflective learners* "prefer to think about it."[12] *Visual learners*, by contrast, tend to "remember best what they see," while *verbal learners* tend to "get more out of words—written and spoken explanations."[13]

To appeal to this range of learning styles, use a combination of supporting materials throughout your speech. For instance, to clarify a point for verbal and visual learners, you could use a spoken definition along with a vivid analogy; to appeal to visual learners, you can also incorporate visual aids (see Chapter 14). One study found that students retained 26 percent of what they heard and 30 percent of what they saw, but those totals increased to 50 percent for information that they heard *and* saw.[14] And asking

thought-provoking questions or providing opportunities to think about a concept can help reflective learners.

To appeal to diverse learning styles in a speech on abstract art, for example, you might begin by defining abstract art and comparing it to other art forms, such as nineteenth-century African masks and traditional Japanese prints. You might then present a few pictures of abstract art pieces (perhaps alongside some non-abstract pieces) and then ask the question "Which pieces are examples of abstract art?" (See Chapter 10 for a discussion of rhetorical questions.)

To appeal to active learners, you can give audience members a chance to do something with your supporting materials. For instance,

THIS IS ACTIVE LEARNING

after using a narrative to help her listeners understand how bees fly, one student invited audience members to manipulate their arms to simulate the motion of bees' wings.

Avoid Long Lists

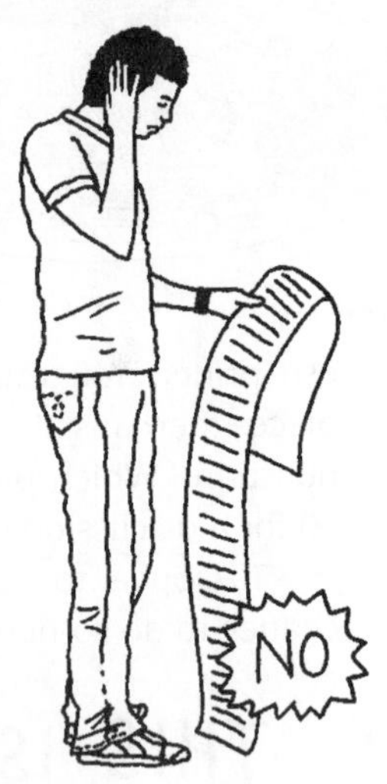

People usually find it difficult to understand and remember long strings of facts, examples, or statistics, especially when they are not presented with any elaboration. Consider this excerpt from a speech entitled "My Hometown":

> There are great restaurants in my town. You can get Chinese food, Italian food, Mexican food, and Ethiopian food. There are lots of places to go. You can go to the lake, the amusement park, the movies, or the ballgame. If you like to exercise, try our running trails, swimming pools, and bicycling paths.

If this speaker followed this pattern for five minutes or more, his presentation would quickly become tedious and forgettable.

To avoid this scenario, select a smaller number of supporting materials (most should take between fifteen and thirty seconds to present), and focus on the materials that *best* develop your main points. The "My Hometown" speech could have been more effective if the speaker had concentrated on the most noteworthy aspects of the town and expanded on them. By focusing on a notable hometown restaurant, the speaker could use examples, and even testimony and analogies, so that audience members could almost see themselves dining in that restaurant and feel as if they could actually taste the food.

Consider Your Audience

Your audience members' knowledge and interests can be exceptionally useful in helping you choose the best possible supporting materials. For example, suppose you want to persuade your listeners to volunteer for community service. If your audience comprises many future teachers, you might offer examples and narratives about service opportunities with young children. Or if many of your listeners enjoy outdoor activities, your supporting materials could relate more to environmental service.

Respect the Available Time

Select supporting materials that you can comfortably fit into the time you have available for your speech. In a five- to ten-minute speech, for instance, you wouldn't have time to use supporting materials that each take one minute or more to present—no matter how interesting and relevant they might be. To illustrate, suppose you were preparing

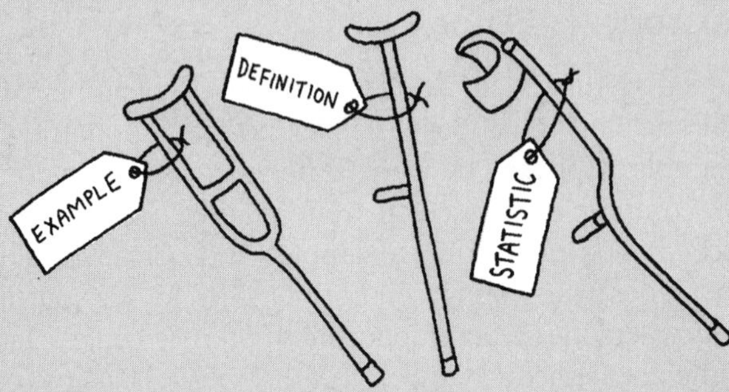

a seven-minute speech about ecotourism in Central America. You may feel strongly tempted to relate a four-minute narrative about the life lessons you learned while traveling throughout Central America. But this narrative would eat up over half of the time allotted for your speech. You would need to either streamline the narrative or replace it with a shorter but equally effective one.

SUMMARY

> "The sum of the parts determines the success of the whole speech."

As the story about Graciela's speech on Title IX illustrated at the beginning of this chapter, the right supporting materials can help you build credibility with your audience and enhance your listeners' understanding of and interest in your topic. To choose the best supporting materials, you can start by understanding the many forms they take—such as examples, definitions, testimony, statistics, narratives, and analogies. You can then apply important guidelines, such as using a variety of types of supporting materials, avoiding long lists of information, considering your audience's interests, and ensuring that your supporting materials don't consume too much of the time available for your presentation. When you use supporting materials, it is important to use a variety of different types of materials so that you can appeal to different learning styles: active, reflective, visual, and verbal.

Key Terms

supporting materials

TYPES OF SUPPORTING MATERIALS

examples
brief examples
extended examples
dictionary definition
expert definition
etymological definition
functional definition
testimony
expert testimony
lay testimony
statistics
narratives
analogy

LOVELY LASHES
BRITNEY'S WORKOUT SECRETS
HOT LIPS
Is your guy cheating?
NICE SHOES
ARE YOU FAT?
IS BEING SMART A TURN-OFF?
IS BEING SMART A TURN-OFF?
NO, DON'T MAKE YOUR BUTT LOOK SMALL
LOGO
$50,000
LOGO
$5,000
ARE YOU COOL?
EAT LIKE THE STARS
SHOP DON'T EAT
COOL NAILS
Does the ALL-CANDY diet work?
—NO.
Cancel your subscriptions to women's magazines now!!!
UPGRADE YOUR MAN
THE SKINNY ON BEING FAT???
Are you too thin?
IS ANIMAL TESTING CUTE?
IS FAT PHAT?
ARE YOU COOL ENOUGH TO READ THIS MAGAZINE?
YES, THOSE DO MAKE YOUR BUTT LOOK BIG
YOU GLOW GIRL!
I'M A ZERO
LOGO
$10,000
OVERWHELMING MASS OF UNORGANIZED INFORMATION
Why??
AAAGH!!?!?
What?

9 ORGANIZING YOUR SPEECH

"Good organization makes the message clear."

Carly stood at the lectern and announced to her audience that her speech would be about magazines targeted at women and teenage girls. She showed her listeners several magazine advertisements featuring gaunt models and explained how listeners could help friends struggling with anorexia or bulimia. One of the ads was for cosmetics, and Carly presented evidence supporting the claim that the testing of cosmetics harms animals. Carly also presented several magazine articles with titles she considered inane—such as "What His Kitchen Tells You about Him" and "Which Spice Girl Are You?" She then contrasted these articles with pieces from more serious magazines published for women.

Carly concluded her speech with a plea for audience members to cancel their subscriptions to women's magazines. Then she sat down, feeling confident that she had scored a success with her audience. During the evaluation of her speech, however, many of her classmates said that they had trouble following her presentation. Some admitted that they found her ideas downright confusing. Surprised and upset by their feedback, Carly didn't realize that she had made an all-too-common mistake: failing to organize her speech clearly.

Carly's story reveals the importance of organization in developing a successful speech. When you organize your ideas clearly, you help your audience see how the different ideas in your presentation fit together—and your listeners then better comprehend your message.[1] They know what to listen for because your organization provides cues to indicate the main ideas. And they don't have to devote their mental energy to figuring out your main points and how all the details in your speech relate to those points.

Good organization is particularly important in oral communication because listeners don't have the luxury of reviewing printed information to understand your message. By contrast, someone who's reading a printed message—whether in a book, a magazine, or online—can go back and reread the text if they're confused. Thus, when giving a speech, you must take special care to help the audience follow your ideas.

...and the next point about the ROMAN EMPIRE is...
What was the last point? It was about the ROMAN EMPIRE???
I ♡ HISTORY
The invention of the toga party.

When you organize your speeches clearly, you also enhance your credibility. Effective organization shows that you have taken the time to prepare your talk.[2]

Organizing a speech is not merely a matter of applying an arbitrary set of rules. Rather, a well-organized presentation imposes order on the set of points that you present in your speech by showing the relationships *between* ideas. Thus, the organizational pattern you select can communicate important information to the audience: What are the most important ideas? Why do you believe that each idea has merit? What evidence are you providing to back up your claims?

In this chapter, we focus on organizing the body of your speech—the part where you present your main points and support them with examples, narratives, testimony, and other materials. To organize a speech effectively, you must learn to group your ideas into a sequence that your audience can easily follow. In the following pages we explore ways to select your main points and structure your supporting materials. We also examine common patterns for arranging main points. And we present some organizing language that you can use to make your speech structure clear to the audience.

SELECTING YOUR MAIN POINTS

The body of your speech should be structured around your **main points**—those few ideas that are most important for your listeners to remember. The body also contains **supporting points**—materials designed to prove or substantiate your main points. A speech body organized around main points and corresponding supporting points helps listeners make sense out of the details of your presentation. By contrast, if you present randomly ordered ideas about your topic (as Carly did), your audience will have trouble determining what is most important and understanding the information you're presenting. Even a five-minute speech requires careful organization, since it can contain fifty or more sentences.

How should you select your main points? The following guidelines can help.

Consider Your Purpose

Make sure that every main point you select relates to the specific purpose of your speech. Consider the following two sets of main points for a speech arguing that the government should not censor radio programs that contain indecent language, such as *The Howard Stern Show*.

FIRST SET OF MAIN POINTS

I. The history of broadcast regulation
II. Background on *The Howard Stern Show*
III. In a free society, people should be allowed to listen to the programs of their choice.

SECOND SET OF MAIN POINTS

I. In a free society, people should be allowed to listen to the programs of their choice.
II. Listeners who find Stern offensive can change the station.
III. Government censorship efforts will be abused.

In the first set, main points I and II are not arguments against government censorship of indecent programming. Thus, they don't relate to the thesis of a speech that argues against censorship. Indeed, the speaker does not address the thesis until the third main point. Conversely, the second set of main points does relate to the speech's purpose: all three points present reasons why the government should not censor such shows.

Take Your Audience into Account

Out of the many relevant main points that you might use to develop your topic, which ones will prove *most* interesting to your audience? Which ones will provide your listeners with the most useful information to *them*?

Consider the following two sets of main points for a speech on backpacking tips.

FIRST SET OF MAIN POINTS

I. Choosing the right backpack
II. Remembering the essential equipment
III. Packing your backpack strategically

SECOND SET OF MAIN POINTS

I. Coping with extreme elevation changes
II. Selecting light, nutritious food for week-long trips
III. Choosing optimal equipment for subzero temperatures

Both sets of main points contain information that fits the topic of "backpacking tips." Thus, they fit the first guideline for main points: they relate to the specific purpose of the speech. However, the question of which set is better depends on the audience. The first set contains basic information that would be appropriate for novice backpackers. The second set contains information that would be more useful for experienced backpackers who are contemplating challenging trips.

Select an Appropriate Number of Main Points

In most situations, effective speeches present two to five main points. In our experience, student speeches typically contain three main points. However, there is no rule that you must have three. You may also have two, four, or five main points if that number gives you the most logical organization of ideas.

Still, most audiences have trouble remembering more than three points. Also, you are unlikely to have enough time to develop that many points. Here are a few suggestions for whittling down your main points to a manageable number.

- See whether any of your main points are related. Perhaps two or more main points can be combined into a single broader category.
- Review your audience analysis. See if any points can be excluded because they will be less effective with your audience.
- Evaluate which points are the most important to developing your topic or thesis. Which do you most want audience members to take away from your speech? Exclude the point(s) that are less essential.

If you find that you only have one main point, consider making that point the topic or thesis of your speech. Then organize the infor-

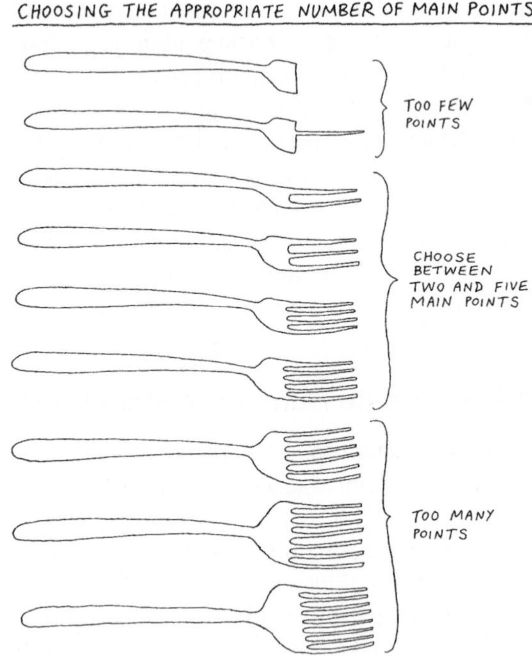

mation you plan to use to support that point into two to five key ideas, which will become your main points.

ORGANIZING YOUR SUPPORTING MATERIALS

Once you select your main points, you need to develop (explain and prove) each one with supporting materials. Supporting materials enable your audience to understand your main points and help prove why you think those main points are valid. In Chapter 8, we discussed a number of different types of supporting materials that you can use, such as examples, descriptions, and evidence. Now we consider how you can organize these supporting materials to help audience members follow your speech.

Subordination and Coordination

The principle of subordination is a key to a well-organized speech. Using **subordination** means creating a hierarchy of points and their supporting materials in your speech. Thus, main points are the most important (or highest) level of subordination, and supporting materials used to develop a main point (called **subpoints**) are subordinate to that main point. In the same way, materials that support subpoints are called **sub-subpoints**, and these sub-subpoints are subordinate to the corresponding subpoint. A well-organized speech also features **coordination**. Each main point is coordinate with other main points—that is, they are at the same level of significance—just as subpoints are coordinate with other subpoints and so on.

Sound confusing? It isn't, really. To see how subordination and coordination work, compare the subpoints (indicated by capital letters) supporting each main point (signaled by roman numerals) in this outline for an informative speech on filmmaking in India:

I. Culture plays an important role in Indian filmmaking.
   A. Indian moviemakers developed a style of their own by the 1950s, based on the teachings of *Natya Shastra* (*Science of Theater*), a 1,000-year-old Hindu book. Entertainment was to embody nine essences: love, hate, sorrow, disgust, joy, compassion, pity, pride, and courage.[3]

B. In Indian culture, women are expected to be closely tied to their families. Thus, female stars are often chaperoned by their mothers, who sit at the edge of the set.[4]

II. There are differences between Indian-made films and films made in the United States.

A. In India, films need not follow the linear, scripted story line that is popular in Western movies. Of any one hundred films made in India, about three will have scripts prepared in advance, according to screenwriter Anjum Rajabali.[5]

B. Many Indian films do not address serious social issues. Director Shyam Bengal notes that mass cinema "is nothing more than a series of continuing sensations. New pictures are made to imitate whatever was most successful previously in order to mop up the largest audience."[6]

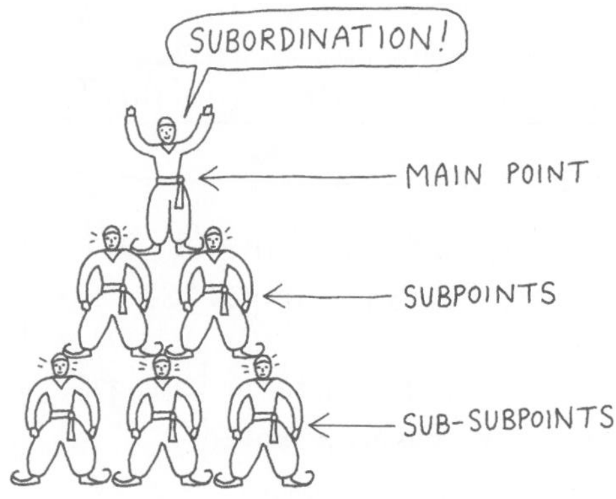

Notice that both subpoints for main point I pertain to the subject of the main point: the role of culture in Indian film-making. These subpoints are *subordinate* to main point I. Then consider main point II. Subpoint IIA supports that main point. However, subpoint IIB does not—because it fails to explain why U.S. made and Indian-made films are different. You can probably think of many American-made films that also have little serious content. Because subpoint IIB is not relevant to the idea that U.S.- and Indian-made films are different, it is not subordinate. Therefore, the speaker should not include it under main point II.

When a Subpoint Doesn't Fit

In developing a speech, you may discover that some of the supporting materials you researched do not relate to any of the main points you selected. Nevertheless, you believe that these materials would improve your speech. What should you do? Consider the following options:

One option is to reword the main point to encompass the additional information. In the first example that follows, the main point is that carpooling can help the environment. Note in this example how subpoint B focuses on saving money, not on helping the environment. It thus does not relate to the main point. In the second example, the speaker has rewritten the main point to make both subpoints subordinate.

FIRST EXAMPLE

I. Carpooling to school helps the environment.
   A. When fewer cars are driven to campus, pollution is reduced.
   B. When students carpool, they spend less money on gas and parking.

A, B, AND C ARE SUBPOINTS

1. Leonardo da Vinci's art had many impacts.

   A. Leonardo's artistic technique was unprecedented.

   B. Leonardo's technique influenced future artists.

   C. Leonardo's art has generated many controversies.

1, 2, AND 3 ARE SUB-SUBPOINTS

C. Leonardo's art has generated many controversies.

   1. Who was the model for the *Mona Lisa*?

   2. Who is to the right of Jesus in *The Last Supper*?

   3. Is the *Vitruvian Man* a geometrical algorithm?

SECOND EXAMPLE

I. Carpooling to school helps the environment *and your pocketbook.*
  A. When fewer cars are driven to campus, pollution is reduced.
  B. When students carpool, they spend less money on gas and parking.

A second option is to create an additional main point to include the supporting materials in question. If you use this option, be sure that you have enough supporting materials to develop a new main point. Also, ensure that the new main point relates to your topic or thesis statement.

ARRANGING YOUR MAIN POINTS

How do you decide the structure in which you'll present your main points during your speech? Familiarize yourself with common patterns of organization and then select the pattern that best suits your speech. In this section, we take a closer look at these patterns.

Spatial Pattern

In a **spatial pattern**, the main points represent important aspects of your topic that can be thought of as adjacent to one another in location or geography. This approach is effective with speech topics that can be broken down into specific parts that relate to each other spatially. You take the audience from one part to the next—much as a museum guide ushers a group from exhibit to exhibit, or much as an anatomy professor decides to lecture about the parts of the human skeleton from head to toe. For example, you could use a spatial pattern to discuss prehistoric cultures that existed around the world:

I. Early *Europeans* adapted to the Ice Age and competed with fellow carnivores for prey.

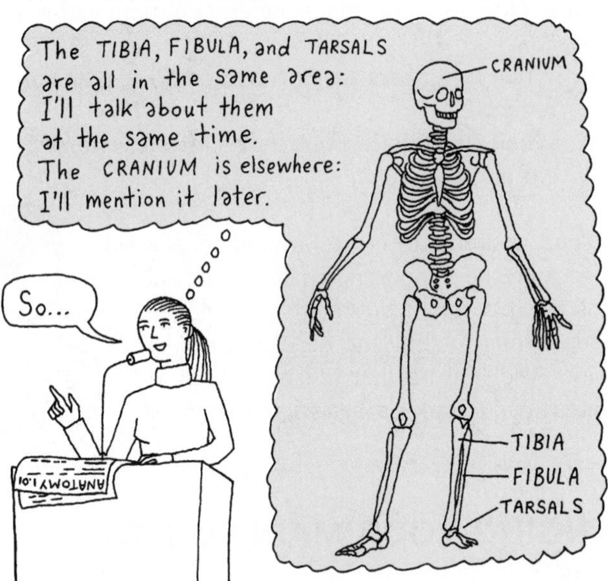

II. Prehistoric *Thais* lived in dense forests.
III. *Australian Aborigines* were the world's first known food processors.

Temporal Pattern

In a **temporal pattern**, you present the information in chronological (time-based) sequence, from beginning to end. Each main point covers a particular point in the chronology. If you are discussing a subject that follows a sequence, such as a historical event or a process, this pattern can help your audience keep track of what you're saying. For instance, a speech discussing the decline and rebound of bald eagles in the lower forty-eight states could use a temporal pattern:

I. In 1963, the bald eagle had nearly disappeared from the lower forty-eight states.
II. In 1972, the pesticide DDT was banned in the United States.

III. During the past thirty years, governments and individual citizens took steps to protect eagles.
IV. By 1995, the bald eagle had made a remarkable comeback.

Causal Pattern

If your speech is explaining a cause-and-effect relationship, a **causal pattern** will help your audience understand the link between particular events and their outcomes. There are two ways to organize main points when you use this pattern. First, if several major causes exist for the situation or phenomenon you are discussing, each main point can cover one of the causes. Second, if there is a chain of events between cause and effect, each main point can become one link in the chain from cause to effect. So to explain why e-commerce has grown in significance, you might use this chain of causation:

I. Internet usage grew rapidly in the 1990s.
II. Businesses took advantage of this new channel of communication by marketing products online.
III. Consumers have increasingly chosen to shop online because of the convenience.

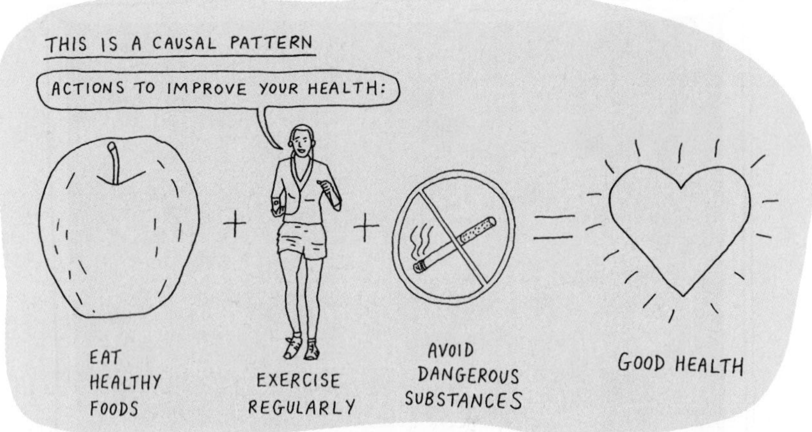

Comparison Pattern

A **comparison pattern** organizes the speech around major similarities and differences between two events, objects, or situations. Each main point discusses an important similarity or difference. This pattern can help your audience learn about a new subject by comparing it to a subject with which they are familiar. To illustrate, you might compare newly discovered planets outside our solar system with the planets in our own system as follows:

I. The orbits of planets outside our solar system often differ from our planets' paths.
II. The size and composition of planets outside our solar system are most likely to resemble Jupiter's.

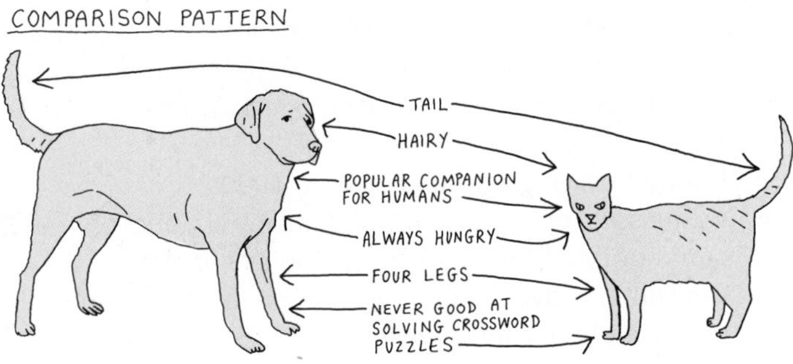

THIS IS A COMPARISON PATTERN

DORM LIFE

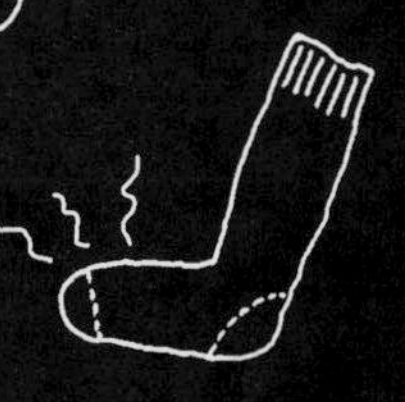

I. College food services will cook for you.

II. You are not responsible for paying bills.

III. You need to get along with your roommates.

APARTMENT LIFE

I. Your own cooking will replace college food services.

II. You and your roommates will become responsible for sharing the bills.

III. You will still need to get along with your roommates.

III. Many planets outside our solar system have moons, as our planets do.

IV. Some planets outside our solar system are in a "habitable zone," as Earth is.

Problem-Cause-Solution Pattern

Consider using a **problem-cause-solution pattern** if you want to ask your audience to take specific action or support a particular policy on an issue. With this pattern, your first main point argues that one or more problems exist. Your second main point covers the cause(s) of the problem. And your third main point develops your proposed solution, which mitigates or eliminates the cause(s). A problem-cause-solution format could help you organize a speech encouraging expanded use of solar energy, as shown in the following example outlines:

I. Fossil fuel energy sources hurt our environment and our pocketbooks.
II. Current energy policies encourage fossil fuel usage.
III. Expanded tax credits for solar technology would promote clean, inexpensive energy.

Criteria-Application Pattern

A **criteria-application pattern** proposes standards for making a judgment about a topic and then applies those standards to the topic. This pattern accommodates two main points. The first establishes the *criteria* (or standards) that you believe listeners should use to make a judgment about your topic. The second main point is the application of those criteria to your speech topic.

One type of speech where this pattern works well is the "hero" speech (explaining why a person is a hero in his or her community or culture). To use this pattern, you could first advocate criteria for heroism. Then you might show why a specific person is a hero, based on those criteria. Here is how one student used this approach in a speech about her cousin, Kyle:

I. If a person overcomes serious hardship while maintaining an optimistic attitude, he or she is a hero.

II. My six-year-old cousin Kyle is a hero because he has maintained a positive outlook on life despite his parents' marital troubles and his father's cancer.

CRITERIA-APPLICATION PATTERN

THE CRITERIA:

A dog has four legs, fur, a tail, and barks.

THE SUBJECT WITH CRITERIA APPLIED:

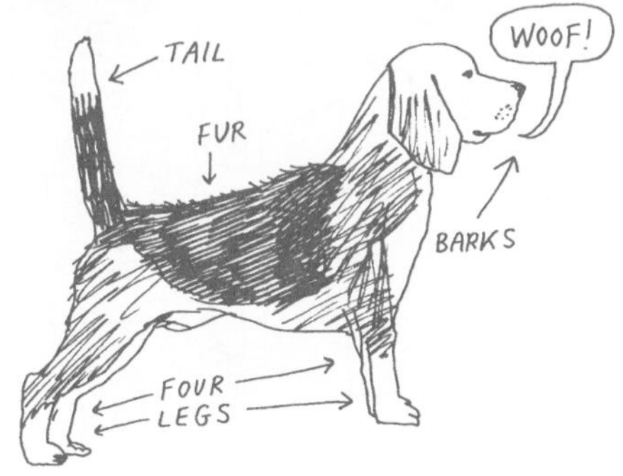

CONCLUSION:

This is a dog.

Narrative Pattern

With a **narrative pattern**, you organize your speech as a story, using characters and a plot to convey your message. You still have a thesis, but you support the thesis with a story rather than a set of explicit main points. The story should have a plot and build to a climax that communicates the main idea of your speech to listeners. Audience members should be able to determine your thesis intuitively from the story and see how the story demonstrates that the thesis is valid.

For example, suppose you want to persuade your audience that smoking should be prohibited. Your narrative could tell the story of a friend, a relative, or a person who you learned about through your research who smoked and died of cancer. You would need to be confident that your audience members were familiar with the scientific evidence linking tobacco to health risks. You'd also have to count on them to understand from the details of your story that you were advocating a ban on cigarettes.

Here is an example of how you could organize a narrative speech on this topic, and how it would compare to a speech using the problem-cause-solution pattern:

Narrative

Introduction

Aunt Amanda was my favorite aunt. She always had time to talk to me, and although she was fifty-six when I was seventeen, she understood what it was like to be a teenager. She never attended college, but she kept telling me that I would be the first person in our family to get a degree.

Body

I. I called Aunt Amanda when I got an A on my first college essay. She tearfully told me that she had been diagnosed with lung cancer and did not have long to live.

II. Aunt Amanda had been a heavy smoker since she was my age. The models in magazine and television ads seemed so glamorous when they smoked. So, my aunt started smoking, and although she tried to quit several times, she never could.

III. Aunt Amanda got so mad at me when I got caught smoking at school. She said that if it was up to her, smoking would be outlawed like any other dangerous drug. She told me that it was not as glamorous as those ads make it seem, and that once you get started, it is almost impossible to stop.

Conclusion

I. Now my Aunt Amanda will never see me graduate from college. I miss her so much. But I will always be thankful that she encouraged me to go to college.

II. And I am even more thankful for her lifesaving message: "Smoking kills like any other dangerous drug, and there ought to be a law against this hazardous product."

Problem-Cause-Solution

Introduction

I. Provide attention-getter (endearing story about Aunt Amanda).

II. State thesis: cigarettes should be prohibited.

III. Establish credibility.

IV. Connect with the audience.

V. Give preview.

Body

I. Cigarette smoking is hazardous to your health. **(Problem)**

II. Tobacco company advertising hooks new smokers. **(Cause)**

III. The federal government should prohibit the sale of cigarettes. **(Solution)**

Conclusion

I. Provide summary.

II. End with clincher: smoking killed my Aunt Amanda, but if we outlaw cigarettes, other families will be spared the loss I have felt.

Categorical Pattern

If the main points you select do not fit any of the patterns mentioned thus far, another option is to use a **categorical pattern**. In this pattern, each main point emphasizes one of the most important aspects of your topic that you want the audience to understand. And each main point supports the specific purpose of your speech. For example, Jodie was presenting an after-dinner speech on the environmental consequences of holiday gift-giving. She used a categorical pattern as follows:

I. Tons of garbage are generated by gift-giving.
II. Thousands of barrels of gasoline pollute the air as we drive gifts to family and friends.
III. Volumes of nondegradable plastics will end up in landfills once kids get bored with new toys.
IV. Seriously, please remember to do your part to protect the environment during the holiday season.

USING ORGANIZING WORDS AND SENTENCES

As the person who has developed your speech, you will know what your main points are, when you are moving from one point to the next, and what part of the speech you are delivering at any point in time. However, without assistance from you, your audience members will have difficulty keeping track of your organization. To see how difficult this task is, watch a speech with two or three classmates and have each person try to outline the speaker's main points. Unless the speech is very well organized, chances are good that you will each have different perceptions of what the main points were.

To make the structure of your speech easy for audience members to follow, you need to insert organizing words and sentences throughout your presentation. The primary types of organizing language include transitions, signposts, and internal previews and summaries.

Transitions

A **transition** is a sentence that indicates you are moving from one part of your speech to the next. A transition usually includes an indication that you have completed one idea and are about to present a new one. Here are some examples of transitions:

- Now that you have learned about wildlife sanctuaries in Belize, let me describe Mayan archaeological sites you can visit.
- The beaches of Belize are very beautiful, but wait until you discover the scenery in the rain forest.

Be sure that your transition introduces a new point *while also* signaling the end of the previous point. Students often have trouble creating transitions that achieve both tasks, as shown by these two failed attempts:

- There are many Mayan archaeological sites you can visit.
- Do you want to find out about some incredible scenery?

Neither of these sentences would make a good transition. The first one only notes the subject of the next main point (archaeological sites), without signaling that the speaker has wrapped up the previous point (wildlife sanctuaries). The second sentence only asks a question pertaining to the main point to follow (scenery in the rain forest). It does not help the audience see that the speaker has finished with the main point about beaches and is moving on to discuss the scenery in the rain forest.

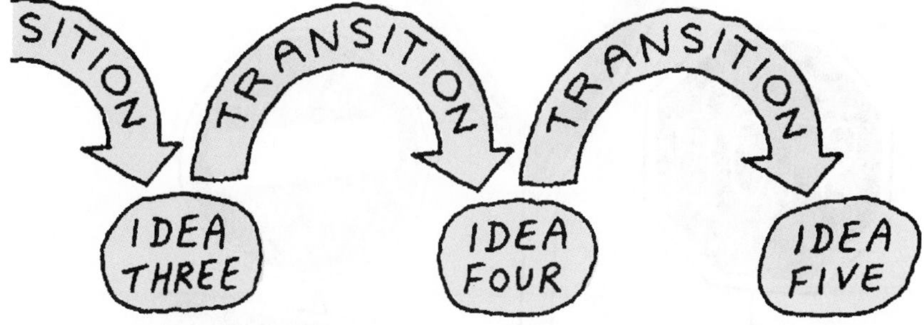

Signposts

Signposts are words or phrases within sentences that help your audience understand your speech's structure. Signposts in a speech serve the same function as their counterparts on a road. Highway signs tell drivers what direction they're traveling in and how the roads are organized. In a similar vein, speech signposts inform audiences about the direction and organization of a presentation.

You can use signposts to show you are at a specific place in your speech (for example, "to preview my main ideas," or "my third point is," or "in summary"). You can also use signposts to indicate that you are about to cite research ("according to") or to indicate that a key point is coming ("if you remember one idea from this speech, I hope it will be that . . ."). You can also use signposts to help your audience understand the structure of your subpoints. For example, in a persuasive speech advocating educational reform, you might have a main point on the causes of poor student performance. You could then write your subpoints with signposts as follows:

- *One cause* of educational failure is inadequate funding of public schools.
- *Another cause* is educators' low expectations for students.
- *An additional cause* of our schools' failure is that athletics receive higher priority than academics.

SIGNPOSTS

YIELD
STOP
DO NOT
ENTER
WRONG WAY

IN SUMMARY
TO PREVIEW MY MAIN IDEAS
IF YOU REMEMBER ONE IDEA FROM THIS SPEECH
ACCORDING TO

Internal Previews and Internal Summaries

In crafting your speech, you may have selected a main point that needs several different points of support or requires considerable detail to develop. To help the audience follow your explanation of such a complex main point, you may want to use an **internal preview**, a short list of the ideas that will follow. Or to help the audience remember what you have just said about the main point, you might use an **internal summary**, a quick review of what you just said about that main point.

For example, in an informative speech on test strategies, suppose that one main point covers test preparation. You might state your main point, followed by an *internal preview*, as shown here:

> Test taking requires good planning and healthy living. *The four steps for test preparation that I will cover are: plan your study time in advance, follow your study schedule, get a good night's sleep, and eat a healthy breakfast.*

In a persuasive speech on campaign finance reform, you might follow a main point on possible solutions with an *internal summary* as follows:

To review my proposed solutions: First, the government should require that all federal elections be publicly funded. Second, an independent commission should be established to enforce campaign financing laws. Finally, you too can be part of the solution by refusing to vote for candidates who accept large contributions.

SUMMARY

"Good organization makes the message clear."

In this chapter, we focused on the importance of a well-organized speech and presented strategies for organizing the body of your speech. Good organization helps your audience understand your message and enhances your credibility as a speaker. Remember the following principles when you organize the body of your speech: Select an appropriate number of main points. Arrange your main points in a pattern that will best convey your ideas to the audience. Organize supporting materials to back up each main point. And use organizing words and sentences to help the audience keep track of where you are in a speech.

Key Terms

SELECTING YOUR MAIN POINTS

main points
supporting points

ORGANIZING YOUR SUPPORTING MATERIALS

subordination
subpoints
sub-subpoints
coordination

ARRANGING YOUR MAIN POINTS

spatial pattern
temporal pattern
causal pattern
comparison pattern
problem-cause-solution pattern
criteria-application pattern
narrative pattern
categorical pattern

USING ORGANIZING WORDS AND SENTENCES

transitions
signposts
internal previews
internal summaries

This is going to be GREAT. I can't wait to see MORE!
EXIT
That was AMAZING. I really ENJOYED myself!
EXIT

10

INTRODUCTIONS AND CONCLUSIONS

"Strong introductions create audience interest; strong conclusions create lasting impressions."

You've finally had time to break away from your schoolwork and go see the latest James Bond movie. You're sitting in the theater, munching popcorn as the curtains open, the lights dim, and the film's opening sequence starts to roll. Every element of that sequence—the music, the visuals, the credits for the movie's title and cast—conveys information about the picture and heightens your desire to see more.

For the next two hours, you're transported into an exciting world. And at the end of the movie, you're left with the lasting sense that you've had a great time. The final close-ups of Bond's face, the swelling of the classic James Bond theme, and the sweeping views of gorgeous scenery as the camera pans back—all of these elements combine to conclude your experience on a satisfying note.

Just as a movie's opening and closing elements powerfully influence the quality of your theater experience, your speech's introduction and conclusion play crucial roles in your audience's reception of your message. An effective introduction builds audience interest, orients audience members to the speech, and establishes your credibility as a speaker, while a strong conclusion leaves them with an enduring impression of your speech.

Your next step after planning the body of your speech is to prepare the introduction and conclusion. Although these elements are shorter than the body, they're just as crucial. After all, you won't get your message across unless your audience is eager to listen. And you want your audience to remember your presentation long after it ends—so they can put into action the information you've imparted to them. In this chapter, we show you how to craft memorable beginnings and endings to your presentations.

INTRODUCING YOUR SPEECH

In public speaking, as in many other situations in life, first impressions are vital. Your introduction creates a first impression of you as a speaker *and* of your message. Scholars have recognized the importance of the introduction for as long as people have discussed speechmaking: Cicero included the introduction as one of six essential parts of a speech,[1] and contemporary scholars note that the introduction is a key opportunity for the speaker to build a bond with the audience.[2]

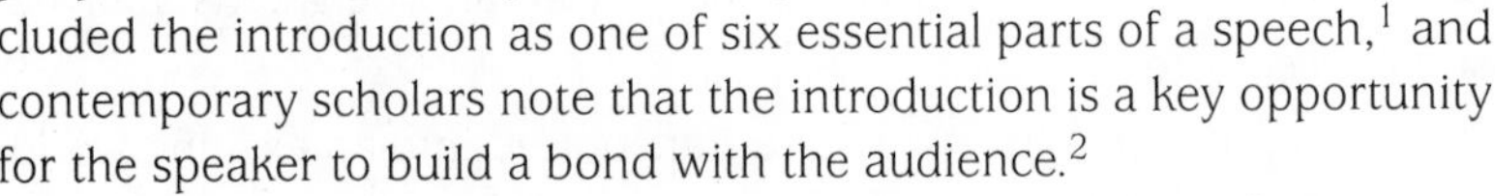

A good introduction thus accomplishes a number of important purposes. Specifically, it

- gains your audience's attention.
- signals the topic and purpose of your speech.

- conveys the importance of the topic for your audience.
- establishes your credibility.
- previews the main points of your speech.

Your introduction must accomplish all this—in a brief period of time. For example, in a five- to ten-minute speech, the introduction should take up no more than one minute. With these kinds of time constraints, there's no doubt about it: your introduction needs to be efficient *and* effective. Let's look more closely at each of the objectives your introduction must achieve.

Gain Your Audience's Attention

Begin your speech with an **attention-getter**—material intended to capture the audience's interest at the start of a speech. People listening to a presentation may have other things on their minds (for example, a problem at home, a distracting sound coming from the next room, worries about an upcoming test or paper). You need to help your listeners redirect their focus from these other matters to you and your message. Otherwise, they won't likely absorb or remember the information you convey in your speech.

How to craft an effective attention-getter? The following guidelines can help.

Tell a Story or Anecdote. Most people love a good story, so opening with one can be a compelling yet comfortable way to begin your speech. If you start your speech with a story, be sure that it relates to your message, takes up an appropriate amount of time, and comes across as believable. Avoid making up a story to open your speech unless you note that you are offering a hypothetical example.

Here is how one student used an anecdote to begin a speech about reforming the No Child Left Behind education law:

> *Time* magazine, May 2, 2005, reported that in the Utah War of 1857–58, President Buchanan sent thousands of federal troops into the territory to install a non-Mormon governor. The people of Utah did not respond well. They spooked the federal livestock, burned federal wagons, and incinerated over 300,000 tons of military provisions. Nearly 150 years later, the Utah legislature sent another message to Washington by becoming the first state to pass a bill that gives schools options for ignoring the No Child Left Behind Act.

Notice how the anecdote about Utah in the 1850s grabs the audience's attention by relating a dramatic, almost over-the-top, historical incident in vivid language and startling details. The story also relates to the speech's topic because in both cases, the state of Utah rebels against a federal mandate.

Offer a Striking or Provocative Statement.

A compelling fact or idea pertaining to your topic can immediately pull the audience into your speech. For example, you might present a surprising statistic or make an ironic statement to defy your listeners' expectations about what they'll hear during your speech. This approach works only if you present a fact or idea that's new, ironic, or counterintuitive to your audience. You are also likely to be more effective if you incorporate vivid language into your striking or provocative statement.

Consider Vaclav Havel, who addressed the people of the former Czechoslovakia when he became their president on New Year's Day, 1990. From 1948 until 1989, Czechoslovakia had been under communist rule, and Havel, a Czech playwright and dissident, had been imprisoned and had his works banned in the 1970s and 1980s. Havel was a leader of the 1989 nonviolent Velvet Revolution that led to his selection as the first popularly elected president in more than forty years in a nation long under the thumb of corrupt, authoritarian communist leaders. Note how Havel offered a striking statement that differentiated him from his unelected predecessors who had controlled the Czech media and propagandized the government's achievements.

> My dear fellow citizens, for forty years on this day you heard from my predecessors the same thing in a number of variations: how our country is flourishing, how many millions of tons of steel we produce, how happy we all are, how we trust our government, and what bright prospects lie ahead of us. I assume you did not propose me for this office so that I, too, should lie to you.[3]

Build Suspense. Consider increasing audience curiosity and anticipation before you reveal your topic. For example, "What will be one of the biggest problems in the next ten years?" or "One of the most exotic vacation spots in the world is unknown to 98 percent of American tourists."

Here's how one student built curiosity in her listeners' minds during the introduction of a speech on rising gas prices:

> Would you like to spend less money on gasoline? I have a solution that does not require drilling in Alaska or importing more oil from the Middle East. You will not need to spend $20,000 on a new hybrid car. My solution does not require an act of Congress; you can apply it yourself on your way home from school.

After this suspenseful introductory statement, the student went on to give ten driving tips that she claimed could improve fuel economy by 20 percent or more.

Let Listeners Know You're One of Them. Consider highlighting similarities between you and the audience or what interests you and the audience have in common. When listeners believe that a speaker is like them, they tend to see him or her as more credible—something that encourages them to pay close attention to the speech. However, to make this type of attention-getter effective, be sure to assert *genuine* common ground. Otherwise, you won't win your audience's confidence.

Here's how one student highlighted common ground in a speech about the importance of understanding the federal government's new food pyramid:

> When I surveyed our class, I discovered that over 70 percent of you agreed with the statement "I try to eat a healthy diet." Like many of you, I have been on a diet more than once, and I do my best to eat my fruits and vegetables. To help us make good dietary decisions, the federal government has created a new food pyramid that contains some useful information but that is also more complicated. The old, familiar pyramid with six basic food groups has been replaced by twelve pyramids containing multicolor regions, supplemented by online calculators. If we can learn to decode it, the new pyramid can help all of us eat more healthily.

Use Humor. Most people enjoy jokes, amusing stories, or other humorous references. A funny or playful attention-getter can be a great way to gain audience interest, break the ice, and enhance your credibility. However, not all humor is created equal. If you begin a speech with humor, the material should relate to your topic. Also, consider your audience members and choose material they will find amusing. Don't tell jokes or stories that may offend some or all of your listeners.

Also note that using humor as your attention-getter can be a high-risk/high-reward approach. If the audience appreciates a joke, your credibility is liable to increase, you'll feel especially confident, and your speech will be off to a great start. Yet, it can be deeply deflating when a joke falls flat. If you have trouble telling jokes or remembering punch lines, you may find that a relevant anecdote from your own life is a better source of humor; almost everyone has told a funny story about something that has happened to them. This more personal approach may help you feel more relaxed and conversational.

Former Texas governor Ann Richards used humor effectively in the introduction to her keynote address at the 1988 Democratic National Convention:

> Twelve years ago Barbara Jordan, another Texas woman, made the Keynote Address to this convention and two women in 160 years is about par for the course. But if you give us a chance, we can perform. After all, Ginger Rogers did everything that Fred Astaire did. She just did it backwards and in high heels.[4]

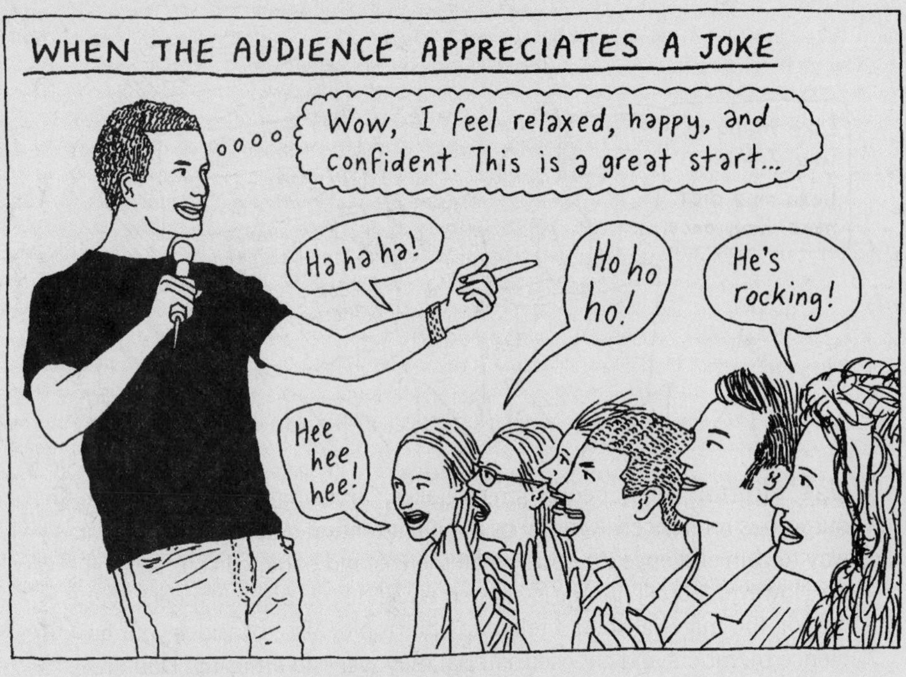

WHEN THE AUDIENCE APPRECIATES A JOKE

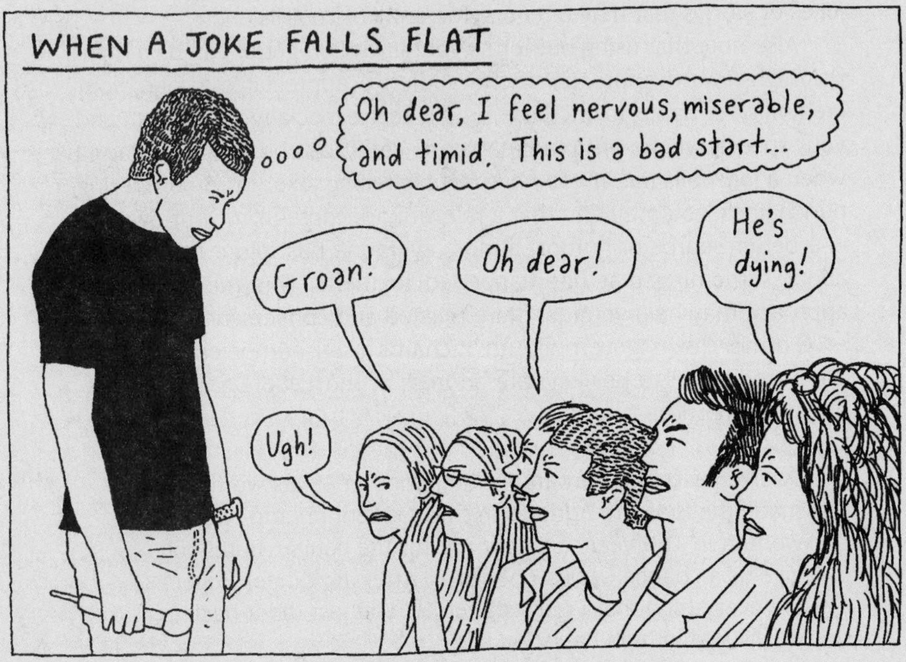

WHEN A JOKE FALLS FLAT

RHETORICAL QUESTIONS CAN RISK DISAPPOINTING ANSWERS

Ask a Rhetorical Question. A **rhetorical question**—one that you want listeners to answer in their heads—can capture your audience members' attention because it gets them thinking about your speech topic. For example, to introduce a speech about the Winter Olympics, you could ask, "What's the first sport that comes to mind when you think about the Winter Olympics?" Make sure your rhetorical questions address something of interest to your audience. And avoid overly general questions ("What would you like to learn about winter sports?"); your listeners won't find them as interesting as more focused queries.

Provide a Quotation. A stimulating quotation that illuminates your topic can make an effective attention-getter—especially if you're quoting someone your audience likes and respects or the quotation is thought-provoking or counterintuitive. For example, here is a quotation from Jon Stewart that could be used in a speech contending that the current campaign financing system offers little chance to less-well-known candidates: "I heard Dennis Kucinich say in a debate, 'When I'm president . . . ' and I just wanted to stop him and say, 'Dude.'"[5]

You can also quote an expert in the field to begin your speech. Consider how this speech on solar energy opens with a quotation:

> According to John Byrne and colleagues at the University of Delaware Center for Energy and Environmental Policy, "The direct comparison of solar electric power and oil on a seventy-year time scale suggests that PV [solar electricity] has a realistic potential of providing energy services in the U.S. that, in energy units, could be 8–15 times more than ANWR (Arctic National Wildlife Refuge) and approximately the same as all known U.S. domestic reserves."[6]

Signal Your Thesis

Once you've riveted your listeners' attention, your next step is to indicate the thesis of your speech. You can use your topic statement for this purpose. Recall from Chapter 6 that your thesis statement is the single sentence that expresses the aspect of the topic you will be emphasizing in your speech; your thesis conveys the speech's "bottom line." Providing this statement early in the speech answers a question in the minds of many audience members—"What will this speech be about?"—and helps focus listeners' attention on your message rather than using their mental energy to figure out what your speech is about.

Your thesis statement should clearly convey your topic and purpose in delivering the presentation—further preparing your audience members to listen. It should also be specific and include a signpost that makes it clear that your attention-getter is finished and you are now revealing your topic.

Consider the following example:

ATTENTION-GETTER

I. The tallest mountain in North America. Grizzly bears eating berries just ten feet from the road. Clean, fresh air that you will not find in "the lower forty-eight."

POSSIBLE THESIS STATEMENTS

II. *Vague thesis statement:* All these features can be found in a pristine wilderness environment.
Or

II. *Specific thesis statement:* You can find all these features in Denali National Park, Alaska, and I hope to convince you to visit Denali.

Notice that the specific thesis statement clarifies that the subject of the speech is Denali and that the presenter's purpose is to persuade his audience to go there.

Show Your Audience "What's in It for Them"

Once you have revealed your thesis, you need to generate audience interest and motivate their active listening. Our former colleague Dr. Gail Sorenson referred to this as WIIFM ("whiff-em")—or "What's in It for Me?" Through WIIFM, you clarify why your message is relevant to and important for your listeners.

To accomplish this goal, provide one sentence or a short paragraph that indicates why the audience should take an interest in your topic. Avoid going on and on. Instead, give listeners just enough to whet their appetite. In the body of your speech, you'll go into more detail about how the ideas or suggestions in your presentation will benefit listeners.

Here are some examples of effective WIIFM statements:

- Drunk driving is not just a problem on somebody else's campus. According to the campus police chief, driving-while-intoxicated arrests at this school have soared by 45 percent over the past decade. And that threatens us all.
- I doubt that many of you have lost sleep over the state budget deficit. It did not make my "Top Ten Worries" list either. But when I read that the governor proposed a 20 percent tuition increase as one means of making up the shortfall, I started to worry. And you should, too.
- Today, we will consider the history of the war between the United States and Mexico in 1846 from a Mexican perspective. This will provide you with an alternative to the romanticized version that many of you were taught in your high school history class.

- My survey showed that 77 percent of this class believes that they are spending too much time on school and work at the expense of their social lives. So, instead of focusing on academics today, let's take a brief look at the art of asking someone for a date.

Establish Your Credibility

Your audience members now know what they'll get out of listening to your speech. Next, you need to answer the question "Why should we listen to *you*? What makes you a credible source on this topic?"

How do you build credibility? The same way your sources of evidence do—by showing that you have relevant experience and education and that you've thoroughly researched the subject area of your speech. You gain even more credibility when your listeners see you as trustworthy and perceive that you have their best interests at heart.

To establish credibility, explain how you have gained knowledge about your topic. Use only one or two sentences and emphasize your most relevant credentials (resist any urge to go over your entire résumé or life history!), and adopt a modest, not superior tone.

A student speaker named Alexandra established her credibility in an informative speech about judging competitive ice skating by emphasizing her own relevant experience. Alexandra was especially qualified to speak on the subject because she had won nearly one hundred awards during her skating career and had also served as a judge at several prestigious skating events in her home state. She might have

discussed her many accomplishments in the sport, but instead she established her credibility in this clear, concise, and modest way:

> I have been active in the sport of ice skating since I was six years old and won my fair share of events. I still love skating, so after retiring from competition, I became certified as a judge and have judged at many competitions during the past two years.

With this information, Alexandra left no doubt in her listeners' minds that she was a good source of information on ice skating. She also held their interest: she summarized her experience without providing excessive detail about specific awards or competitions, which would have meant little to her audience.

Preview Your Main Points

A **preview** is a brief statement of the main points you will be developing in the body of your speech. It lets your audience members know what main ideas to expect and helps them visualize the structure of your speech—the sequence of ideas you'll present. Your preview should consist of no more than one sentence per main point.

To differentiate the main points in your preview, include *signposts* (for example, *first*, *next*, *finally*) to help your audience grasp the structure of your speech. Also, avoid the use of *and* or other connecting words while previewing a single main point.

Consider the following two previews that Alexandra might use in her speech about judging ice skating:

WEAKER PREVIEW

The rules of judging and the ways you can judge, along with the many controversies over Olympic judges, are all interesting aspects of judging competitive skating.

STRONGER PREVIEW

Today, we'll look at *three major topics* about judging competitive ice skating: *first*, we'll look at rules for judging the event, *followed by* tips you can use to score the performances yourself, and, *finally*, controversies in the judging at previous Olympics.

Both of these previews offer information about the main points to be developed. However, the first preview is much less explicit. It mentions the three points Alexandra plans to cover, but it runs them together in a single sentence. Thus, it doesn't help the audience understand the structure of the speech. This preview also contains no hints indicating that Alexandra is previewing her main points. This statement could just as easily be an attempt to connect with the audience. By contrast, the strong second preview signals the speech structure clearly, making it easy for Alexandra's audience to recognize exactly what the main points will be and in what sequence she will cover them.

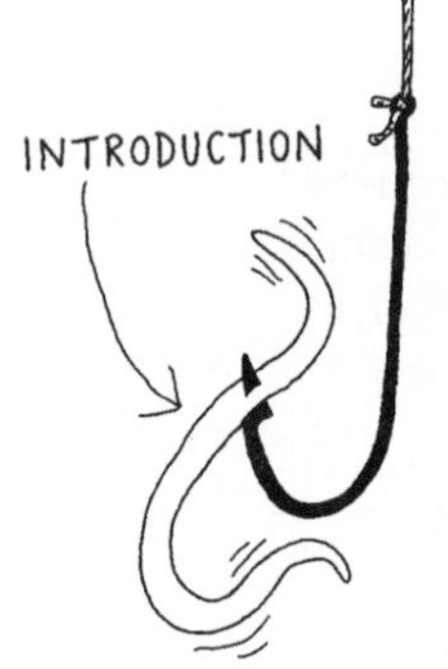

CONCLUDING YOUR SPEECH

While your introduction helps you set the stage for your speech, your conclusion serves another equally important purpose: it helps you sum up the message you developed in the body of your speech and leave a memorable impression in your audience members' minds. Don't use the conclusion to develop new ideas about your topic or further expand on points you've already made. Instead, use it to highlight content that you have already presented. A good conclusion generally takes one minute or less (few sins of a speaker are worse than saying "in conclusion" and then continuing to speak for several more minutes). Your conclusion should start with a transition, summarize your main points, and finish with a clincher—a memorable idea. We examine each of these elements in this section.

Transition to Your Conclusion

After presenting your final main point, insert some transitional language that signals you're ready to wrap up your presentation. For example, a persuasive speech encouraging students to participate in a campus food drive might offer this transition to the conclusion:

FINISH YOUR SPEECH WITH A BANG

> Today, *we have seen* how important it is for every member of this class to participate in our annual campus food drive.

In this example, the use of the phrase *we have seen* signals that you're finished with the main part of your speech and are ready to move on to the next part.

Here's another example of a transition into the conclusion:

> I hope *you have learned more* about the first cultures to inhabit the Americas.

Summarize Your Main Points

The first part of your conclusion is a **summary**, a brief review of your main points. The summary is similar to the preview of your main points that you offered in your introduction, except that here you are reminding the audience of what you said instead of telling them what ideas you'll present. You may summarize in a single compound sentence that covers each main point or restate each main point in a complete sentence. In either case, your goal is to remind the audience of your main ideas one last time. An effective summary helps listeners remember your message by enabling them to put your speech together in their own minds.

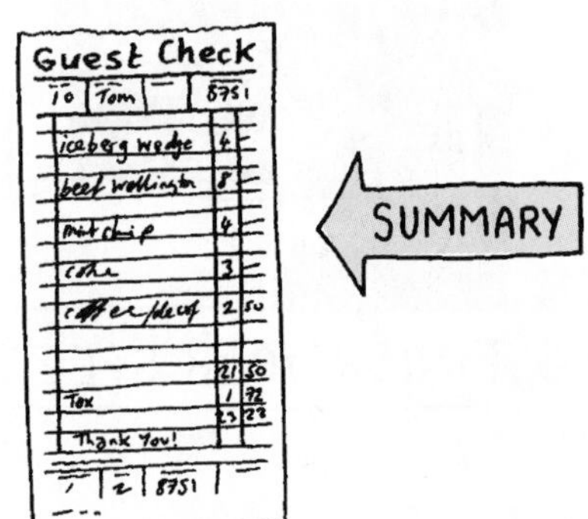

Be sure that your summary includes each main point from your speech. That way, you'll break the speech down into manageable sections for your audience members and remind them of the presentation's structure.

Here is how Alexandra might summarize her main points during the conclusion of her speech about judging ice skating:

> Today, *we have covered* three major topics about judging competitive ice skating. First, we considered the main rules for judging ice skating. Then, we considered some tips for you to use if you want to score at home. Finally, we considered controversies in the judging at the recent Winter Olympics.

Note how Alexandra made a clear reference to each main point and used the past tense to help the audience recognize that she was reviewing her points rather than developing new material.

Finish with a Memorable Clincher

Finish your conclusion with a **clincher**, something that leaves a lasting impression of your speech in your listeners' minds. Once your speech ends, audience members will have countless demands on their time and attention. To make your presentation memorable, select and word your clincher carefully.

The clincher should take up only about thirty seconds in a five- to ten-minute speech. Below are several ways to craft a good clincher.

Tie Your Clincher to the Introduction. If you began your speech with a compelling anecdote or example, consider extending it in your clincher. One speech asking audience members to serve as volunteer tutors began with the story of Hector, a twelve-year-old at risk of dropping out of school because he had fallen behind his classmates. The presenter effectively touched again on Hector's story in her clincher:

> Remember Hector, the boy who was on the verge of dropping out in sixth grade? Ana, a student at this university, became his tutor and role model. Today, Hector has a B average in high school and has applied to several colleges. There are many more Hectors in our local schools, and your help as a tutor will make sure that there is a happy ending to their stories too.

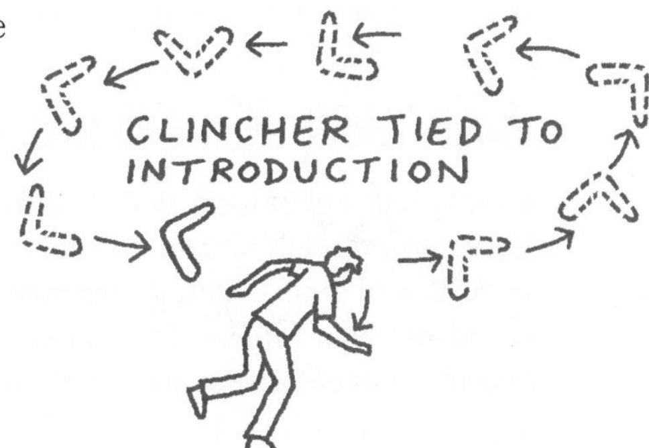

End with a Striking Sentence or Phrase. There may be a single sentence or phrase that effectively sums up your speech. Advertisers and political campaign managers often use this technique because the results are easy to remember. For example, an advertiser refers to a product as "The One," or a campaign manager describes his candidate as possessing "the right stuff for the job." We do not recommend ending your speech with a trivial phrase or a catchy tune. However, do consider using memorable, relevant phrasing to conclude your speech.

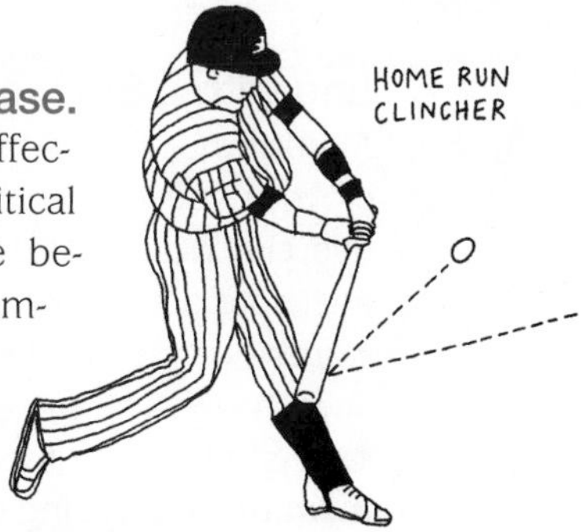

For example, one student used the following clincher to end her informative speech about the mental health benefits of running:

> So, I hope you will remember that running is not just good for your body, but it's also great for your mind.

And a speech about Hmong history effectively concluded with a theme that had been evident in each main point:

> The name Hmong means "free." And no matter what continent we are living on, that is what we will always be—a free people.

Conclude with an Emotional Message. Recall a speech or presentation that ended by touching your emotions. If you're like most people, that speech left more of an impact on you than one merely using cold hard facts. Often, a clincher that delivers an emotional charge makes a speech particularly memorable—especially in a persuasive or commemorative presentation. For example, one student concluded a tribute to a beloved pet in this way:

> My mind flooded with memories: finding him as a tiny kitten and nursing him to health with my own hands. He became my best friend. I let him go lovingly, with the same arms that held him fast as a baby. Good-bye, my friend—I'll never forget you.

End with a Story or Anecdote.

A story that illustrates the message of your speech can make an effective clincher. Consider the following anecdote about Albert Einstein that a student used as her clincher in a speech advocating greater efforts to raise students' self-esteem and prevent them from dropping out:

> Over one hundred years ago, there was a boy who was considered "backward" by his teachers. They said the boy was mentally slow and adrift forever in his foolish dreams. His father said that when he asked the headmaster what profession his son should adopt, he was told, "It doesn't matter, he'll never make a success of anything."[7]
>
> Who was that hopeless student? Believe it or not, his name was Albert Einstein. We must never give up on the mind of a child. Educators must convince every student that he or she is valued and capable of learning. Not a single dropout should be acceptable.

SUMMARY

> "Strong introductions create audience interest; strong conclusions create lasting impressions."

In this chapter, we provided ideas for crafting effective introductions and conclusions for your speeches. You learned that a good introduction has several purposes—including capturing your audience's attention, indicating your thesis, conveying the importance of your topic for audience members, establishing your credibility, and previewing your main points. And you discovered that an effective conclusion transitions smoothly from the body of your

speech, helps your audience remember your main points, and enables you to leave a lasting impression on listeners. There are many strategies to choose from in developing your introduction and conclusion, so you have room to be creative. By tailoring these elements of your speech to your audience and allotting the right amount of time to each, you stand an excellent chance of delivering an effective presentation.

Key Terms

INTRODUCING YOUR SPEECH

attention-getter
rhetorical question
preview

CONCLUDING YOUR SPEECH

summary
clincher

OUTLINING IS USEFUL (AND FUN)

11 OUTLINING YOUR SPEECH

> "A good outline strengthens organization and preparation."

Once you have delivered a few speeches, you will certainly be on your way toward developing better skills. You might even begin getting over any speech anxiety you felt when you gave your first presentation. And, with several speeches under your belt, you may begin to find opportunities to personalize your approach to speech assignments—that is, to develop a style that works best for you. While your public speaking instructor may assign you a speech with a specific purpose (informing, persuading, or marking a special occasion), he or she will often ask you to select the subject matter for your speech and decide how to organize your ideas. By making these kinds of choices yourself, you have the opportunity to put your own stamp on your speeches and to add life and energy to the proceedings.

At the same time, you want to ensure that your presentations are always clear, well organized, and well supported. **Outlining**—organizing

DNA AS METAPHOR FOR SPEECH OUTLINE, BUT IT'S ALSO JUST FINE IF YOU THINK THIS DRAWING LOOKS LIKE TWO PIECES OF TWISTED SCOTCH TAPE WITH SOME IDEAS IN BETWEEN, AS THAT GETS ACROSS ALMOST THE SAME MESSAGE

the points of your speech into a structured form—can help you immensely in doing that. Outlines are valuable tools: they help you lay out the sequence and hierarchy of your ideas, so you can see if your speech flows logically and covers the subject matter adequately. Thus, you can think of an outline as representing the "structural DNA" of your speech. You can also use your outlines to practice your delivery and therefore present your speech with confidence and flair. In most speech situations, an outline can help you further polish your skills—even seasoned presenters find outlining highly useful!

TYPES OF OUTLINES

Most speech instructors suggest creating two versions of an outline for each presentation you prepare. Your **working outline** (also referred to as a detailed or preparation outline) contains all of the points in your speech written in full sentences or detailed phrases (though this type of outline doesn't typically transcribe your speech word-for-word). The main ideas are indicated by roman numerals, and supporting ideas are indented and noted with capital letters (subpoints), numbers (sub-subpoints), lowercase letters (sub-sub-subpoints), and so on. Your detailed outline thus depicts the hierarchy of the ideas in your speech—that is, what your main points are and which details support each of these main points. In addition, where you are quoting evidence, you will include the citation and quote the author word-for-word.

Your working outline should be specific enough that if you woke up with laryngitis on the day of your speech, another classmate could use your outline to deliver your speech. Your instructor will likely require you to turn in a working outline to accompany many of your in-class presentations. You should also use this outline when you begin practicing your speech.

While your working outline is most useful for first organizing your thoughts and rehearsing your speech, a briefer **speaking outline** (also known as an extemporaneous or a delivery outline) is preferred while you're actually presenting to an audience. As you're delivering your talk, you can refer to the speaking outline to remind yourself of

THIS IS AN OUTLINE

I. How an outline helps speakers organize their thinking

   A. Shows relationships between ideas

      1. SHOWS IDEAS IN THE ORDER OF PRESENTATION
      2. SHOWS WHICH IDEAS ARE MORE IMPORTANT THAN OTHERS

II. How outlines can improve presentations

THIS IS A MANUSCRIPT, NOT AN OUTLINE

Today, I will discuss the major ways that outlines are especially important tools for public speakers.

First, outlines show relationships between ideas by showing ideas in their presentation order and showing which ideas are the most important.

Second, outlines help improve speakers' presentations

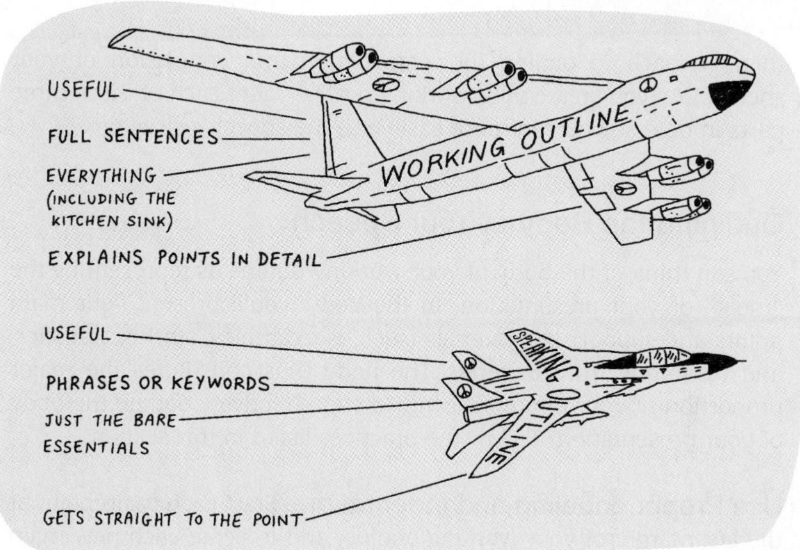

your presentation's structure and key ideas. You can even use it to remind yourself of delivery guidelines by including reminders such as "SPEAK SLOWLY" or "ADD EMPHASIS HERE!" In your speaking outline, you may also choose to include word-for-word quotations for evidence you'll be presenting, so you can be sure you're quoting your sources correctly.

You should prepare your speaking outline after you have become comfortable practicing your speech with your working outline. Once you are familiar with your working outline, a briefer speaking outline can help you deliver a conversational, natural presentation.

In this chapter, we show you how to create a working outline and then a speaking outline. We also discuss three common levels of detail used in each type of outline—sentence, phrase, and keyword. Finally, we provide examples of working and speaking outlines from an actual speech.

CREATING YOUR WORKING OUTLINE

A working outline consists of three main sections: the introduction, the body, and the conclusion of your speech. (Note: most instructors will recommend that you outline the body of your speech first and then go back to outline the introduction and conclusion of your speech.) As you create your working outline, label each of these three parts in bold so you can more easily see the speech's structure.

Outlining the Body of Your Speech

You can think of the **body** of your working outline as representing the "meat" of your presentation. In the body, you'll present your main points and supporting materials (such as examples, stories, statistics, and testimony from experts). The body thus constitutes the major proportion of your entire speech. How to effectively outline the body of your presentation? Follow the practices listed in this section.

Use Proper Labeling and Indentation. Start each main point at the left margin of your working outline, and indicate each new main point with a roman numeral. Label your subpoints with capital letters, and indent them in this part of your outline. If you develop a subpoint further with two or more different supporting ideas, indicate each of these sub-subpoints by arabic numerals, and indent the sub-subpoints another step beneath the subpoint they support. Typically, you'll want to include between two and four subpoints for each main point, and the same number of sub-subpoints for each subpoint (you must *always* include a minimum of two subpoints supporting each main point and two sub-subpoints supporting each subpoint).

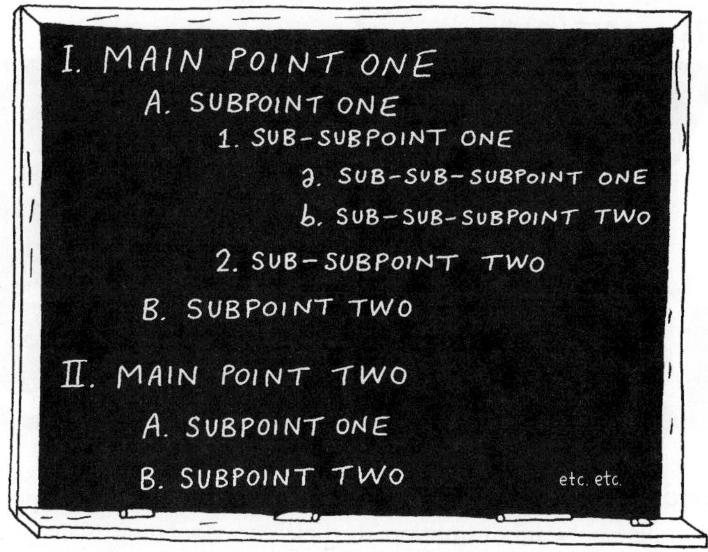

Use Full Sentences or Detailed Phrases. To ensure that you have enough information while practicing your speech, express your main ideas, subpoints, and sub-subpoints in full sentences (some instructors may prefer detailed phrases). In addition, a more detailed outline will be useful for your instructor if he or she asks you to turn in a copy of your working outline. If your working outline is insufficiently detailed, your instructor may misinterpret the points you want to make or (worse) conclude that you haven't put enough effort into preparing your speech.

SUBORDINATION

Check for Subordination. In a well-organized speech, supporting materials show **subordination** to their corresponding main points. Thus, be careful that each subpoint is relevant to the main point it's supposed to support and that each sub-subpoint relates to its corresponding subpoint. How can you tell whether your supporting materials show appropriate subordination to the corresponding point? Complete the following sentence for each of your supporting materials:

> "This supports the point I am making because ________."

If you can't come up with a logical way to complete this sentence, you may need to reexamine your supporting materials and find ways to make them more clearly relevant. For example, you might want to move a subpoint to a different place in your outline where the idea fits better. Or you may decide to reword a main point or subpoint so that the supporting material more clearly explains or expands the idea it is meant to support. Finally, you could consider developing a supporting example or explanation into a main point.

Include Full Information for Citations, Quotations, and Other Evidence. When you use evidence to support a claim, you need to include in your working outline all the information about the source of your **evidence**—the author, his or her qualifications, the source publication or Web page, and the date of publication. And if you are quoting a source, be sure to present the information word-for-word and enclose the information in quotation marks to remind you that you are using someone else's words.

For example, here's how you would outline evidence for a commemorative speech about Cammi Granato, captain of the 1998 and 2002 U.S. Olympic Women's Hockey Team. In this case, the evidence is used as subpoint A, which supports a main point about the beginnings of Granato's hockey career:

I. Cammi Granato got an early start on her hockey career.
   A. Cammi Granato honed her skills by playing hockey with her brothers. According to Ken Campbell, senior editor for *Hockey News*, in *American Hockey Magazine*, December 1997: "The Granato kids painted lines on the floor, set up nets, and played two on two, Tony and Cammi against Donnie and Robbie. 'Those games got pretty intense,' Tony recalls. 'But Cammi hung right in there and she never backed down. She was one of the most tenacious kids I've ever seen.'"

Insert Transitions. Using **transitions**—words, phrases, or sentences that indicate you are moving from one part of your speech to another—helps you keep on track and makes it easier for listeners to follow along. At minimum, include transitions:

- between the introduction and body.
- as you move from one main point to the next.
- between the body and conclusion.

On your outline, indicate a transition by labeling it and placing it in brackets, as shown in the following example:

[TRANSITION The food and scenery in Belize may be a new adventure, but you will find the language very familiar.]

Outlining Your Introduction

After you've outlined the body of your speech, turn to outlining the **introduction**. In Chapter 10, we identified the five parts of an introduction: the attention-getter, the topic or thesis, a connection with the audience, your credibility, and a preview. When you have prepared each of these parts of your introduction, write each one in your work-

ing outline. The structure of the introduction should look like this on your outline:

INTRODUCTION

I. Attention-getter
II. Topic or thesis statement
III. Connection with the audience
IV. Speaker's credibility
V. Preview of main points

Note that your instructor is likely to ask you to write each element of your introduction word-for-word in this part of your working outline or to add in keywords you intend to say for each one.

Outlining Your Conclusion

Once you've finished outlining your introduction, do the same for the **conclusion** of your speech. Just as the introduction grabs your listeners' attention, your conclusion should end your speech on a strong note. Start by outlining the two parts of the conclusion that we discussed in Chapter 10: a summary of your main points and a clincher. When you have prepared these two parts, write them down in sentences or phrases on your outline and indicate each with a roman numeral. The structure of the conclusion should look like this on your working outline:

CONCLUSION

I. Summary of main points
II. Clincher

Creating a Bibliography

Your instructor may require you to include a **bibliography**—a list of the sources you cited in your speech—at the end of your outline. A bibliography should not include sources that you discovered during your research but did not quote or use in your speech. Some colleges consider including unused sources in your bibliography to be academic dishonesty and will take strict disciplinary action against students who commit this kind of wrongdoing.

In your bibliography, include full citations for sources you referred to in your outline. And remember: even if you create a bibliography for the end of your detailed outline, you'll still need to properly attribute all evidence within the outline and when delivering your presentation.

Your instructor will likely require you to use a particular style of documentation in your bibliography; two of the most common are those recommended by the American Psychological Association (APA) and the Modern Language Association (MLA). Regardless of which style you use, make sure to follow your instructor's requirements for the bibliography.

Inserting the Title, Specific Purpose, and Thesis

Some instructors may also ask you to write the title, specific purpose, and thesis of your speech at the top of your working outline to guide

BOGUS BIBLIOGRAPHIES = BIG TROUBLE

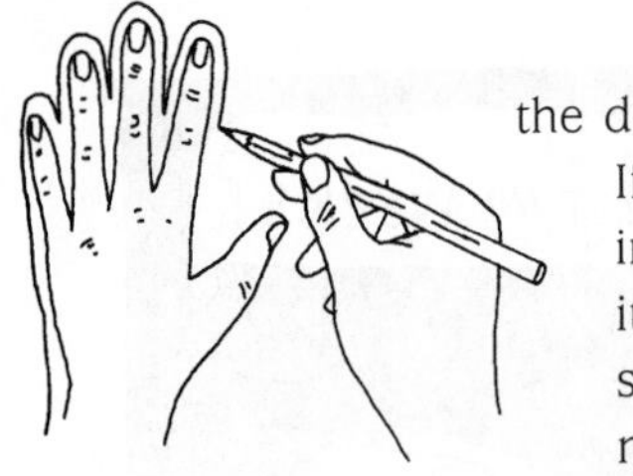

the development of your main and supporting points. If your professor has requested this information, indicate the title of your speech and type or write it out in relatively large or bold type. Indicate your speech's specific purpose and thesis at the left margin, as shown in the example below:

TRANSLOCATION AND ANIMAL INSTINCTS

SPECIFIC PURPOSE To inform my audience about the process of animal translocation and explain the challenges to its success.

THESIS Animal translocation, a process in which human beings relocate a threatened species to a new and, ideally, better habitat, is sometimes a necessary but also challenging process.

A Sample Detailed Outline

Robin McGehee of William Carey College developed a speech titled "A Deadly Mistake," in which she advocated steps for reducing prescription-drug errors. In this section, we show the working outline of her speech, with updated evidence, along with annotations highlighting key concepts covered in this chapter.

SAMPLE WORKING OUTLINE

A DEADLY MISTAKE

Your instructor may require a written specific purpose statement; the speech itself begins with the introduction.

SPECIFIC PURPOSE To persuade my audience that prescription drug errors are a serious health threat in the United States, requiring their personal efforts to reduce the problem, accompanied by new governmental policies.

INTRODUCTION

I. On July 15, 1994, Megan McClave underwent tonsillectomy surgery. Four days later, she was dead. The reason? According to the May 1995 *Ladies Home Journal*, she died because her pharmacist made a deadly mistake—accidentally filling a prescription for the painkiller Demerol from a bottle of Roxanol, a brand name for the powerful painkiller morphine. Megan followed the directions for taking her prescription and swallowed enough morphine to shut down her entire respiratory system. Everyone makes mistakes, but this was a deadly mistake that could have been avoided.

Robin begins with an anecdote to gain the audience's attention.

Source citation for the anecdote.

II. I hope to convince you that prescription drug errors (PDEs) should be reduced through individual and governmental action.

III. Library and interview research indicate that Megan's tragedy was only the tip of the iceberg.

IV. My research revealed that seven class members currently take one or more prescription drugs and that most of us have friends and loved ones who are taking prescription medications. We are all at serious risk if drug errors are made.

V. To analyze the issue of prescription drug errors, let's consider the consequences of drug errors, some causes of these errors, and some urgent and immediate solutions.

Robin includes the five components of the introduction: attention-getter; thesis; connection with the audience; credibility; and preview.

[TRANSITION Let's start by analyzing the seriousness of the problem.]

Transition from introduction to body.

BODY

I. The costs of drug errors include disease, dollars, and death.
   A. Megan's case is not rare.
      1. A study of common pharmaceutical agents, reported in the August 2002 *Journal of Toxicology*, found that therapeutic errors

Proper citations to research material used to support a point.

Subpoints and sub-subpoints are indented properly.

were reported for more than ninety-five thousand children under six years of age; 86 percent of these errors were acute.

2. The *Washington Post*, April 25, 2001, reported a study by Rainu Kaushal and colleagues at Boston's Brigham and Women's Hospital: "Hospitalized children experience potentially dangerous medication errors three times as often as adults."

B. Children are not the only group at risk: Nearly one million elderly patients used at least one of eleven medications that should always be avoided by the elderly, according to the U.S. Agency for Healthcare Research and Quality in the February 2002 edition of *Drug Utilization Review*.

C. On October 3, 1995, *USA Today* reported that prescription drug–related problems cost approximately $75.6 billion each year.

D. Deaths are an even more tragic cost.

   1. According to an Institute of Medicine report, *To Err Is Human: Building a Safer Health System*, 2000, the annual number of lives lost to medication errors exceeds seven thousand—more than the number of Americans who die from workplace injuries each year.
   2. In the April 25, 2001, issue of the *Washington Post*, David Brown provided a tragic example of a nine-month-old girl who died at Children's Hospital in Washington, D.C.: a misplaced decimal point in an order led to her getting ten times the intended dose of morphine.

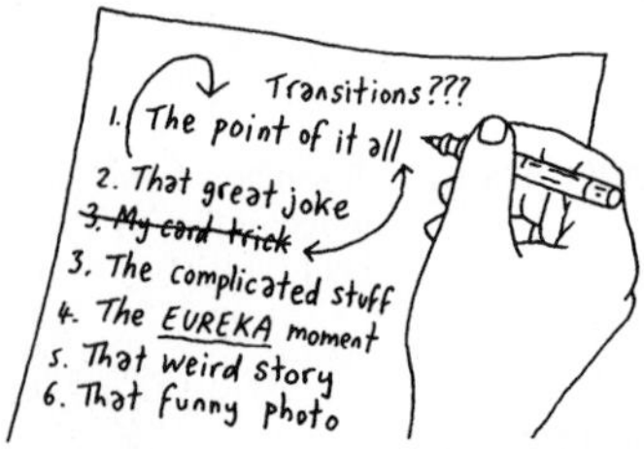

[TRANSITION Drug errors are causing needless death and suffering. Why do these deadly mistakes continue?]

II. The causes of prescription drug errors are threefold.
   A. One cause: lack of reporting requirements.
      1. According to Michelle Meadows, in *FDA Consumer*, May–June 2003, "Since 1992, the [FDA] has received about 20,000 reports of medication errors. These are voluntary reports, so the number of medication errors that actually occur is thought to be much higher."
      2. When drug errors are not reported, we receive no explanation of why or how a pharmacist could confuse medicines, and the pharmacist remains licensed to practice and is able to make more mistakes in the future.
      3. We cannot save patients unless we learn from pharmacist mistakes and implement precautionary measures.
   B. Another cause: the trust we place in medical professionals.
      1. People in the health-care professions are among the most trusted individuals in our society.
      2. Have we come to trust these human beings too much?
         a. Pharmacists, like other workers, may get tired, bored, or distracted.
         b. Pharmacists may assume that someone else is ensuring that prescriptions are properly filled.
      3. Economic pressures are making pharmacists' jobs even harder.
         a. According to *American Druggist* in January 1998, "HMOs, with their eye on the bottom line, pay pharmacists less for each drug they dispense than insurers did in the past."
         b. This forces pharmacists to scramble to fill as many prescriptions as possible.

Note the parallel wording of the three main points.

The terms *one*, *another*, and *a third* signpost subpoints on the cause of the problem.

c. William Campbell, dean of the School of Pharmacy at the University of North Carolina, calls this situation a "doomsday machine" (same article).

C. A third cause: failed communication—noted by Kevin Doherty, Alissa Segal, and Patrick McKinney in *Consultant*, February 2004—including poor handwriting, misinterpreted directions, and misplaced decimals.

Transition links main points II and III.

[TRANSITION There are many causes of drug errors, but are there solutions? Yes.]

III. The solutions to prescription drug errors depend on both individual and government efforts.

The words *first*, *second*, and *third* signpost the three aspects of Robin's solution.

A. First, a nationwide drug error reporting system should be implemented.

1. The Institute of Medicine of the National Academies made this recommendation in *To Err Is Human*, 2000, "A nationwide mandatory reporting system should be established by building upon the current patchwork of state systems and by standardizing the types of adverse events and information to be reported."

2. Pennsylvania Senator Arlen Specter has introduced Senate Bill 2766, which includes grants for states to establish medication error reporting systems that follow federal guidelines.

3. As customers of the health-care profession and citizens of the United States, we should ask Congress to pass legislation with sufficient funding for every state to implement a sound reporting system.

B. Second, computerized systems can further reduce error according to Janet Corrigan, director

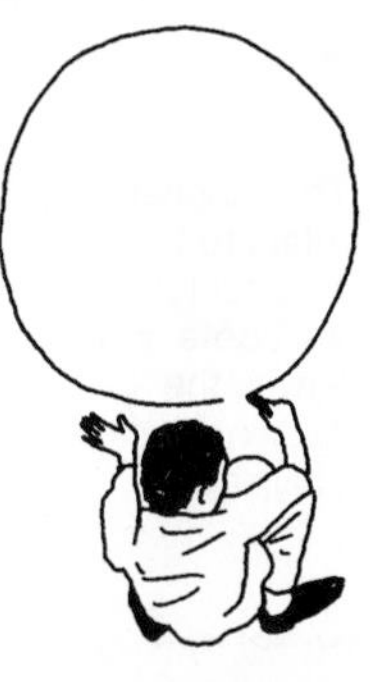

of the Institute of Medicine's Board on Health Care Services, who testified before the Senate Special Committee on Aging, May 3, 2001.

1. Since the mid-1990s, the Agency for Healthcare Research and Quality has funded numerous evaluations of computer monitoring systems that prevent and detect adverse drug events (ADEs).
2. The results are promising—from 28 to 95 percent of ADEs can be prevented.

C. Third, I will distribute a wallet-sized card provided by the American Pharmacy Association with reminders of action you can take to reduce the risk of drug error:

1. Write down the name, dose, and purpose of the drug when it is prescribed.
2. Introduce yourself to the pharmacist.
3. Read the prescription label carefully to be certain that you have received the proper drug.
4. Ask the pharmacist any questions you have, and get a phone number you can call if you have questions later.
5. Use this card as a quick reference when having a prescription filled, and it may save your life or the life of a loved one.

[TRANSITION In conclusion, I hope that you have become more aware of the prescription drug error problem in the United States.]

Transition from body to conclusion.

CONCLUSION

I. Today, I described the deadly consequences of drug errors, focused on some causes of these errors, and presented immediate solutions. The prescription errors that pharmacists are making are serious, but we *can* do much to reduce these deadly mistakes.

Efficient summary of main points.

The clincher refers to the introductory anecdote and leaves the audience with a challenge.

II. Remember Megan McClave and her family, and how a young life was lost because of a deadly mistake that could have been avoided. If the pharmacist had been more careful, or Megan's family had known the right questions to ask, this girl would be alive today. Are you going to ask these questions the next time you or a loved one needs a prescription filled? Or will you just walk out the door and take your chances? Let's not allow these needless deaths to continue.

Bibliography

Full citation of sources in the references section. (Check with your instructor on his or her preferred citation format.)

M. Belson, and G. Bauer, "Therapeutic Errors in Children," *Journal of Toxicology: Clinical Toxicology* 40 (August 2002): 607.

D. Brown, "Study Looks at Children, Drug Errors," *Washington Post*, April 25, 2001, A19.

K. Doherty, A. Segal, and P. McKinney, "The 10 Most Common Prescribing Errors: Tips on Avoiding the Pitfalls," *Consultant* 44 (February 2004): 173.

"Drugs Wrongly Prescribed to Millions of Elderly," *Drug Utilization Review* 18 (February 2002): 15.

Institute of Medicine, *To Err Is Human: Building a Safer Health System* (Washington, D.C.: National Academy Press, 2000).

D. McLellan, "Megan Won't Wake Up," *Ladies Home Journal* May 1995, 132.

M. Meadows, "Strategies to Reduce Medication Errors," *FDA Consumer* (May–June 2003). http://www.fda.gov/fdac/features/2003/303_meds.html (accessed November 29, 2004).

"Prescription Misuse Costs Nation Billions," *USA Today*, October 3, 1995, D4.

M. Slezak, "*Good Housekeeping* Examines Rx Errors," *American Druggist* 215 (January 1998):19.

U.S. Senate Special Committee on Aging, *Concerning Patient Safety and Medication Errors,* 107th Congress, 1st Sess., 2001, 16.

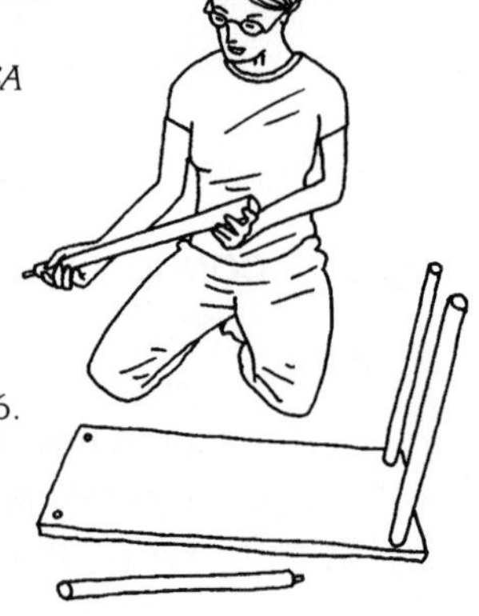

CREATING YOUR SPEAKING OUTLINE

In most public speaking situations, **extemporaneous delivery** gets you the best results. To give an extemporaneous presentation, you speak from limited notes rather than reading word-for-word from a manuscript or delivering your speech from memory. Extemporaneous delivery allows you the freshness of choosing your words as you speak, while the briefer outline notes serve as useful reminders of your main and supporting points in case you lose track.

To deliver the most effective extemporaneous presentation possible, transform your working outline into your briefer speaking outline, which is made up of short phrases or keywords as opposed to full sentences. Prepare the speaking outline only *after* you've practiced your speech several times with your working outline and have become thoroughly familiar with the ideas in your presentation. Then use the speaking outline for your final practice sessions and for delivering your speech.

Formatting Your Speaking Outline

Prepare your speaking outline on 5-by-7-inch note cards or on regular $8^1/_2$-by-11-inch paper. Keep your points brief, using only quick phrases or one or two keywords for each point. The more you've practiced your speech using your working outline, the more useful the speaking outline will be as a reminder while you're delivering your speech.

Because you'll refer to this outline as needed while giving your presentation, make it easy on the eyes. If you use a word processor to create the outline, double-space and select a large font size. If you handwrite your outline on note cards, write neatly and leave space between each line.

IF YOU NEED TO CHECK YOUR NOTES DURING YOUR SPEECH... ...WHICH OUTLINE WOULD YOU PREFER TO READ?

Base your speaking outline on your working outline. Use a similar structure by indenting subordinate points and using roman numerals, capital letters, and numbers. Number each note card or page of your speaking outline—this will help you reassemble the outline quickly if you happen to drop your pages or cards while walking up to the front of the room or delivering your speech.

Note that your instructor may have specific requirements about the form and length of your speaking outline. Check to ensure that your outline meets these requirements.

Elements of Your Speaking Outline

Your speaking outline should be a condensed version of your working outline that retains all of your points, subpoints, and source quotations. Indicate main points and supporting points in no more than a sentence, and trust yourself to develop these ideas conversationally while delivering your speech. Include the following elements in your extemporaneous outline:

- *Main points.* Write each main point as a brief phrase or as one to three keywords. Stating your main points in similar words or parallel structures will signal to your listeners that these points are important.

- *Subpoints and sub-subpoints.* Write just enough to remind yourself of the key idea.
- *Evidence.* When providing evidence for your claims in your speaking outline, include necessary citation information and consider including word-for-word quotes or evidence from the original source.
- *Difficult words.* If you'll be using words that are difficult to pronounce or remember, include them in your speaking outline. For example, in the sample outline on page 327, if the speaker wanted to include complex names of medications, such as "acetazolamide," she would insert pronunciation notes.
- *Transitions.* Include a brief reminder of each transition in your speech. These reminders don't need to be word-for-word, but make them detailed enough to indicate to your audience that you're done with one idea *and* you're moving on to the next. Consider using brackets to set your transitions apart from your points.

THE ART OF BEING COMFORTABLE AND ONLY LOOKING AT YOUR NOTES ONCE IN A WHILE

- *Delivery notes.* In the margin, consider jotting down **delivery reminders** for handling speaking challenges effectively. For example, write "SLOW DOWN!" in places where you tend to rush or "LOOK UP!" if you often read from your notes rather than making eye contact while presenting. Consider writing "KEY POINT" or "EMPHASIS!" to remind yourself to use voice or gestures to highlight an

important idea. Try writing "COVER WHEN DONE!" as a reminder for what to do after you've finished using a visual aid. To make reminders stand out, circle them, write them in capital letters, use a different colored ink, or highlight them.

A Sample Speaking Outline

Here is a speaking outline of Robin McGehee's speech, "A Deadly Mistake." Compare this outline with her working outline (see pages 316–22). Notice how Robin used keywords and abbreviations to condense her ideas. She inserted direct quotations word-for-word and showed these quotations in boldface. Finally, she included delivery reminders.

SAMPLE SPEAKING OUTLINE

A DEADLY MISTAKE

INTRODUCTION

Look up

I. Megan McClave anecdote: experienced pharmacist gave her Roxanol (morphine), not Demerol.
II. Reduce PDEs through indiv. + govt. action.
III. Research: Megan = tip of iceberg.
IV. Survey—7 taking PD and most have friends and loved ones taking PD. All at risk.
V. Consequences, causes, solutions.

Pause

[TRANSITION Let's start by analyzing problem.]

All five parts of the introduction are included, but limited to keywords.

Abbreviate "prescription drug errors" as *PDEs*.

Remember to include a transition to body of speech.

BODY

I. Costs = disease, dollars, and death.
   A. Megan's case not rare.
      1. **Errors in 95,000+ children under six; 86% acute,** *Journal of Toxicology*, August 2002.
      2. **"Hospitalized children experience potentially dangerous medication errors three times as often as adults,"** *Washington Post*, April 25, 2001, study by Rainu Kaushal et al. @ Brigham and Women's Hospital.
   B. **About one million elderly using 1 of 11 risky medications,** U.S. Agency for Healthcare Research and Quality, *Drug Utilization Review*, February 2002.
   C. **Drug-related problems approx. $75.6 billion/year,** *USA Today*, October 3, 1995.
   D. Deaths.
      1. **7,000+ deaths annually, > workplace deaths,** Institute of Medicine report, *To Err Is Human*, 2000.
      2. **9-month-old girl died at Children's Hospital in D.C.—misplaced decimal point,** *Washington Post*, April 25, 2001.

Include evidence citations.

Robin's detailed outline is condensed to keywords with abbreviations. She trusts herself to explain the details.

Slowly

[TRANSITION Errors cause needless deaths, why do they continue?]

II. Causes of PDEs are threefold.
  A. Lack of reporting requirements.
    1. Reporting limited—**"Since 1992, the [FDA] has received about 20,000 reports of medication errors. These are voluntary reports, so the number of medication errors that actually occur is thought to be much higher,"** Michelle Meadows, *FDA Consumer*, May–June 2003.
    2. No reporting = no improvement.
    3. Learn from mistakes + precautions.
  B. Trust in med. care pros.
    1. Most trusted in society.
    2. Pharmacists: human errors, tired, distracted.
    3. Economic pressures.
      a. **HMOs pay less per drug dispensed,** *American Druggist,* January 1998.
      b. Pharms. fill as many RXs as possible.
      c. **A "doomsday machine,"** William Campbell, dean of the Pharmacy School at the University of North Carolina (same source).
  C. Communication errors: **poor handwriting, misinterpreted directions, misplaced decimals,** Doherty, Segal, and McKinney, *Consultant,* February 2004.

[TRANSITION Many causes, but are there solutions? Yes!]

III. Solutions: indiv. and govt. efforts.
  A. Nationwide reporting system.
    1. **"A nationwide mandatory reporting system should be established by building upon the current patchwork of state systems and by**

standardizing the types of adverse events and information to be reported," Institute of Medicine, *To Err Is Human*, 2000.

2. Sen. Specter, Bill 2766.
3. Pressure Congress: legislation with enough $ for reporting system in every state.

Look up

B. Computerized systems. Janet Corrigan, director of Inst. of Med. Board on Health Care Services, Senate Special Committee on Aging, May 3, 2001.
   1. **Evaluations of reporting systems by Agency for Healthcare Research and Quality.**
   2. **Promising: 28–95% prevention.**

Explanation of subpoints and sub-subpoints is very brief.

C. Wallet-sized card from Am. Pharmacy Assn.
   1. Write down name, dose, purpose.
   2. Intro. self to pharm.
   3. Read label, check for proper drug.
   4. Ask questions, get phone number.
   5. Use card as reference.

[TRANSITION In conclusion, hope you are more aware of PDE problem.]

CONCLUSION

I. Summary: consequences, causes, solutions to PDEs.
II. Remember Megan. Don't let it happen again.

SUMMARY

> "A good outline strengthens organization and preparation."

In this chapter, we explained the importance of outlining and showed you how to develop and use a working outline and a speaking outline to organize your ideas, practice your presentation, and ultimately deliver an effective speech. A working outline shows the structure of your speech and the hierarchy of your ideas, as well as full quotations for all evidence you'll provide in your speech. This outline also includes notes for transitions and visual aids. Use your working outline to practice your speech until you're thoroughly familiar with it.

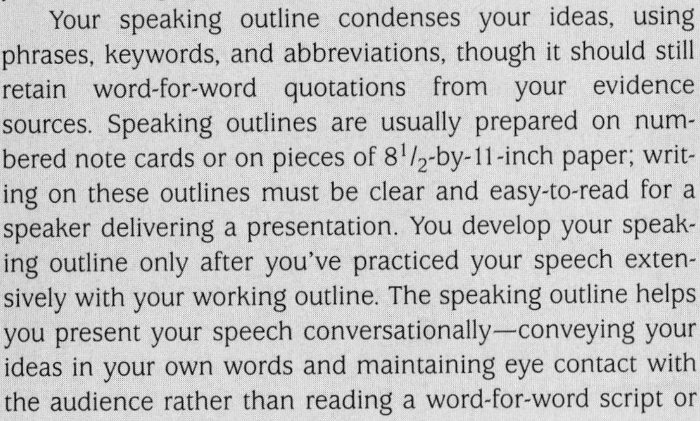

Your speaking outline condenses your ideas, using phrases, keywords, and abbreviations, though it should still retain word-for-word quotations from your evidence sources. Speaking outlines are usually prepared on numbered note cards or on pieces of $8^1/_2$-by-11-inch paper; writing on these outlines must be clear and easy-to-read for a speaker delivering a presentation. You develop your speaking outline only after you've practiced your speech extensively with your working outline. The speaking outline helps you present your speech conversationally—conveying your ideas in your own words and maintaining eye contact with the audience rather than reading a word-for-word script or reciting your presentation from memory. The speaking outline also serves as a handy reminder if you lose your place while delivering your speech, if you need to quote evidence during your talk, or if you want to remember certain delivery tips (such as adding emphasis to a particular point while presenting your speech).

Key Terms

outlining

TYPES OF OUTLINES

working outline
speaking outline

CREATING YOUR WORKING OUTLINE

body
subordination
evidence
transitions
introduction
conclusion
bibliography

CREATING YOUR SPEAKING OUTLINE

extemporaneous delivery
delivery reminders

As a civilian volunteer with my local police department, I've seen how policemen handle perps, run informants, and deal with certain problem neighborhoods where those people won't help the policemen yet they want the policemen to help them...
09/11/01
PERP? PERPLEX??
PERPETUAL???
PERPENDICULAR????

12 LANGUAGE AND STYLE

"Choose your words carefully."

Marvin was eager to present his speech about law-enforcement techniques in large cities to his public speaking classmates. A civilian volunteer with the local police department, he had forged close bonds with the police officers there and hoped to become a homicide investigator one day.

In delivering his speech, Marvin drew on the terminology and style of talking that he had come to know through his experiences at the department. For example, he made frequent references to the "policemen" on the force and described what it was like to "handle perps" and "run informants." At one point in his presentation, he also mentioned "problems of law enforcement in certain neighborhoods. These people don't want to help the police, but they feel justified demanding more service from policemen." When Marvin sat down after concluding his speech, he felt confident that he had conveyed his credibility and had met his objective: informing the audience about his topic.

Yet the students in Marvin's class had mixed reactions to his talk. Many found him credible because of his volunteer experience and his wide vocabulary of police terms and slang. Others, however, found some of his slang impenetrable. Several women in the audience also resented his use of *policemen* instead of *police officers*. Some listeners found the phrase *certain neighborhoods* insensitive because it seemed to be a veiled reference to socioeconomics or race. These same audience members also saw the word *service* as laughable in the light of recent episodes of excessive police violence featured on the national news.

Clearly, Marvin failed to get his message across to many people in his audience—in large part because of the words he chose. If he had used the same language in talking to an audience of police officers, he might well have had more success. But his classmates comprised diverse students who had very different perspectives on law enforcement than police officers have—and who used very different language. Marvin failed because he didn't adapt his word choice to these listeners' expectations. When it comes to giving speeches, your word choice can matter far more than you might think.

Another great example of the importance of **word choice** (also known as **diction**) can be found in Martin Luther King Jr.'s "I Have a Dream" speech, which we discussed in Chapter 2. When King presented this address on August 28, 1963, at the March on Washington, he didn't give it an official title. Only later did people start calling it the "I Have a Dream" speech. Why has this phrase endured in people's memories? It was an exceptionally powerful expression that

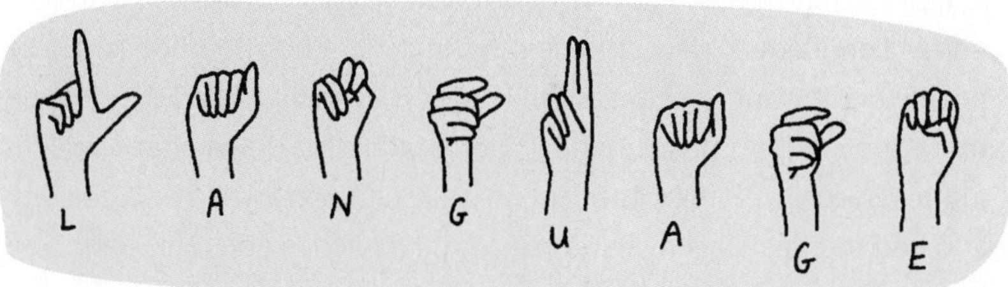

encapsulated King's vision of a time and place free from prejudice and discrimination. Nearly forty years after his death, people still experience profound emotion when they recall this expression. If King had calmly used the words *I hope* instead of *I have a dream*, he would have had much less impact on his listeners.

An average speech may contain hundreds or even thousands of words. And every one of them matters. Selected carefully, your words can help you connect with your audience and get your message across clearly. Used thoughtlessly, they may confuse, offend, bore, or annoy your listeners—preventing them from absorbing your message. In this chapter, we examine the importance of choosing the right words for your speeches, and the difference between oral and written language. Then we explain how to use language to present your message clearly, express your ideas effectively, and demonstrate respect for your audience.

THE IMPORTANCE OF LANGUAGE AND WORD CHOICE

Even if you don't think of yourself as much of a reader or a "word" person, you still make thousands of word choices every day: when talking with friends and family, taking notes in class, writing e-mails, making phone calls, and sending text messages. You probably try to choose your words carefully in each of these situations. After all, you know that your words have a lot of power. They can inform, inspire, and uplift others. But they can also confuse people (for example, if you've used jargon or slang that others might not understand), and they can hurt others (for instance, if you've used biased language).

Your word choice reflects on you as a speaker. In earlier chapters, we introduced the concept of a speaker's *ethos*, or personal credibility, and explained how ethos can influence an audience's perception of the presenter's message. Your words

and phrases convey your ethos to your listeners because they say something about you as a person.

How do you use words in ways that clarify your message and enhance your credibility? Along with using appropriate and considerate language, you can explain technical terms and use helpful audiovisual aids (for clarity) and effectively incorporate such terms into your speech (to enhance credibility).

A student speaker named Gillian applied these practices while delivering an informative presentation about armor plating used during the Ottoman Empire. Gillian showed photographs depicting the armor worn by soldiers and their horses. She also used technical terms in a way that the audience would understand. For instance, at one point

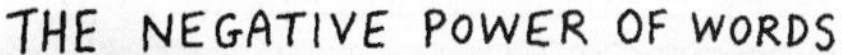

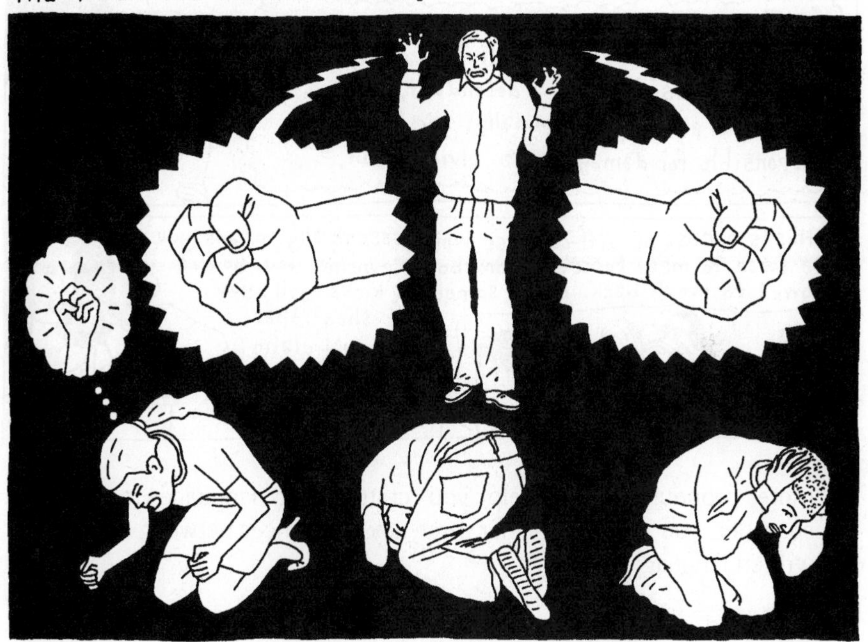

she discussed a "gilded copper chanfrein," which she immediately explained was "forehead armor for the horse—like the helmet a soldier might wear." By using the correct technical terminology, Gillian showed authority and gained credibility in the eyes of her audience. And by explaining these terms through devices such as analogies ("like the helmet a soldier might wear"), she made her message accessible without coming across as condescending to her listeners.

DIFFERENCES BETWEEN ORAL AND WRITTEN LANGUAGE

You may have noticed that words and sentences can come across quite differently when you hear them spoken aloud, as opposed to when you read them to yourself. In a public speaking context, that difference between spoken and written language is usually even

more pronounced. To help you craft better language for your speeches, you should consider three key differences between oral and written language:

- *Oral language is more adaptive.* Writers seldom know exactly who will read their words, or in what context; the best they can do is to take educated guesses and make language choices accordingly. When you speak before a live audience, however, you can get immediate feedback that is virtually impossible for a writer. Thus, you can observe your audience members during your presentation, interact with them, and *respond* to the way they are receiving your message. Because a speech is a live, physical interaction and audience feedback is instantaneous, you can adapt to the situation, such as by extending or simplifying an explanation if listeners seem confused or choosing clearer or simpler language.
- *Oral language tends to be less formal.* Because writers have the luxury of getting their words down on paper (or on screen) and then going

I do try and wear stuff by unknown designers.

BJÖRK IN HER SWAN DRESS

back to make changes, they typically use precise word choice and follow the formal rules of syntax and grammar. This careful use of language aligns well with most readers' expectations. In most speech situations, however, language choices tend toward a somewhat less formal style. Because listeners lack the chance to go back and reread your words, you will usually want to use shorter and less complicated sentences (of course certain speech situations, such as many political settings, require elevated sentence structure and word choice). Effective oral language is also often simpler and less technically precise than written language. Thus, consider incorporating appropriate colloquialisms, conversational tone, and even sentence fragments into your speeches.

- *Oral language incorporates repetition.* Most writing teachers and coaches advise their students to avoid repeating themselves or being *redundant* by covering the same ground more than once. But in speaking situations, repetition can be an especially effective tool because your listeners can't go back and revisit your points—your words are there and then suddenly they are gone. Because most audience members won't take notes (especially outside of a classroom setting), there is nothing for listeners to rely upon except their own memory of your words.

As a speaker, you can help your listeners remember your message by intentionally repeating keywords and phrases throughout a presentation. If an audience hears certain words often enough, they will remember them.

DENOTATIVE AND CONNOTATIVE MEANING

In addition to using words to express your message clearly and to enhance your credibility, you need to be aware that words can have two very different kinds of meaning. By understanding these differences, you can select your language more strategically to exert the impact you want. In the sections that follow, we take a close look at this notion of two different meanings: denotative meaning and connotative meaning.

Denotative Meaning

The **denotative meaning** of a word is its exact, literal dictionary definition. When you use a word that has one dictionary definition (and that is not overly technical), you can pretty well expect that your audience will understand what you mean. But many words have several dictionary definitions. In these cases, you may need to take steps to avoid confusion.

Consider the word *run.* According to *Merriam-Webster's Collegiate Dictionary*, *run* has numerous def-

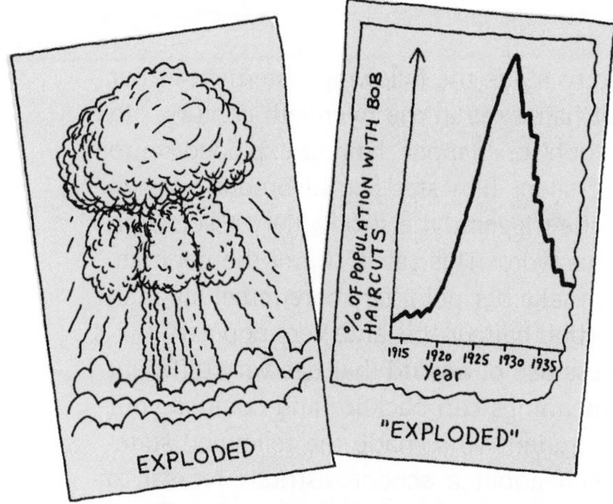

initions. It can be a verb meaning "to go faster than a walk," a noun meaning "an unbroken course of performance" (such as "a good run of profits this year"), and an adjective meaning "being in a melted state" (for instance, "that butter's run"). Suppose you wanted to use the word *run* in a speech to refer to a successful series of victories by your school's track team. If you said, "We've had a great run this season," your listeners may wonder if you're referring to a specific running race or to a string of victories scored by the team against opponents during the season. In this case, you may want to avoid the risk of confusing your audience by saying, "We've consistently trounced the competition during this season" instead of "We've had a good run this season."

Connotative Meaning

In addition to denotative meanings, many words also have **connotative meanings**—associations that come to mind when people hear or read the word. A word's connotative meanings may bear little or even no resemblance to its denotative meanings. For example, the word *dog*, when used as a noun in a statement about stocks, may connote a poor investment opportunity—yet the literal meaning of the noun *dog* is a specific type of canine.

By using words in your speeches deliberately for their connotative meanings, you can make a powerful impression on your audience. For

example, a student named Betty made the following statement in her presentation on the history of hairstyles in the twentieth century: "In the roaring 1920s, the short 'bob' or 'flapper' haircut exploded on to the scene through the rise of silent film star Louise Brooks." When Betty used the verb *exploded*, she triggered the strong, fiery association that most people have with this word. This savvy use of the connotations of *exploded* helped Betty make her point far more forcefully than if she had merely said that the bob haircut "became very popular."

On the other hand, careless use of a word that has very different denotative and connotative meanings can backfire and confuse your audience. Consider Albert, a student who made the following statement in an impromptu speech about a school district's refusal to lower the student/teacher ratio for class size in elementary schools: "That kind of decision really demonstrates some bigotry by the school board." The word *bigotry* literally means the state of mind of a person who is intolerantly devoted to his or her personal opinions or prejudices—the meaning that Albert intended in his comment. Unfortunately, many people have come to associate the word *bigotry* with racial prejudice. Albert did not intend a racial connotation—he just wanted to say that he thought the school district was unreasonably wedded to its decision about class size. Unfortunately, many students in Albert's class had experienced the pain of racial prejudice firsthand. Thus, they inferred from Albert's use of *bigotry* that issues of race underlay the school board's decision—which wasn't true. If Albert had analyzed his audience more carefully, he might have known to avoid using the word *bigotry*—because of its potentially misleading connotative meaning.

PRESENTING YOUR MESSAGE CLEARLY

You can't get your message across to your audience unless you present it clearly. To make your message as clear as possible, use language that's understandable, concrete, proper, and concise.

Understandable Language

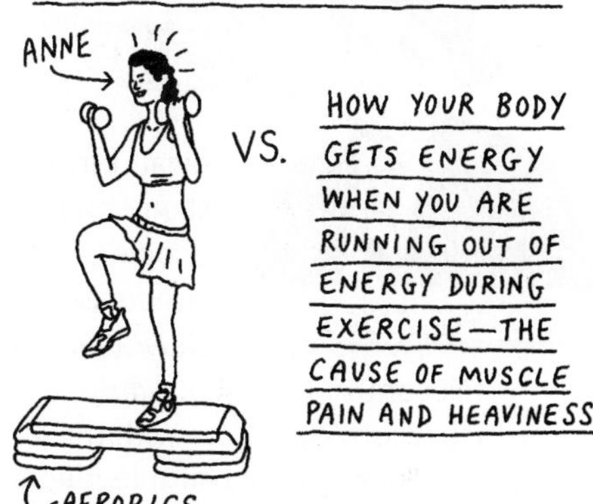

Understandable language consists of words that your listeners find *recognizable*. In most situations, the best ways to ensure that you're using understandable language are to choose words that reflect your audience's language skills and to avoid technical terms beyond your listeners' comprehension. For example, if a cell biologist gave a talk to a room full of English majors, she would quickly confuse her listeners with terms such as *ribosomal DNA* and *anaerobic cellular metabolism*. Yet those terms could be appropriate in a speech delivered to a group of experts or insiders—for example, when giving a paper to scientists at a biology conference.

Thus, you need to analyze your audience to determine what language your listeners will recognize. Audience members' educational background can suggest their general vocabulary level. Meanwhile, demographic information and stories about listeners' life experiences can help you predict what language the audience will understand.

I fear those big words which make us so unhappy.

JAMES JOYCE

Also take care in using **jargon**—specialized or technical words or phrases familiar to people in a specific field or group. Jargon includes technical terms as well as abbreviations, acronyms, slang, and other esoteric expressions. For example, people in the field of telecommunications use jargon extensively—including expressions such as *FTTP* ("fiber to the property"), *3G* ("third-generation telecom networks"), *CapEx* ("capital expenditures"), and *first-tier ops* ("telecom operators with the largest market share").

Here are two simple guidelines for deciding whether to include a particular instance of jargon in a speech:

- *If you can say something in plain language, do so.* Unless you see a pressing reason to use jargon—such as to clarify an important point or bolster your credibility—use widely accessible words.
- *If you do use jargon, explain it.* By clarifying your use of jargon, you can gain whatever advantages it offers while still maintaining your audience's understanding.

For example, a student named Patrick was giving a speech in his public speaking class on safe horseback riding practices. Most of his fellow students had grown up in the city and had had little exposure to horses. In explaining the steps required to prepare a horse for a trail ride, Patrick said, "Be very careful about how you tack up your horse—that is, how you put the bridle and saddle on." He guessed (correctly) that many of his listeners wouldn't understand the phrase *tack up*. By using the term—which is common among people who ride horseback—he gained credibility as someone familiar with his topic. And by explaining it, he helped his audience understand the information.

Concrete Words

Whenever possible, strive to use concrete words instead of abstract ones. What's the difference? **Concrete words** are

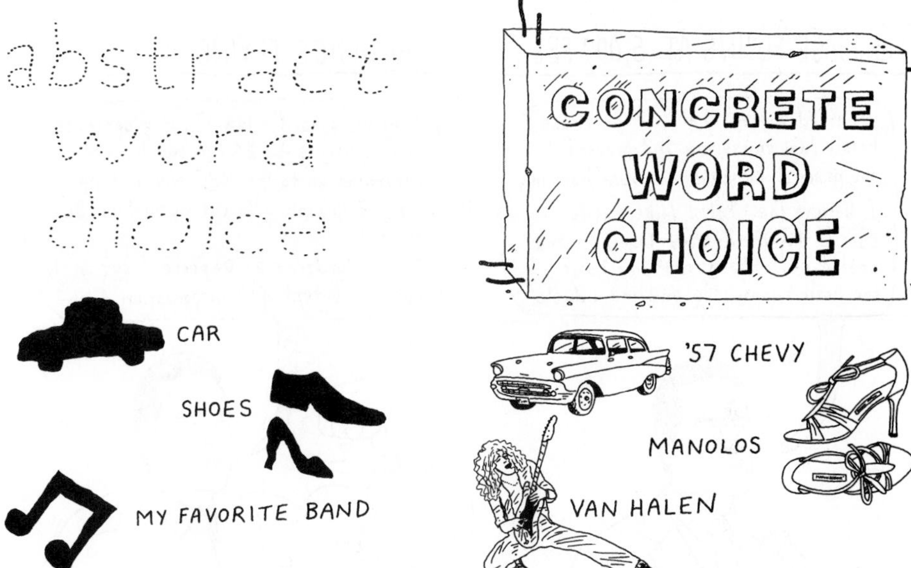

specific and suggest exactly what you mean. **Abstract words**, on the other hand, are general and can be confusing and ambiguous for your audience. Consider these four sentences, which range from abstract to concrete:

> This past week, Jane arrived in a vehicle. *(abstract)*
>
> Four days ago, Jane arrived in a car. *(less abstract)*
>
> Last Tuesday at noon, Jane arrived in a blue Toyota. *(more concrete)*
>
> Last Tuesday at noon, Jane arrived in a 2001 blue Toyota Corolla. *(most concrete)*

Only the third and fourth sentences convey in specific terms how and when Jane arrived. If this information is relevant to the presentation, these sentences would help the speaker convey more information than the first and second sentences.

This is not to suggest that you should never use more general language. In fact, some situations clearly call for a more general language style. In the language of speech writers, this is the difference

LANGUAGE FLYING AT 5,000 FEET

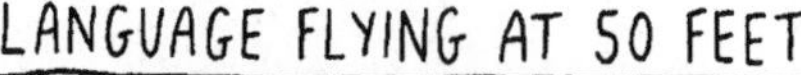

between speaking from "five thousand feet, as opposed to fifty feet." Sometimes you will want to describe a concept or theory from a much bigger perspective (hence the term *five thousand feet*), and thus give the audience the *big picture* or the *grand vision*, invariably using more general language.

Proper Use of Words

The audience's understanding of your message will improve if you use words that correctly express the point you want to make. Incorrect word choice can confuse listeners or undermine your credibility. For example, if a speaker described the long period of reduced economic activity and widespread unemployment in the United States from 1929 until the early 1940s as a *recession*, he would not be using the word correctly. Why? That downturn was actually a full-blown economic *depression*—a far worse and more damaging state of affairs than a mere recession. In this case, misuse of *recession* could give a false impression of that era to audience members too young to know

USE PROPER WORDS

about it. Using the word improperly could also raise serious questions about the speaker's credibility among audience members who experienced or are familiar with the devastating effects of what became known as the Great Depression.

Failure to use words correctly can also produce unintended humorous results—often at your own expense. For example, one student delivering a speech on "grunge rockers" accused them of "immortal behavior." The audience laughed, knowing that grunge rockers don't actually live forever and that the speaker probably meant "immoral behavior." Though this speaker's listeners laughed, the joke was on him: most of his audience members probably lost some respect for him.

Concise Language

Because audience members cannot reread or rehear portions of your speech, they have only one chance to grasp your ideas—during the actual presentation. For this reason, make sure that each of your sentences expresses just one thought. Although long sentences linking different ideas may be understandable in print, they're hard to follow in a speech. As a rule of thumb, aim to be *concise*; that is, use the fewest words necessary to express an idea. When you outline your speech, focus on making your points in the fewest words possible. Of course, you may occasionally want to add words or phrases to incorporate color, eloquence, wit, or humor into your talk. However, make certain you have a good reason to insert those extra words.

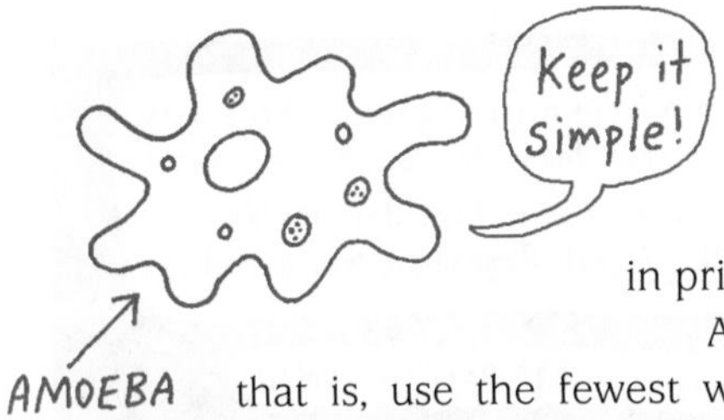

The term for unnecessary words in a presentation is **verbal clutter**, extraneous words that make it hard for the audience to follow your message. Here are three examples:

- "The death penalty cannot deter crime *for the reason that* murderers do not consider the consequences of their actions."
- "*Regardless of the fact that* you disagree with the government's position, you cannot dispute the FCC's ruling."
- "If we are to *make contact* with our bargaining opponents, we have to find a mutually acceptable schedule."

You could easily revise those sentences to eliminate verbal clutter:

- "The death penalty cannot deter crime *because* murderers do not consider the consequences of their actions."
- "*Although* you disagree with the government's position, you cannot dispute the FCC's ruling."
- "If we are to *meet* with our bargaining opponents, we have to find a mutually acceptable schedule."

EXPRESSING YOUR IDEAS EFFECTIVELY

Words have great power to move an audience, especially when used vividly. Empower your own language through the use of repetition, hypothetical examples, personal anecdotes, vivid language, and similes and metaphors.

Repetition

Repetition—saying a specific word, phrase, or statement more than once—helps you grab your audience's attention and leave listeners with enduring memories of your speech:

> At the end of the battle, every soldier was killed. Every soldier.

This use of repetition draws listeners' attention to the fact that all the soldiers *on both sides of the conflict* died at the end of the battle. It thus drives home a sobering point that the speaker wants to make.

To get the most from repetition, use it sparingly. If you repeat too many statements in your speech, your listeners won't be able to discern the *really* important points in your presentation.

OVERUSING REPETITION

GOOD USE OF REPETITION

You can also use repetition by returning to a point later in a speech to provide a gentle reminder to your audience. In the following example, a student named Allyson employs this technique in a speech about trekking across Russia:

> When most people think about mountains in Russia, if they know anything, they think about the Urals. These are old mountains, stretching some twelve hundred miles from north to south. The mountains themselves are covered with taigas—large forests that blanket the area. . . .
>
> As I mentioned a few minutes back, these twelve hundred miles of Ural Mountains are an impressive sight, with all sorts of wildlife, including wolves, bears, and many different game birds.

Later in her speech, Allyson again repeated the north to south distance ("twelve hundred miles") to emphasize the challenges of backpacking through the vast Ural mountain range.

Finally, you may want to repeat a point through *rewording* it, making the point again but in different words. Rewording is useful when the original point could be confusing, because it gives your audience another option for grasping what you mean. Rewording is similar to the technique you use to explain jargon. Here's one example:

> According to the engineering report, the shuttle booster rockets had systems failure with the cooling system, not to mention serious problems with the outer hatch doors and the manually operated crane. Put another way, there were at least three mechanical problems we know of with this last shuttle mission.

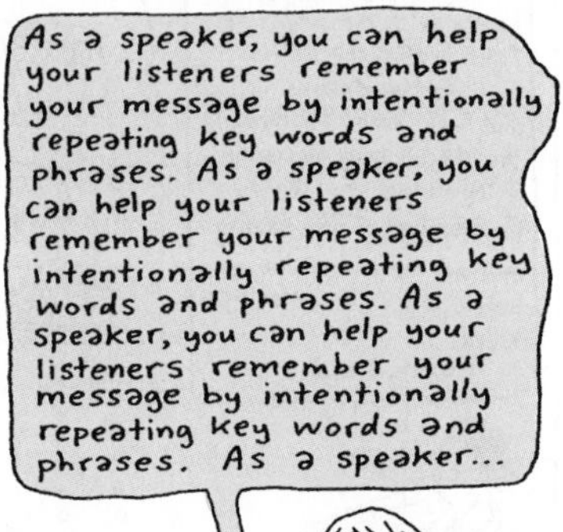

Rewording works particularly well in those parts of your speech where you enumerate a list or make a technical statement that might be difficult for your audience to follow.

Hypothetical Examples

With technical, complicated messages—as well as policy statements and points in a speech where you particularly want to focus your audience's attention—consider using **hypothetical examples**. These are imagined examples or scenarios that you invite your audience to think about. Hypothetical examples can help your listeners follow a complicated point that you present immediately afterward.

For instance, a student named Blake wanted to inform his audience about the legal test for defamation of character. He introduced his presentation with the following hypothetical example:

> Suppose a television news crew was shadowing a paramedic team to record their average day, and the paramedics were called out to a highway accident. Now suppose the camera crew taped the whole rescue, and the reporter talked to a badly injured victim who was sedated with painkillers. Under the influence of the painkillers, the victim said many foolish things, including some unkind words about her employer. Would the news station be justified in broadcasting the whole story—including everything the victim said to the reporter? What would the victim's rights be here, if any? This scenario suggests the difficulty of determining whether defamation of character has taken place.

Personal Anecdotes

Illustrating a concept with *personal anecdotes* (brief stories) can help you further build credibility and reassure your listeners that you're not judging them. Adam, a sophomore in a speech class, used the following personal anecdote in a speech about phobias:

MY BLACK BELT CEREMONY

> Phobias come in many different forms—and most, if not all, can be cured with therapy and/or medication. I know this, because I've lived with one of these myself. Although you would not know it to look at me today, I once had a horrible fear of flying. Just the thought of getting near a big jet used

> to give me the shakes. Sweaty palms. The works. It was a real problem. But a half year of therapy—which included taking some flights with someone I really trusted—cured me of the fear.

Adam illustrated one type of phobia in a way that gave him credibility (he spoke from experience). His personal anecdote also helped him demonstrate that he took his subject seriously. And it enabled him to avoid offending audience members who may have struggled with similar fears.

You can achieve similar effects with anecdotes about events that your listeners may have experienced personally. In a speech on credit card debt, a freshman student named Jackie sought common ground through the following anecdote:

> You really have to be careful about these credit cards. You get on somebody's mailing list right after you're out of high school and starting college. Suddenly your mailbox is filled with offers of free credit cards. And they don't have a service charge for the first three months. You can get credit up to five thousand dollars. Just a minimum payment each month. Hasn't that happened to most of you in this room? It happened to me, too. And we all know how fast that credit card debt can pile up!

Vivid Language

Vivid language grabs the attention of your audience with words and phrases that appeal to all the senses—touch, hearing, taste, smell, and sight. The following examples from an autobiographical presentation illustrate the difference between ordinary and vivid word choice. In the first example, Jamie describes his childhood years with his family in relatively uninspiring language:

> I remember those mornings at home only too well. Mom would call us if we overslept. She was downstairs making breakfast, every morning at eight o'clock sharp. My brothers and I would fight to be the first into the bathroom.

Now consider this more vivid version of Jamie's story:

> Mornings were memorable in my house. It was always cold in the room I shared with my brothers. With no curtains on our windows, light would stream in, poking us in the eyes before Mom ever called us down for breakfast. The smell of bacon wafting upstairs did the rest. Routinely we shoved one another, forming a line outside the bathroom, knowing Mom would demand to know if we had washed up before coming to the table.

The second version conveys the same basic information as the first. However, it paints a more graphic picture of the scene, with stronger **imagery**—mental impressions—for the audience. We can *see* the bright light. We can also smell the bacon and hear Mom's voice.

To use vivid language, select descriptive words that evoke pictures, smells, textures, sounds, and flavors in your listeners' minds. But use such language sparingly. If you overuse it, it may lose its effect.

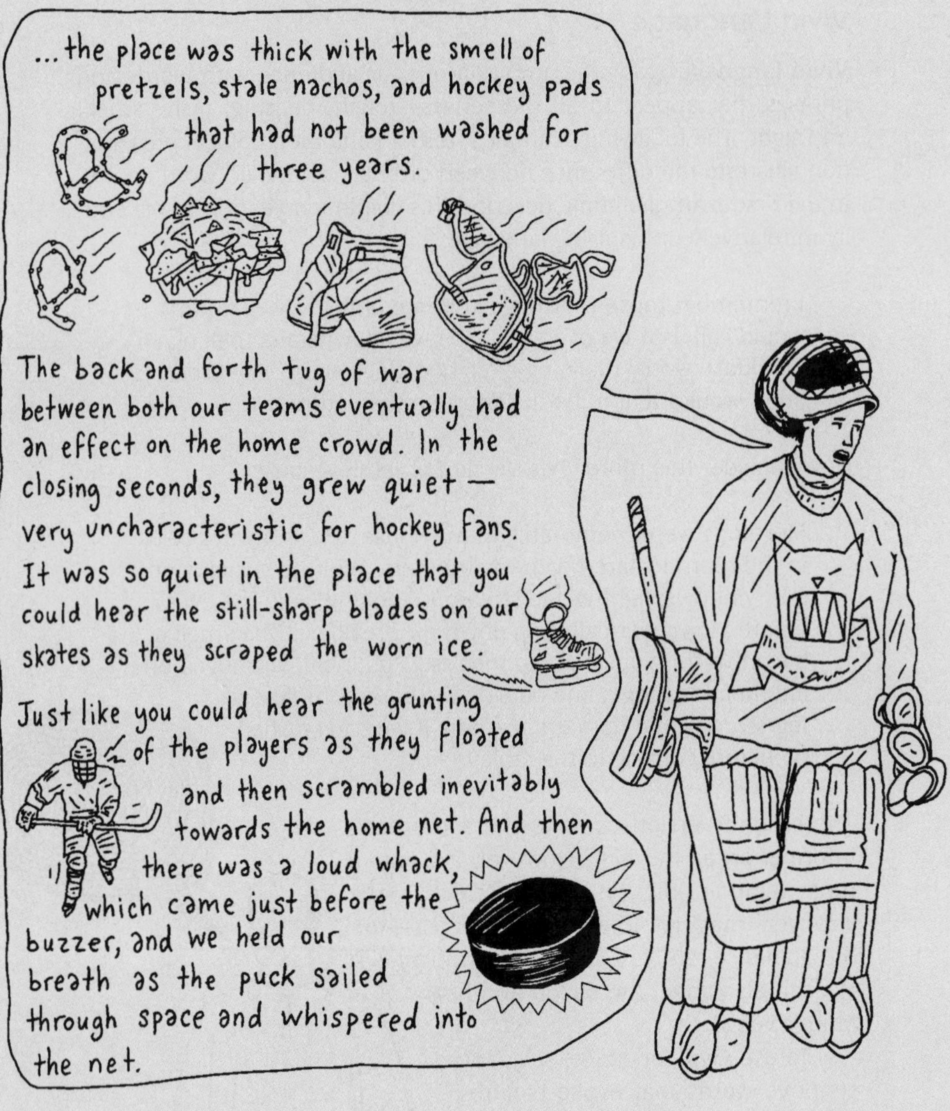
...the place was thick with the smell of pretzels, stale nachos, and hockey pads that had not been washed for three years.
The back and forth tug of war between both our teams eventually had an effect on the home crowd. In the closing seconds, they grew quiet — very uncharacteristic for hockey fans. It was so quiet in the place that you could hear the still-sharp blades on our skates as they scraped the worn ice.
Just like you could hear the grunting of the players as they floated and then scrambled inevitably towards the home net. And then there was a loud whack, which came just before the buzzer, and we held our breath as the puck sailed through space and whispered into the net.

Similes and Metaphors

Similes and metaphors suggest similarities between objects that are not alike. **Similes** make explicit comparisons and contain words such as *like* or *as*. Here are three examples (the similes appear in italics):

- His mind works *like an adding machine.*
- After bumping her head, she fell *like a tree.*
- The baby's crying was *as sweet as music* to his ears.

Metaphors make *implicit* comparisons. They suggest connections between objects that are not alike by identifying one object with the other. The comparisons, however, are not meant to be taken literally. Here are three examples:

- My willpower is *my shield against temptation.*
- Her life was *a journey along a path filled with obstacles.*
- Technology is *the engine driving this economic boom.*

Similes and metaphors can add color, vividness, and imagery to your speech. But when you use these devices, be sure the comparison makes sense. For example, if you said, "The baby's crying was as sweet as candy to his ears," you wouldn't be making sense. People don't listen to candy; they taste it.

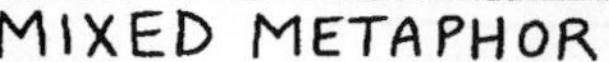

Likewise, avoid mixing comparisons—that is, using more than one metaphor or simile at a time. Otherwise, you might produce some unintentionally funny statements. Here's an example of a mixed metaphor:

> Outlawing the possession of marijuana paraphernalia was exactly the *bullet* the House of Representatives needed to *cook* the new drug bill and *drive* it over to the Senate.

And here's an illustration of a mixed simile:

> The new father floated *like a butterfly*, bouncing off the delivery room walls *like a rubber ball*.

When used properly, metaphors and similes can help your audience understand one idea through its reference to another.[1] Metaphors can also help listeners experience a new idea "in terms that resonate with their past experience."[2]

CHOOSING RESPECTFUL AND UNBIASED LANGUAGE

When you use respectful language in your speeches—words, phrases, and expressions that are courteous and don't reflect bias against other cultures or individuals—you deliver far more effective presentations. Why? Your audience members remain open to your ideas and view you as trustworthy and fair. In this way, you gain immense personal credibility.

By contrast, using **biased language**—word choice that suggests prejudice or preconceptions about other people—erodes your credibility and distracts your audience from listening to your message. For these reasons, avoid language that suggests you're making judgments about your listeners' or someone else's race, ethnicity, gender, sexuality, religion, or mental or physical ability. In the rest of this section, we present ideas for keeping biased language out of your speech.

Avoid Negative Stereotypes

Negative stereotypes are critical generalizations about characteristics that members of a group can't change—for example, their race, ethnicity, or gender—and about characteristics central to a person's identity, such as religious beliefs. Negative stereotypes rest on the false assumption that characteristics shared by some members of a group are shared by all members of the group.

Stereotyping can come into play when speakers make claims beyond the facts that their evidence proves—by generalizing about their topic. Suppose a presenter offers only a few examples of persons who received jobs through affirmative action policies but who didn't have the skills or experience required for the jobs. The speaker argues that those few examples prove that everyone who benefits from affirmative action is unqualified. The speaker would be making a claim without proof and thus perpetuating a negative stereotype.

Take special care to use arguments that avoid negative stereotypes with topics that are loaded with potential for controversy. For example, if you wanted to argue against affirmative action, you could claim that race or gender should play no role in any hiring decisions. Or you could advocate stronger remedies for reducing discrimination in society—thereby acknowledging that discrimination does exist.

Use Gender-Neutral References

Experts in grammar openly advocated the use of the generic *he* as early as 1553,[3] and by 1850, this preference was legally supported (*he* was said to stand for *he* and *she*).[4] By the 1970s, however, modern linguists began questioning the generic use of masculine pronouns because they reinforced gender-based stereotypes.

Using gender-neutral references can be challenging at times. For instance, suppose you keep saying *he or she* in a speech about jobs that can be held by men and women—such as chief executive officer (CEO), nurse, or high school principal. Occasional use of *he or she* is fine, but frequent use could get tedious for your audience. How would *you* react if you heard a speaker say, "A good president keeps his or her meetings organized, listens to his or her employees, and puts his or her company's needs first"? Happily, there are ways to work around any awkwardness with pronouns. Using plurals where appropriate can help: "Good *presidents* keep *their* meetings organized, listen to *their* employees, and put *their* company's needs first." Or, if a singular pronoun is appropriate in your speech, alternate the use of *she* and *he* from paragraph to paragraph or from example to example.

Also avoid gender-specific nouns or noun phrases, such as *poetess, chairman, congressman, cleaning lady*, and *fireman*. Instead, look for **gender-neutral terms**—words that do not suggest a specific gender—such as *poet, chair, congressional representative, cleaner*, and *firefighter*.

Make Appropriate References to Ethnic Groups

To show respect for your audience, use the noun or phrase preferred by a particular ethnic group when you are referring to that group. For example, *African American* is commonly preferred to *black* or *Afro-American*. Sometimes, people from a group may use more than one name to refer to themselves—for example, *Latino/Latina* and *Chicano/Chicana* or referring to themselves from their country of origin. If you are uncertain about which term to use in such a case, ask friends or classmates who are members of that group which name they prefer.

When ethnicity is relevant to your audience, be sure to refer to ethnic groups correctly. Not all people from Laos are Hmong. A visiting professor from Nigeria is not African American. And people from Puerto Rico or Spain are not Mexican Americans. Moreover, when a word comes from a language that uses different masculine and feminine forms, pay attention to those forms. For example, author Ana Castillo is a Chican*a*, not a Chican*o*. Attentiveness to such distinctions during a speech will pay big dividends in the form of appreciation from your listeners.

Steer Clear of Unnecessary References to Ethnicity, Gender, Sexuality, or Religion

When a person's ethnicity, religion, sexuality, or gender is not relevant to a point you are making, there's no need to mention it in your speech. Including it can only hurt your credibility. For instance, if you

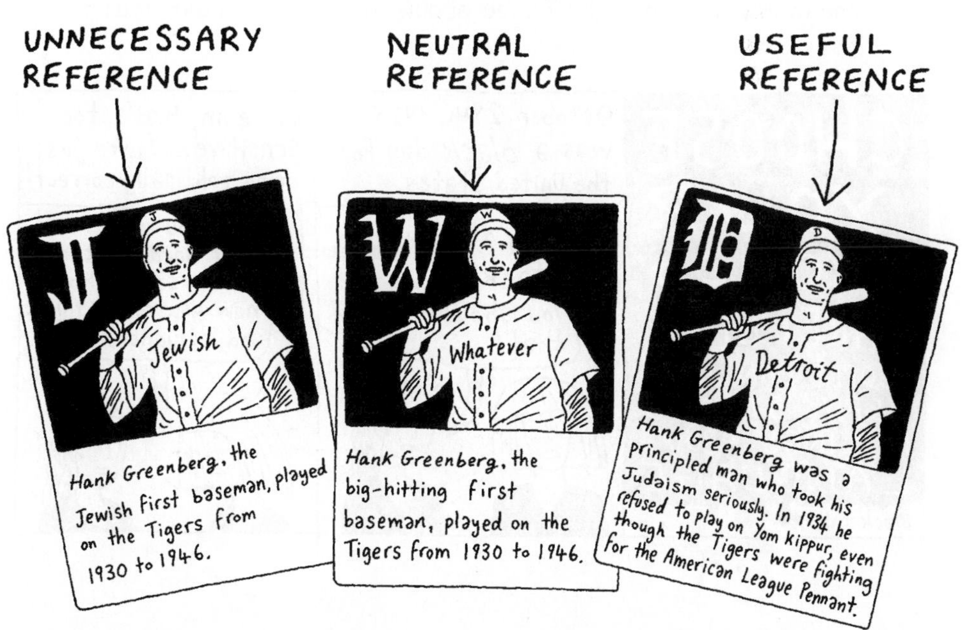

say "the *Chinese American* judge," "the *Jewish* baseball player," "the *male* first-grade teacher," or "the *lesbian* CEO," listeners may believe that you find it odd for a judge to be Chinese American, a baseball player to be Jewish, a man to be a first-grade teacher, or a lesbian to run a company. On the other hand, in an informative speech about baseball great Jackie Robinson, you *would* probably want to refer to his African American heritage. Why? Robinson was subjected to many forms of racism and broke the "color barrier" when he joined the Brooklyn Dodgers in 1947. His enduring legacy stems just as much from his experiences as an African American as it does from his talent as a ballplayer. Thus, it would be appropriate and even necessary to acknowledge his race during your speech.

A Note on Appropriate Speech and Political Correctness

The notions of "appropriate speech" and "political correctness" have made it even more difficult for people to know how to avoid bias in their speeches. What do these terms mean exactly? The idea behind appropriate speech is that words have tremendous power to influence the ways that people think of, feel about, and treat each other; thus it

is important to avoid—as often as possible—words that could cause harm or pain to others, especially in terms of a person's or a group's identity.

Some critics, on the other hand, argue that efforts to encourage appropriate speech often go too far. Rather than protecting certain vulnerable people from hurtful speech, critics argue that these guidelines limit people's precious rights to freedom of expression by establishing strict rules of "political correctness"—written or unwritten codes of conduct requiring language that reflects a politically and socially liberal view.

The best way to avoid the debate over appropriate language and political correctness entirely is to simply support your position on an issue—no matter what it is—with credible evidence and logical reasoning. Otherwise, your listeners will likely perceive you as prejudiced. Saying something like, "We all know that affirmative action programs give jobs to unqualified women and minorities" would instantly reveal bias and a lack of thought about your topic. On the other hand, you could build a much stronger case on the controversial topic of affirmative action by making careful word choices and offering solid and unbiased evidence such as compelling examples, credible statistics, and solid expert testimony.

SUMMARY

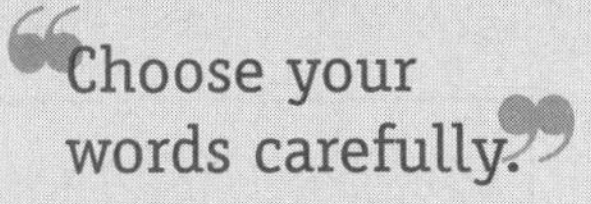

As Marvin's story early in this chapter revealed, your word choice can make or break the effectiveness of your speech. In this chapter, we explained how to use language specifically to clarify your message, captivate your audience, and enhance your credibility. Key practices include understanding the denotative and connotative meanings of words and evoking those meanings strategically. We also offered ideas for presenting your message clearly—including using understandable language and concrete words, employing words properly, and adopting concise language. And we suggested that to infuse your speech with color and evocative imagery, you can use devices such as repetition, hypothetical examples, personal anecdotes, vivid language, and similes and metaphors. Finally, we addressed the importance of using unbiased language so as to show respect for your listeners. Suggestions on this front include avoiding negative stereotypes, using gender-neutral references, referring to ethnic groups properly, and avoiding references to ethnicity, gender, sexuality, or religion that are irrelevant to a point you're making.

Key Terms

word choice
diction

DENOTATIVE AND CONNOTATIVE MEANING

denotative meaning
connotative meaning

PRESENTING YOUR MESSAGE CLEARLY

jargon
concrete words
abstract words
verbal clutter

EXPRESSING YOUR IDEAS EFFECTIVELY

hypothetical examples
vivid language
imagery
similes
metaphors

CHOOSING RESPECTFUL AND UNBIASED LANGUAGE

biased language
negative stereotypes
gender-neutral terms

Er... um...
You gentle
R... R... Romans...
Grrr!
Boo!

Alas, I shall be undone henceforth if I go on with delivery such as this.
Oh, piteous spectacle!
Hiss!

Friends, Romans, countrymen, lend me your ears...
Peace there! Let us hear him.
Hark at him!

Methinks there is much reason in his saying.
Bravo!

13 DELIVERING YOUR SPEECH

"How you say something is often as important as what you say."

Hannah, a student in a political science class, just finished delivering an oral presentation of her essay advocating more fiscal conservatism in the federal government. An experienced writer, she had structured her speech clearly and concisely. In just eight minutes, she commented on a wide range of issues—including federal income taxes, entitlement programs, and the national debt. She had carefully outlined her speech and delivered it using a small stack of note cards. And she used several helpful visual aids, such as charts showing government spending on various social programs.

Though Hannah had worked hard to develop a well-organized speech, she received only a B− from her instructor on the presentation. When she asked why, her professor explained that while the content of the speech was excellent, her **delivery**—the combination

of verbal and nonverbal communication skills used to present the speech—was less than ideal. The instructor explained that Hannah had spoken too fast and in a monotone, and she had fussed too much with her note cards. In addition, she had turned her back on her audience while pointing to and discussing her visual aids.

Hannah's experience reveals a major lesson for all public speakers: how you say something can be as important as what you say. Why is effective delivery so crucial in public speaking? It helps make your speech compelling and memorable. In an age when audience members may be easily distracted by their many responsibilities, even the most carefully researched and clearly organized talk may not be enough to hold their attention. Speakers today need every advantage they can get to capture—and keep—their listeners' interest. And skillful delivery can give you that edge. Think about it: in your lifetime, you may have listened to dozens or even hundreds of speeches. Of these, how many did you find truly memorable? And what made them so outstanding? If you're like most people, you'll realize that the best speech you've ever heard not only contained valuable ideas, but was also delivered in ways that held your attention and that had you remembering the speech long after it was over.

In fact, delivery is what comes to mind for most people when they think of speechmaking. Though audience analysis, research, preparation, and practice all play vital roles in public speaking, it's how you deliver your speech that determines whether you find success with many audience members.

In this chapter, we discuss speech delivery—focusing on the various ways you can present a speech as well as the verbal and nonverbal skills you need to deliver a powerful, evocative, and exciting presentation.

SELECTING THE RIGHT MODE OF DELIVERY

Imagine yourself standing before an audience, preparing to make an address. How will you actually deliver your speech? Will you read from a manuscript? Recite from text that you've memorized? Speak extemporaneously from an outline?

In most classroom settings (as well as many settings outside of class), speaking extemporaneously from an outline will allow you to achieve the best possible results. This delivery mode enables you to adopt a natural, conversational style that audiences appreciate. Yet there are certain situations where you may want to read from a manuscript or recite your speech word-for-word from memory. Below, we examine each of these three delivery modes in turn, starting with reading from a manuscript.

Reading from a Manuscript

In this delivery mode, you give your speech by reading directly from a script—a typed or handwritten document containing the entire text of your speech. As you read, you typically do not deviate from your script or ad-lib.

Delivery from a script is particularly appropriate when speakers or speech writers need to choose their words carefully. The word-for-word manuscript delivery ensures that listeners hear *exactly* what you want them to.

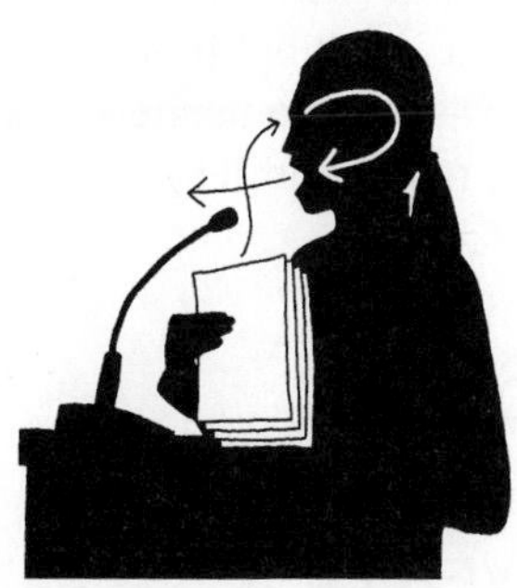

READING FROM A MANUSCRIPT

MEMORIZING FROM A MANUSCRIPT

SPEAKING FROM AN OUTLINE

For example, public speakers often use this mode of delivery in press conferences. Imagine a lawyer approaching the microphone to "make a statement" to the press about his client, a professional athlete accused of wrongdoing. The lawyer reads directly from a carefully prepared manuscript to ensure that his specific words are heard and reported in the news—no deviations and no surprises. By closely controlling his message, he stands a better chance of controlling what journalists say about him or his client—and therefore influencing public perceptions.

Still, reading from a script has its disadvantages. To begin with, the script itself becomes a prop—something you can hide behind as you read. And like other props, it can limit your eye contact with the audience.

In addition, when you read from a script, you tend to speak in more of a monotone voice rather than sounding as if you're conversing with your listeners. Some listeners may find the resulting impersonal quality dull, while others may even consider this mode condescending. Consider the words of one student: "To tell you the truth, I almost found it insulting. If all [the speaker] wanted to do was read to us, he could have just given us the notes and let us read them ourselves."

ONLY SPECIFIC, FORMAL SITUATIONS CALL FOR MANUSCRIPT DELIVERY

Memorizing from a Manuscript

To recite a speech memorized from a script, you learn your script word-for-word and deliver it without looking at any text, notes, or outline. You behave like an actor on the stage or the screen who memorizes dialogue and recites the words in a *performance*. When would you want to deliver a speech by memorizing from a script? Memorization is only advisable when you are called on to deliver a precise message, and you are already trained to memorize a great deal of text and deliver it flawlessly.

This delivery mode does offer some advantages over reading from a script. Specifically, there's no barrier between you and your audience, so you can maintain eye contact with listeners throughout your speech. This allows you to be more natural with gestures and in using visual aids. And like reading from a manuscript, you can control your word choice by precisely repeating what you've memorized. In fact, memorization was a key feature of classical rhetorical training, but in contemporary thought it is no longer considered the best form of speech preparation and delivery in most situations.

MEMORIZED DELIVERY CAN COME ACROSS AS SLICK... AND NOT IN A GOOD WAY

Why? Because this mode of delivery also has distinct disadvantages. For one thing, memorized presentations often come across as slick and prepackaged—or "canned." Listeners may view the speech as a stale performance delivered the same way every time, regardless of the audience. As a result, they may take offense or lose interest.

Memorizing is also very challenging—especially with a long speech. In addition, people who speak from memory are typically wedded to their text; the presentation can grind to a halt if the speaker forgets so much as a single word or sentence.

Because this delivery mode's disadvantages outweigh its advantages, we recommend avoiding it unless you have a specific background in memorizing large bodies of text (as a trained actor, for example) *and* your speech situation requires it.

ANOTHER DOWNSIDE OF MEMORIZATION

Speaking from an Outline

In this mode of delivery—the preferred mode in most speech situations—you deliver your speech by referring to a brief outline that you prepared in advance. Typically, you will initially want to prepare and practice with a full-sentence working outline. Next, like most speakers, you'll want to condense the working outline into a briefer speaking outline (complete with delivery cues) recorded on sheets of paper or note cards (for more information on outlines, see Chapter 11).

You should be able to glance at this brief outline and instantly remember what you want to say. And if you've made the note cards easy to read (for example, by using large print and spaces between lines), you can maintain eye contact with your audience.

You can speak from an outline in either of two ways. Most commonly, speakers will do this *extemporaneously*, meaning they will write the speech outline ahead of time, learn the material in the outline, and then speak spontaneously in the presentation with only the outline available for reference. In different situations, however, you may be called upon to speak and have no time to prepare a written outline, as is the case with an *impromptu* speech. Even with this kind of spontaneous speaking situation, however, you will still be speaking from an outline—albeit one that you keep in your mind and refer to while you speak, as you would with a physical outline in an extemporaneous situation. In fact, in impromptu speaking situations, you might even want

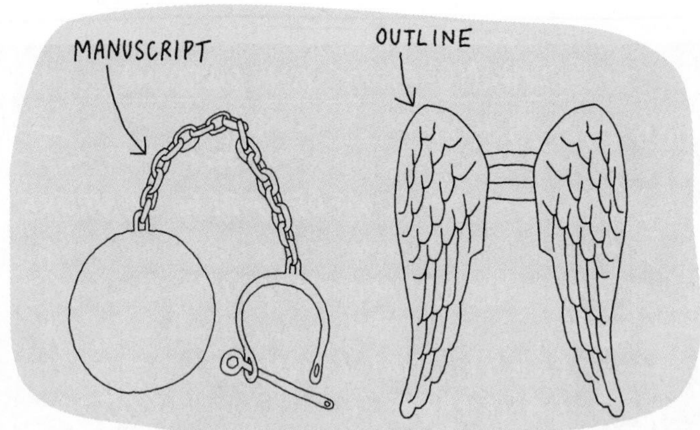

to write down two to four main points on a piece of scrap paper before walking to the front of the room or standing to give your speech.

Speaking from an outline offers the best aspects of reading from a script and memorizing your speech while avoiding the disadvantages of those two other delivery modes. You can glance quickly at the outline just long enough to spur your memory, so there's no barrier between you and your audience, and your eye contact does not suffer. Also, you don't have to worry about forgetting your place, because the outline is at hand to remind you.

Equally important, when you speak from an outline, your delivery becomes more *conversational*. You sound as if you are talking with your listeners, instead of reading a speech *at* them. Finally, with this delivery mode, you choose your words flexibly, as you do during a conversation. Thus, you can adapt your message as needed to the audience at hand. For instance, if you notice that a listener looks confused, you can provide further explanation for the point you're discussing.

Of course, speakers need to practice delivering from their outlines to give the best possible presentation. This practice is extremely beneficial in more than one way; research indicates that practice and preparation can lessen the anxiety that speakers also feel when it is time to present.[1]

NONVERBAL DELIVERY SKILLS

USING VOCAL DELIVERY SKILLS

To deliver a high-impact speech, you need to think about more than just your mode of delivery. In addition to selecting the right mode, you must draw on **vocal delivery skills** (use of volume, tone, rate, variety, and articulation) and **nonverbal delivery skills** (use of gestures, eye contact, facial expressions, body movement, and overall physical appearance) to convey meaning. In this section, we explain how to use key elements of vocal delivery skills to deliver a successful presentation; in the next section, we move on to nonverbal delivery skills.

Volume

Volume refers to how loud or soft your voice is as you deliver a speech. Some speakers are not loud enough, while others are too loud. A guiding rule for volume: be loud enough so everyone in your audience can hear you, but not so loud as to drive away the listeners positioned closest to you.

Most speakers' biggest challenge in terms of volume is speaking loudly enough. Since audience members don't have the option of "turning up the volume," you will need to provide that volume yourself when there is no microphone available. If you speak too softly and don't project enough, your listeners may have trouble hearing you, or they may see you as timid or uncertain—which could damage your credibility.

Yet speaking too loudly presents a different set of problems. A student named Jason once gave an informative presentation in one of our classes. During his speech, many listeners in the front row began leaning back in their chairs. He was speaking so loudly that his listeners were trying to put some distance between themselves and him.

When you begin preparing your delivery, think about your volume level. How loud is your natural speaking voice? If you aren't certain, ask some friends or relatives to give you an assessment. Then consider your audience for the speech presentation—as well as your speaking forum. How will the size of the audience or the room affect you? Finally, focus on visual cues from your audience while you deliver your speech to help you determine whether your volume level is appropriate, and adjust your volume as needed.

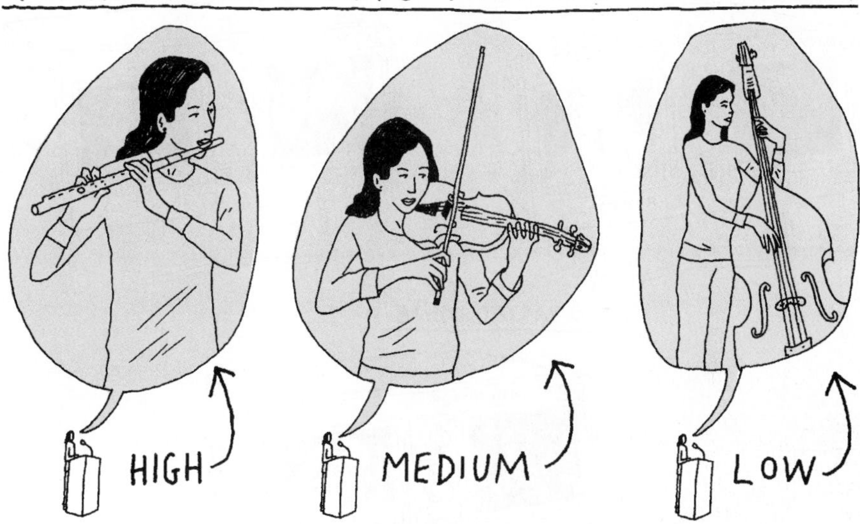

Tone

The **tone** of your speaking voice derives from *pitch*—the highs and lows in your voice. If you can mix high and low tones and achieve some tonal variety, you'll add warmth and color to your vocal delivery. By contrast, if your tone never varies (called speaking in a *monotone*), listeners may perceive your presentation as bland, boring, or even annoying (in the case of a relentlessly high-pitched voice).

How much tonal variety should you aim for to make your voice interesting and enticing? Follow this guiding rule: use enough tonal variety to add warmth, intensity, and enthusiasm to your voice, but not so much variety that you sound like an adolescent whose voice is cracking. As you practice your speech, try dropping your pitch in some places and raising it in others. If you're not sure whether you're achieving enough tonal variety, practice in front of a trusted friend, family member, classmate, or colleague. Then solicit his or her feedback.

Additionally, consider using *inflection*—raising or lowering your pitch—to emphasize certain words or expressions. For instance, try a

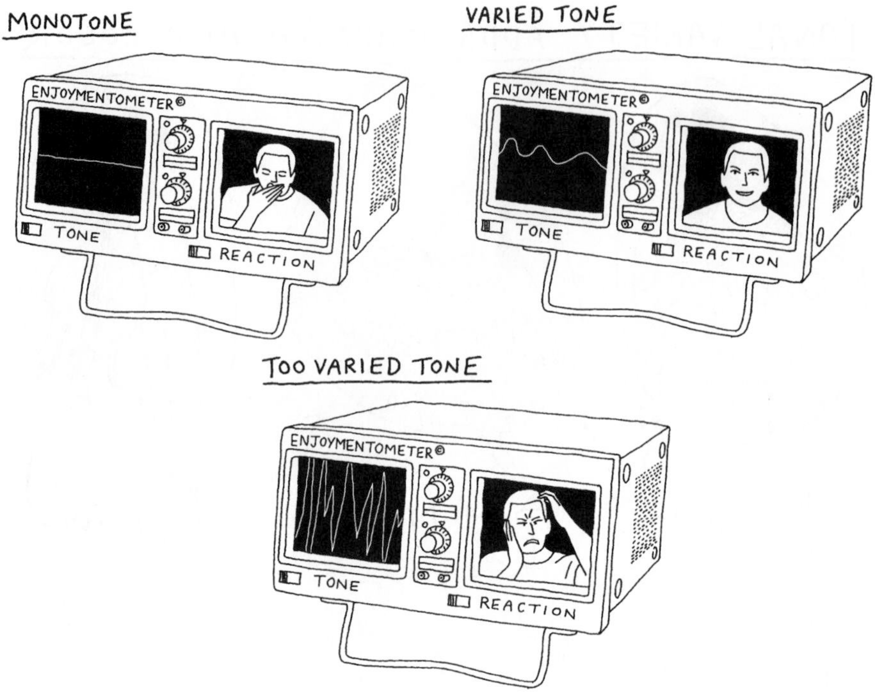

MONOTONE

VARIED TONE

TOO VARIED TONE

lower pitch to convey the seriousness of an idea or end on a higher pitch if you are posing a question. Like italics on a printed page, inflection draws attention to the words or expressions you want your audience to notice and remember.

Rate of Delivery

Your **rate of delivery** refers to how quickly or slowly you speak during a presentation. As with other vocal delivery skills, going to one extreme or another (in this case, speaking too quickly or too slowly) can hurt your delivery.

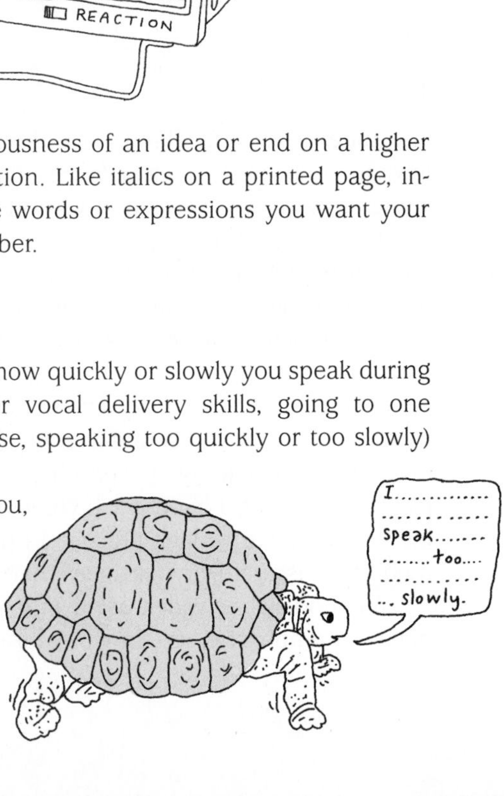

Consider the example of Lou, a student at Harvard University who had a very slow rate of delivery. While giving a talk during a seminar on

music theory, he noticed that many of the students (as well as the teacher) seemed inattentive. He also became aware that those listeners who *were* paying attention began interrupting him—not with questions about the content of his speech but with queries about his next point. Clearly, they were trying to move him along—which probably meant they were irritated and distracted.

Do you fall into the "slow speaker" category? Do people tend to finish your sentences for you—during conversations or while you're delivering a public address? Although people who try to finish your statements may seem rude, their behavior sends an important signal that you need to step up your rate of delivery. Fail to catch that signal, and you risk losing your audience's interest and appreciation.

Of course, swinging to the other extreme—talking too fast—presents the opposite problem. Overly fast talkers tend to run their words together, particularly at the ends of sentences—preventing their audiences from keeping up with what they're saying. Listeners often have a difficult time following fast talkers not because they are disinterested or impatient, but simply because they cannot comprehend what is being said. And in the worst case scenario, potentially interested audience members can transform into defeated listeners in the face of a fast talker's verbal onslaught (see page 106).

The guiding rule for achieving an appropriate rate of delivery is this: speak fast enough to keep your presentation lively and interesting, but not so fast that you become inarticulate. You can also ask a friend or relative to listen to you and give you feedback about your rate of delivery. Finally, resist any temptation to speed up your delivery to fit an overly long speech into the allocated time. Instead, shorten the content of the presentation.

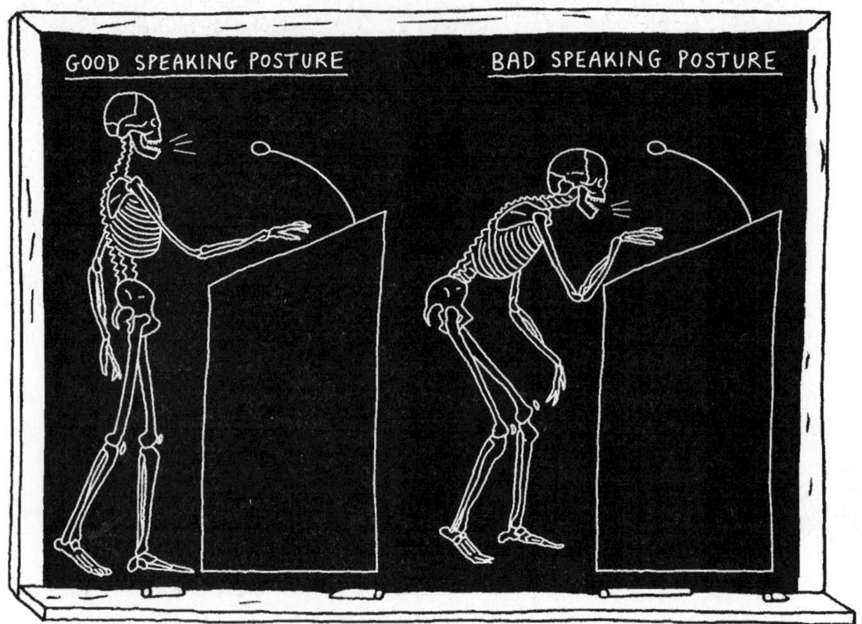

Projection

Have you ever observed someone singing without a microphone and wondered how the person's voice managed to reach people near *and* far? What about actors on a stage who speak their lines quietly yet still can be heard by everyone in the theater? These individuals use **projection**—"booming" their voices across their speaking forums to reach all the members of their audiences.

To project, use the air you exhale from your lungs to carry the sound of your voice across the room or auditorium. Projection is all about the mechanics of breathing. To send your voice clearly across a large space, first maintain good posture: sit or stand up straight, with your shoulders back and your head at a neutral position (not too far forward or hanging back). Also, exhale from your diaphragm—that sheet of muscle just below your rib cage—to push your breath away from you.

Articulation

Articulation refers to the crispness or clarity of your spoken words. When you articulate, your vowels and consonants sound clear and

distinct, and your listeners can distinguish your separate words as well as the syllables in your words. The result? Your audience can easily understand what you're saying.

Articulation problems are most common when nervousness increases a speaker's rate of delivery or when speakers are being inattentive. Whatever the cause of any articulation issues you may have, focus on this rule to get better results: when you deliver a speech, clearly and distinctly express all the parts of the words in your presentation. This advice applies to the vowels and consonants of your words as well as each syllable, and make sure not to round off the ends of words or lower your voice at the ends of sentences.

Pronunciation

Pronunciation refers to correctness in the way you say words. Are you saying them in a way that has been commonly agreed to? Pronounce terms incorrectly, and your listeners may have difficulty understanding you. Equally troublesome, they may question your credibility.

Elizabeth, a banking professional, related this story about the problems that can arise when a speaker mispronounces words:

> In my job I was required to work with lawyers, because they drew up the trust documents for their clients. I worked with lawyers, but I was no lawyer myself. Sometimes they can be a little arrogant about their position, thinking that if you didn't go to law school, you shouldn't be working in a law-related field. I worked hard to earn their respect. But I noticed that when I used some legal terms or words with them, they occasionally would look at each other and smile. Like they were sharing a private joke. One such word was *testator*. That's the person who creates a testament like a trust or a will. Whenever I used that word, I always said "TES-tah-tore," so that it sounded like it would rhyme with "matador." And the lawyers would smirk—but nobody ever corrected me. Some time later I was embarrassed to learn that the word is pronounced "tes-TAY-ter."

In some situations, mispronouncing people's names and place names can offend your audience. A student named Gabriel learned this lesson the hard way when he pronounced the last name of renowned Mexican American labor organizer Cesar Chavez as "SHAH-vez," instead of as "CHA-vez." Two-thirds of the students in Gabriel's class were Latino. Many of them concluded that Gabriel hadn't cared enough about his topic to find out how Chavez's name was pronounced.

How can you ensure that your pronunciation is accurate? The guideline here is simple: if you're not certain how to pronounce a word you want to use in your speech, find out how to say it *before* you deliver your presentation. Ask classmates or coworkers how the word is pronounced. Better still, refer to your dictionary, which likely provides phonetic pronunciations for each word as well as a general guide to pronunciation.

Pausing

Used skillfully, **pausing**—leaving gaps between words or sentences in a speech—affords you some significant advantages. It enables you to collect your thoughts on a subject. It also reinforces the seriousness of your subject, because it shows that you're choosing your words care-

fully. Pausing can help you create a sense of importance as well. If you make a statement and then pause for the audience to weigh your words, your listeners may conclude that you've just said something especially important.

To get the most from pausing, use it judiciously—every so often rather than after every sentence. Otherwise, your listeners may wonder if you're having repeated difficulty collecting your thoughts, or they may think you're being melodramatic. In either case, your audience will begin to take you less seriously.

When pausing during a speech, it's best to fill those pauses with silence rather than **verbal fillers** such as *you know* and *like* or **verbal tics** such as *um* and *ah*. Here's an example of what verbal fillers do to a speaker's delivery:

> *And so,* the library was closed . . . *you know.* But I had to study somewhere. *But* . . . I didn't get to study there, *and* . . . *but* . . . I had to go somewhere . . . *but* . . . *and* . . . I tried the dorm reading room. *And, like* . . . it was so quiet there, *you know*?

And here's an example of what verbal tics sound like:

> *Um* . . . the purpose of my speech is . . . *ah*, to . . . *um* make you see how . . . *um* . . . dangerous this action . . . *ah* . . . really is.

Everyone uses verbal fillers or tics at some point while giving speeches—it's hard *not* to. But using them too often can distract your listeners or make them wonder if you're tentative or ill-prepared. The best way to avoid overusing tics and fillers is by learning to be more aware of when you do use them. How? Try speaking in front of a friend who is holding a clicker or other low-level noisemaker; have your friend use the noisemaker every time you use a filler or tic; at first you may be surprised how often you do so, but with some practice you will develop better awareness and better habits.

USING NONVERBAL DELIVERY SKILLS

By augmenting your vocal delivery skills with nonverbal skills during speeches, you stand an even greater chance of connecting with your audience and leaving a lasting impression. In this section, we discuss specific elements of nonverbal delivery: eye contact, gestures, physical movement, proxemics, and personal appearance.

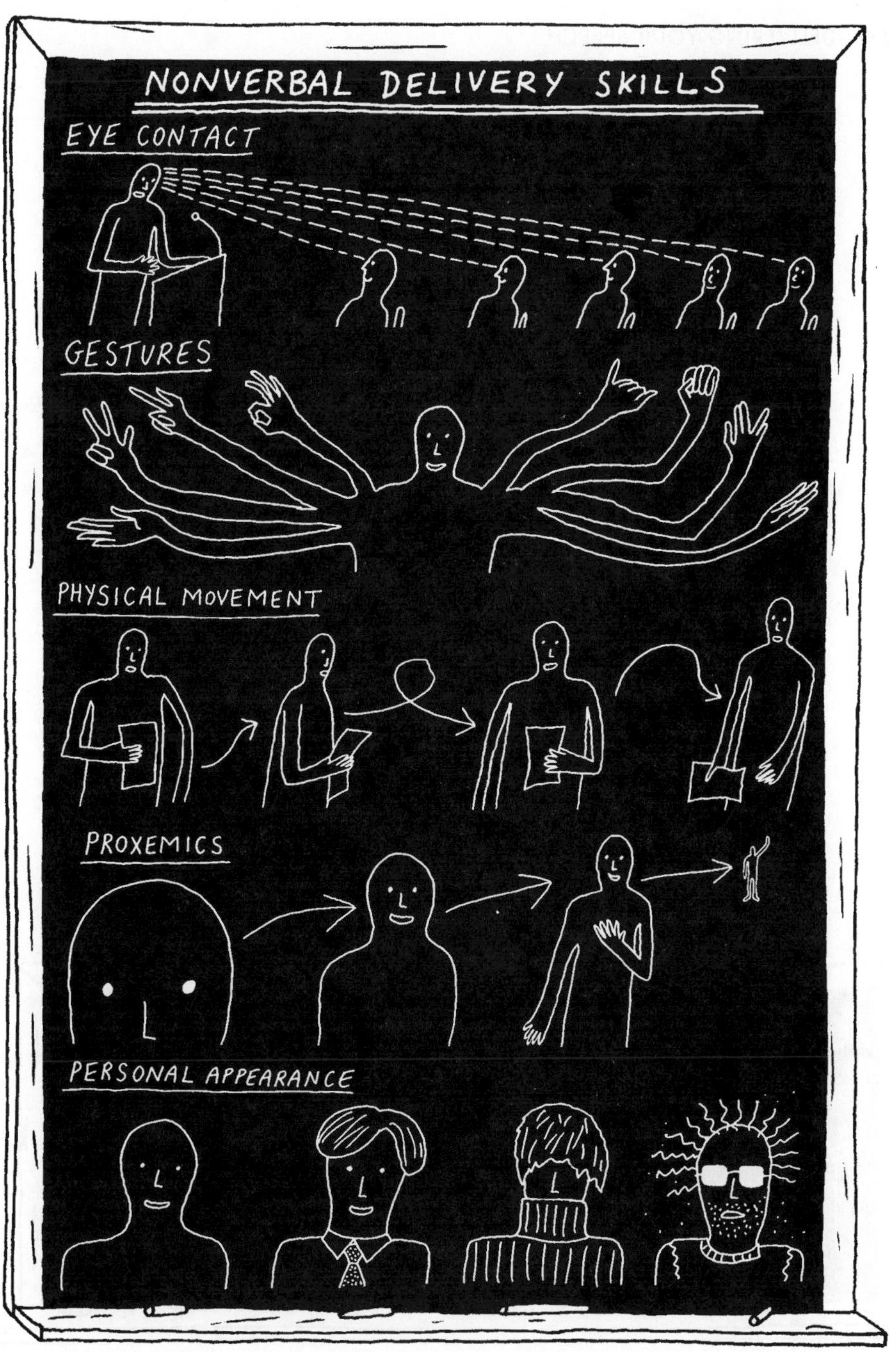
NONVERBAL DELIVERY SKILLS
EYE CONTACT
GESTURES
PHYSICAL MOVEMENT
PROXEMICS
PERSONAL APPEARANCE

Eye Contact

To understand what **eye contact** is, you may find it helpful to think first about what it is not. Eye contact is not you looking at your audience members while they look at something else. Nor is it the audience looking directly at you while you stare at your notes or nervously gaze at the ceiling for some divine guidance on what to say next. Rather, with true eye contact, you look directly into the eyes of your audience members, and they look directly into yours.

Eye contact enables you to gauge the audience's interest in your speech. By looking into your listeners' eyes, you can discern how they're feeling about the speech (fascinated? confused? upset?). Armed with these impressions, you can adapt your delivery if needed; for example, by providing a few more juicy details about a particular main point if you notice that your listeners look fascinated and hungry for more, or by re-explaining a key point if listeners look confused or overwhelmed.

Eye contact also helps you interact with your audience. For instance, by glancing at a particular listener, you may notice that he or she seems eager to ask a question, so you can then stop and field queries from the audience.

Finally, eye contact helps you compel your audience's attention. Father Paul, a wise Episcopalian priest, once confided a secret of his

effective sermonizing technique: "When I speak, I look right at my congregation. And when I do that, I make them look at me too. And it is harder not to listen to me when I do that . . . precisely because of that!"[2] When you and your audience establish eye contact, it becomes difficult for listeners to look away or mentally drift as you're talking.

From the audience's perspective, eye contact is critical for another reason entirely: in Western cultures, many people consider a willingness to make eye contact evidence of a speaker's credibility—especially truthfulness. An old saying holds that "the eyes are the windows of the soul," meaning that our eyes can betray who we really are or what we really think or believe. Of course, just because

someone makes eye contact doesn't necessarily mean that he or she is telling the truth. Likewise, a speaker's failure to look directly at the audience may stem from causes other than dishonesty, such as nervousness or shyness. Still, as long as people *believe* that the eyes reveal the soul, they will associate a lack of eye contact with deception. To communicate honesty, expertise, and confidence, maintain frequent eye contact with your audience.

How you use eye contact depends on the size of your audience. With small audiences, try to establish and sustain direct eye contact with each listener at various points in your speech. With large audiences, this isn't practical. Therefore, you'll need to use a technique called **panning**. To pan your audience, think of your body as a tripod, and your head as a movie camera that sits atop the tripod. Imagine yourself "filming" everyone in the group by moving your "camera" slowly from one side of your audience to the other. With this technique, you gradually survey all audience members—pausing and establishing extended eye contact with an individual listener for a few moments before moving on to do the same with another listener.

IF YOU WANT TO BE BELIEVED, LOOK AT YOUR AUDIENCE, NOT THE FLOOR.

Panning with extended eye contact gives your audience the sense that you're looking at each listener, even if you aren't. And it still enables you to gauge your audience members' interest, hold their attention, and interact with individual listeners if needed.

Gestures

Gestures—using hand movements to emphasize a point, pantomime, demonstrate, or call attention to something—can add flair to your speech delivery, especially when your gestures seem natural rather than overly practiced.[3] At the same time, be aware that gestures can also backfire. For one thing, not all your listeners will interpret the same gesture—a clenched fist, an open palm, a raised forefinger—in the same way.[4] For example, some people see a fist as a symbol for violence, while others consider it a show of forcefulness or determination. If an audience member interprets a particular

gesture differently from what you intended, you may inadvertently send the wrong message to that person.

Another consideration is that gestures may communicate a message that is not consistent with your verbal speech message. Former President George H. W. Bush used the same gestures in nearly every presentation—often enough that creating a parody of his delivery style was easy work for comedians such as *Saturday Night Live*'s Dana Carvey. The gestures—alternating a jabbing fist with a thrusting open-palmed hand—may have proved effective during addresses calling for strength (for instance, a presentation urging Congress to "get tough" on crime). But when Bush wanted to communicate tenderness or sympathy—for instance, while expressing grief for the victims of a hurricane or when speaking lovingly of his family—the jabbing fist (which Bush perhaps used out of habit) sent the wrong message.

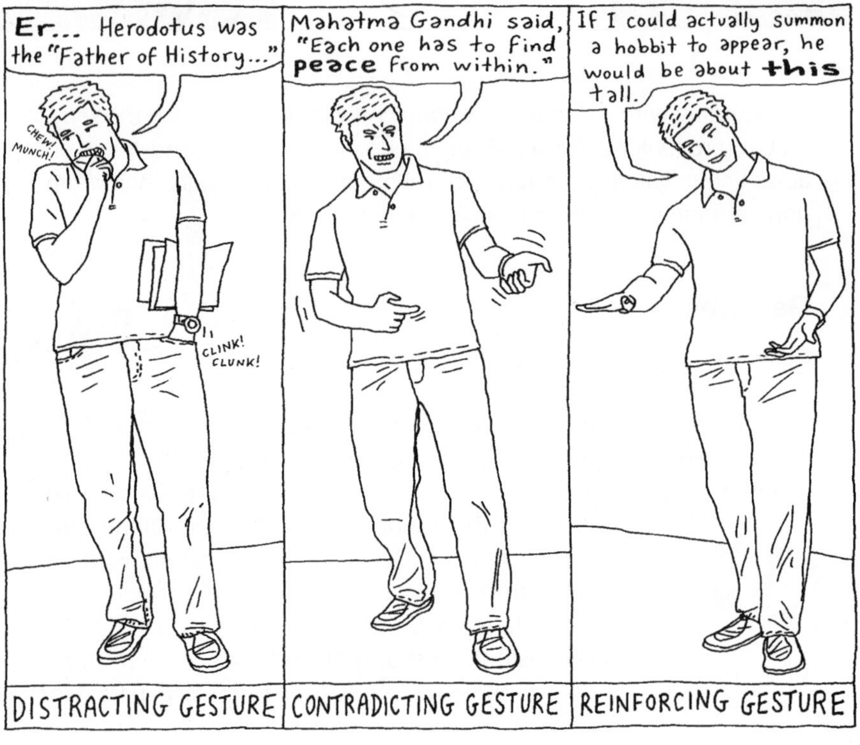

In addition to ensuring that your gestures reinforce your spoken message, avoid using distracting gestures born of nervousness—such as stuffing your hands in your pockets, jingling keys or change in your pockets, and fiddling with a watch, ring, or pen. These behaviors can distract audience members to the point that they'll start focusing more on your gestures than on your speech.

To get the most from gestures, follow these guidelines:

- Use gestures deliberately to emphasize or illustrate points in your speech.
- Remain aware that not all audience members may interpret your gestures in the same way.
- Make sure your gestures reinforce your spoken message.
- Avoid nervous, distracting gestures.

Physical Movement

Physical movement describes how much or how little you move around while delivering a speech. Not surprisingly, standing stock-still (sometimes referred to as the "tree trunk" approach) isn't very effective; nor is

TOO MUCH MOVEMENT IS DISTRACTING

MOVEMENT EMPHASIZES TRANSITIONS AND ENGAGES LISTENERS

shifting or walking restlessly from side to side or back and forth ("pacing") in front of your audience. A motionless speaker comes across as boring or odd, while a restless one is distracting and annoying.

Instead of going to either of these extremes, strive to incorporate a reasonable amount and variety of physical movement as you give a presentation. Skillful use of physical movement injects energy into your delivery *and* signals transitions between parts of your speech. For example, when making an especially important point in your presentation, you can take a few steps to the left in front of your audience, then casually walk back to your original spot when you shift to the next major idea.

How much physical movement, if any, is right for you? Move as much as necessary to invigorate your speech (even if you must come out from behind the podium or lectern), but not so much that you confuse or distract your audience.

Finally, a brief note about speaking from a lectern or podium. Although the lectern might make you feel somewhat more comfortable, it usually acts as a barrier between you and your listeners. Thus, unless you must be at the lectern because of a microphone, we recommend that you come out from behind it at least part of the time, and thereby interact more fully with your audience. When you are at the lectern, be sure to avoid gripping the sides or top tightly with your hands; such a grip adds tension to your body and will be clearly visible to audience members.

AVOID STAYING ROOTED TO ONE SPOT

Proxemics

Proxemics—use of space and distance between yourself and your audience—is related to physical movement. Through proxemics, you control how closely you stand to your audience while delivering your speech.

The size and setup of the speech setting can help you determine how best to use proxemics. For example, in a large forum, you may want to come out from behind the podium and move closer to your audience, so listeners can see and hear you more easily. Moving toward your audience can also help you communicate intimacy;[5] it suggests you're about to convey something personal, which many audience members will find compelling. Research has also shown that audiences perceive not only a strong association between closeness and intimacy, but also between closeness and attraction,[6] and closeness as an indication of the immediacy/nonimmediacy of the speech message.[7]

THE POETICS OF SPACE (A.K.A. PROXEMICS)

Of course, different people have different feelings about physical proximity. While some welcome a speaker's nearness, others consider it a violation of their personal space or even a threat. Culture can also influence a person's response to a speaker's proximity. In some cultures, people consider physical closeness downright offensive or invasive.[8] In others, people consider it essential to positive relationships.

To determine how much space to put between you and your listeners, consider your audience's background, the size and setup of your forum, and your ability to move around the forum. When speaking, move close enough to your audience to interact with them and allow them to see and hear you—but not so close as to violate any listener's sense of private space.

Personal Appearance

By **personal appearance**, we refer to the impression you make on your audience through your clothing, jewelry, hairstyle, grooming, and other elements influencing how you look.

Personal appearance in a public speech matters for two reasons. First, many people in your audience will form their initial impression of you *before* you even say anything—just by looking at you. Be sure that your appearance communicates the right message about you! Second, studies show that this initial impression based on appearance can be long lasting and very significant.[9] If you make a negative first impression because of a sloppy or otherwise unappealing appearance, you'll need to expend a lot of time and effort to win back your audience's trust and rebuild your credibility.

The rule for personal appearance is to do what is appropriate for the audience you are addressing, given the occasion and the forum. If you're addressing a somber and formally dressed audience while eulogizing the life of a fallen friend, don't show up in brightly colored, casual garb and loud jewelry. Likewise, if you're delivering a presentation to a potential client in an industry known for its relaxed and playful corporate culture, consider "dressing down" for the occasion rather than donning a blue pin-striped suit and power tie.

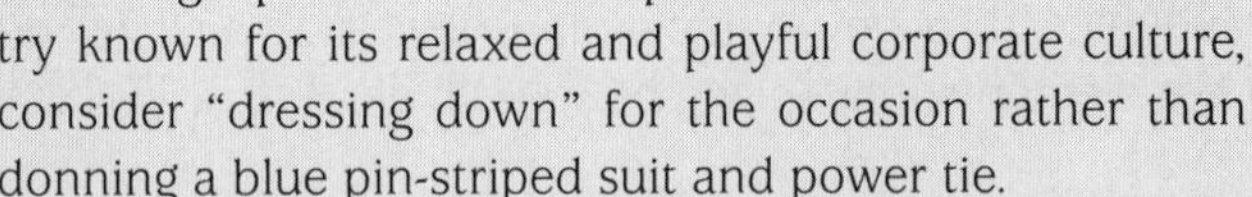

But in any speaking situation, you should always strive to look presentable through good grooming (tidy hair, nails, makeup, etc.) and an overall tidy appearance (avoiding holes in clothing, clothes that are inappropriately revealing, etc.). That way, you show respect for the audience, the situation, and yourself.

SUMMARY

> "How you say something is often as important as what you say."

As Hannah's story at the beginning of this chapter shows, how you deliver your speech and the verbal and nonverbal skills you use while making your presentation can spell the difference between success and failure. In this chapter, you learned the pros and cons of three modes of delivery—reading from a script, reciting from a memorized text, and speaking extemporaneously from an outline—and learned that extemporaneous delivery is preferred in most contemporary settings. You also discovered how to use many different elements of vocal delivery—voice volume, tone, rate of delivery, projection, articulation, pronunciation, and pausing—to create more impact in your speeches. And you learned how to use elements of nonverbal delivery—eye contact, gestures, physical movement, proxemics, and personal appearance—to further captivate and engage your audience. By using the right delivery mode as well as the right blend of verbal and nonverbal skills, you can get your message across to your listeners—and leave them wanting more.

Key Terms

delivery

USING VOCAL DELIVERY SKILLS

vocal delivery skills
nonverbal delivery skills
volume
tone
rate of delivery
projection
articulation
pronunciation
pausing
verbal fillers
verbal tics

USING NONVERBAL DELIVERY SKILLS

eye contact
panning
gestures
physical movement
proxemics
personal appearance

...and now, if you'll look this way.
MOTOR
HARLEY-DAVIDSON
CYCLES
claire
RRRRUMBLE!
Cool!

14 USING AUDIOVISUAL AIDS

"Listening can lead to understanding; seeing can lead to believing."

Phil couldn't wait to deliver his speech about Harley-Davidson motorcycles to the rest of his public speaking class. The purpose of the speech was to inform his audience of the difference in quality between American-made motorcycles and machines made in Japan and Germany. A longtime Harley owner, Phil felt strongly that if his audience could actually *see* a Harley up close and *hear* the distinctive rumble of its engine, they would understand his point in a more visceral way. But how could he provide this experience without actually driving his Harley into the classroom?

Phil considered other possibilities, such as playing a recording of a Harley engine being revved up, showing enlarged photos of different Harley models, or playing some video footage he had taken from a recent motorcycle convention he had attended. He knew that these

audiovisual aids would all help him convey the unique character and quality of Harley-Davidson bikes. But to his mind, they still weren't as potent as showing his listeners an actual motorcycle. He decided to put some more thought into the situation and to talk with his wife, Claire, about it.

That evening, after listening to Phil's concerns, Claire had an idea about how she could help. She agreed to park the family Harley outside the classroom windows during Phil's talk. When the day of the speech arrived, Phil opened the window shades and invited his classmates to stand near him as he extolled the virtues of Harley motorcycles. Outside, Claire pointed to various parts of the bike as he mentioned them. Members of the audience had to shift their gaze from Phil in the classroom to Claire standing outside (looking a bit like Vanna White as she gestured and walked around the bike). But they saw enough to understand what he was saying, and they immediately grasped his passion for Harleys (not to mention his wife's love for him!). Through creative use of audiovisual aids—in this case, an actual bike and an assistant who focused his listeners' attention on various aspects of the machine—Phil was able to deliver an exceptionally engaging and interesting speech.

In this chapter, we take a close look at audiovisual aids, examining their advantages, the many different forms they can take, and strategies for using them effectively.

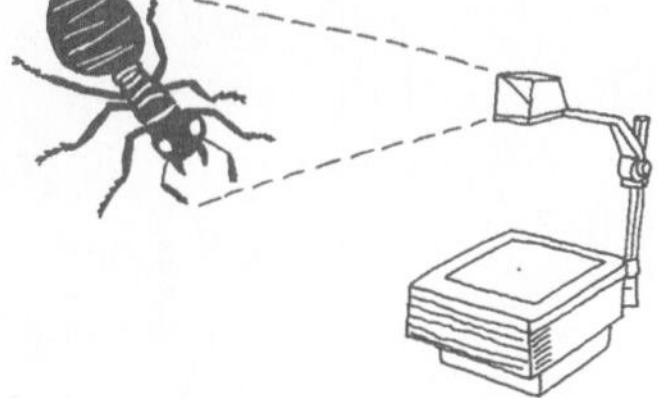

WHY USE AUDIOVISUAL AIDS?

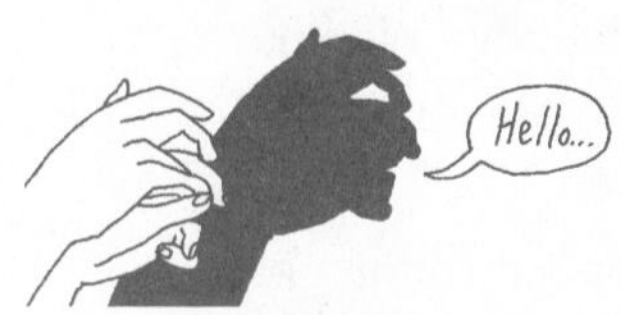

An **audiovisual aid** is anything (in addition to your spoken words) that the members of your audience can see or hear that helps them understand and remember your presentation. Speech communication experts have long believed that listeners are much more likely to grasp spoken facts and concepts if presenters also provide visual and other nonverbal cues.[1] Indeed, as early as

the 1950s, studies showed that the use of audiovisual aids in a speech could increase learning by as much as 55 percent.[2]

Consider your own learning experiences over the years. For example, how did you come to understand difficult math concepts? Did your teacher expect you to know how to solve complex problems after merely lecturing you about algebra or geometry? Or did she *illustrate* the problems and concepts on the chalkboard—with plenty of examples? Most likely, you found the illustrations helpful—even essential—for grasping the concepts. Likewise, if you studied a language not native to you, did your teacher merely lecture you about the language in your native tongue? Or did he model the language for you, demonstrating correct pronunciation and accent and perhaps playing recordings of native speakers using the language? Again, you probably found the demonstrations and recordings crucial for mastering the basics of the new language.

Savvy use of audiovisual aids can gain you several important advantages as you deliver a speech. These include the following:

- *Adding interest.* A colorful and attractive audiovisual aid can help you spice up any presentation, especially one on a slightly dry topic. For instance, a financial-services salesperson giving a talk on retirement savings displays a photo of an older couple looking relaxed, happy, and healthy aboard their yacht. The salesperson could also play a brief audio snippet of the couple explaining how the company's services improved their quality of life.
- *Simplifying a complex topic.* If you are giving a speech on a technical or complicated topic, an audiovisual aid can help you simplify your message so your listeners can better understand you. For example, a student giving a presentation on how to skydive shows a drawing of a simplified parachute, with labels highlighting each key part of the equipment.
- *Helping your audience remember your speech.* Many individuals find visual information much easier to recall than spoken information. Thus, the right audiovisual aids can help

you ensure that you leave a permanent impression on your listeners. To illustrate, a speaker who had been sharing a lengthy list of statistics about the impact of climate change on the planet's ecosystems helps his listeners remember his point by displaying a line graph showing the rise in the number of extinctions over the past two hundred years.

TYPES OF AUDIOVISUAL AIDS

An audiovisual aid can provide both audio and visual assistance simultaneously (as in a video recording of an exotic bird singing), audio assistance only (such as a recording of a Harley-Davidson motorcycle engine), or visual assistance only (for example, a photograph of a person on a surfboard). Traditional aids include the speaker's own person, assistants, objects, drawings, photographs, charts and graphs, and overhead transparencies. Computer and information technology have opened the door to even more sophisticated video, audio, and digital aids. Below, we take a closer look at each type of audiovisual aid.

The Speaker

You yourself can be an effective visual aid, particularly if your topic calls for an explanation of an action. Consider Zoya, a student who

YOU CAN BE YOUR OWN VISUAL AID

loved rock climbing and gave a presentation on the sport's basics. During her speech, she covered some of the most common climbing moves and provided tips for taking lessons and finding the best climbing spots for beginners. To illustrate what she was talking about, Zoya wore the same clothes, special shoes, and equipment (such as a harness, belay device, and carabiners) that she used while climbing. Through her attire, she thus served as a visual aid.

In addition to wearing clothing or other apparel or equipment related to your topic, you can also be a visual aid by demonstrating or acting out an aspect of your speech topic. Shenille, a college sophomore in a speech class, prepared an informative presentation about three styles of African dance. She described each one and then demonstrated them by dancing briefly before the audience.

Assistants

If serving as an audiovisual aid yourself would complicate things too much or prevent you from interacting with your audience, consider asking someone else to reinforce points from your speech or to help you demonstrate. For example, in speeches about life-saving techniques and the use of CPR, lifeguards teaching new recruits often ask an assistant to role-play the victim of a drowning accident, concussion, heart attack, or stroke. The lifeguard then demonstrates techniques and procedures on the assistant while the class watches. As we saw earlier in the chapter, using an assistant can also help you surmount unique challenges in using audiovisual aids—such as how to show a motorcycle to a classroom of students.

Objects

Any object can be a visual aid. For example, in a speech about James Bond movies, one student presented a collection of posters depicting all the actors who ever played 007,

from Sean Connery to Daniel Craig. And in a January 2007 speech, Apple's CEO, Steve Jobs, used the iPhone—a multipurpose mobile phone—to unveil a new generation of products from his company.[3] To make sure his audience members could see the very small iPhone from a distance, Jobs showed close-ups of the phone on a giant screen behind him. The images illustrated how to use the phone to make calls as well as connect to the Internet, record streaming video, download and play music files, and take and send photographs.

Of course, Jobs was speaking to an immense audience and needed projection technology to make the iPhone accessible to all his listeners. If you want to use a small object as a visual aid in a speech to your classmates, you won't likely need the same technology. Instead, consider walking closer to the audience and holding the object up for them to see.

But what if you have the opposite challenge: your object is too large or unwieldy to present in its entirety to your listeners? This situation calls for equally creative problem-solving. Consider Alan, a student who once gave a speech about the "physics of bowling." He

explained everything about bowling—including the science behind the holes drilled into the balls, the effect of the rotation and angle of the bowler's arm on the ball's momentum, and the ball's impact on the pins. Naturally, Alan couldn't bring an entire bowling alley into the classroom. So, he came up with an ingenious alternative. He showed his audience three bowling balls—all with different kinds of holes. Then he rolled each of the balls down a slanted table and into the hands of an assistant. As he rolled the balls, he pointed out to his audience how each ball's speed and path differed based on its design and his technique.

ABSTRACT ART

Printed Materials: Maps, Charts, Graphs, Drawings, and Photographs

Printed materials—such as maps, charts, graphs, drawings, or photographs—can also help you simplify complex information for your audience.

MAP OF COUNTRY SHAPED LIKE ELEPHANT HEAD

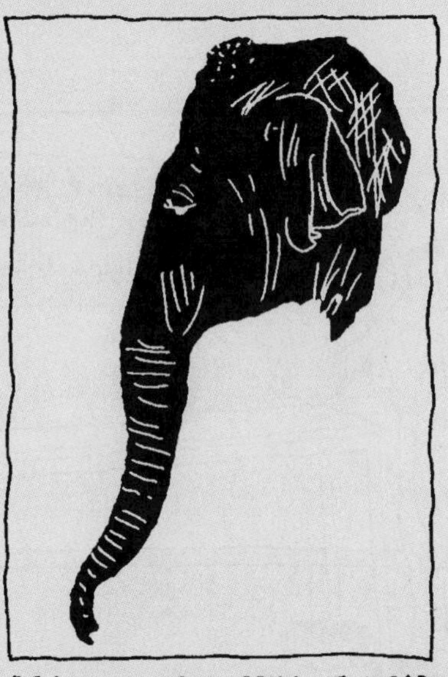
DRAWING OF ELEPHANT HEAD

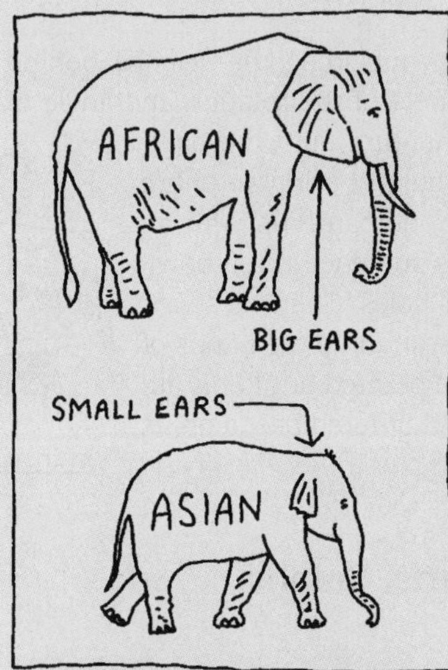

CHART SHOWING HOW TO TELL AFRICAN FROM ASIAN ELEPHANTS

YOUNG WOMAN HOLDING A PHOTO OF A THAI ELEPHANT

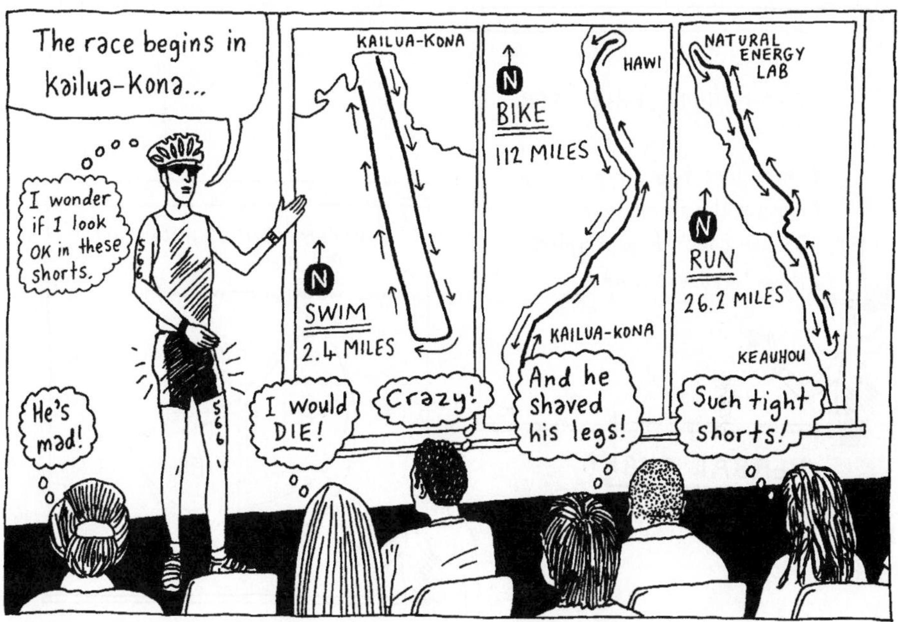

A **map** is a visual representation of geography and can contain as much or as little information as you wish. In addition to the map itself, you can add highlighting or labels to make the map more useful to your listeners. For example, if you're giving a talk on the architecture of a particular city, you could show a map with the most important buildings labeled. And in a presentation about competing in the Ironman triathlon in Hawaii, a speaker could use a map to show the route traveled for the race.

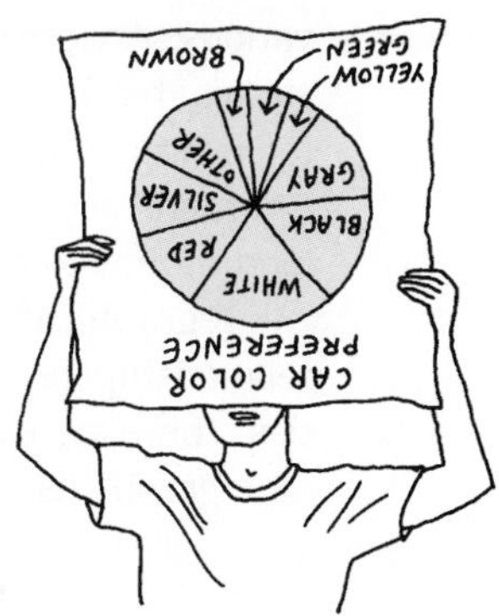

A **chart** is any graphic representation that summarizes information and ideas. There are three basic types of charts: *verbal, pie,* and *flowcharts*.

A **verbal chart** uses words arranged in a certain format to explain ideas, concepts, or general information. For example, you could use a verbal chart to list the key ideas or most important "takeaways" from your speech, such as the steps in last-minute

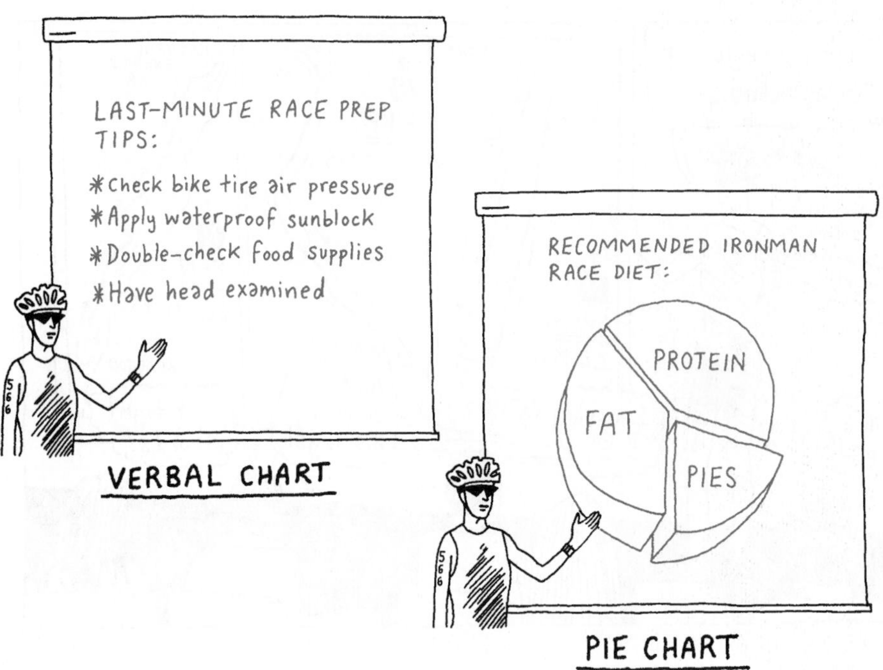

race preparation for the Ironman competition or a list of the parts that make up a motorcycle engine. A **pie chart** resembles a sliced pie and can help you clarify how proportions and percentages relate to one another. For instance, you could use a pie chart to show the percentages of different types of foods in a doctor-recommended diet for triathletes, or to show how much your town spent in a given year on various services such as education or road repair. A **flowchart** demonstrates the direction of information, processes, and ideas. You might, for example, use a flowchart to show the steps in preparing for the Ironman race or the process that a bank uses to decide whether to lend money to a mortgage applicant.

A **graph** can also help your audience visualize and understand the relationship between different numbers, measurements, or quantities. There are two main types of graphs: **line graphs** and **bar graphs**. Line graphs use lines plotted on a pair of axes to show relationships

HOW TO BECOME AN IRONMAN COMPETITOR:
BUILD ENDURANCE BASE OF FITNESS
INCREASE LENGTH OF WORKOUTS AND DISTANCES
MIX IN SPEED WORKOUTS
STUDY THE SPECIFIC RACE COURSE
PREPARE FOR RACE NUTRITION
DEVELOP MENTAL TOUGHNESS AND COMMITMENT
BEGIN GRADUAL TAPER OF WORKOUTS AS RACE APPROACHES
RACE WEEK TAPER (LIGHT WORKOUTS & TOP OFF ON CARBS)
RACE DAY: Ready, set, go!
12 TO 16 WEEKS
566

FLOWCHART

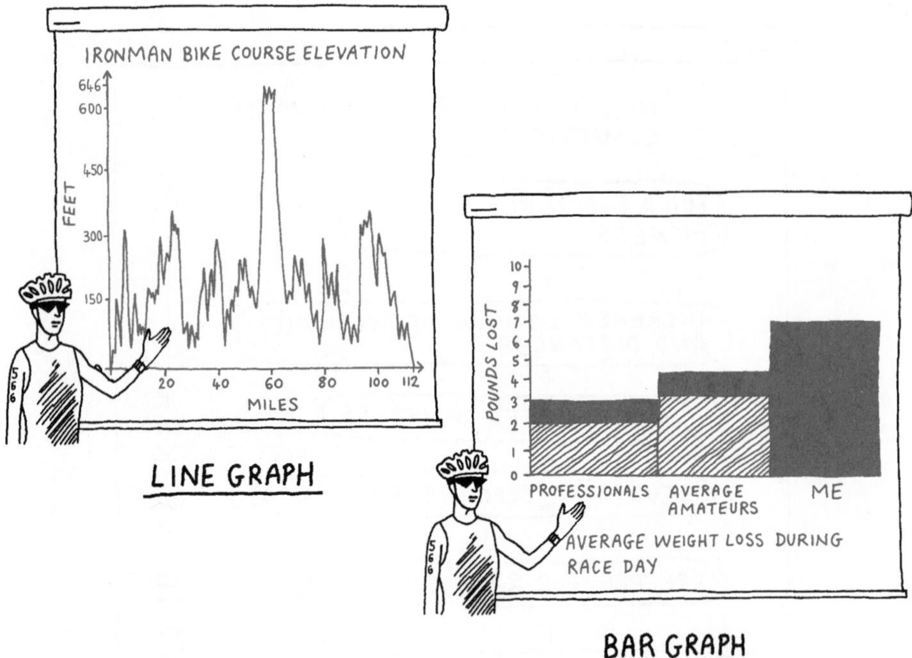

between two elements. For example, you could use a line graph to show the various elevations of the Ironman race or how much profit a company made over a ten-year period. Bar graphs consist of parallel bars of varying height or length that compare several pieces of information. For instance, you could use a bar graph to compare the weight loss of three different triathletes in a series of races.

Maps, charts, and graphs illustrate quantitative information. But sometimes you want to provide a visual depiction of what you're describing in your speech. In this case, a **drawing** or **photograph** may be your best choice of audiovisual aid. Photographs can help you provide an exact depiction. For example, if you're giving a speech about the *Mona Lisa*, you could provide a photograph of the painting and use it to point out certain aspects of Leonardo da Vinci's technique. Drawings enable you to emphasize and de-emphasize certain details about your topic. For instance, in a speech about how mosquitoes spread malaria, you could provide a drawing of the insect that details

PHOTO OF COMPETITOR

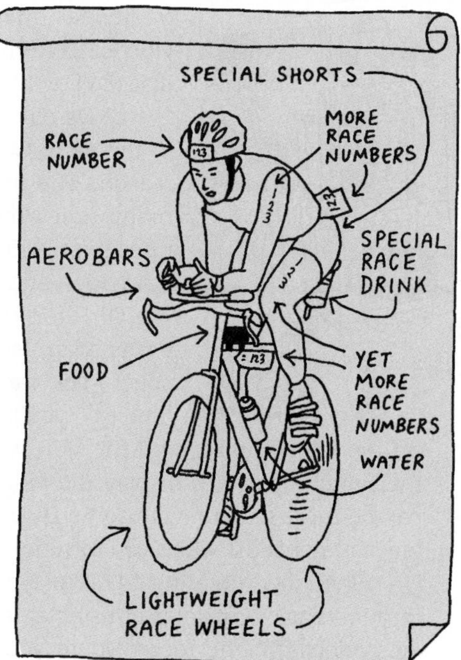

ANNOTATED DRAWING OF COMPETITOR

its proboscis as the tool for spreading disease. As with maps, you can add labels or other types of highlighting to a photograph or drawing to focus your audience's attention on specific details.

Videos and DVDs as Audiovisual Aids

In many speech situations, you may want to use video clips to vividly explain, demonstrate, or illustrate a key point. Although in recent years it has become possible to integrate such video into presentations using computer software and a digital projector, it may often be more convenient or downright necessary to show video using more

traditional means—a television set and a videocassette recorder (VCR) or a digital video disc (DVD).

DVDs still dominate the market for video in the early twenty-first century, and for good reason. The small plastic diskettes can store many times more information and extra features than VHS tapes, with simple menu-driven navigation and superb picture quality.

On the other hand, using a VCR can be easier than using a DVD player in one key respect—you can cue to the specific spot on the tape that you'll want to play. Then you can turn off the television or even the VCR while you begin your speech and then press "play" to display the video at the appropriate time. This can be more difficult with some DVD players, since cuing to a specific place may be lost when you turn the unit off.

When incorporating a DVD player or VCR in a presentation, keep in mind basic principles of using aids: make sure to practice with the aids, ideally in the room where you will be presenting and on the same equipment. Avoid tripping over power cables during your speech (consider taping such cables to the floor), and focus on showing brief clips only.

Digital Visual Aids

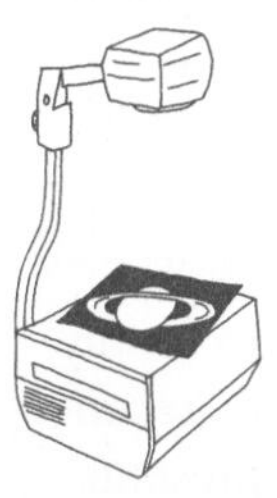

In the past, public speakers presented most of their visual aids on printed pages, marker boards, or flip charts, or projected them on a wall from slide or overhead projectors. Software programs in laptop and desktop computers have revolutionized the use of such aids. Today, you can use this type of software to create tables, charts, graphs, and even illustrations. Digital cameras and cell phones have further transformed the world of visual aids—by enabling you to download digital photos or video from the device to your computer. Once you create these visual aids, you can

print or project them in black and white or in vibrant colors. Digital presentations have become extremely widespread on college campuses, in communities across the world, and especially in business settings.

The most commonly used presentation software is Microsoft PowerPoint. In all likelihood, you will have experimented with this tool already. The latest version is enormously user-friendly and very accessible for novices. Whether you use PowerPoint or another product, you can display your presentations to an audience on your computer monitor or use a **digital projector** to show them on a screen or blank wall. You can also print your presentations as black-and-white or color documents, as slides, or as transparencies for display on an overhead projector.

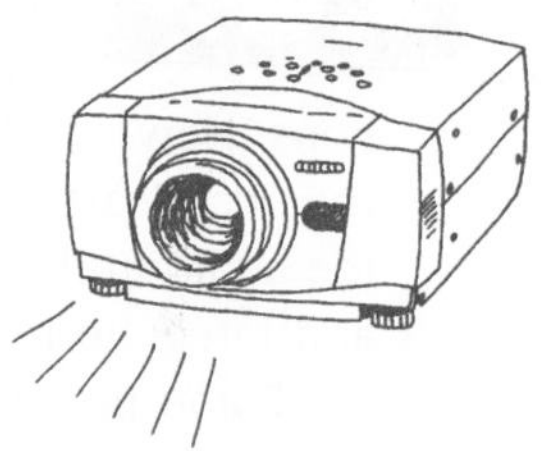

Other technological advances can enable you to do creative things with artwork, photographs, and video. For example, in earlier years, public speakers had to take photographs with a film camera and then use a scanner to convert their image into digital form and download it to a computer program. Today, digital cameras do all of those tasks at once, and even allow for limited video. These functions are also increasingly available on cell phones. The picture resolution on a phone is not as high as it might be with a more expensive camera, but many people find it relatively simple and quite convenient to capture pictures or video on a cell phone and transfer them to a computer program for later use as a visual aid.

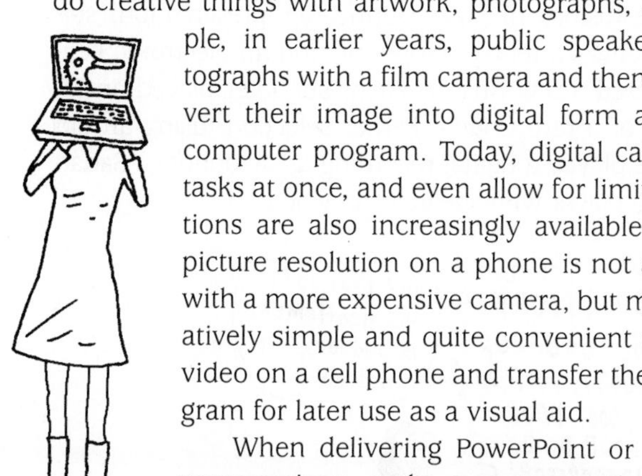

When delivering PowerPoint or other sorts of digital presentations, make sure to practice a number of times with your slides, just as you would with speech outlines. To guard against any surprises, check that your media will work with the computers in the speech setting before it's time to speak and bring hard copies of your aids with you on the day of the presentation. Even better, be ready to speak without your aids if necessary. Finally, remember that *you* need to be the center of attention, not your slides. Help your listeners focus on you and your message by avoiding reading from your slides, by maintaining eye contact with listeners, and by not writing out virtually everything you plan to say so that it appears on-screen.

Technology and Audio Aids

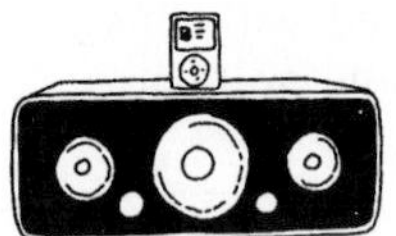

Recent technologies have also made it easier to use audio aids in your presentations. For example, by using portable MP3 players such as Apple's iPod, you can integrate sound and music into your presentations. How? You insert the player into a small speaker stand, which can broadcast the audio over a very large forum. You can also store the audio in the same laptop you're using for presentation software, and integrate music or sound effects into your visual presentations.

Some presentations may benefit from multiple audio aids. A student named Justine knew this when she gave an informative speech to her classmates on the history of jazz. During her presentation, she showed actual instruments—a tenor saxophone and an electronic keyboard—and demonstrated a few riffs on each. She later played an LP phonograph recording of a rare Charlie Parker selection (using an old record player). And she played a digital recording of saxophonist Sadao Watanabe from an MP3 player with speakers attached.

USE AUDIO SPARINGLY

AUDIENCE ANALYSIS AND AUDIOVISUAL AIDS

Because audiovisual aids become part of the message you are sharing with listeners during your speech, your analysis of that audience should drive your selection of those aids. Three aspects of audience analysis—forum, demographics, and prior exposure—merit special consideration when choosing audiovisual aids.

Forum

Consider the **forum** as you're mulling over which audiovisual aids to use. Where will the audience listen to your speech? Is the forum equipped to handle audiovisual aids? For example, are there outlets available for a laptop computer and computer projector, a slide projector, a television monitor, or a video/DVD player? If you want to visit a Web site during your presentation and show it to your audience, is wireless access available? If you plan to use printed visual aids, do you have access to poster boards, flip charts, marker boards, or chalkboards?

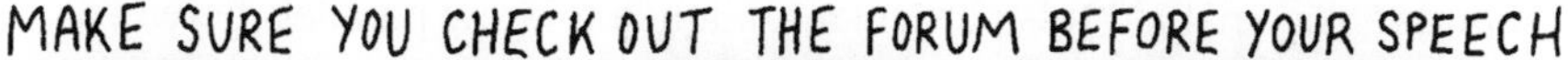

Demographics

Think about the *demographics* of your audience. Demographics—such as listeners' age, gender, and place of birth—can easily predetermine audience members' response to a particular audio or visual aid.

For example, in a presentation comparing the war in Iraq to the conflict in Vietnam given to an audience of mostly middle-aged men and women from the baby boomer generation, a speaker juxtaposed photos of American troops in Iraq with news photos taken during the United States military action in Vietnam during the 1960s. As she showed and discussed the slides, the speaker also played a quiet soundtrack featuring music from the sixties rock group The Doors in the background. This presenter knew that many of her listeners had children who were old enough to serve in the military and that they all remembered the Vietnam War. Her choice of photos and music enabled this particular audience to draw parallels between Iraq and Vietnam—which was her purpose in giving the speech.

On the other hand, how would the speaker want to change her audio and visual aids if the audience was comprised of traditional college-aged students? She would probably want to keep the visuals the same since she would want to establish a powerful connection between the two conflicts by showing images from both. Yet considering that audience members usually have strong visceral connections to popular music from their own era, the speaker might want to start

with more contemporary songs that comment on the Iraq war—such as music from the Dixie Chicks, Green Day, or System of a Down—before transitioning into the Doors song from the Vietnam era. That way the speaker would pull audience members in with familiar songs before showing connections to the past.

Prior Exposure

Prior exposure to certain audiovisual aids may positively or negatively influence your audience's response to those aids. Consider Crystal, a student who gave a persuasive speech opposing abortion. She knew from interviews that many of her listeners identified themselves as pro-choice. Therefore, she avoided using graphic photos or images of abortion procedures, which these audience members had already seen many times and would likely find offensive. Instead, Crystal chose other visual aids to make her argument that all life has value. For example, she showed pictures of healthy infants and the children and young adults they grew up to be. While she may not have persuaded all her listeners to change their viewpoints on abortion, her speech nevertheless proved thought provoking and held her audience's attention.

How can you determine whether your audience has had prior exposure to the audiovisual aids you're considering—and what that exposure implies? Ask the same kinds of questions we introduced in Chapter 5:

1. *"Has my audience seen or heard this aid before?"* If so, proceed to the next question.
2. *"What was the result of this prior exposure?"* Were listeners persuaded to take the action the speaker advocated? If not, proceed to the next question.

3. *"Why was the prior exposure ineffective?"* Ask yourself how you can avoid repeating the mistakes made by the previous presenter who failed to persuade his or her audience through those particular aids.

GUIDELINES FOR PREPARING AUDIOVISUAL AIDS

As you prepare audiovisual aids for your presentation, keep these guidelines in mind:

- *Make sure your aids support your point*. Is your point something that can be enhanced by specific images or sounds? For example, if you're giving a speech on a particular city's architecture, a map would strongly support your message. A recording of a song about that same city would be less relevant to your speech.
- *Consider your audience.* Your analysis of the forum, audience demographics, and listeners' prior exposure can help you select appropriate aids. Ask yourself: of all the possible aids for this speech, which one or combination of several would work best with this audience?

- *Test the size of visual aids.* Make sure each visual aid is large enough to be seen by everyone in your audience. Remember: the bigger your audience, and the farther it is from you and your visual aid, the larger the aid should be.
- *Test the legibility of visual aids.* Check whether numbers, letters, words, sentences, and graphics in your visual aids are each legible—that is, easily distinguished at a distance. For instance, ask a classmate, friend, or roommate to view a poster or projected slide from a distance and to tell you whether he or she can see everything on the visual aid. If not, continue refining the aid—for example, by stepping up font size and adding white space between elements.
- *Test the volume and clarity of audio aids.* Be certain your audio aids will be loud enough *and* clear enough (that is, free of static or other "noise") so that all your listeners can hear them.

TIPS FOR HOW A CANDIDATE CAN SPIN A POLITICAL CRISIS

- Deny, deny, deny.
- Accuse your opponent of the same thing.
- Do the "mea culpa."

WRONG

TIPS FOR HOW A CANDIDATE CAN SPIN A POLITICAL CRISIS

- Deny, deny, deny.
- Accuse your opponent of the same thing.
- Do the "mea culpa."

RIGHT

- *Create contrast.* On visual aids, contrast increases readability. To create contrast, place dark colors against a light background or light colors against a dark background. For example, if you decide to use PowerPoint to create slides, make sure the numbers or words on your slides are dark against a lighter background—or white against a dark background.
- *Keep your aids simple.* An audiovisual aid works best when your listeners can simply glance at it or hear it once and quickly grasp what you're trying to communicate. If they

THIS VISUAL AID IS NICE & SIMPLE

have to stare at it, see it more than once, or listen to it several times, the aid is too complex and detailed. And you need to think about how you can simplify it.

- *Practice using your aids.* Create your audiovisual aids while developing your speech—and then practice using them as you rehearse your presentation. Don't put yourself in the risky position of needing to create aids "on the fly" while delivering your speech.

- *Be prepared to speak without aids.* As many hapless public speakers have discovered, technology can fail just when you need it most. Imagine how you'd feel if, during a key point in your speech, you turned on your computer to project an important photo and the device didn't work. To avoid this scenario, always prepare a hard copy of any audiovisual aids you plan to present through computers or other technology or equipment. To further cover yourself, make sure you practice giving your speech without using the aids.

BE PREPARED TO SPEAK WITHOUT AIDS

USING AUDIOVISUAL AIDS DURING YOUR SPEECH

Skillful development of your audiovisual aids isn't enough to ensure a successful speech. You also need to use the aids correctly during your presentation. Otherwise, you risk making all-too-common mistakes—such as distracting your audience by leaving aids for display after you're finished with them, or losing eye contact with your listeners while discussing an aid. The following strategies can help you exert maximum impact with your audiovisual aids.

Make Sure Everyone Can See and Hear Your Aids

Position stereo speakers so that all your listeners can hear the audio recordings you're playing. Position a computer screen so everyone can see it. Place a printed graph, chart, or picture prominently on the wall or flip chart, so your entire audience can view it.

Control Audience Interaction with Your Aids

To avoid distracting your audience unnecessarily, do not show or play an aid until you are ready for listeners to see or hear it. Then, when you're finished presenting the aid, put it away or shut it off. This strategy keeps your audience's attention focused on you instead of your aids—and helps ensure that listeners don't miss important parts of your speech.

You can control audience interaction with your aids in several ways. For example, if you are using an audio recording, cue up the desired track ahead of time so you can play it promptly when you're ready. Avoid playing a tape or CD as background music to your speech. If you plan to tape or pin a chart to the wall, do so in advance, but fold half of the display over the other half and tape or pin it down. That way, you'll block the audience's view until you are ready to refer to the chart in your speech. At that point, undo the tape or pin, and reveal the entire aid.

Use the same technique when displaying a series of images on successive sheets of a flip chart. Insert blank sheets between each sheet containing an image. When you finish with one image, flip the page so all your audience sees is a blank page.

This technique also works well with overhead transparencies, slide shows, and computer images in a PowerPoint presentation. Remove each image after you've discussed it, leaving a blank screen, or turn the equipment off and refocus the audience on you.

What about handouts? To ensure that they're informative rather than distracting for listeners, issue clear instructions about how to use them. For example, pass handouts out face down and tell the audience not to look at them until you say so. Explain that you don't want listeners to get ahead of you. Of course, there will always be somebody in the audience who ignores this instruction and takes a peek. To keep these individuals focused on your speech, watch your audience during your presentation. Look for listeners who are paging through the handouts. Then adjust your delivery by increasing your volume or moving closer to those audience members to draw their attention back to you.

Maintain Eye Contact

Many inexperienced speakers look at their visual aids during their presentation instead of maintaining eye contact with their audience. Of course, you need to glance at visual aids as you present them—especially if you're referring to something specific on an aid. But this should be *only* a glance—not a gaze.

MAINTAIN EYE CONTACT WITH YOUR AUDIENCE, NOT YOUR VISUAL AID

Remember the Purpose of Your Aids

Treat your audiovisual aids as tools that supplement your speech—not the main vehicle for delivering your speech. Your presentation contains your message, and you are the messenger. If you forget this, you risk seeing your audience focus on your aids instead of you. For instance, many inexperienced salespeople rely too heavily on brochures and handouts during a presentation. They assume—mistakenly—that good marketing materials are all they need to sell a product or a service. But a brochure can't answer listeners' questions or interact spontaneously with them. Only a human being can connect with audiences in these crucial ways. The best speakers understand that audiovisual aids support a speech—not the other way around.

SUMMARY

> "Listening can lead to understanding; seeing can lead to believing."

In this chapter, you saw how the right selection and strategic use of audiovisual aids enhances your audience's interest, comprehension, and retention of your speech. Aids can take many forms—including the speaker him- or herself and an assistant, as well as objects, printed materials such as maps, charts, graphs, photos, and drawings. Newer technologies offer speakers many compelling presentation tools, including audio and video recordings and digital aids. You can display audiovisual aids in a variety of ways—such as in printed form or through presentation software and other technology. To get the most impact from your aids, you need to develop them with your audience's needs in mind. Then use them judiciously during your presentation to support your points—not to deliver your message for you. A key point to remember is that audiovisual aids supplement your message, but they can never replace you; *you* are the messenger!

Key Terms

WHY USE AUDIOVISUAL AIDS?

audiovisual aid

TYPES OF AUDIOVISUAL AIDS

map
chart
verbal chart
pie chart
flowchart
graph
line graph
bar graph
drawing
photograph
digital projector

AUDIENCE ANALYSIS AND AUDIOVISUAL AIDS

forum
prior exposure

POOL RULES
NO
NO
NO
NO
NO
OK. Can I have your attention please...

15 INFORMATIVE SPEAKING

> "Effective informative speakers share information in an accessible, understandable, and compelling manner."

Suppose you work as a lifeguard at an inner-city municipal swimming pool frequented by toddlers and their parents. The program director has asked you to give a presentation to the parents about swimming safety rules for children. Your task is to prepare an informative speech that presents knowledge or information to an audience. An informative presentation teaches the audience something and increases listeners' understanding, awareness, or sensitivity to your topic. As a lifeguard, you might inform your audience members about swimming safety for children by explaining and demonstrating the proper use of personal flotation devices, correct swimming and breathing techniques, and first-aid tactics such as the Heimlich maneuver and mouth-to-mouth resuscitation.

Your goal in this informative speech would be to teach the concepts and practical skills of water safety as well as to capture and maintain your audience members' attention so that they retain the information in your talk. Though the presentation is primarily informative, it may also contain a bit of persuasive power. After all, when parents have a clearer understanding of the rules of water safety, they'll be more likely to follow those rules as well as help their children practice them.

In this chapter, we take a close look at informative speaking. First, we examine specific techniques for informing. Next, we consider the common types of informative speaking. Finally, we address how to develop an informative speech, including strategies for analyzing your audience and simplifying complex information in your presentation.

TECHNIQUES FOR INFORMING

Most informative speeches rely on one of the following techniques for conveying information: definition, explanation, description, demonstration, or narrative. While some topics may lend themselves best to one of these techniques, in truth you will most often use a blend of techniques in your informative presentation.

Definition

Through **definition**, you break something down by its parts and explain how they add up to identify the topic. In short, you explain the essence, meaning, purpose, or identity of something. That "something" could be

- an object—for example, "What is a lever?"
- a person or group—for instance, "Who are the Hutus?"
- an event—such as, "What was the Diet of Worms?"
- a process—for instance, "What is bookkeeping?"
- an idea or concept—for example, "What is obscenity?"

*JUSTICE POTTER STEWART, CONCURRING OPINION ON *JACOBELLIS V. OHIO* (1964).

As we discussed in Chapter 8, there are four different types of definitions. An example of each is shown in the following table, which demonstrates how you might use each of the four types to define the word *obscenity*.

TYPES OF DEFINITIONS

Type	Explanation	Example
Dictionary	The meaning of a term as it appears in a dictionary.	*Merriam-Webster's Collegiate Dictionary*, Eleventh Edition, defines *obscenity* as "something that is obscene"—that is, "disgusting to the senses."
Expert	Comes from a person or an organization that is a credible source of information on your speech's topic.	According to Chief Justice Burger of the U.S. Supreme Court in the 1973 case *Miller v. California*, obscenity is expression that appeals to a "prurient" (sick or unhealthy) interest in sex or sexual matters, in a "patently offensive way," and which, when taken as a whole, "lacks serious literary, artistic, political, or scientific value."
Etymological	Understanding a word or concept by tracing its roots in the same or other languages.	The word *obscenity* may derive from the Latin word *obscaenus,* combining the prefix *ob* (meaning "to") and the word *caenum* (meaning "dirt," "filth," "mire," and "excrement").
Functional	Defining a concept by examining how it is applied or how it functions.	In practice, American law recognizes obscenity as hardcore pornography (and ironically, not as violence, disease, or other social ills).

Explanation

Through **explanation**, you provide an analysis of something for purposes of clarity and specificity by tracing a line of reasoning or a series of causal connections between events. In this process of interpretation, you may also offer examples to illustrate the information you're sharing. For instance, you might use explanation to help your audience understand

- what causes climate change.
- how a bill becomes a law in the U.S. Congress.
- what events and decisions led up to the outbreak of World War II.
- how the engine in a hybrid car works.
- what stages a couple experiences as they form and maintain an intimate relationship.
- how photosynthesis works.

Explanation works well when you're giving a speech about a process (such as how photosynthesis works), tracing the emergence of an important event (such as World War II), or explaining how an interesting object works (such as a hybrid engine).

Description

When you use **description**, you use words to paint a mental picture for your listeners so they can close their eyes and imagine what you are saying. If you provide sufficient information and detail, your audience may be able to experience vividly what you describe, and through multiple senses. For example, you might decide to use description to help your audience understand

- what the aurora borealis looks like.
- how it feels to complete a perfect snowboard run in fresh powder.
- what it's like to meet someone in person for the first time after corresponding over the Internet.
- how you felt when you got your driver's license.
- what the call of a blackbird sounds like.
- how your city would look if people stopped littering.
- what it is like to attend the Burning Man festival in Nevada.
- the sights, sounds, and smells of a family dinner in your home country.
- the feeling of a freshly applied tattoo.

You can exert maximum impact through description by using vivid language, audiovisual aids, and details that evoke the senses of sight, sound, smell, touch, and taste. This can be especially effective if you use it is as a subpoint to engage listeners' imaginations and place them in the middle of what you're describing.

Demonstration

You might choose to provide a **demonstration** of a topic if your goal is to teach your audience how a process or a set of guidelines works—as with the water-safety speech discussed at the beginning of the chapter. Demonstrations often call for both physical modeling and verbal elements, as you lead the audience through the parts or steps of whatever you are demonstrating. Your audience learns by watching

your modeling and listening to your words. Because physical modeling often requires the use of props and visual aids, be sure to practice using these aids before you give your speech. And since you'll be teaching your audience, you need to be confident that you know your topic thoroughly.

Demonstrations could be helpful for a wide range of informative speeches. For example, you might use a demonstration to show your listeners how to

- take apart and rebuild a computer.
- create paper origami sculptures.
- make a video blog.
- saddle a horse.
- milk a goat.
- breakdance.
- practice self-defense.
- prepare a baby's bottle.

For some of these demonstrations, you could bring the needed props to your speech forum. For instance, to demonstrate how to prepare a baby's bottle, you could easily use an actual bottle and formula, and perhaps even bring in a small microwave oven for use during your speech. For other demonstrations, you may need to improvise with your props. To illustrate, you could show how to saddle a horse by bringing in a barrel-shaped object and a saddle and demonstrating how you would position the saddle, tighten the girth, and so forth.

Demonstration coupled with repetition of the speech message has proven especially effective as a learning and memory-enhancement tool. For example, an organization called *Per Scholas* provides job training for low-income individuals. This program has been spectacularly effective with helping to train computer-repair technicians who have little or no previous formal education. The practice of demonstrating the repair process and repeating the message has been key to the success of this program.[1]

Narrative

A **narrative** is a story. When you use a narrative in an informative speech, the story enables you to both share information and capture the audience's attention. The story itself can take the form of a personal remembrance, a humorous anecdote, or perhaps a serious account of an event that happened in someone else's life—all told in a way that informs the audience about your topic. Used skillfully, narratives can help "humanize" a speaker for listeners and thus enhance the speaker's credibility, or ethos.

When might you decide to use narrative in an informative speech? Anytime you want to get your point across in an engaging, memorable way. For example, you could use narrative to:

- *Open a speech on the drama and dangers of the Daytona 500.* A poignant introductory story about Dale Earnhardt (known as "The Intimidator") and his death in 2001 from a crash could help win your listeners' attention and stir up their emotions right from the start.
- *Emphasize the importance of communication in sustaining intimate relationships.* An entertaining narrative about a misunderstanding that you and your romantic partner ultimately cleared up through skillful communication could help you get the point across in a lighthearted but meaningful way.
- *Help your listeners appreciate the need for careful preparation before a job interview.* A story about how your friend failed to research the dress code of a company he was interviewing with—and showed up in overly casual attire—could leave a lasting impression on your listeners.

Using narrative effectively takes careful thought and preparation. You need to make sure the story supports your message, rather than just throwing in a narrative simply to entertain or captivate your audience. Thus, select stories—and the details that go into them—based on audience analysis. To illustrate, if you were giving a speech about the Daytona 500 to an audience composed of many people who had little knowledge of the race, you might need to explain who Dale Earnhardt was and why he remains such an important figure to NASCAR fans. Even if you know the elements of the narrative well, you may also want to research background information and specific details of the story and weave the information you found through your research into the speech.

Finally, remember that telling a compelling story in a way that also informs and educates your audience is a bit of an art. You want to come across as casual and natural (rather than over-rehearsed) but also authoritative. That requires extensive preparation and practice. It's almost as if you have to carefully practice . . . acting unrehearsed. In fact, using narrative in a speech can be a risky call, but if you can pull it off well it offers you and your audience real rewards.

TYPES OF INFORMATIVE SPEECHES

Informative speeches seek to share information, explanations, or even ideas with an audience. Unlike persuasive speeches that seek to make an argument and therefore confirm or alter an audience's beliefs or actions, informative speeches are meant to give audience members knowledge they might not have possessed before the speech. Informative speeches can be about a wide range of topics: specific objects, individuals or groups, events, processes, and ideas. In this section, we take a closer look at each of these types of informative speeches.

Objects

If you're giving an informative speech about an object, you have a virtually unlimited range of possibilities to choose from. The one thing all objects do have in common, though, is that they're not human. The following table shows just a small sampling of the much larger universe of possible objects your speech could address.

TYPES OF OBJECTS SUITABLE FOR AN INFORMATIVE SPEECH

Type	Examples
Mechanical/Technological	motorcycle blender cell phone weapons system
Natural	flowering plant river elephant planet
Cultural	painting building book gourmet dish
Personal	jacket credit card ice skate necklace

In giving an informative speech about a particular object, you could use a number of different techniques. For example, suppose you're preparing a presentation about the benefits of chocolate—which is a food and therefore an object. In this case, you could easily use description to inform your audience about chocolate. You might, for instance, describe the smooth, creamy texture and sumptuous flavor of a high-quality chocolate truffle and the feeling of well-being that can come from eating it.

But depending on the purpose of your speech, you can use one or more of the other techniques as well. For example, you could use

- *definition* to clarify what chocolate is and how it differs from other consumable products derived from cacao beans.
- *explanation* to trace the process by which chocolate bars are made.
- *demonstration* to show how you might bake a chocolate cake.
- *narrative* to convey chocolate's popularity as a romantic gift.

Finally, note that an informative speech about an object may also have elements of process in it—especially if that object has moving parts. For instance, to deliver a presentation on how a motorcycle operates, you might explain how the bike's fuel and transmission systems work together to create the process of acceleration.

Individuals or Groups

Giving an informative speech about an individual or a group offers an equally wide range of possibilities. People are consistently fascinated by others, as we can clearly see from the popularity of celebrity-focused magazines, "reality" television, and the booming trend of personal memoirs. Human subjects, then, can make for fascinating informative topic material because of extraordinary physical or emotional characteristics or compelling life stories. Groups, likewise, are collections of people with whom your audience can identify; these can include famous politicians in the same party or musical performers who capture tremendous amounts of attention. To illustrate, you could focus your talk on

- *a famous politician, entertainer, sports star, explorer, or artist.* For example, you might give a speech about Winston Churchill—a prominent British politician who eventually became his country's prime minister during the Second World War.

A FAMOUS POLITICIAN

AN UNSUNG HERO

- *an unsung hero*—a person or group who did something great but never won recognition for their accomplishment. For instance, you could tell your audience about a member of a small tribe in the forests of Burma who survived persecution by the ruling junta.

- *a tragic figure whose life provides a cautionary tale.* For example, you might discuss John F. Kennedy Jr.'s untimely death in a plane crash as a lesson about the importance of safety and preparation in private aviation.

A TRAGIC FIGURE

- *an influential political party, artistic movement, sports team, or musical group.* For instance, you might discuss the adversities and triumphs of the 1999 U.S. Women's Soccer Team, which won that year's World Cup Championship.

AN INFLUENTIAL SPORTS TEAM

As with objects, you could easily use description to deliver your informative speech about an individual or a group. For example, if your speech focused on Senator Obama, you could describe his personal qualities as well as his leadership style. You might also use narrative to tell a story about a defining experience in Obama's life. Or you could use explanation to trace the events that led to his decision to become a public servant.

Remember that while you will never be able to describe all of a person's life experience in a single speech, you can use life events to make a larger point about a person's character—what kind of person he or she is. You could even support such claims by using narratives supplied by the person's family, friends, associates, and even critics or enemies.

A presentation on a person or group might effectively incorporate information about an object or a process as well. Consider a talk on renowned inventor Thomas Edison. To convey Edison's innovative spirit, you could discuss not only the life experiences that led to his great achievements, but also several of his most famous inventions—objects such as the light bulb and the phonograph. Or, you could lay out the process by which he developed one of his best-known inventions—including how he resolved problems that surfaced while designing a particular invention.

Events

An event is a notable or exceptional occurrence, either from the present time or from some point in the past. Here are just a few examples of events on which you could focus an informative speech:

- the signing into law of a constitutional amendment to lower the voting age to eighteen years
- the discovery of a new planet or species
- the outcome of a high-profile murder trial
- the publication of an important new book
- an underdog's surprising victory over the frontrunner in a sporting event
- the emergence in the business world of a new and different kind of company
- the unearthing of new evidence suggesting the origins of humankind
- a wedding, funeral, or religious ritual in your family
- the Republican or Democratic National Convention
- the Banzai Pipeline Surf Invitational
- a commemoration of a tomb of the unknown soldier
- your town's extraordinary Fourth of July celebration
- Diddy's thirtieth birthday party in Long Island, New York

How do you decide what event would make a good topic for an informative speech? Look for events that your audience will consider exciting, newsworthy, historically important, or interesting because they are unfamiliar or surprising.

In delivering an informative speech about an event, you could easily use narrative to tell the story of how the event unfolded. You could also use description to explain how the event affected a group of people. Or, you could employ a blend of both narrative and description. For instance, suppose you were presenting a speech about what it was

like to earn your driver's license. You might include a funny story about how your nervousness during the driving test caused you to knock over a trash barrel by the side of the road—something many listeners might identify with. You could then use description to help your audience appreciate how getting a license is an event that marks many young people's transition from adolescence to adulthood or perhaps a turning point for someone who had moved from an urban area where a car was not necessary to a suburban area where it is.

Processes

Imagine that you're filing a tax return, changing a tire, planting a vegetable garden, or giving a friend a haircut. Or maybe you're thinking about how two countries resolve a border dispute, how Major League Baseball owners and the players' union negotiate the baseball salary cap for each team, or how marriages are arranged in a particular culture.

Each of these is a process—a series of steps or stages that lead to a particular outcome. You can detect processes both at the level of

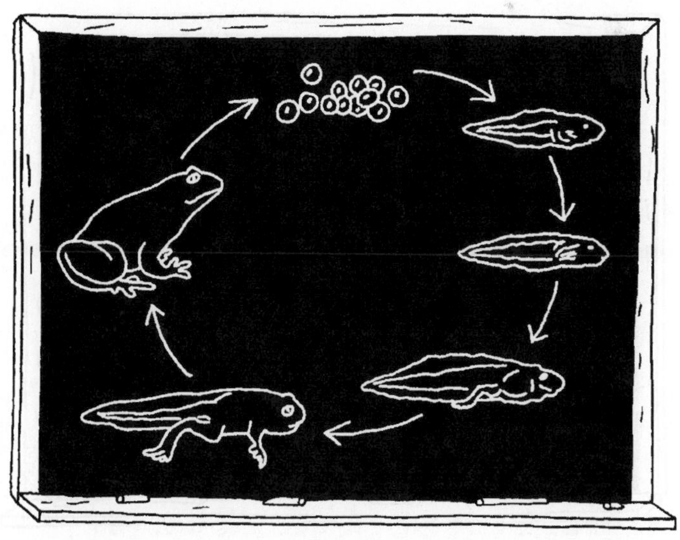

something localized and simple, such as changing a tire, and at a much broader level, such as the ways in which changes in labor and immigration laws and trade policies affect the cost of automobiles (including those same tires!) in different countries and markets. Thus, we sometimes suggest that processes can be seen at both the micro and macro levels (the view of a process from fifty feet or one from five thousand feet). Many of the informative presentations you may find in a speech class will lean towards the micro level, something easier to explain and grasp; but that shouldn't discourage you from trying a topic such as the ways in which global warming occurs. When presented as a process, even larger topics can still be digestible for most audiences.

Remember that some topics do not lend themselves well to a discussion of process—simply because of their sheer technical nature (for example, a speech about how changes in the tax code affect the concept of the alternative minimum tax). Does this mean you should avoid a technical topic? No; but it does mean that if you are selecting

a topic because it *is* process oriented, focus on subject matter that is within your audience's level of understanding, and try to break down the topic into smaller parts before you show how those parts work together as part of a larger process.

When you deliver an informative speech about a process, you will probably want to walk your listeners through the steps that make up the process, explaining how those steps are carried out and in what order.

Depending on your goal, use a variety of techniques to inform your audience about a particular process. For example, if you want listeners to understand how a particular object is made or how it works, you might use explanation to clarify what each step is and how it leads to the creation of the object.

By contrast, if your goal is to teach audience members how to perform the process themselves, combine both explanation and demonstration—that is, verbally and physically model the steps of the process.

To illustrate, suppose you're giving an informative speech about waxing to remove unwanted hair. You would probably want to explain how waxing works, and what the various stages are that lead to the

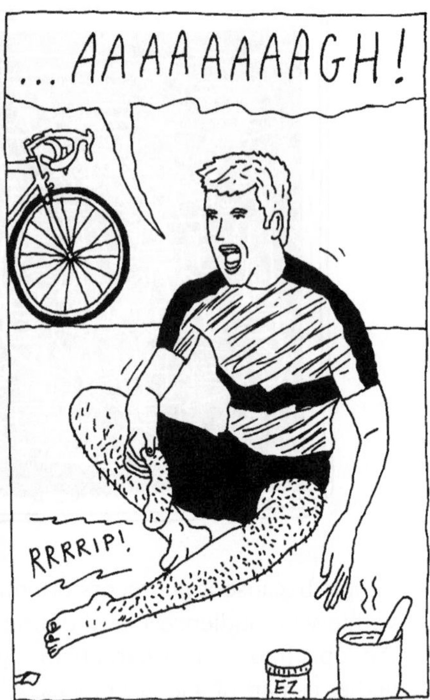

final (albeit painful) result. As one student did, you might then demonstrate by showing photos or a video from an actual waxing session with an aesthetician. If you were particularly brave, you could even wax part of your own leg to demonstrate.

In deciding which process to focus on in an informative speech, take care to avoid overused topics (such as how to make the perfect PB + J sandwich), topics related to alcohol (such as how to make Jello-shots or brew beer at home), or how to interpret dreams. Instead, think about processes that would be interesting and fresh for your listeners. Also, consider how you might discuss the impact of an important process. For instance, suppose you're informing your audience about how the baseball farm system works. In this case, you could add interest to the topic by using a narrative to convey how the process changes young players' lives by giving them a shot at the big leagues.

Ideas

An idea is a theory, a principle, a belief, or perhaps a value. Ideas are relatively abstract compared to other informative speech topics, such as an object, a person, or a process. For example, it's harder to describe the notion of "freedom of speech" than it is to explain what the aurora borealis looks like or how a motorcycle engine works. The idea of "freedom of speech" is more difficult to explain for two reasons: First, it's an idea and not a physical object or process; second, there are limits to "freedom of speech"—indeed, this concept has several subtleties that restrict its application in many situations (for example, it is illegal to incite certain kinds of violence or to threaten to kill another person).[2]

Some ideas are also loaded because people have difficulty agreeing on their meaning. Consider the notion of "terrorism." The meaning of terrorism seems obvious to many after the 9/11 attacks and their repercussions. But are all violent acts against civilians or noncombatants terrorism? Are nation-states guilty of terrorism when their troops accidentally kill civilians? Why do people say things like "One man's terrorism is another man's freedom fight?" Like freedom of expression, terrorism is a more complex and abstract notion than it may originally appear.

Here are some additional ideas that may constitute topics for an informative speech about an idea:

- family values
- fairness
- the economic impact of globalization
- Murphy's Law ("if something can go wrong, it will")
- the disadvantages of technology
- "It's better to give than receive."
- the separation of church and state
- free agency in professional sports

Because ideas are so abstract, it's important to select an idea carefully as you consider topics for an informative speech. Otherwise, you may fail to connect with your audience during your presentation. Be sure to consider your audience's interests and level of education while weighing potential ideas to discuss in your speech. For example, if you want to inform your listeners about the economic impact of globalization, think about how much your audience already knows about the topic. If their knowledge is scanty, you'll need to provide more background on globalization during your speech, or you may decide to select another topic with which your listeners are more familiar.

Also ask yourself whether your audience members have had prior exposure to the idea you want to discuss in your presentation. If they have—and did not find the idea compelling—you may want to consider selecting a different topic.

Finally, consider how you might make particularly abstract ideas more understandable to your listeners during your presentation. In a talk on the impact of globalization, for example, you could draw the following analogy: "Globalization is like agriculture. In agriculture, the more evenly you spread seeds across a large field, the more certain you can be that crops will grow in every corner of the field. Likewise, the more you allow commercial activity to flourish across many countries, the more you'll encourage economic well-being among the world's populations."

Most informative speeches about ideas require the use of definition and/or explanation, both of which enable you to clarify the meaning of the idea you're discussing and to examine its various ramifications. For instance, while the meaning of terrorism is hotly debated in academic and political circles, most people define it as some form of calculated violence (or the threat thereof) against civilians or noncombatants, all for the purpose of creating mass anxiety and panic while publicizing a political or social agenda.[3] An informative speech on terrorism might *begin* with that definition. But to further *clarify* the idea of terrorism for your audience, you could separate each part of the definition and explain it individually. For instance, to clarify what "publicizing a political or social agenda" means, you could offer several examples of groups who have committed violent acts and then used the resulting publicity to advance their causes.

DEVELOPING YOUR INFORMATIVE SPEECH

To develop an informative speech, you use the same strategies described in earlier chapters. Those strategies include analyzing your audience's background and needs, deciding which supporting materials to include, and determining how to organize the content of your talk. In this section, we focus on how to analyze your audience and how to select a technique that will help you organize your informative speech. Appropriate audience analysis and organization help ensure that you prepare a solid foundation and structure for your speech.

Analyzing Your Audience

As with any type of public presentation, audience analysis is essential for developing a successful informative speech. Yet analyzing your audience for an informative presentation raises unique challenges. Specifically, you'll want to focus on where and how your audience is situated for the informative presentation, your audience's specific demographics, and especially on common ground between you and your audience.

To analyze your audience, start by considering the characteristics of your speaking situation. If you are presenting an informative speech in class, note any requirements for the topic, format, and content of the presentation. If you're planning to deliver your speech outside of class, consider the occasion for your speech. Also note the forum (the setting where you will be speaking), the time of day intended for your presentation, the size of your audience, and the expected length of your speech.

Next, remember to examine audience **demographics**—particularly those most likely to influence your listeners' interest and disposition toward your topic. These may include political affiliation, group membership, occupation or academic major, race, ethnicity, gender, sexual orientation, income, age, religious affiliation, and family status—just to name a few.

Also look for common ground you might have with your audience—such as shared values, interests, and experiences. By noting common ground while developing an informative speech, you can incorporate strategies to strengthen your credibility, or ethos.

Selecting a Technique

Your audience analysis also informs your choice of technique—or organizational pattern—for delivering the informative speech. Which technique would *most* help you inform your audience about your topic: definition, explanation, description, demonstration, narrative—or a combination of these? Your choice of technique is crucial, because it helps you decide how you'll develop and organize the main points and supporting materials in your presentation.

For example, suppose you were considering using demonstration to present your informative speech. In this case, you would want to ask yourself the following questions:

- *Forum*: "Where will the audience be situated—and will there be ample space for me to move around as I give my demonstration?"
- *Audience size*: "How many people will be in my audience—and will they all be able to see and hear my demonstration?"

You should also consider audience size and details of the speaking forum when planning audiovisual aids for your informative speech. If you anticipate a small audience and cramped space, a PowerPoint presentation may be unnecessary; showing objects or offering simple handouts might create a more intimate setting. In a bigger forum with a large audience, you may be best served by projecting PowerPoint slides on a large screen—or even several large screens—combined with adequate amplification of your voice. When speaking in such situations, make sure you plan carefully where you will stand; you may want to stand in the center of the room, directly before the screen or screens, and control the audience's interaction with the audiovisuals by making the screen go blank after each point is made.

Conversely, let's say you were considering using explanation or description to deliver your speech. In this case, you would focus more on demographics to analyze your audience. Look for anything in your listeners' backgrounds and characteristics that may make it difficult for audience members to understand the explanation or description you're planning to offer in your speech. For instance, if you're planning to describe a Hmong wedding ceremony and your listeners have no knowledge of Hmong culture, you'll need to provide more details in your description. Or, if you're planning to explain the events leading up to the assassination of U.S. president John F. Kennedy, and your listeners are too young to have lived through the event, you'll want to provide a fuller explanation than you would for an older audience. Of course, cultural background and age are not exhaustive examples of demographics. You'll need to consider other characteristics as well to develop an effective informative speech.

What if you're thinking about using narrative to present your speech? Common ground becomes particularly important in this case. To tell a story that will interest and move your listeners, it helps if you have had some of the same life experiences or share some of the same values. When you and your audience have common ground, listeners will find it easier to believe you and identify with the narrative you're presenting.

PATTERNS FOR ORGANIZING AN INFORMATIVE SPEECH

Organizational Pattern	Pattern Description	Example
Spatial	Describes or explains elements or events as they occur in space.	A speech to explain the trajectory of a meteor that may come dangerously close to the earth.
Temporal	Moves from the beginning to the ending by referencing points in time.	A speech that describes a negotiation process, breaking down each of the bargaining steps as they occur in time.
Causal	Explains the roots of a phenomenon or process.	A presentation that explains how fossil fuel emissions contribute to global warming.
Comparison	Presents major similarities and differences between two items.	A speech that compares the global reach and power of the United States with that of ancient Rome.
Criteria-Application	Presents the topic as a condition (or series of conditions) that must be met in order for a conclusion to follow.	A speech to explain how U.S. troops might be withdrawn from Iraq if certain criteria or benchmarks are met.
Narrative	The speech as story, with characters and plot.	A speech to describe racism by relating a personal instance involving a hate crime directed at or witnessed by the speaker.
Categorical	Main points constitute separate topics, each of which supports the thesis.	A presentation to explain running a marathon, breaking it down into separate categories for training, nutrition, technique and style, and mental preparation.

CLARIFYING AND SIMPLIFYING YOUR MESSAGE

As you prepare your informative speech, focus on clarifying and simplifying your message as much as possible. You'll help your audience understand and thus retain your message.

Clarity is something you'll want to strive for in every informative speech, no matter what your topic is or who your listeners are. If you present a message that's confusing or use words that have vague meanings, it will be hard to connect with your audience.

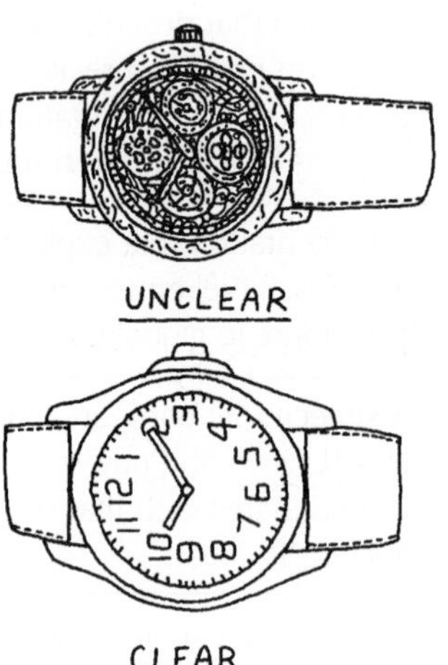

In addition to clarifying your message, your audience analysis will help you decide how much you should simplify your informative speech. For example, if listeners have little knowledge of your topic, and the topic is complex, simplicity will be vital. A student named Jean once gave an informative presentation on a complex, experimental genetic treatment doctors and research scientists could use to fight cancer. Her audience was made up of students in her speech class—few of whom had sufficient background to follow the technical details in her speech. Jean wisely simplified things by reducing "treatment" to "gene therapy." She then further simplified her topic by describing a simple three-step process for introducing genes into cells to prevent disease.

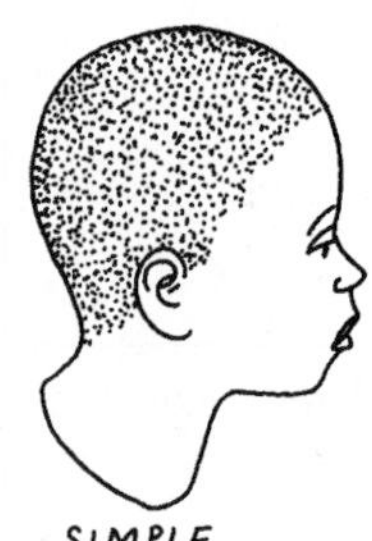

To clarify or simplify complex messages, consider the following techniques:

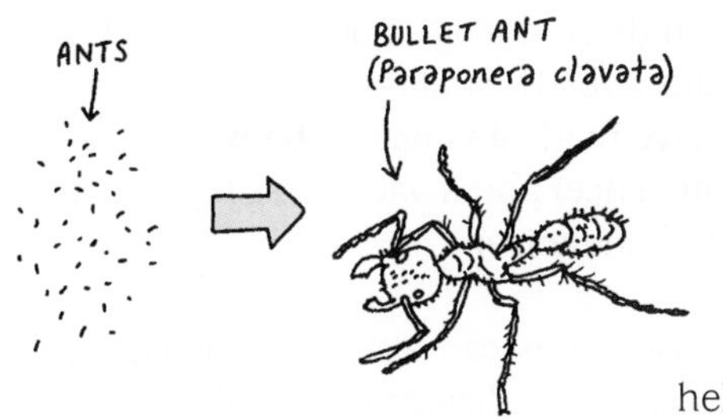

Move from General to Specific. Ask yourself: "At a minimum, what do I want my audience to take away from my speech? What basic message should the audience carry away?" Your answer can help you narrow down a general or broad topic to a specific, simpler one—as in Jean's speech on gene therapy.

Reduce the Quantity of Information You Present. An informative speech may contain a tremendous amount of information for the audience to hear, process, and remember. An old adage still rings true here: "Less is more." Look for ways to pare down the details you present. Obviously, a speech about gene therapy could contain huge volumes of information. Jean effectively reduced the quantity of information she presented by boiling the details down to a three-step process.

Make Complex Information Seem Familiar. You can further clarify a complex message by using definition to explain difficult-to-follow terms and ideas. You can also avoid **jargon**—technical or insider terminology not easily understood by people outside a certain

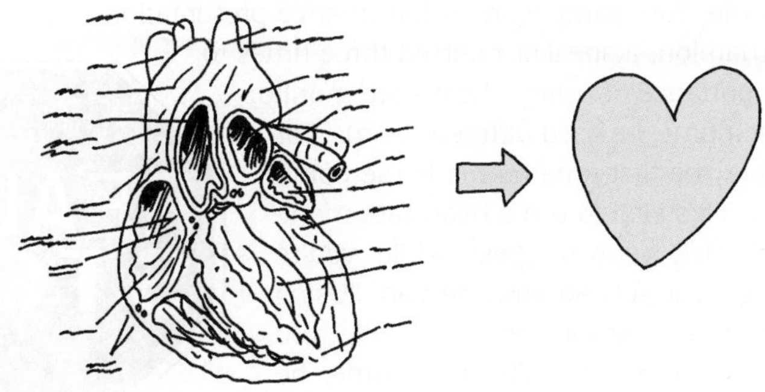

group or field. In addition, you can draw analogies between complex ideas and things your listeners are already familiar with and understand.[4] For example, Jean could have made an analogy between gene therapy (a new concept for her audience) and a vaccine against polio (something probably familiar to her audience).

Use Audiovisual Aids. Audiovisual aids can also help you clarify and simplify your message. For instance, a diagram of the three-step gene-therapy process Jean was describing could enable her listeners to better envision the process and thus remember it. Likewise, if you were giving a speech on various bird calls, you could play a recording of a particular call instead of relying only on lengthy descriptions or demonstrations of what the call sounds like.

Reiterate Your Message. Through *reiteration*, you clarify a complex message by referring to it several times, but with different words each time. For example, in an informative presentation about training for a triathlon, a speaker referred three times to the importance of using a heart-rate monitor. But each time, he used different words. For example, the first time he made the point, he said, "It's vital to use a heart-rate monitor to track your progress while you're training." The second time, he said, "Using a heart-rate monitor can really help you track your progress." The third time, he

said, "The more you use the monitor, the more information you'll have on how you're progressing." By reiterating key points, you help your audience remember your message.

Repeat Your Message. Conveying a key point several times using the same words can also help you ensure that your audience understands your message. For example, while introducing the gene-therapy process, Jean could say something like, "This three-step process offers the best hope for treating cancer in the future." Then, in the conclusion of her speech, she could say, "Let me repeat: this three-step process offers the best hope for treating cancer in the future."

SAMPLE INFORMATIVE SPEECH

SPIDER SILK: A MIRACLE MATERIAL DERIVED FROM . . . GOATS?

Rachel Parish
Southeastern Illinois College

Student Rachel Parish gave this informative speech in the 2007 finals of an annual national tournament hosted by Phi Rho Pi, a group that fosters public speaking and debate for junior and community college students throughout the United States. In this speech about an object, Rachel explains the astonishing strength and versatility of a material that may surprise her listeners—spider silk. Rachel's speech is organized categorically, or by topic, with the main points describing spider silk's properties, the means of producing it, and a number of its applications.

In the classic book *Charlotte's Web*, we find the story of a loving spider saving pitiful Wilbur from becoming bacon through messages spun in her webs. However, this is not the first time that such power has come from such a seemingly delicate medium.

In ancient Greece, spider webs were used to stop bleeding in open wounds. Aborigines use spider silk in small fishing lines. And how could we not mention Peter Parker's amazing ability to swing from buildings and catch the bad guys, all through the power of the web?

Now that last example may be fictional, but Spider-Man's formidable weapon, the web, is no less amazing in real life. Spider silk is one of the strongest fibers known; it is incredibly fine and tough, and as the November 9, 2006, *London Daily Mail* tells us, "When woven into a fiber, it is weight-for-weight five times stronger than steel." •

• Rachel's attention-getter includes stories and compelling facts.

So we know that spider webs or spider silk is tough, and over the past decade we found it to have both practical and medicinal benefits for us. However, to date we've never actually seen any of the benefits. Why? Well, gathering large quantities of spider silk has been relatively impossible until now. You see, while we may not have a real-life Spider-Man, we do have Spider*goat*. This is a transgenic goat that's producing spider silk on a much larger scale than Charlotte ever could. •

• "What's in it for them": a startling fact about goats plus the benefits of spider silk.

Today, we'll learn the value of spider silk and how these scientifically altered goats are allowing its once unavailable advantages to become a reality. First, we'll look at the background of spider silk; second, the goat's role in production; and finally, its current and future uses. •

• Rachel quickly gives her thesis and previews her three main points—organized topically.

Let's first learn the value of spider silk and how these goats are allowing its once unobtainable potential to be a reality. According to BBCNews.com, July 12, 2006, "Spider silk has been admired by scientists for decades due to its unique combination of strength, toughness, flexibility, and light weight; its thickness is less than one-tenth the size of a human hair, but it has 400,000 pounds per square inch of strength. To put this in perspective, if you built a massive spider web where each strand was the width of a pencil, you could catch a 747 jumbo jet in full flight.

So if spider silk is indeed the strongest fiber on earth, why haven't we taken advantage of this miracle material before? The June 16, 2006, *Science and Technology* tells us that "spiders are incredibly hard to farm so silk can be harvested, mainly due to a spider's nature." • Basically, if you put two spiders together in a confined space, due to their cannibalistic nature, you'll suddenly find yourself with only one spider.

• Rachel establishes her sources' credibility here and throughout by citing publication title and date. She could add even more credibility by including consistently the author's name and credentials.

In addition, even when they are contained properly, you can only milk so much silk from a spider. A study this past November by Randy Lewis of the University of Wyoming showed that even when dealing with large spiders, on a good day you can only gather 1.5 mg of silk. Thus, even if you could get the cannibals to get along, a spider farm capable of raising enough useful silk would simply be impossible. •

• Here and throughout, Rachel offers a variety of supporting materials, mainly examples, expert testimony, and statistics.

However, all that has now changed. Last year, Nexia Biotechnologies—a Canadian research firm—began looking at normal farm goats as the key to bringing spider silk to the masses. According to Christopher Helman, in Forbes.com, February 19, 2001, Jeffrey Turner, a geneticist at Nexia, discovered that the silk gland of spiders and the milk gland of goats were almost identical, but the goat's is obviously much bigger. At the turn of the millennium, Nexia began implanting spider genes into goats in order to breed "spider goats" capable of producing spider silk in large enough quantities for commercial use. The end result was Webster and Pete, the first two goats born with the spider web gene.

So now that we've looked past the roadblocks to cultivating spider silk by showing the creation of a feasible silk resource thanks to Webster and Pete here, let's examine the process by which the spider gene was passed on to the goats. • According to the January 15, 2006, issue of the journal *Nature*, "Spider silk starts out as a substance called scleroprotein, which shoots out from the spider's web

• An effective transition signals the end of a previous point and introduces the next one.

spinnerets. . . . [I]t dries into a thread, and when this thread hardens we end up with something that looks a little more familiar to us."

When Nexia discovered that the silk glands of spiders were similar to goats' mammary glands, Nexia applied this discovery to dairy goats. Taking a goat embryo, Nexia injected the spider gene controlling the creation of silk into the goat's mammary cells. These cells then took effect and activated the female goats when they started lactating, or creating milk for their young. When the lactation period in the goat is over these cells stop functioning and stop producing silk until the goat starts lactating again. According to *Materials Today*, December 2002, Jeffrey Turner reports that each transgenic goat is "capable of making 'literally miles' of this spider silk–based material." Fifteen thousand goats could produce enough silk to meet projected medical and industrial demands. Plus, because they're not cannibalistic, we're able to farm goats on a large scale. •

• Rachel offers this explanation of a process within her larger topical organization.

However, the spiders do have one advantage: the goats can't spin the silk they produce, so then there's a weaving process. As explained in the October 10, 2006, airing of *Modern Marvels* on the History Channel, "The goats are milked as they normally would be, then the milk is put into a centrifuge that spins rapidly. This causes the silk fibers to separate from the milk so they can be extracted. Salts are then added to the silk fibers to help them harden. Once this step is completed, you have what researchers have dubbed 'bio-steel.'" According to the June 3, 2006, *Journal of Biological Chemistry*, this new silk made from spider-enhanced goats is the same strength and composition as normal spider silk. The method is environmentally safe and the goats are not harmed in any way during the milking process. •

• Rachel shows solid audience analysis by anticipating listener concerns: the process is environmentally safe and doesn't harm the goats.

So we've examined the background of spider silk, its genetic switch to goats, and how it has evolved into bio-steel. But what benefits can we anticipate from this evolution? Will the use of goat silk bring us from the research lab to the battlefield and the operating room? •

• Questions act as a transition and keep listeners involved.

Biotech Week, December 13, 2006, reports that bio-steel is now being used to construct bulletproof clothing for soldiers and police. Dr. Randolph Lewis, a biologist at the University of Wyoming, stated in the same issue of *Biotech Week* that Kevlar, the most popular fiber used in bulletproof vests, is very difficult to make and requires a chemical processing that is highly damaging to the environment. Unlike Kevlar, spider silk bio-steel is made in water-based conditions and it's completely biodegradable. • In addition, in tests performed in early 2006 at the University of Wyoming, it was proven that when woven into a bulletproof vest, spider silk was stronger and more durable than the now-outdated Kevlar.

• Rachel returns to the theme of environmental safety.

Yet bio-steel's most promising benefits are medicinal rather than military. According to the Royal College of Surgeons of England, in "Secrets of the Spider Web," March 9, 2007, "the demand for spider silk in the medical profession is high with a myriad of potential uses such as scaffolds, bone grafts, or ligament repair." The real strength of bio-steel as an internal support is its great wall strength and its ability to naturally dissolve over time without the need of additional surgeries. In addition, the spider silk bio-steel can be used as wonderful, durable, and biodegradable stitches that can be used in the most delicate of areas due to the material's thinness and strength. What's more, as *Science*, June 23, 2006, reports, spider silk bio-steel provokes a very low immune response when introduced into the body. What does that mean for us? Well heavy immune responses cause rejection of artificial medical implants, thus making bio-steel a much more successful option than any previous materials. •

• By outlining bio-steel's medical uses, Rachel again shows what's in it for listeners.

The main challenge for researchers is breeding enough goats to meet the demand for bio-steel. However, according to the October 31, 2006, *CBC News*, "If breeding continues as is, then the University of Wyoming's herd of goats alone will be bountiful enough to meet commercial demands by the end of 2008." In 2006 they produced over 5,200 pounds of spider silk, and just this past August the UW researchers received a quarter-million-dollar grant from the Department of Defense to expand their output, so the future of goat bio-steel looks very promising.

Today we looked at the background of spider silk, the goat's role in production, and finally its current and future applications. We can see the value of goat bio-steel for both military and medicinal uses, and in time perhaps we could imagine America's favorite web slinger changing from Peter Parker to Pete and Webster. •

• The conclusion brings the speech full circle with a reference to Spider-Man.

SAMPLE INFORMATIVE SPEECH

PRECISION-GUIDED TUMOR KILLERS

Elvia Anguiano
Moraine Valley College

Elvia's informative speech focuses on an experimental cancer treatment that may improve on current chemotherapy techniques. She uses a categorical (topical) pattern to explore the current methods and to describe the benefits, pitfalls, and possibilities for this new treatment. By praising the possible benefits of the technique while also exploring some potential drawbacks, Elvia informs her audience ethically by showing different sides of the topic.

Have you ever heard one of those parodies of medicine ads before? You know, one that goes something like: "If you suffer from back pain, then *BelieveAll* is the right medication for you. Before taking *BelieveAll*, ask your doctor. Some side effects include insomnia, kidney infections, heart attacks, infertility for men and women under thirty-five, uncontrollable flatulence, and spontaneous self-combustion." •

• Humorous attention-getter will connect with many audience members.

Parodies like these can be very funny, but real side effects are not. As many cancer patients will probably tell you, one of the scariest things about having cancer is the treatments themselves—because of their horrible side effects.

But it may no longer have to be this way. Today, I'm here to tell you about an experimental new method of chemotherapy—precision-guided tumor killers, or PGTKs • — and the possibility of its eradicating tumors more effectively than traditional chemotherapy, without all the horrible side effects. •

• By using the acronym "PGTK," Elvia creates a memorable label. Since the label itself is a kind of jargon, she makes sure to explain this acronym a second time, later in the speech.

• Elvia offers a precise statement of her topic.

So that you may all get an idea of the importance of this new method, keep the following estimates in mind: the National Cancer Institute's Web site, accessed September 30, 2006, estimated that in 2006 there would be more than 1.3 million new cases of cancer and over 500,000 deaths in the U.S. alone. Furthermore, an article in the March 23, 2007, *Chicago Tribune* noted that, as of right now, one in twenty people worldwide has cancer. By 2020, that number will be one in nineteen. Think of the hundreds of people you have seen today, all the people here that could now have cancer or one day have cancer. •

• Elvia offers statistics about cancer rates to show relevance to listeners.

So that you may all better understand PGTKs, you need to learn a little bit more about traditional chemotherapy, what PGTKs are, how they work, and finally their future potential and current limitations. •

• Elvia offers a preview of main points.

Today chemotherapy is one of the most commonly used methods to fight cancer. To understand why its use has become so widespread, we need to learn what it is, how it works, and why it has such horrible side effects. To begin with, chemotherapy was first developed in the 1950s—as reported by the Web site of the American Cancer Society, accessed November 27, 2006—when some people were accidentally exposed to mustard gas in a government weaponry experiment and the exposure resulted in a lowered white cell count. This intrigued the scientists, who then injected mustard gas into cancer patients and were shocked at the remarkable improvements. This discovery led to the development of many other drugs that now treat cancer. Today, chemotherapy is a mixture of many of those drugs.

• Elvia offers a quick internal preview.

Now that we know what chemotherapy is, we will move on to how it works. • According to the American Cancer Society Web site, accessed September 30, 2006, chemotherapy may be administered into the body through three different methods: a pill, a shot, and through an IV. The chemotherapy then courses through the body, seeking any cells in the process of reproduction. It then poisons those cells so that when they try to reproduce, or split, they are unable to and therefore die off.

Although chemotherapy has been very effectively attacking cancer for the past sixty years, there is one major drawback: chemotherapy cannot tell the difference between actively reproducing cells of cancer and those of normal tissue. This is why so many chemotherapy recipients suffer such horrible side effects, including fatigue, nausea and vomiting, pain, hair loss, blood clotting problems, and effects on vital organs. •

• An effective explanation of the chemotherapy process and its drawbacks.

Now that we know a little bit more about traditional chemotherapy, we may move on to the new method: precision-guided tumor killers, or what I referred to earlier as PGTKs. These are hollow spheres that are 1,000 times smaller than the size of a pinpoint. PGTKs are filled with small doses of chemotherapy and are studded with aptamers on the outside. According to Dr. Omid Farokhzad, aptamer researcher and assistant professor at Harvard Medical School, quoted in the August 2006 issue of *Popular Science*, "aptamers are like the GPS in your car. They allow the direct delivery of the PGTKs to cancer cells, leaving all normal cells in the body alone." •

• Analogy helps clarify a potentially complex idea—aptamers are like a car's GPS.

PGTKs are designed to work in a very similar way to chemotherapy. The PGTKs are injected into the body. They then course through the blood searching for any cancer cell, using their GPS system. Once they find a cancer cell, they latch onto that cancer cell in a similar way to standard chemotherapy. After a while, the cancer cells absorb the PGTKs. Inside, the PGTKs open up and release the chemotherapy. Once poisoned, the cancer cells burst and die off. •

• Explanation of the process of the PGTKs' function highlights advantages as compared to the earlier explanation of traditional chemotherapies.

Having learned what the PGTKs are and how they are designed to work, we may now focus on why they may prove more effective and better tolerated than traditional chemotherapy. According to an April 10, 2006, issue of the *Proceedings of the National Academy of Sciences*, researchers compared these chemo-loaded nanoparticles to regular chemotherapy in mice with prostate cancer. They found that after a single injection of the PGTKs, complete tumor reduction was observed in five of seven mice with a survivability of 100 percent. In contrast, two of seven mice in the chemotherapy group had complete tumor reduction with survivability of only 57 percent.

Thus far, Dr. Farokhzad's research has been most effective in targeting prostate cancer cells. As he noted in an interview published in the November 10, 2005, issue of *Nano World News*, "we wanted to focus on a cancer model where a localized tumor has a localized way of being treated in clinical practice." And Dr. Farokhzad's research has been well-received in the medical and scientific communities; in the last several years he and his colleagues have published numerous articles in leading peer-reviewed medical journals, including the July 2006 issue of the *American Journal of Drug Delivery*, the February 2007 issue of *Biomaterials,* and the October 2007 issue of *Nanomedicine*. •

• Citing several peer-reviewed sources helps to support Elvia's credibility.

Expressing his high hopes for the future of PGTK therapy, Dr. Farokhzad noted in *Science Central News* on May 11, 2006, that "Our system is both significantly more effective than traditional chemotherapy and remarkably less toxic, allowing the long list of chemotherapy side effects to shorten significantly, and allowing cancer patients to continue with their current lifestyles." Venture capitalists seem to agree. The November 27, 2007, issue of *Red Herring*, a business and technology magazine, reported that a biotechnology company called Bind-Biosciences, cofounded by Dr.

Farokhzad, had raised approximately 16 million dollars in a second round of venture capital funding—all for the purpose of developing these nanoparticles further. The same article added that demand in the United States for nanotechnology-based medicines could grow to 39 billion dollars by 2011 and up to 82 billion dollars by 2016.

Having learned about PGTKs, it is time to look into the future potential and current limitations of this new system. Although the future uses for the PGTKs are focused mainly on treating cancer, they are not limited to it. Since the PGTKs really are hollow spheres, the medicine inside can vary. Also, researchers are working toward a system whereby the aptamers' target can be changed—just like the target on your GPS—expanding the use of the PGTKs to other diseases and procedures. For example, if you fill the PGTKs with small doses of Carbatrol and target the aptamers to nerve cells in the brain, you could treat epilepsy. Or, as reported on the National Cancer Institute's Web site, accessed October 1, 2006, if you fill the PGTKs with mercury and target a specific organ in the body, you could make CT scans and other imaging procedures much more accurate and the diagnosis of doctors much more accurate.

• Elvia acts as an ethical informative speaker by noting drawbacks of PGTKs.

Although the promise of PGTKs is extraordinary, there are some drawbacks. • As Professor Miqin Zhang—a material scientist at the University of Washington in Seattle—stated, one drawback is that the PGTKs must remain separate to do their job. If they should join together, they become toxic to healthy tissue. Another drawback that Professor Zhang mentions is that at different stages of development, cancer cells have different molecular makeup. So, the PGTKs could easily detect an early stage of cancer using their GPS system, but they may not be so successful at a later stage of cancer. Keeping these drawbacks in mind, scientists continue to do their research and their testing to confirm their findings.

Looking back, we've learned a little bit more about traditional chemotherapy. We've learned about a new system known as PGTKs, their future potential, and current limitations. • Cancer patients suffer enough with the pain and fear of having cancer. They should not have to increase their pain and suffering because of treatments that are supposed to save their lives. Perhaps one day you or someone you know may have cancer, and in fact, you probably will know someone who does. Just remember that neither you nor they may have to suffer or die; should this treatment be perfected and approved, patients will gladly take it. The ads for these new medicines would not need to be parodied as yet another treatment with horrible side effects. Instead this could be a case where the medicine is actually better than the side effects. •

• "Looking back . . ." indicates the start of the conclusion, followed by a summary of main points.

• Clincher is a compelling hypothetical story that reconnects with the introduction.

SUMMARY

"Effective informative speakers share information in an accessible, understandable, and compelling manner."

As the opening example about the speech on water safety suggested, informative speaking is about teaching your listeners something and increasing their awareness of your topic. You probably use informative speaking many times during a typical day—whenever you're defining, explaining, describing, demonstrating, or telling a story about something. Whether you're speaking informatively in everyday situations or delivering a formal presentation to a class or other type of audience, you can greatly enhance your effectiveness by applying the key practices presented in this chapter.

First, know how and when to use the five techniques for informative speaking: definition, explanation, description, demonstration, and narrative. Second, decide on the type of

informative speech you want to give—whether it will be about an object, an individual or a group, an event, a process, or an idea. Third, use audience analysis to decide which technique you should use to organize your speech and how much to simplify your message.

When you apply these practices, you improve the odds of achieving your purpose in giving an informative speech. You enable your audience members to learn something new and important, and you hone their understanding, awareness, or sensitivity to your topic.

Key Terms

TECHNIQUES FOR INFORMING

definition
explanation
description
demonstration
narrative

DEVELOPING YOUR INFORMATIVE SPEECH

demographics

CLARIFYING AND SIMPLIFYING YOUR MESSAGE

jargon

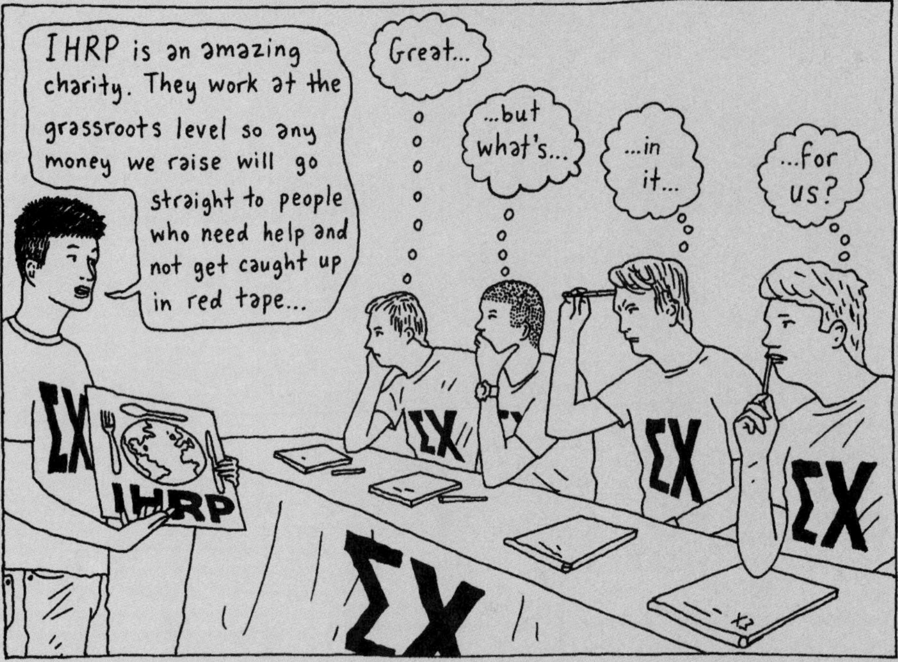

IHRP is an amazing charity. They work at the grassroots level so any money we raise will go straight to people who need help and not get caught up in red tape...

Great...

...but what's...

...in it...

...for us?

IHRP

ΣX

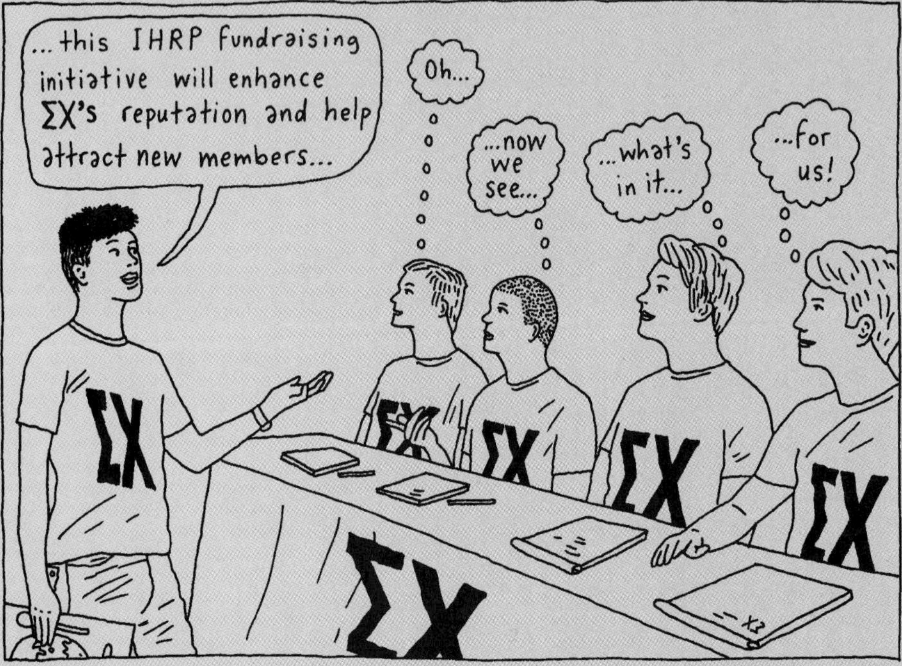

...this IHRP fundraising initiative will enhance ΣX's reputation and help attract new members...

Oh...

...now we see...

...what's in it...

...for us!

ΣX

16 PERSUASIVE SPEAKING

"Good persuaders make strategic choices in an ethical manner."

Jorge was excited: he had recently joined a fraternity at the university he attended, and he had an idea that he couldn't wait to share with the leadership council. His thought? To have the fraternity conduct a large fundraising drive for an international hunger-relief program. Jorge had read an article in the newspaper about the program and considered it a very worthy cause. Moreover, when he was a child, his family had always supported such programs, and he knew how important such aid was to people in need. He felt certain that the fraternity would be interested in the project.

During a council meeting, he presented his idea to the fraternity's leaders, complete with statistics showing how aid programs help mitigate hunger throughout the world. He even provided a detailed breakdown of the work needed to conduct the fundraiser. But to his surprise, he got a lukewarm response. Though the council members seemed somewhat interested during his presentation, they were non-committal about dedicating the required resources to the project. And in the weeks following his speech, he didn't hear back from them; they just didn't seem to share his enthusiasm for the project.

Jorge didn't realize it, but he had made an error that's all too common among people seeking to persuade others to adopt their ideas: he had neglected to explain how his proposal would benefit his listeners—a key element in any persuasive speech. For example, during his presentation to the leadership council, Jorge could have pointed out that by conducting the fundraising drive, the fraternity not only would help ease hunger, it would also enhance its reputation on campus and in the wider community. As a result, the fraternity would probably attract more members, solving a problem of declining membership that it had been experiencing in recent years. Because Jorge hadn't answered his listeners' question "What's in it for us?" he failed to deliver that crucial bit of motivating power that makes a speech truly persuasive.

As Jorge discovered firsthand, knowing how to speak persuasively is a vital skill for all areas in life. Consider your own situation: Do you want to get a new policy adopted on campus? advance in your career? influence members of your community to support an important cause? get your roommate to listen to the music you want to hear? win a major contract for your company from a new customer? get an extension on the deadline for a late paper? In these and many other cases, you'll need to master the art of speaking persuasively if you hope to generate the outcomes you want.

In this chapter, we introduce the topic of persuasive speaking. We start by explaining the nature of a persuasive

speech. Then we show you how to select an appropriate thesis, main points, and supporting materials based on your audience analysis. We also consider the ethical obligations of a persuasive speaker and present several strategies for organizing a persuasive speech. In Chapter 17, we'll go into more detail about specific methods of persuasion.

THE NATURE OF A PERSUASIVE SPEECH

In a **persuasive speech**, you attempt to influence your audience members' beliefs, attitudes, or actions. To do so, you should consider three distinguishing characteristics of persuasive speeches.

Persuasive Speeches Attempt to Influence Audience Members

When giving a persuasive speech, you always want to make a specific impact on your listeners based on your desired outcomes. One approach is to encourage listeners to adopt your point of view on a topic. For example, you might seek to convince your classmates that your college's general education requirements are excessive or that people should offer more alternatives to alcoholic beverages at parties.

If audience members already agree with your perspective, you may try to *strengthen their commitment*. For instance, your classmates may already concur that there are not enough healthy food and drink options in campus vending machines. You could seek to convince them to take immediate action to address the problem.

If many members of the audience disagree with your perspective on an issue, you may attempt to *weaken their commitment to their viewpoint*. For example, suppose you oppose capital punishment, but many class members favor the death penalty in murder cases and

believe that death sentences should be carried out promptly. Rather than trying to convince your listeners that the death penalty is wrong (an objective you are unlikely to achieve), you could instead try to persuade them that delays in executions can help innocent people go free. To do so, you could point out that in recent years a number of death-row inmates have been found innocent thanks to new DNA technology developed years after a guilty verdict. If it weren't for execution delays, these inmates would have been wrongly put to death.

You may also seek to persuade audience members to *take a specific action*. Asking students to drink less caffeine, serve on the college's library improvement committee, or vote for an activity-fee increase would be examples of this type of speech.

Persuasive Speeches Utilize Strategic Discourse

To give an effective persuasive speech, you use **strategic discourse**—the process of selecting arguments that will best achieve your rhetorical purpose in an ethical manner. Aristotle wrote that rhetoric involves "observing in any given case the available means of persuasion."[1] What he meant was that, with any persuasive speech topic, there are many arguments you might make to support your thesis. Your job is to present the most strategic discourse possible; that is, to select the arguments *most* likely to persuade your particular listeners.

To make such selections wisely, you must understand the audience's perspective on your topic. For example, suppose you want to persuade your classmates to comparison-shop for student loans. You assume that your audience is aware of recent news reports suggesting that the lenders recommended by some colleges do not offer the best loans for students. But if your classmates don't believe this is a problem at your school, you will need to supply proof. Otherwise, your listeners probably won't go to the trouble of shopping around for a new loan.

Analyzing your audience can also help you select the right blend of ethos (credibility), logos (logic), or pathos (emotion) as you present your appeal. (Ethos, pathos, and logos are introduced in Chapter 17.) For instance, Jorge could have enhanced his ethos with the fraternity council members by telling them about his family's success in supporting aid programs—presenting a more persuasive argument by bolstering his credibility. And he could have intensified the pathos in his speech by painting a disturbing picture of what might happen if hunger became more widespread *and* if the fraternity's membership continued to decline.

Persuasive Speeches Advocate Fact, Value, or Policy Claims

In any persuasive speech, you will make one of three types of claims: a fact claim, value claim, or policy claim.

Fact claims assert that something is true or false. Factual claims that are debatable can make especially strong persuasive speech topics. For example, is human activity indeed the primary cause of climate change and global warming? Has the 1996 federal welfare reform law decreased poverty in the United States? Do first-person shooter video games cause players to commit violent crimes? Because each of these questions is debatable, you could come up with an argument supporting either a "yes" or "no" answer.

Value claims attach a judgment (such as good, bad, moral, or immoral) to a subject. Examples of persuasive speeches making these claims include "Physician-assisted suicide is immoral," "The war in Iraq is not worth the costs," "The Bush administration's tax cuts have been good for the United States," and "It is unfair to deny marriage to same-sex couples."

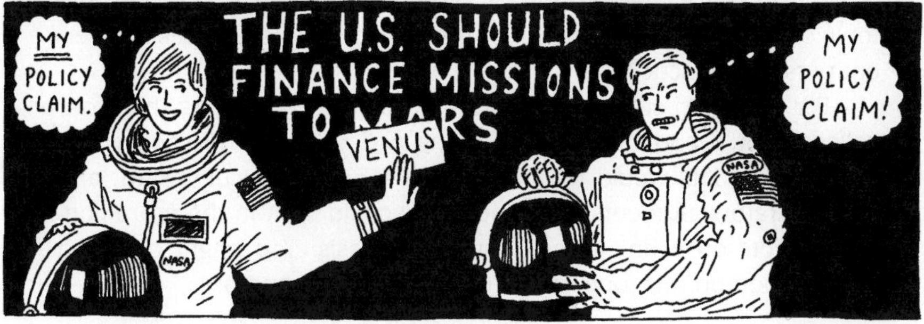

Whereas many people can reach agreement on factual claims when presented with enough evidence, value claims are more challenging for persuaders to make. Audience members' ideas of right and wrong may be deeply held and stem from fundamental religious or philosophical beliefs—and thus be difficult to change. If you decide to make a value claim in a persuasive speech, select one that your audience is at least open to considering. For example, with enough evidence, you could probably convince your classmates that more rigorous graduation requirements would be good for the university. By contrast, you'd probably stand little chance of significantly changing their views on abortion.

Policy claims advocate action by organizations, institutions, or members of your audience. Examples include arguing that your state legislature should raise the minimum wage or that your listeners should invest in stocks, eat more vegetables, or volunteer to assist with disaster relief.

Now that we've considered the nature of a persuasive speech, let's take a closer look at the strategic decisions you need to make when crafting a presentation intended to persuade.

FRAMING YOUR ARGUMENT BASED ON AUDIENCE DISPOSITION

Your listeners' disposition—their attitude toward your topic—should affect your approach to persuading them. As we discussed in Chapter 5, your audience may be hostile, sympathetic, or neutral toward the topic of your speech. And each of these dispositions requires a different persuasive tactic.

For example, suppose you want to convince listeners that your college should adopt an open parking policy. Under this policy, the best parking lots would no longer be reserved for faculty, staff, and administrators. Students and employees could park in the more convenient lots on a first-come, first-served basis. You might deliver a presentation on this topic to several different audiences:

- a committee of faculty and administrators
- a student senate meeting
- a group of students who live on campus, most of whom do not own cars

Although you want to advocate open parking with each of these audiences, you wouldn't present the same speech to all three. Faculty and administrators may have a hostile disposition toward your idea, because the current arrangement provides them with designated staff

parking in prime locations. They might even believe that the current policy is fair, since they had to park in remote locations back when they were students. On the other hand, student senate members are likely to have a sympathetic disposition, because they would probably appreciate open parking themselves and they need to take pro-student positions to get reelected. Finally, students who don't have a car may have a neutral disposition, given that parking policies do not directly affect them. They may support student rights in general, but they may not be motivated to invest much time and energy promoting open parking.

To draft an argument or thesis that will persuade each audience to support your idea, consider which proposals they are open to accepting and which they will reject without further consideration. Audience members have a **latitude of acceptance**, which is the range of positions on a given issue that are acceptable to them. They also have a set of positions that are unacceptable, which is their **latitude of rejection**.[2] Moreover, if your listeners are very concerned about the issue you'll be discussing in your speech, their latitude of acceptance

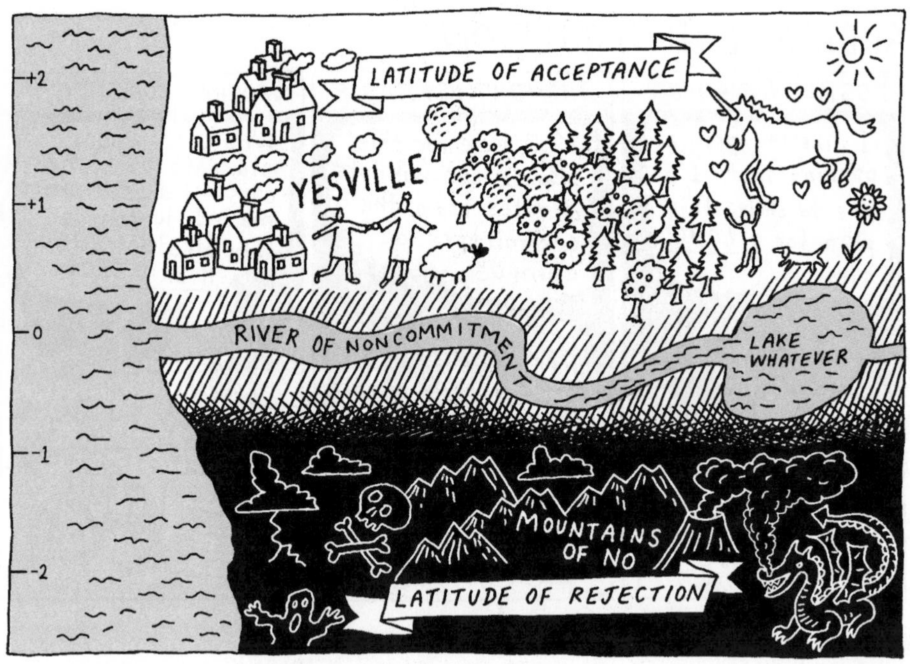

will be narrower. If the issue is not very important to them, they will be open to a broader range of positions.[3]

Therefore, you're most likely to persuade your listeners to change their minds if the position you take on your speech topic falls within their latitude of acceptance and if they do not feel strongly about the issue under discussion. Conversely, you won't likely persuade audience members if your position falls within their latitude of rejection and if they have very strong viewpoints on your topic that differ from yours. Under these conditions, your speech may even produce a **boomerang effect**—pushing your listeners to oppose your idea even more vigorously than they already do.[4]

How does all this work in practice? Let's return to the example of your effort to promote open parking on campus. If you are addressing the faculty and administration (a hostile audience), a speech advocating a change to open parking is likely to fall within these listeners' latitude of rejection. Thus, it would be counterproductive to take that position in your speech. However, your audience analysis might reveal that these listeners would be willing to try the policy for a week or convert a single faculty lot to open parking. If these options fall within their latitude of acceptance, consider framing your thesis around one of them.

Conversely, when you address the student senate (a sympathetic audience), you can ask for much more. Their latitude of acceptance may include not only a vote in support of your proposal, but also a willingness to give their time to your campaign. Thus, for this audience, you could select an ambitious thesis—such as asking student representatives to pass a resolution declaring their support *and* to meet with college administrators to promote your idea.

Finally, you would take still another approach for the students who do not drive to campus (a neutral audience). If you asked them to sign a petition advocating open parking, that would probably fall within their latitude of acceptance because they likely support benefits for

BOOMERANG EFFECT NIGHTMARES

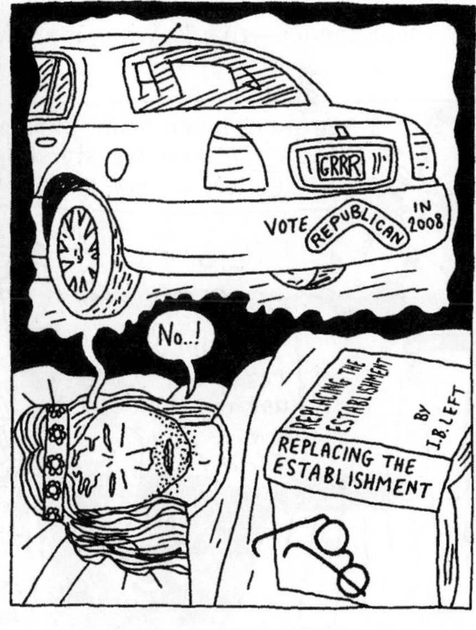

students and because signing such a document requires little effort on their part. However, if you asked them to pass out flyers, this greater demand on their time might fall within their latitude of rejection.

INCORPORATING PERSUASIVE STRATEGIES

Once you have used your audience analysis to select an appropriate thesis, it's time to select main points and subpoints that will support your argument. In this section, we discuss some strategies for approaching this task.

Relate Main and Supporting Points to Your Audience

No matter what your thesis is, there will typically be a wide variety of main points and subpoints you might use to support it—far more than you'll have time to present in a five-to-ten-minute speech. Therefore, select only those points that will be most persuasive to your audience. Your message is more likely to succeed when it is relevant to the audience—that is, when it answers their question "What's in it for

me?"[5] You can show relevance by indicating how accepting your thesis will satisfy your listeners' needs, connect with their values, or benefit them in some specific way. In this section, we take a closer look at these three forms of relevance.

Appealing to Your Audience's Needs. Audience members have **needs**—objects they desire and feelings that must be satisfied. Human needs powerfully affect how we behave and how we respond to one another's ideas. Experts from previous eras, such as psychologist Abraham Maslow[6] and social critic Vance Packard,[7] have identified specific sets of needs, and these needs continue to be emphasized in many persuasive appeals.

The most basic human needs are physiological: we require food, drink, health, and shelter to survive. Once we've had these needs met, we attend to safety needs, which include economic security and protection from danger. If our physiological and safety needs are fulfilled, we seek to satisfy social needs, including love and friendship. From there, we strive for self-esteem, the feeling that comes from being respected and valued as contributing members of society. Finally, to satisfy what Maslow called self-actualization needs, we seek opportunities for creativity, personal growth, and self-fulfillment.

If you can relate your message to your listeners' various needs, then you'll be more likely to persuade them to support your idea. Audience members will be inclined to listen closely and ultimately agree

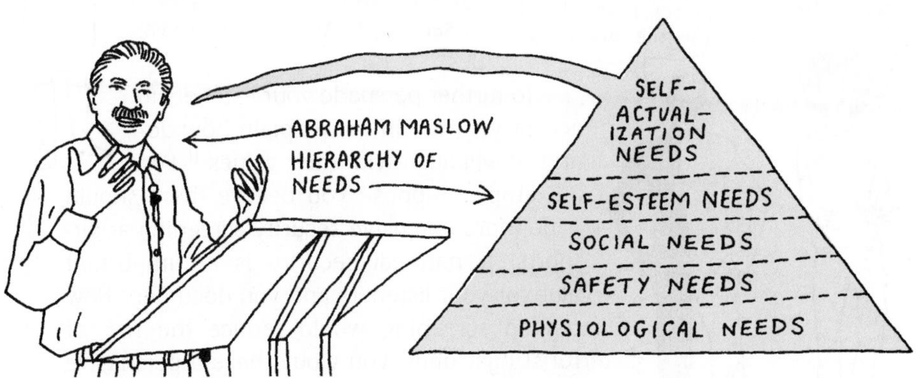

with you because your message speaks to their concerns and shows them how these concerns can be addressed.

For example, let's say you want to give a speech persuading your classmates to exercise more often. Exercise fulfills a number of different needs: it can improve people's health, help them perform better at work and school, increase their self-esteem, mitigate the dangers that come with obesity, and (if done in a social setting) provide opportunities to forge friendships and meet romantic partners. How do you know which of these needs to focus your message on? Determine which ones are most important to your audience members. Are they most concerned with getting better grades? losing weight? meeting interesting new people? Find out by asking questions in casual conversations, formal interviews, or in written surveys or questionnaires. Then craft your appeal accordingly, by selecting main points and subpoints focused on the particular needs you've identified.

Connecting to Your Listeners' Values. **Values** are "core conceptions" of what is desirable for our own life and for society.[8] They guide peoples' judgments and actions.[9] Each of us has values that guide how we live; for example, being helpful, honest, logical, imaginative, or responsible. We also have ideas about what kind of society we want to live in, such as one that offers equality, freedom, happiness, peace, or security.[10] All of these are values.

To further persuade your listeners to accept your argument, explain how doing so will align with their values.[11] For example, suppose you believe there should be more extensive security screening at airports. If national security is an important value for your listeners and you document how extended screening would reduce the risk of terrorist hijackings, you would have a persuasive argument.

VALUES GUIDE AUDIENCE JUDGMENTS— AND SOMETIMES VALUES ARE IN CONFLICT

On the other hand, suppose your audience favors efficiency and liberty. To persuade these listeners, you will need to explain how the screening you're advocating would not slow down airport lines and could be done with minimal intrusion on travelers. If you could prove a high risk of terrorist hijacking, you could also argue that even though efficiency and liberty are generally important values, *in this case*, the value of national security is paramount.[12]

Demonstrating How Your Audience Benefits. Audience members weigh the costs and benefits whenever they are deciding whether to take action in response to a persuasive appeal.[13] They are

most likely to support your proposal when you show how they will benefit by doing so.[14]

To step up your persuasive power, help your listeners visualize themselves experiencing the benefit they'll gain if they take the action you're advocating. Here is how one speaker showed the audience how they could benefit by volunteering their time for young children:

> I hope you can spare some time to help the young children in our community. You do not need to drive downtown to help out. Students can volunteer to read to children at the Day Care Center in our library at story hour each day. The next time you are using the library in the afternoon, walk past the center and see what a good time the kids and your classmates are having. Share a story from your culture or a book you loved as a child. If you enjoy volunteering, you can even sign up for a community service course and earn academic credit.

Acknowledge Listeners' Reservations

In analyzing your audience, you may discover reasons that your listeners are opposed to your thesis or at least uncommitted or neutral towards it. To address their reservations, consider using a **two-sided argument**. In a two-sided argument, you acknowledge an argument *against* your thesis and then use evidence and reasoning to refute that argument. For example, suppose you want to see a ban on alcoholic beverages at all campus sporting events. In this case, you know that fans who drink responsibly will likely oppose your idea, as will athletic department administrators concerned about the revenues that would be lost if alcohol sales were banned. To address responsible drinkers' reservations, you could acknowledge that they themselves aren't causing a problem, but then argue that the harm caused by irresponsible drinkers is so great that a ban is needed. To deal with administrators' reservations, you could agree that it's important for sports programs to raise revenues but then suggest alternative ways of doing so that don't involve alcohol sales.

TWO-SIDED ARGUMENT

A well-presented two-sided argument can help you change your audience members' attitudes in favor of your thesis and can strengthen your credibility.[15] That's because people are more likely to support an idea if they know that its proponent cares about their concerns and understands their views.

Focus on Peripheral Beliefs

You'll be more likely to persuade your audience members if you avoid threatening their core beliefs. **Core beliefs** are viewpoints that people have held closely, often for many years. Such beliefs are particularly immune to persuasion—especially through merely one speech.[16]

Beliefs that audience members have not held quite so closely or for quite so long are **peripheral beliefs**. People may form peripheral beliefs by hearing a news report, reading a book or magazine, or listening to a statement made by a political or religious leader. These beliefs are more open to change by a persuasive message. Thus, you can boost your chances of success if you focus your appeal on your listeners' peripheral beliefs.

For example, suppose you want to persuade various groups of people at your college to devote one Saturday morning to work on a campus beautification project. You first address the Campus Peace and Civil Liberties Coalition. Its members typically devote Saturday and Sunday mornings to antiwar activities. If you argue that their antiwar position is less important than campus beautification, you won't likely gain volunteers, since you'd be attacking their core beliefs. On the other hand, the coalition members' belief that antiwar activities must take place *every* Saturday and Sunday morning is more peripheral. You would have a better chance of winning these listeners' support if you maintained that devoting just one Saturday morning to do something to benefit the campus community would be a worthy cause—and that the coalition members could quickly return to their regular schedule of antiwar demonstrations afterward.

You can further enhance your persuasiveness if you show audience members how they can stay true to their core beliefs. For instance, let's say you want to persuade your listeners to invest in the stock market. Some audience members may oppose stock investments because they strongly believe that large corporations harm the environment. For these listeners, you could suggest investing in companies that are developing alternative energy sources. This action would enable them to stay true to their core belief.

ETHICAL PERSUASION

As we noted in Chapter 3, a public speaker must be ethical as well as effective. You want your audience members to accept your thesis, but you should earn their support with honest—not deceptive—persuasion. In this section, we highlight important ethical considerations for persuasive speakers.

Help Your Audience Make an Informed Decision

Ethical speakers help their listeners reach well-informed decisions, rather than manipulating them into agreement. Unfortunately, some persuaders use unethical tactics. For example, one study found that a detailed description of a single individual who had been on welfare for sixteen years exerted a greater influence on an audience's perceptions of welfare recipients than statewide statistics showing

that 90 percent of welfare recipients go off the rolls within four years.[17] Use of vivid evidence that depicts an atypical situation would constitute an unethical half-truth, unless the speaker informed the audience that the situation described is not the norm.

To persuade ethically, present solid, truthful claims that support your thesis. Scrupulously avoid arguments based on faulty reasoning, and include all key facts you know of that would help your audience carefully weigh what you're proposing. Remember, you can always address counterarguments to your position by using a two-sided argument.

Research Your Facts

As a public speaker, you have an ethical duty to research your topic so you can be sure the facts you present to your audience are accurate. If your research reveals that a fact is supported by a consensus of credible sources, you can confidently use that fact in your speech. Conversely, if you find that the "jury is still out" on a claim you wish to make, don't present that point as an established fact. Instead, acknowledge that the point is being debated. Then use a two-sided argument to show why you believe that the support for your side outweighs the support for the other side. If you find that few credible sources support your claim and most sources disagree, do not include that point in your speech. Research other arguments for your position instead.

Note Any Biases

If you stand to gain some sort of reward if the audience accepts your thesis, then you can't help but be biased toward the thesis. And your listeners should know about this. For example, if you would receive a commission if your listeners purchased a product you were promoting, or you'd receive extra credit if you recruited students to participate in a professor's study, your audience members deserve to know that information. They will also be more likely to respect you if you're honest enough to reveal such biases.

Attribute Your Research Properly

Include citations *every* time you present ideas that you found from other sources. Make sure that quotations and paraphrases are accurate and that they represent the original author's point of view.

ORGANIZING YOUR PERSUASIVE SPEECH

In Chapter 9, we presented several patterns for organizing the main points in the body of your speech. In a persuasive speech, you want to choose a pattern that will clearly convey your message *and* maximize your persuasive

impact. To select the most effective pattern, consider whether you will be making a fact, value, or policy claim in your speech.

Organizing Fact Claims

If you're planning to make a fact claim, you will be seeking to prove that something is true or false. In this type of persuasive speech, consider using a causal, comparison, or categorical pattern, depending on the main points you'll be presenting.

Causal Pattern. Many fact claims argue that one thing causes another. If this describes your fact claim, a causal pattern is ideal. To illustrate, here is how a presenter might organize a speech claiming that fast food causes health problems:

THESIS Fast-food restaurants are a significant cause of health problems in the United States.

MAIN POINTS

I. Low prices encourage frequent fast-food consumption.
II. Fast-food meals are high in fats and calories.
III. High-fat, high-calorie foods cause obesity, diabetes, and heart disease.

Comparison Pattern. When you want to claim that two situations are similar or different, a comparison pattern can help you support that claim. Here is an example of how a student used this pattern to persuade his fellow classmates that they should vote in upcoming elections because the candidates had substantively different positions on issues that affected the lives of many students:

COMPARISON PATTERN

THESIS There are significant differences between the two candidates for the legislature in our district.

MAIN POINTS

I. One candidate does not support the minimum wage; the other proposes an increase.
II. One candidate believes taxpayers already spend too much on colleges; the other supports increased financial aid.
III. One candidate opposes contraceptive distribution at campus health centers; the other proposes to make them readily available.

Categorical Pattern. Sometimes each main point in your speech will reflect a different reason that you believe your fact claim is true. In this case, you can use a categorical pattern to organize your

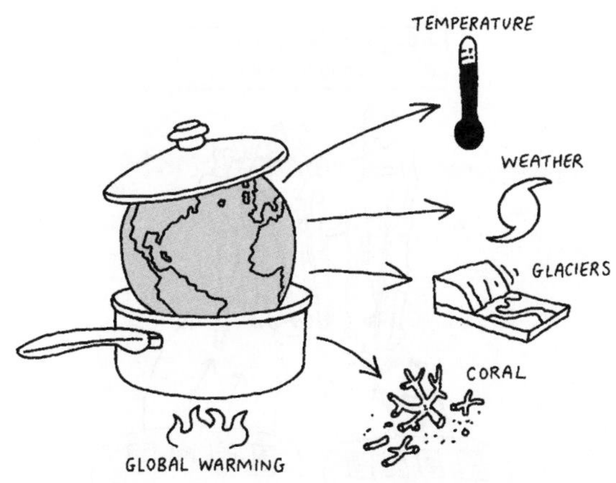

CATEGORICAL PATTERN

presentation. Consider the following example from a speech intended to convince listeners that global warming is actually happening:

THESIS The earth is experiencing global warming.

MAIN POINTS

I. The changes in ocean temperature are consistent with computer models of global warming.
II. Extreme weather is on the rise.
III. Glaciers on every continent are contracting.
IV. Coral reefs are disintegrating.

Organizing Value Claims

In making a value claim in a persuasive speech, you attach a judgment to your subject and then try to get the audience to agree with your evaluation. Two organizing patterns—criteria-application and categorical—can help you.

Criteria-Application Pattern. Recall that a criteria-application pattern has two main points. One establishes standards for the value judgment you are making. The other applies those standards to the subject of your thesis. Here is how you could use this pattern in a persuasive speech on the value of community service in college:

THESIS Community service is a valuable part of the college experience.

MAIN POINTS

I. A college education should provide students with several benefits.
   A. New knowledge and skills
   B. Preparation for the workforce
   C. Participation in new experiences
   D. Clarification of students' values and their place in the world

II. Community service provides college students with the opportunity to gain all these benefits.
   A. It leads to higher grade-point averages and stronger communication skills.
   B. It provides valuable work experience and a chance to discover career interests.
   C. It offers an opportunity to experience new situations and work with people from diverse backgrounds.
   D. It encourages students to consider their values and see how they can help society.

Categorical Pattern. In some persuasive speeches, you may decide that it isn't necessary to explain how each main point supports the value judgment you are making because your audience already understands each point's relevance. In this case, you can use a categorical pattern.

To illustrate, suppose you want to convince your audience that advanced driver-training courses are beneficial. Your listeners probably know that they could judge the value of a driver-training course by considering factors such as reduced accident risk and lower insurance premiums. Therefore, you could organize your main points in a categorical pattern, such as the following:

THESIS Advanced driver-training courses are beneficial.

MAIN POINTS

I. They reduce the risk of accidents.
II. They lower drivers' insurance premiums.
III. They lower drivers' maintenance and gas costs.
IV. The savings gained from the course exceed the cost of the course.

Organizing Policy Claims

When you advance a policy claim, you call for action. You might want audience members to do something in particular, or you may want to convince them that an organization or institution (such as state or local government) should take a particular action. For this type of persuasive speech, you can use any of these three organizational patterns: motivated sequence, problem-cause-solution, or comparative advantage.

Motivated Sequence. Developed by Alan Monroe over seventy years ago, this pattern remains popular.[18] It follows the stages of thinking that people often go through while solving a problem or considering new ideas.[19] A **motivated sequence** aims to establish five main points, as shown in the following example from a persuasive speech encouraging students to study abroad:

MAIN POINTS

I. *Attention* (creating a willingness to listen to your message). Few members of our class are looking forward to final exams next month. Do you think it would be more exciting if your finals were happening in Rome, Beijing, Sydney, or Buenos Aires?
II. *Need* (identifying a need relevant to your audience). Every member of this class plans to get a job after graduation. The job market is highly competitive.
III. *Satisfaction* (showing how your proposal will fulfill the need you identified). Participation in our college's Study Abroad Program will strengthen your credentials on the job market. Employers report that they are more likely to hire a candidate with international experience.

IV. *Visualization* (helping listeners form a mental picture of the benefits of your proposal). Imagine that you have returned to the United States after an amazing semester in Spain or Japan. At an interview for a job you really want, the interviewer asks if you have experience with other cultures. You answer yes, and you see the interviewer's interest perk up. The next day, the company makes you an offer.

V. *Action* (clarifying what you want listeners to do). Attend an informational session on next year's Study Abroad Program in the Student Union next Wednesday. You can learn more about the exciting options open to you, hear from past participants, and ask questions. After that, I hope you will decide to make Montreal, Mumbai, or Madrid your home for next fall.

Problem-Cause-Solution Pattern. This pattern can be especially helpful if you are asking the audience to support a policy change by an organization or institution. Since your ultimate goal is new behavior on the part of the organization or institution, the problem-cause-solution pattern builds to the action you are advocating. Recall that with this pattern, the first main point demonstrates a problem that needs to be addressed. The second shows how current policies are not sufficient to eliminate the cause of the problem. And the third presents a solution that can minimize the problem.

Here is an example of how a speaker might use this pattern in a persuasive speech advocating expanded federal funding for embryonic stem cell research:

THESIS Federal funding for embryonic stem cell research should be expanded.

MAIN POINTS

I. Humanity is plagued by devastating diseases.
II. Federal regulations limit funding of embryonic stem cell research.

III. Expanded federal funding improves the likelihood of finding cures and treatments for many diseases.

In the first main point, the speaker would establish that a *problem* exists—by showing the nature and extent of serious diseases. In the second main point, he or she would explain how current federal policies in part *cause* the problem by setting limits on research that could mitigate disease. In the final main point, the speaker would show how expanded funding of embryonic stem cell research would provide a *solution* to the problem of disease.

Comparative Advantage Format. This format shows why the policy you are advocating would be more beneficial than existing policies. You would typically use it when there is no glaring problem or issue at stake but there *is* a reason that your proposal would be better than the status quo. Examples include arguing that the U.S. penny should be abolished or that college students should have a minor as well as a major.

With this format, the first main point on your speech outline explains your solution. Then each subsequent main point identifies one advantage that your solution offers compared with the status quo. The subpoints for each advantage should include proof that your proposal would produce that benefit.

For instance, a speaker who wanted to persuade college students that they should have a minor could use the comparative advantage format as follows:

THESIS You should graduate with a minor.

MAIN POINTS

I. *Solution*: Research available minors on campus and select one that interests you.
II. *Advantage*: You can focus your studies on a subject you enjoy.
III. *Advantage*: You can strengthen your qualifications in your chosen career.
IV. *Advantage*: You can open the door to new career possibilities.

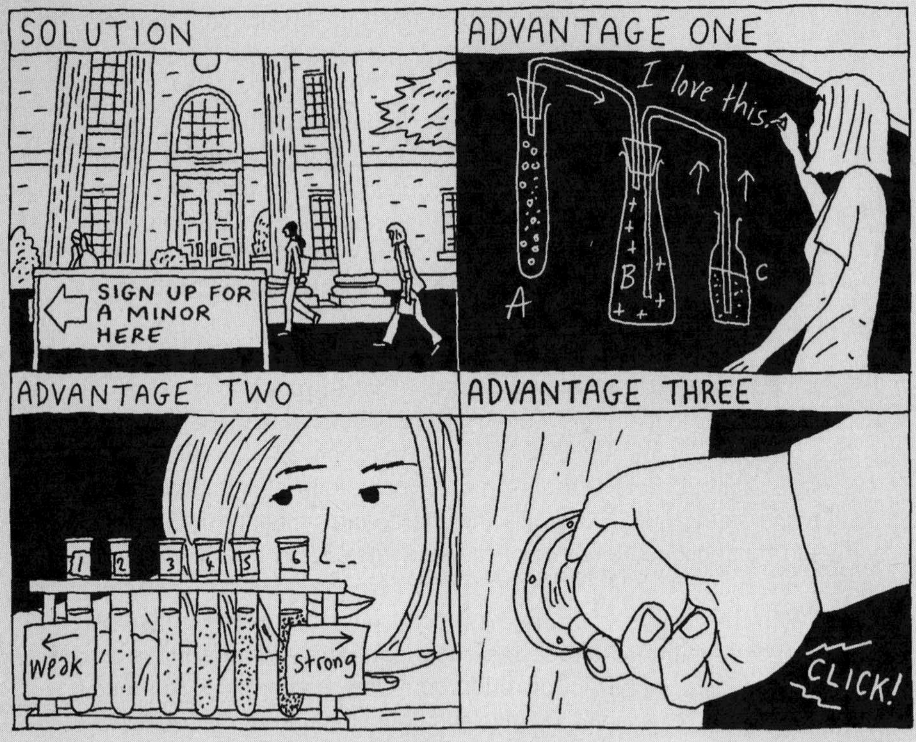

SUMMARY

> "Good persuaders make strategic choices in an ethical manner."

In this chapter, you learned how persuasive speakers strengthen or weaken their audience's commitment to a particular topic or motivate their listeners to take a particular action.

You also discovered strategies for developing an effective persuasive speech, including choosing a thesis based on your listeners' disposition, relating your message to the audience's needs and values, demonstrating how listeners will benefit if they support your proposal, addressing resistance to your ideas, and steering clear of listeners' core beliefs.

Additionally, you found advice for developing your message in an ethical manner, by helping your listeners make an informed decision, researching your facts thoroughly, disclosing any bias that you have, and properly attributing all your research sources.

Finally, you learned strategies for organizing your message, depending on whether you are making a fact, value, or policy claim.

Key Terms

THE NATURE OF A PERSUASIVE SPEECH

persuasive speech
strategic discourse
fact claims
value claims
policy claims

FRAMING YOUR ARGUMENT BASED ON AUDIENCE DISPOSITION

latitude of acceptance
latitude of rejection
boomerang effect

INCORPORATING PERSUASIVE STRATEGIES

needs
values
two-sided argument
core beliefs
peripheral beliefs

ORGANIZING YOUR PERSUASIVE SPEECH

motivated sequence

INTRO
DNA evidence proved my uncle was innocent.
CLICK!
ETHOS
I am credible.
CRIME + JUSTICE
DNA EVIDENCE
PRISON & PEOPLE
WRONGFUL CONVICTION IN AMERICA
INCARCERATION FACTS
JUSTICE NOW (& THEN)
INCARCERATION
THE EXONERATED SPEAK
AFTER PRISON?
LOGOS
My reasoning is sound.
2000
2001
2003
2004
PATHOS
At the time my uncle wrote to me and said: "They say I am free, but all I can feel is the huge weight of reality squashing down on me. They can't give me back those years ..."

17 METHODS OF PERSUASION

> "Persuasion happens when credible speakers provide good reasons and touch audience emotions."

Maya was both excited and nervous about delivering her upcoming persuasive speech. In her presentation, she planned to ask the audience to lobby for states to provide compensation for former convicts who are exonerated by new DNA evidence. She felt passionately about the topic. Three years earlier, her uncle, David, had been released from a twenty-two-year imprisonment after DNA tests revealed that he hadn't committed the murder for which he was jailed.

But Maya knew she would face a challenge in persuading her listeners. After all, not many people are wrongly imprisoned, so why should her audience members take time out of their busy lives to lobby state governments for a new policy? In short, why should they care?

To build the most persuasive case possible, Maya decided to use three powerful tools: ethos (demonstrating her credibility), logos (presenting sound reasoning for her claims), and pathos (evoking intense emotion in her audience). She established her credibility by citing trusted researchers' findings on the accuracy of DNA testing and the inaccuracy of eyewitness accounts (which typically lead to wrongful convictions). She demonstrated solid reasoning for her proposal by presenting statistics about the difficulties exonerated prisoners face in finding paid work after their innocence is proven. And she evoked her listeners' compassion and empathy for exonerees by describing the harsh realities David had been enduring since his release from prison—including long stretches of unemployment.

Maya's presentation proved a resounding success. By skillfully blending ethos, logos, and pathos, she captured her listeners' attention. And she convinced them that exonerees deserve to be compensated for the ordeal they had suffered because of errors in the justice system. By the time Maya wrapped up her speech, some students were even jotting down the tips she was sharing for how to lobby state governments to introduce a new exoneree compensation law. Clearly, they had embraced her proposal and intended to take the action she recommended—solid evidence that she had given an effective persuasive speech.

You can use these strategies as successfully as Maya did. In Chapter 17, we discuss the use of ethos, logos, and pathos to create an effective speech.

ETHOS: YOUR CREDIBILITY AS A SPEAKER

Since ancient times, people have recognized that a speaker with **ethos—credibility**—has far more persuasive power than one without. A credible speaker is seen as knowledgeable, honest, and genuinely interested in doing the right thing for his or her audience. Ethos can help you win your audience's trust and persuade them to embrace your viewpoint. But what is credibility, exactly? By taking a closer look at what it consists of, we can get a deeper understanding of this crucial persuasive tool.

Understanding the Elements of Credibility

The ancient Greek philosopher Aristotle believed that practical wisdom and virtue are major components of ethos. Modern communication scholars use the term **competence** to refer to practical wisdom and **trustworthiness** instead of the word *virtue*. When audience members perceive a speaker as competent (knowledgeable and experienced) about his or her subject as well as trustworthy (honest and fair), they find it easier to believe the speaker's claims.[1]

Aristotle also urged public speakers to exhibit **goodwill** toward their audiences—by wanting what is best for their listeners rather than what would most benefit themselves.[2] According to contemporary researchers, speakers who demonstrate goodwill:

- understand their listeners' needs and feelings.
- empathize with their audiences' views (even if they don't share them).
- respond quickly to others' communication.[3]

Building Your Credibility

When you're just starting out as a public speaker, your audience members may not immediately recognize your credibility. You'll need to build your ethos through what you say during your speech—and how you say it. Here are some helpful strategies:

- *Build credibility with your introduction.* The introduction to your speech provides a crucial opportunity to build your credibility. The introduction is where you can outline your experience and education as well as the research you've conducted on your topic. All of this helps demonstrate your competence. During your introduction, you also connect with your listeners by explaining how your topic relates to them, which shows you have their best interest at heart.
- *Build credibility through word choice.* The words you select for your speech can also demonstrate your understanding of your listeners and thus your goodwill toward them. Throughout your speech, use respectful language to refer to people who disagree with you. For example, "Some of you may not share my thinking on this, and that's okay. There are lots of ways to look at this issue."
- *Build credibility through strong evidence, organization, and delivery.* When you provide evidence for your claims, you indicate that you have carefully researched your topic, which communicates your competence. When you present a well-organized speech, you show that you care about helping your listeners follow your ideas, and that conveys goodwill. And when you practice effective delivery skills while making your presentation—for example, by interacting comfortably with the audience—you're more likely to come across as trustworthy.

BUILDING CREDIBILITY

...their recent data suggests that nearly 15% of U.S. youngsters and one-third of adults are obese...

BUILDING CREDIBILITY through STRONG EVIDENCE.

Avoiding Loss of Your Credibility

You have many strategies at hand for enhancing your credibility during a speech. But there are just as many ways to make a misstep and erode your ethos while you're giving a talk. Anytime you say something that shows a lack of competence, trustworthiness, or goodwill, you damage your credibility. Consider former vice president and 2000 Democratic presidential candidate Al Gore. Speaking on CNN in March 1999, Gore said, "During my service in the United States Congress, I took the initiative in creating the Internet."[4] Critics immediately noted that the Internet actually had its beginnings in 1969 and used Gore's statement as a sign that he tended to pad his résumé—which brought his competence and trustworthiness into question. Although what Gore meant was that through his efforts in Congress he had worked to create an economic and technological environment that would support the expansion of the Internet, the damage to his ethos had been done. Long after the election was over, comedians, bloggers, and political opponents continued to parody Gore's claim about creating the Internet.

Another example of lost credibility occurred in a campaign speech by Virginia Senator George Allen in the summer of 2006.

While Allen was speaking, he noticed a college student who had been filming his campaign tour on behalf of the opposing candidate, James Webb. The senator said the following: "This fellow here, over here with the yellow shirt, Macaca, or whatever his name is. He's with my opponent. He's following us around everywhere."[5] The term *macaca* is a racial slur against African immigrants in certain European cultures.[6] Although Allen later claimed that he had no idea what the word *macaca* meant and issued an apology to the student, the statement greatly damaged Allen's political career. Columnist Kathleen Parker wrote that "singling out a young person for ridicule—a lone Democrat in a crowd of rowdy Republicans—is behavior unbecoming a gentleman, a senator, and certainly a president."[7] Before this comment, Allen had a double-digit lead in his race for reelection to the Senate, and he was on the short list of potential presidential nominees for 2008. After his speech, the gap between Allen and his opponent narrowed. George Allen ultimately lost the senatorial election, and he was no longer mentioned as a strong presidential candidate.

Once a speaker's credibility has come into question, it's very difficult to repair the damage. Thus, before giving a speech, examine the language you intend to use, and make sure that it communicates competence, trustworthiness, and goodwill. However, even a bulletproof ethos isn't enough to deliver an effective speech. You also need to deliver a solid set of facts to prove the claims you're making.

LOGOS: THE EVIDENCE AND REASONING BEHIND YOUR MESSAGE

Reliable facts can further strengthen your credibility and help your audience members make well-informed decisions—key effects of ethical public speaking. Sound reasoning that supports your claims is also essential if you hope to persuade audience members to change their beliefs or behaviors. When you present trustworthy facts to back your

A BUNCH OF LOGICAL PEOPLE

If you gain, you gain all; if you lose, you lose nothing. Wager, then, without hesitating, that He exists.
BLAISE PASCAL

This isn't magic—it's logic—a puzzle. A lot of the greatest wizards haven't got an ounce of logic; they'd be stuck here forever.
HERMIONE GRANGER

The length of life takes the leading place among inquiries about events following birth.
PTOLEMY

No one will be free until nerd persecution ends.
GILBERT (*REVENGE OF THE NERDS*)

I am an omniverous reader with a strangely retentive memory for trifles.
SHERLOCK HOLMES

That is a most illogical attitude.
Mr. SPOCK

claims and clearly show how those facts have led you to those claims, you use **logos** effectively.

For example, suppose you want to deliver a persuasive speech arguing that diet soft drinks do not actually help people lose weight, a claim that might seem counterintuitive to many of your listeners. To convince them that you know what you're talking about, you'll need to supply proof, or **evidence**, of your claim. To

further strengthen your logos, you'll have to show that the conclusions you've drawn from the evidence make sense. Is your train of thought logical? Or are you using **fallacious (faulty) reasoning** to twist or distort the facts in your favor?

In the following sections, we discuss how to use evidence and reasoning to build a persuasive message and how to avoid several common logical fallacies.

Using Evidence

When your audience analysis suggests that listeners may not accept a claim you want to make, you'll need to supply proof. One of the best ways to do that is to research evidence from credible sources (see Chapter 7) and then present that evidence in your speech. To use evidence effectively, apply the following principles:

Identify Your Sources and Their Qualifications. Indicate who your source is for each piece of evidence you present, along with his or her qualifications, before providing the evidence during your speech. Concrete documentation strengthens your credibility.[8] To ensure your *sources'* credibility, use facts provided by unbiased experts.[9]

Give Listeners New Evidence. Use audience analysis to determine what evidence is likely to be new to your listeners. Facts that they're not yet familiar with are more likely to increase their perceptions of your credibility.[10]

Provide Precise Evidence. Precise evidence consists of specific dates, places, numbers, and other facts. Here's an example of this kind of precision:

> A study by Sharon Fowler and her colleagues at the University of Texas Health Science Center found that the risk of becoming obese or overweight for regular soft drink drinkers consuming 1–2 cans daily is 32.8 percent. For those who consume a comparable amount of diet soft drinks, the risk is 54.5 percent.[11]

This citation provides a specific percentage as well as the lead researcher's name and affiliation.

Look for Compelling Evidence. Audiences are more likely to be persuaded by compelling evidence that includes concrete or detailed examples. Such evidence engages listeners' senses, helps them visualize the point you're presenting, and increases the likelihood that listeners will remember the information.[12] For example, in your speech about diet sodas, you could include a compelling anecdote about a student who gained weight after switching from sugared to diet soft drinks.

Characterize Your Evidence Accurately. Carefully word your claim so it accurately reflects what your evidence proves. For example, if all the facts you've gathered strongly support the idea that diet drinks don't help people lose weight, then use those very words to state your claim about the drinks—rather than saying something like "Diet soft drinks aren't as healthy as people think."

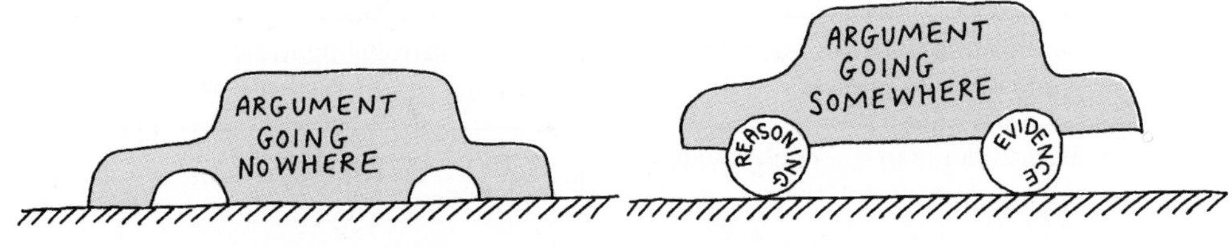

INDUCTIVE REASONING

Using Reasoning

Reasoning is the line of thought that connects the facts you present and the conclusions that you draw from those facts. Persuasive speakers typically use **inductive reasoning**—generalizing from facts, instances, or examples and then making a claim based on that generalization. The following table shows several examples of inductive reasoning from everyday life.

EXAMPLES OF INDUCTIVE REASONING

Fact	Claim
At three different locations at this university, food service was slow.	All food service outlets at this school are slow.
Ahijah is good at football.	Ahijah would be good at soccer.
Sarah waits until the last minute to study or write papers.	Sarah is struggling in her classes.
Two students in the back row just fell asleep.	This is a boring class.

There are four types of inductive reasoning: example, comparison, causal, and sign. Let's explore each type in detail and consider how to use them effectively.

Example Reasoning. When you use **example reasoning**, you present specific instances to support a general claim. Your goal is to persuade the audience that your examples supply sufficient proof of your claim.

For instance, here's how you could use example reasoning to argue that endangered species are making a comeback:

> The Fortymile caribou herd, which ranges from central Alaska to the Yukon Territory, was down to 5,000 members in the 1970s. Now the number is up to 46,000.[13] In California, the number of peregrine falcons has increased from two known pairs to more than 150.[14] And there are now more than 6,000 breeding pairs of bald eagles in the lower 48 states, far more than the 400 pairs in the 1960s.[15]

To use example reasoning skillfully, be sure to provide enough instances to persuade your audience that your general claim is reasonable. The more examples you can find, the more confident you can be that your claim is correct.

Of course, in a short speech, you may have time to present only three or four examples to back up your argument. In this situation,

REPRESENTATIVE EXAMPLES

CLAIM: FORMERLY ENDANGERED SPECIES ARE THRIVING ACROSS THE U.S.A.

you'll need to choose the most **representative examples**—that is, examples that are typical of the class they represent. To illustrate, if you wanted to present an even more compelling case that endangered species are making a comeback, you might want to cite three very different species that come from a variety of regions in North America.

If you're planning to use example reasoning in a speech you're researching, think about counterexamples your audience may consider. For instance, some listeners may argue that while certain species are recovering their populations, others are still endangered. Thus, they may view your claim that "endangered species are making a comeback" as inaccurate. If such counterexamples have merit, you may need to revise your claim to "*some* endangered species are making a comeback."

NONREPRESENTATIVE EXAMPLES

CLAIM: FORMERLY ENDANGERED SPECIES ARE THRIVING ACROSS THE U.S.A.

Comparison Reasoning. When you use **comparison reasoning**, you argue that two instances are similar, so that what you know is true for one instance is likely to be true for the other. For example, if you argued that long-term prohibition of marijuana can't succeed because prohibition of alcohol failed, you would be using this type of reasoning.

For comparison reasoning to work, your audience must agree (or be persuaded) that the two instances are in fact comparable. To illustrate, suppose you can show that marijuana use is similar to alcohol use and current marijuana law closely resembles earlier alcohol-prohibition law. By emphasizing these similarities, you can make a more convincing argument that marijuana prohibition will likely prove just as ineffective as alcohol prohibition did.

To further strengthen your comparison reasoning, make sure your audience accepts the "known facts" as true. For example, perhaps your listeners would argue that alcohol prohibition in the United States wasn't actually a failure if it reduced alcohol consumption significantly. In this case, you might have to note other ways in which prohibition could be considered a failure. For example, it led to the rise of organized crime, as entities such as the Mafia took over bootlegging operations to counter government raids on speakeasies.

Many speakers have used comparison reasoning to make the case for or against the war in Iraq. For example, Secretary of State Condoleezza Rice argued that:

> Just as America's soldiers of yesteryear made priceless contributions to the security of Europe following World War II, and then to the security and prosperity of Asia in the next decade, the professionalism and commitment of our soldiers will help countries like Afghanistan and Iraq recover from years of tyranny. . . .[16]

Conversely, Nebraska Senator Chuck Hagel contended:

> [N]ow we are locked into a bogged-down problem, not unsimilar, dissimilar to where we were in Vietnam. The longer we stay, the more problems we're going to have.[17]

If Rice could draw direct parallels between the reigns of Saddam Hussein and Adolf Hitler, and between the efforts of U.S. soldiers rebuilding Baghdad and the U.S. army's support of the Marshall Plan in Berlin after World War II, she could then make a more convincing argument that Iraq's reconstruction will be as effective as that of postwar Germany. Conversely, Hagel could argue that the United States will face an outcome in Iraq similar to that in Vietnam by establishing similar challenges in both situations: a protracted conflict with complex rules of engagement amidst a foreign culture.

Causal Reasoning. When you use **causal reasoning**, you argue that one event has caused another. For instance, you would be using

causal reasoning if you claimed that playing violent video games leads children to get involved in violent and illegal activities.

You can strengthen your causal reasoning in several ways. One way is to explain the link between cause and effect. For example, you might contend that when children play violent games, they empathize with the violent character they control in the games. Thus, they are more likely to emulate that character in their everyday lives. Another way to use causal reasoning effectively is to support the cause-effect link with evidence from credible sources. For instance, you could use quotations from the American Academy of Pediatrics or the American Psychological Association to bolster your argument about violent video games' impact on children's behavior. Finally, you could show a correlation between the cause and effect; for example, by presenting statistics indicating that as the number of hours children spend playing violent video games increases, so does the number of violent incidents in which they get involved.

When using causal reasoning, be sure you're not committing a **post hoc fallacy**. This fallacy takes its name from the Latin phrase

post hoc ergo propter hoc, meaning "after this, therefore because of this." The fallacy lies in the assumption that just because one event followed another, the first event caused the second. But a correlation, in itself, does not prove causality. It may be true that children who play violent video games commit more crimes; however, the games may not necessarily have caused the criminal activity. There may have been other causes at work. For example, perhaps children who play violent video games tend to live in families with absent parents, and it's the parents' absence (not the games) that leads to the youngsters' entry into criminal activity. Still, if you can show that research consistently finds a link between the games and young people's criminality, you'll strengthen your argument.

Also watch out for **reversed causality**, in which speakers miss the fact that the effect is actually the cause. For example, in the video game scenario we've been following, it may be possible that children who are predisposed to violence choose to play such video games, rather than the games' causing their violence.

Sign Reasoning. When you use **sign reasoning**, you claim that a fact is true because indirect indicators (signs) are consistent with that fact. For example, you might claim that college tuition is increasing, as evidenced by students working longer hours.

This type of reasoning is most effective if you can cite multiple consistent signs of the fact that you are claiming. For instance, you could strengthen your claim that tuition is rising by also noting an increase in student loans and a higher rate of students dropping out of school. But as you're researching your speech, look for signs *inconsistent* with your argument. To illustrate, if you discover that students are

SIGNS OF RISING TUITION

spending more money on entertainment and clothes, you may find it more difficult to convincingly claim that signs prove tuition is rising.

Now that you've considered several types of reasoning that can help you support claims in a persuasive speech, let's look at several examples of faulty reasoning—the logical fallacies that can trip up unwary speakers or be misused by unethical ones.

Avoiding Logical Fallacies

Reasoning is fallacious (faulty) when the link between your claim and supporting material is weak. We have already discussed several fallacies in this chapter and in Chapter 3 on ethics: the hasty generalization from too few examples, the ad hominem attack on a presenter instead of on the issue raised in the speech, the post hoc fallacy when the link between two events is coincidental rather than causal, and the reversed causality fallacy. In this section, we highlight several additional common fallacies you'll want to avoid in your speeches.

Ad Populum Fallacy. You've committed the **ad populum fallacy** (also known as the **bandwagon fallacy**) if you assume that a statement (such as "the earth is 10,000 years old" or "the United States is losing the war in Iraq" or "the San Francisco 49ers will win the Super Bowl") is true because many people believe it is true.

AD POPULUM FALLACY

The problem with basing the truth of a statement on the number of people who believe it, is that most people have neither the expertise nor the time to conduct the research needed to arrive at an informed opinion about the big questions of the day. For this reason, it's best to avoid using public opinion polls to prove "facts."

Straw Person Fallacy. You commit the **straw person fallacy** if you replace your opponent's real claim with a weaker claim you can more easily rebut. This weaker claim may sound relevant to the issue, but it really isn't. You're presenting it just because it's easy to knock down, like a person made of straw.

During the impeachment trial of former U.S. president Bill Clinton, some of his defenders committed this fallacy when they argued that an extramarital affair is part of private life and not a sufficient justification for impeaching a president. However, Clinton's political opponents maintained that whether the president had had an affair

was irrelevant: the important thing was that he had lied under oath, an action that *did* justify impeachment in their minds.

Slippery Slope Fallacy. You've fallen victim to the **slippery slope fallacy** if you argue against a policy because you assume (without proof) that it will lead to some second policy that is undesirable. Like the straw person fallacy, this type of argument distracts the audience from the real issue at hand. Here's one example of a slippery slope argument:

> We can't legalize same-sex marriage, because the next thing you know, people will be marrying their pets.

In this example, the speaker can't support his or her claim: in states or nations that have extended marriage rights to gay men and lesbians, no one has in fact tied the knot with Fluffy or Fido.

SLIPPERY SLOPE FALLACY

False Dilemma Fallacy. You fall prey to the **false dilemma fallacy** if you claim that there are only two possible choices to address a problem, that one of those choices is wrong or infeasible, and that therefore your listeners must embrace the other choice. For example:

> Either we keep our broken-down Social Security system or we privatize it. The current system will be bankrupt by 2041, so we'd better privatize.

FALSE DILEMMA FALLACY

The weakness in a false dilemma argument is that most problems have more than just two possible solutions. To illustrate, in the Social Security example, additional options for addressing the system's financial problems include raising the retirement age and slowing the rate of increase in Social Security benefits.

Appeal to Tradition Fallacy. You've committed the **appeal to tradition fallacy** if you argue that an idea or policy is good because people have accepted or followed it for a long time. For example:

> We must continue to require general education courses at this college. For the past fifty-three years, the students at State U have taken general education.

APPEAL TO TRADITION FALLACY

This argument is weak because it offers no explanation for why the tradition of general education courses is a good thing in the first place. To strengthen the argument, the speaker would need to show how general education requirements offer more benefits to students than they would gain by taking additional classes in their major or taking more classes of their choice.

PATHOS: EVOKING YOUR LISTENERS' EMOTIONS

When you stir your listeners' feelings, you enhance your persuasive power. Indeed, some experts have referred to human emotions as "the primary motivating system of all activity."[18] Thus, a heartwarming example of a person who benefited greatly from taking an action you're recommending in your speech may be even more compelling than a statistic about the number of people who could benefit.

When used with ethos and logos, **pathos**—or emotional appeal—helps you put a "human face" on a problem you're addressing. But don't try to appeal to feelings alone. If you failed to also build your credibility and make a logical connection between your point and the emotion you are invoking, you would be neither logical nor ethical (even if you succeeded in persuading some of your audience members). Recall the old adage "with great power comes great responsibility," and don't use emotional appeal to manipulate your audience. History is replete with persuaders (witness Adolf Hitler) who used pathos to achieve unethical and even horrific ends.

Humans have the capacity to experience a wide range of different emotions, including empathy, anger, shame, fear, and pity. And each of these feelings provides an opportunity to enhance your use of pathos in a persuasive speech. For example, in a presentation in which she advocated greater freedom in doctor selection for Health Maintenance Organization (HMO) patients, a speaker used this emotional appeal:

> Trey McPherson was born with half of his heart shrunken and nearly useless, a condition that causes most children to die in infancy.
>
> Fortunately, Trey was not one of these victims, because he was treated by a leading pediatric heart surgeon. After two surgeries, Trey's parents were able to experience the joy of seeing their ten-month-old son climb out of his crib at the hospital. Except for a bandage on his tiny chest, it was difficult to tell that Trey had recently experienced open-heart surgery. Unfortunately, many babies are not as fortunate as Trey. Although this skillful surgeon's patients have far-above-average survival rates, many pediatric cardiologists in the New York area find their "favorite surgeon is frequently off limits because of price if a child belongs to an HMO."[19]

This example evokes a variety of emotions. It stimulates listeners' *anger* and *pity* at the thought of small children denied the best available care. It prompts them to *empathize* by imagining how they would feel if a loved one with a serious disease were forced to accept low-quality medical care. And it brings *joy* at the thought of how Trey's parents must have felt when their child recovered from surgery.

But notice that this emotional appeal is accompanied by sound reasoning. The speaker provides evidence that Trey's case is not unusual, which justifies the anger she evokes.

Conversely, a speaker would commit a hasty generalization fallacy (see Chapter 3) by presenting an example that represents a very rare occurrence. And the speaker would also be making an unethical appeal if she failed to establish a logical connection between her proposed course of action and the feelings she is stirring up. For example, if having access to a wider selection of physicians would do little to help families in Trey's situation, this speech would merely be an emotional ploy to manipulate the audience into accepting her argument.

A **fear appeal**—an argument that arouses fear in the minds of audience members—can be a particularly powerful form of pathos.[20] But to be effective, a fear appeal must demonstrate a serious threat to listeners' well-being.[21] And to be ethical, it must be based on accurate information and not exaggerated specifically to make your argument sound more persuasive.

A fear appeal is also more likely to succeed if your audience members believe they have the power to remedy the problem you're describing.[22] Consider messages by National Park Rangers advocating safe storage of food in parks. The rangers provide statistics showing how often bears have broken into cars or tents when people have left food out. They augment these statistics with videos depicting bears smashing car windows and climbing inside the vehicles to get food. These images usually strike fear into viewers' hearts. But then the rangers show how easy it is to store food safely in lockers or bear-proof canisters. Because audience members realize they *can* readily adopt these practices, they *do* adopt them.

SAMPLE PERSUASIVE SPEECH

EXTRA CREDIT YOU CAN LIVE WITHOUT

Anna Martinez
California State University–Fresno

Anna Martinez selected student credit card debt as the topic of her persuasive speech. Based on her survey of the audience, she determined that it would not be feasible to argue that students should not use credit cards. She selected a different thesis that was within their latitude of acceptance: to encourage students to be more careful credit card consumers.

Anna's speech is targeted to an audience of college students, and she refers to information gleaned from her survey to support her points. Anna consistently uses evidence to support her claims. And she has a clearly organized speech in a problem-cause-solution format.

There is a dangerous product on our campus. It is marketed on tables outside the student union and advertised on the bulletin board in this classroom. Based on my audience survey, it is likely that most of you have this product in your possession right now. By the end of my speech, this product may be costing you more than it is right now. The dangerous product is credit cards. •

• Suspense-building attention-getter.

Today, I would like to discuss the problems created by college students' credit cards and hopefully persuade you to be a careful credit card consumer. If your credit card situation is anything like mine—and over two-thirds of this class indicated that they are currently carrying a balance on one or more cards—take note: you can save money.

My husband and I paid for our own wedding. More accurately, we used our credit cards to charge many of our wedding expenses. And thanks to Visa, we are still paying for our wedding every month! We have saved money with some of the suggestions I will present today, and you can do the same.

To that end, let's cover some of the problems created by students' credit card debt, then analyze causes of the problem, and finally consider steps you can take to be a careful credit card consumer. •

• Anna includes her thesis, connects with the audience, establishes credibility, and previews her main points.

We'll start with a look at the problems created by these "hazardous products."

Credit card debt on campus is a significant and growing problem.

Many students have credit card debts. According to Matthew Scott, in *Black Collegian*, April 2007, "College financial aid provider Nellie Mae reported that 76 percent of undergraduate students had credit cards in 2005, with an average balance of $2,169. An alarming 25 percent of undergraduates had credit card balances totaling $3,000 or more." In *Business Week*, September 5, 2007, Jessica Silver-Greenberg noted that "the freshman 15, a fleshy souvenir of beer and late-night pizza, is now taking on a new meaning, with some freshmen racking up more than $15,000 in credit card debt before they can legally drink." If you are not sure how your own balances compare, you are not alone. The previously mentioned Nellie Mae study found that the average balance reported by students was 47 percent lower than the average balance computed from data provided by credit bureaus. •

• Anna consistently uses research sources to support her points.

High credit card use can change our lives for the worse. According to the April 2007 *Black Collegian* article, Rhonda Reynolds of Bernard Baruch College built up $8,000 worth of debt and was unable to make even the minimum payment. Her account went into collections. *Business Week*, March 15, 1999, provided another example. Jason Britton, a senior at Georgetown University, accumulated $21,000 in debt over four years on sixteen cards! Jason reports that "when I first started, my attitude was 'I'll get a job after college to pay off all my debt.'" Then he realized that he was in a hole because he could not meet minimum monthly payments. He had to obtain financial assistance from his parents and now works three part-time jobs. •

• Supporting material: examples.

You probably do not owe $20,000 on your credit cards, but even smaller balances take their toll. Robert Frick, associate editor for *Kiplinger's Personal Finance Magazine*, March 1997, states that if you make the minimum payments on a \$500 balance at an 18% interest rate, it will take over seven years to pay off the loan and cost \$365 in interest.

High credit card debt can also haunt your finances after you graduate. Matthew Scott, previously cited, notes that credit bureaus assign you a credit score, which is "your economic report card to the rest of the world." That score will "determine the interest rates you pay for many forms of credit and insurance." He also notes that prospective employers will check your credit score and use that number to decide whether or not you are responsible.

Many people in this class are carrying student loans, which will need to be paid back upon graduation. When you add credit card debt to student loan payments, rent, utilities, food, that payment on the new car you want to buy, family expenses, etc., the toll can be heavy. Alan Blair, director of credit management for the New England Educational Loan Marketing Corporation, in a 1998 report on the corporation's Web site, noted serious consequences for students who cannot balance monthly expenses and debts, including "poor credit ratings, inability to apply for car loans or a mortgage, collection activity, and at worst, a bankruptcy filing." •

• Relating the problem to a college audience.

Don't let this happen to you. After all that hard work earning a degree and finally landing a job where you don't have to wear a plastic name tag and induce people to get "fries with that order," the last thing any of us need is to be spending our hard-earned money paying off debt, being turned down for loans, or, worse yet, being harassed by collection agencies.

Credit card debt is hazardous to students' financial health, so why are these debts piling up? Let's move on to the causes of this problem. •

• Transition to main point II.

The reality is that credit card issuers want and aggressively seek the business of students like ourselves. As Jessica Silver-Greenberg writes in her previously cited September

2007 article, "over the next month, as 17 million college students flood the nation's campuses, they will be greeted by swarms of credit-card marketers. Frisbees, T-shirts, and even iPods will be used as enticements to sign up, and marketing on the Web will reinforce the message."

Card issuers actually troll for customers on campus because student business is profitable. Daniel Eisenberg, writer of the column "Your Money" for *Time* magazine, September 28, 1998, notes that "college students are suckers for free stuff, and many are collecting extra credit cards and heavier debts as a result." Eisenberg refers to a U.S. Public Interest Research Group survey, which found that students who sign up for cards at campus tables in return for "gifts" typically carry higher unpaid balances than do other students. Jessica Silver-Greenberg, in an October 15, 2007, *Business Week* article, writes that "college kids are a potential gold mine—one of the few growing customer segments in the saturated credit-card market. And they're loyal, eventually taking three additional loans, on average, with the bank that gives them their first card." •

• Supporting material: explanation of why card issuers market to students.

Companies use "sucker rates" to induce students to apply for credit. *Business Week*, March 15, 1999, wrote "credit card marketers may advertise a low annual percentage rate, but it often jumps substantially after three to nine months. First USA's student Visa has a 9.9% introductory rate that soars to 17.99% after five months. Teaser rates aren't unique to student cards, but a 1998 study by the Washington-based U.S. Public Interest Research Group found that 26% of college students found them misleading."

So it appears that credit card companies will not stop demanding student business any time soon. What can we do about it?

My proposed solution is to be a careful credit card consumer.

Why not get rid of your credit cards before it's too late? All right, maybe you won't go for that solution. My survey indicated that most of you enjoy the flexibility in spending that credit cards provide. •

• Anna notes that her listeners are likely to reject her strongest suggestion. Anna then advocates a solution within her audience's latitude of acceptance.

So here are some other ways you should be credit card smart. One practice is to shop carefully for the best credit card deals. The companies that are not spending their money giving away pizzas and iPods on campus may be able to offer you a better deal. In her September 7, 2007, *Business Week* article, Silver-Greenberg recommends that you beware of offers from South Dakota or Delaware corporations. Those states are "considered 'safe harbors' for credit card companies because they have no cap on interest rates or late payment [fees]."

A second solution is to read the fine print on credit card applications to learn what your actual interest rate will be. Alison Barros, a staff writer for the Lane Community College *Torch*, October 29, 1998, quoted Jonathan Woolworth, consumer protection director for the Oregon Public Interest Research Group, who wrote that "students need to read the fine print and find out how long those low interest rates last. Rates that are as low as 3% can jump to 18% within three months, and the credit card company doesn't want the student to know that."

Here is an example of the fine print on an ad that begins at 1.9% and soon rises. If you read the fine print, you note that the rate can rise to more than 20%. •

• Anna shows a visual aid here.

• *Second* and *third* are examples of signposts.

Third, even if you can only make the minimum payment on your cards, pay your bills on time. • Silver-Greenberg's September 5 article indicates that students' "credit scores can plunge particularly quickly, with one or two missed payments, because their track records are so short." She further cautions students to be aware of "universal default" provisions in their credit agreements—these provide that if you miss a payment on one card, other credit card companies can also raise your interest rate (even if you have paid those cards on time), perhaps to 30%. *Business Week*, March 15, 1999, cautions that "because students move often and may not get their mail forwarded quickly, bills can get lost. Then the students fall prey to late fees." •

• Adapting the solution to a college audience.

Finally, you can keep money in your pocket and out of the credit card company's by paying attention to your credit report. If any agencies are "talking trash" about you with inaccurate information, be sure to have it corrected.

To sum up these solutions, even if you do not want to stop using credit cards, there are many ways to be a careful credit card consumer. Shop for a good rate and be careful to read the fine print so you know what the rate really is. Know what you owe, and take the responsibility to make payments on time. •

• Internal summary of main point III.

This morning, we have learned about a hazardous product on campus—credit cards. We have noted the problem of high student credit card debt, analyzed some of the causes of this problem, and considered several methods for being a careful credit card consumer. •

• Summary of main points.

If your instructor offers you a chance for extra credit in his or her class, take advantage of the opportunity. But when a credit card issuer offers you a free T-shirt or phone card if you will sign up for their extra credit, just say no. When you pay off a credit card with a 19.9% interest rate, that "free" T-shirt could turn out to be the most expensive clothing you will ever buy. •

• Clincher sums up Anna's speech with irony.

SAMPLE PERSUASIVE SPEECH

WOMEN WITH DISABILITIES: HOW TO BECOME A BOAT ROCKER IN LIFE

Sue Suter

Sue Suter, the former U.S. Commissioner of Rehabilitation and President of the World Institute on Disabilities Services, delivered this speech to the New Zealand Rehabilitation Association Conference on Ethics in Rehabilitation in 1993.

Unlike classroom speakers, who should precisely follow the format presented by the instructor and textbook, professional speakers tend to develop their own unique style of crafting a speech. Nevertheless, Ms. Suter does an excellent job of modeling good public speaking practices. Her speech below—excerpted from the longer version that Suter delivered—is organized topically around main ideas. She uses diverse supporting materials (including examples, studies, poetry, humor, and anecdotes). And she relates her speech to the audience, indicating how each person can take an active role as a "boat rocker."

I'd like to begin with a favorite quote of mine that applies here. It's from a book called *What's Right with America*. And it says:

> Most of us Americans sail steadily through life on an even keel. But there are some, very few Americans who are boat rockers. They go through life making a fuss when things aren't right. And fighting the fights for us that we don't always fight for ourselves.

Ladies and gentlemen, this not a "woe is me" speech. It is, however, about boat rocking. And it is about universal truths that women with disabilities have learned through a common experience. •

• Suter uses a quotation to gain audience attention and then reveals her topic.

A few days ago, while preparing for this speech, a friend and I talked about differences between the women's rights and the disability rights movements. At one point, my friend asked the question: which I considered myself first—a woman, or a person with a disability? I said that I thought of myself as a woman first. That's an important distinction. One that's too often lost on those who are not members of the disability community. •

• Main idea: gender matters.

I contracted polio when I was two years old. I don't remember it. But I do remember my parents telling me about the advice that the doctor gave when it was time to take me home from the hospital. He told them, "just put her in bed. She's going to be staying there the rest of her life."

When I was in college, I decided to go after a master's degree in clinical psychology. But my career counselor advised against it. He warned that it was hard enough for a woman with a disability to get married. Having an advanced degree would only intimidate a man more.

When our son was born, the day before he and I were to leave the hospital, a social worker visited me to inquire how I was going to possibly care for a newborn infant. •

• Supporting material: examples of gender- and disability-based stereotypes.

These were well-meaning professionals who believed that they knew what was best for me. But my life would be much different, and I probably wouldn't be with you today, if their advice had been followed.

Many articles about people with disabilities assume that gender has no influence. It does. As one interviewee put it, using a metaphor from baseball, "I'm a disabled woman now; two strikes. I'm almost out." Actually, there are three strikes against women with disabilities. The dual discrimination as women and as people with a disability. Plus, as William John Hamma and Betsy Rogovsky noted in their research, there's a special treatment meted out when the two intersect.

In a study of 130 undergraduate students in the United States, each was asked to describe what they saw in two photographs. One showed a forty-five-year-old man in a wheelchair. Most students imagined the cause of his disability as related to war, or job, or sports-related injuries—highly admirable. When they were shown a picture of a woman in a wheelchair, no one mentioned wars or jobs or sports. Instead, their answers centered on carelessness, like falling down stairs, or diseases—perhaps, by implication, diseases that were contagious. In other words, signs of weakness. •

• Supporting material: a study.

Judy Heumann has often noted that "women with disabilities, in the richest and the poorest countries, are the poorest of the poor." That's a reality. Another reality is the impact of labels. Passive, child-like, lacking minimal skills.

Even the absence of labels takes its toll. The images of being independent, leader, married, child-bearer, sexual, or an employer. When a group of college students was asked in a survey to describe women with disabilities, none of those attributes were listed. Why?

Many of the women with disabilities in this room can claim those same titles as their own. I'd like to add my name to theirs. But why don't others see these qualities? Women with disabilities are seen neither as mothers and nurturers, nor as professionals. Women who write about women with disabilities call this rolelessness!

The American comedian, Lilly Tomlin, once played a character named Crystal. She was quadriplegic. And she asked her doctor, "What about sex?"

"I think you can have a baby."

"That's not what I asked." •

• Supporting material: a wry and humorous example.

Rolelessness. Women with disabilities are seen as asexual beings. Women with disabilities can have a baby. That's biology. The tough part is imagining that people with disabilities are capable of sexuality. There's a lot of truth to the old saying, "hormones know no handicap." •

• Main idea: disabled people are ordinary people.

Overcoming rolelessness means revealing that we are ordinary. I'll say it again. Overcoming rolelessness means revealing that we are ordinary. We must fight the Third Reich mentality that says the greatest goal is the perfection of the human race. •

• Style—use of repetition and also the phrase "Third Reich mentality."

. . .

More than anything else, the world needs to rediscover the normal. Disability is a normal part of being human. People with disabilities are ordinary people. This is not a form of denial. It is a fundamental recognition of our undeniable worth and our inseparable membership in the human race.

Yet women with disabilities are often devalued by the institutions they should be able to count on most—their families and the women's movement. One feminist activist said, "Why study women with disabilities? They reinforce traditional stereotypes of women being dependent, passive, and needy."

To that I ask, who is an accomplice to that image? Who is abandoning the universal ideals of freedom and dignity for all women in exchange for the easy path of appeasement? Appeasement has been defined as feeding your friends to the alligator in hopes that he'll eat you last. Everyone loses with that strategy.

. . .

Part of demonstrating our ordinariness means getting involved in situations that have nothing to do with disabilities. It's not enough to be invited to serve on a subcommittee for architectural accessibility. We need to aggressively seek positions on the finance committees and planning committees, as well. To get involved with parent-teacher groups. To volunteer at the local shelter for homeless people. To run for office. In essence, to claim a shared ownership in every issue that everyone holds in common.

Breaking into those roles takes an empowering action called cliff jumping. •

• Main idea: the importance of cliff jumping.

There's a poem by S. Wilde that reads:

"Come to the cliff," he said.
I said, "I am afraid."
"Come to the cliff," he said.
I went.
He pushed me.
And I flew. •

• Supporting material: a poem.

One of my first experiences with cliff jumping came when I attended my first day in junior high. My first day in a regular classroom after six years in a special ed school. There were a tense few moments of wondering how I'd be accepted. I was scared to death. Then my teacher took one look at me and said in front of the whole class, "What the hell happened to you?" Talk about an ice breaker. But later I figured it ended up being one of the best introductions I ever had. The disability issue was handled right up front. That freed up the rest of the time for me to get to know my classmates, and for us to find that we had many more similarities than differences . . .

Another kind of cliff jumping happened well into my professional career. I moved from running a relatively small state rehabilitation agency to head up the Rehabilitation Services Administration in Washington, D.C. And it was one of the best decisions I ever made. It overcame a kind of geographical isolation I hadn't recognized existed. •

• Supporting material: examples of cliff jumping.

I commuted to Washington, because my husband and son were in Springfield. I cried for a week before I started the job. I hated leaving my family. But I learned that careers grow when people are willing to risk leaving their own backyard. And we made it an adventure for our family.

Finally, I returned to Illinois. I was recruited by the governor to run the state's Department of Public Aid. And then I became the first person with a disability to be nominated by a major party to run for a statewide office.

That was tough. Getting out to meet people. Wondering how they'd welcome me. Having to crawl into small commuter planes that are rightfully "puddle jumpers," so that I could make the next engagement. Riding in parades and waving, because I couldn't walk; riding in a car while other candidates walked and shook hands along the parade route went against every instinct I felt, but it was an accommodation I had to accept. I was also hoisted onto haystacks to address crowds.

We lost a close election. Yet looking back on all of it, one impression especially touched me. Most people, I'm convinced, saw the real Sue Suter. A major party candidate fighting in a tough election. Not some cripple to pitied. That revelation meant a lot.

Cliff jumping is a part of being normal. Every time is scary. But they are among the most empowering events in our lives, because they free us from the emotional impoverishment of isolation. And because they give us the freedom to follow our conscience and our dreams. And perhaps most importantly, they free us from labels. •

• Main idea: the importance of role models.

. . .

There's [a] lesson we can learn from the deaf community. It's about the fact that history is a vast warning system. Most of the speeches you'll hear in this conference will center on the evolution of the disability movement. Progress, one step at a time. Yet history can also be cyclical.

Years ago, almost 50 percent of all teachers for the deaf in the United States were deaf themselves. More than teachers, they were imparters of a graceful language of signs that were rooted in the deaf community; they were role models for entire generations of young deaf students.

Then, in 1880, the renaissance came to an abrupt end. At an international conference of rehabilitation professionals—much like this one—the school of thought called oralism won the day. American Sign Language was discouraged. Speech acquisition was made paramount, so many schools no longer used deaf teachers; they were now considered bad role models of communication. And perhaps the most blatant wrong committed at the Milan Conference of 1880 was that not a single deaf teacher was allowed to vote on the changes.

It was not so long ago that stories filtered from our own Illinois School for the Deaf about a young deaf girl who asked a hearing dorm counselor if she was going to die soon. She was nearing graduation, and she had only seen a few deaf adults. What happened to the others? This is an extreme example. But it points out the vital importance of role models. •

• Supporting material: an anecdote.

I never had a role model when I was growing up. I remember what my father said to me when I was in the second grade. He loved me very much. He wanted me to be prepared for the future. So he warned me that I would probably never get married. He told me that I should become a clinical psychologist. I eventually did. Then he said that I should work to be the best, so that I could be independent, because some day there might not be anybody around to take care of me.

Hard words for a seven-year-old girl to hear. But my father loved me. And he wanted me to be prepared. What a difference it would have made, for myself and my parents, if there was a family next door where the mother also wore braces. A role model. A person with a disability who was married, who raised children, who was nurturing and independent in her own right. Maybe even a corporate leader.

Middle class college students aren't the only ones who need to know that those labels can also belong to a woman with a disability. People like you and me need that affirmation, as well. Would having a role model like that next door have changed my life? Maybe not. But it would have made me feel better. More normal. More ordinary.

. . .

We can dwell on the injustices of dual discrimination. We can churn until we turn a rut into a grave. Or we can empower ourselves: •

• Main idea: empowering actions audience members should take.

- by holding claim to our citizenship in the community of humanity . . .
- by reaching beyond parochial disability issues that others feel safe in allowing us to govern . . .
- by wrestling for control over the language that defines us . . .
- by treating the needs of women with disabilities as civil rights issues . . .
- by empowering ourselves as full-fledged citizens . . .
- and by simple acts of ordinary living that can mentor and nurture others looking for a role model. •

• Audience involved in solutions.

If there's one thought that I'd like to leave with you, it's that we can make a difference. I've seen it happen over and over.

For example, when women with disabilities in Chicago reached their limit putting up with poor health care, the Rehabilitation Institute of Chicago opened a new Women's Center. And with the help of their executive director, Judith Panko-Reis, the Center has recently received a hundred-thousand-dollar grant to keep the operation alive.

A few years ago, there was a bill in our state legislature to increase wages for personal attendants, so that high turnover rates could be reduced. Many prominent rehabilitation organizations came to the legislative hearings in support of the bill. But it was one consumer, named Terry Gutterman, who made the issue understandable to legislators by simply asking them to "imagine giving the keys to your house to fourteen different people in a single year." That message got through—I believe—in large part because of one small action by one person. The bill passed.

Groups and individuals make a difference. And I believe with all my heart that it can happen again. We women with disabilities have the same hopes and dreams and ambitions as our nondisabled sisters. We are neither weak or heroic. We are normal. And we are boat rockers. •

• Clincher—relating back to boat rocking theme from introduction.

SUMMARY

"Persuasion happens when credible speakers provide good reasons and touch audience emotions."

Once you have selected a topic for your persuasive speech, analyzed your audience, and chosen an effective thesis, you need to develop a message that compels your listeners to accept your thesis—and your ultimate goal of changing or strengthening audience beliefs, attitudes, or actions. You can do this by combining ethos, logos, and pathos.

Through ethos, you establish your credibility as a speaker. The audience must perceive that you are competent and trustworthy, and that you have their best interests at heart. You can also avoid losing credibility by avoiding statements that raise doubts about your knowledge, honesty, or goodwill.

Through logos, you present the sound reasoning behind your claims, using examples, comparisons, cause-effect relationships, or signs, and avoiding common logical fallacies such as ad populum and slippery slope.

Through pathos, you further strengthen your persuasive power by evoking your audience members' emotions—not to manipulate your listeners but to move them in an ethical and responsible manner to take the action you're proposing or adopt the belief you're advocating.

Together, ethos, logos, and pathos can help you win your listeners' heads (their reason), hearts (their emotions), and hands (their commitment to action). Master these three tools, and you'll greatly enhance your prowess as a persuasive speaker.

Key Terms

ETHOS: YOUR CREDIBILITY AS A SPEAKER

ethos (credibility)
competence
trustworthiness
goodwill

LOGOS: THE EVIDENCE AND REASONING BEHIND YOUR MESSAGE

logos
evidence
fallacious (faulty) reasoning
inductive reasoning
example reasoning
representative examples
comparison reasoning
causal reasoning
post hoc fallacy
reversed causality
sign reasoning
ad populum (bandwagon) fallacy
straw person fallacy
slippery slope fallacy
false dilemma fallacy
appeal to tradition fallacy

PATHOS: EVOKING YOUR LISTENERS' EMOTIONS

pathos
fear appeal

Mein Skol, Dein Skol, Alle Vakkera Flikka Skol!

He was a noble warrior...

Eeek!

This is a day of commemoration...

18 SPECIAL-OCCASION SPEAKING

"Whether to mark a celebration, a milestone, or a passing, we all participate in special-occasion speaking as speakers or listeners."

Speeches that praise, celebrate, memorialize, or otherwise commemorate special occasions have a long history. A Sumerian tablet dating back to about 2000 B.C.E. records the funeral utterances of Ludingirra, a teacher and poet, as he laments the loss of his father and his wife by eulogizing (or memorializing) their achievements and personal qualities. Indeed, **epideictic** rhetoric—speaking that praises or blames—was one of the three genres of oratory identified by the fourth-century B.C.E. Greek philosopher Aristotle.[1] Speakers typically used this form of address to celebrate timeless virtues during occasions such as funerals or holidays.[2] And ever since Aristotle's lifetime, people around the world have continued to use public speaking to help themselves and others celebrate joyous occasions, mourn the passing of loved ones, honor friends' or colleagues' achievements, and observe other milestones in their communities.

Think about the times you've been moved by a speech marking a special occasion. Perhaps on the most recent Memorial Day, you heard a speaker praising soldiers who fought in World War II and remembered your grandfather's tour of duty in Europe during that conflict. Maybe you've attended a gathering to observe the passing of another September 11 on the calendar, and the speaker's words helped you reflect once again on the magnitude of the terrorist attacks. You might also have attended a wedding, clapping and cheering along with the other guests as friends and relatives of the bride and groom offered toasts to the new couple. And if you've excelled at your job, perhaps you've been presented with an award, along with words of praise from your boss, during a department meeting or party. If you've attended a formal dinner for your company or a community

PERHAPS A GREAT WEDDING TOAST PUT THIS COUPLE'S MARRIAGE ON THE RIGHT TRACK.

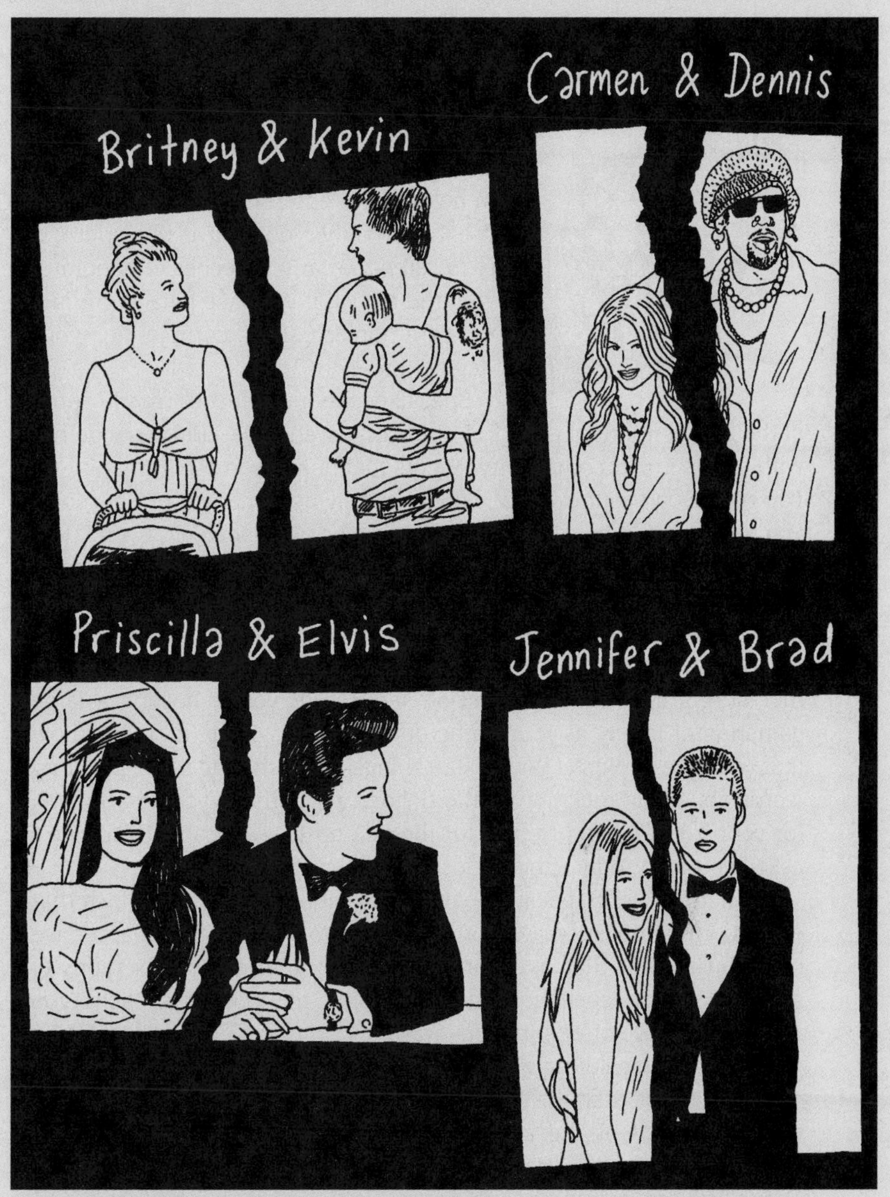

WITH THE RIGHT WEDDING TOAST, PERHAPS THESE COUPLES WOULD HAVE STOOD A BETTER CHANCE OF MAKING IT.

organization, you may have listened to an after-dinner speech—a traditional presentation designed to entertain an audience after a meal. Certainly, you'll have the opportunity to listen to many speeches of congratulation and advice if you take part in graduation ceremonies after completing your college degree.

Special-occasion speeches mark some of the most important events in our lives—events that bring us together with others in our community; events that unite us in our humanity. As you go through your own life, you'll not only hear many such speeches; you will probably be called on to give one or more yourself. Even if you never have to deliver a formal presentation in an official capacity (such as at work or in a civic setting), you will almost certainly be invited to "say a few words" at various points in your life. For example, your grandmother might ask you to say good-bye to your deceased grandfather during an intimate graveside service. Or you're hosting a large gathering of family at your home during Thanksgiving, and you know that your guests expect you to start things off by sharing some inspiring words about the meaning of the holiday. Or perhaps you've arranged for your friend's band to play for the first time at a local pub, and he's asked you to introduce the performers to the crowd.

Whatever your special speaking occasion, you'll have to face that ever-daunting question: "What am I going to say?" In this chapter, we help you answer that question. We start by introducing six types of special-occasion speeches and discussing the purposes each type serves. Then, we offer some general guidelines for speaking at a special occasion. After that, we go into detail about each of the six types of special-occasion speeches, providing tips tailored to each type. And finally, we revisit a few preparation and delivery strategies discussed earlier in this book.

TYPES OF SPECIAL-OCCASION SPEECHES

Although there are various types of special-occasion speeches, the six most common are:

- *Speech of introduction.* Sometimes referred to as "the speech before the speech," this is a brief presentation designed to prepare an audience for the "main event"—a speaker, a performance, or an activity that will follow. A speech of introduction provides context and gives credentials for the main speaker or performer.

- *Speech of presentation.* Awards, honors, and special designations often require speeches before they are conferred. A presentation speech explains the background and significance of the award and the reasons that the recipient is deserving of it.

- *Speech of acceptance.* Recipients of honors, awards, or designations are often expected to give a short presentation of their own—something beyond a simple thank you. Recipients typically express gratitude for the award, extol the award's significance to them and others, and acknowledge others' support and contributions.

- *Speech to memorialize or eulogize.* A eulogy comments on the passing of an individual, celebrates his or her life, and often shares personal reflections and stories about the deceased. A speech to memorialize uses the same approach but is expanded to honor the sacrifice and heroism of a group of individuals—often on a significant anniversary, such as Veterans Day or September 11.

- *Speech to celebrate.* Events that represent rites of passage—such as christenings, graduations, weddings, reunions, and retirements—often demand celebration speeches. These may take the form of a toast or special observance that focuses the audience's attention on the milestone achieved and recognizes the joy and pride the participants feel.
- *After-dinner speech.* At times, a speaker needs to use humor and good storytelling to lighten the mood of an occasion or soften up an audience. Though these presentations are called "after-dinner speeches" (in the tradition of Mark Twain), they can follow or precede a meal. Light in tone, they can help a speaker entertain his or her listeners or set the stage for an event that follows the meal, such as a fundraising effort for a charitable cause.

At some events, you'll hear more than one type of special-occasion speech being delivered. Consider the Academy Awards—what most of us call the Oscars. This star-studded annual event begins with a *speech of introduction*. A master of ceremonies—perhaps Ellen DeGeneres, Jon Stewart, or Billy Crystal—prepares the audience for the main event, often acknowledging the honored tradition of the Oscars while also telling jokes to loosen up the crowd. At some point during the evening, a well-known actor gives a *presentation speech* before announcing a lifetime achievement award for a long-famous director or producer. Recipients of Oscars and lifetime achievement awards deliver *acceptance speeches* thanking the academy, exclaiming how much the award means to them, and acknowledging (sometimes seemingly endlessly) the support they've received from their families and colleagues. And later in the evening, a presenter might *eulogize* a recently departed luminary from the motion-picture industry.

Each type of special-occasion speech serves a unique purpose and evokes a different mood. But the six types all have something in common as well: to deliver them effectively, you apply certain common skills (such as evoking your listeners' emotions and being mindful of their expectations) no matter what type of speech you're giving. The following guidelines can help you establish a basic foundation of knowledge before we explore strategies tailored to each of the six types of speeches.

GENERAL GUIDELINES FOR SPECIAL OCCASIONS

A handful of general guidelines can boost your chances of delivering an effective special-occasion speech, no matter what type you'll be giving. These guidelines include appealing to your audience's emotions, ensuring that your delivery suits the mood of the occasion, adapting your speech to your audience's expectations, evoking shared values, and respecting time constraints.

THE ELEMENTS OF AN EFFECTIVE SPECIAL-OCCASION SPEECH
IT APPEALS TO EMOTION
Love really is a many-splendored thing...
There is always death and taxes...
Wow, I'm genuinely surprised...
...we will remember them...
IT SUITS THE MOOD OF THE OCCASION
...this truly is a happy day...
...this truly is a sad day...
...what an honor...
...this truly is a day for reflection...
IT IS ADAPTED TO AUDIENCE EXPECTATIONS AND EVOKES SHARED VALUES
...without my amazing team I would be nothing...
...to serve in their memory is a great honor...
...and now for an embarrassing story...
...but now I need to cheer you up with a happy story...
IT RESPECTS TIME CONSTRAINTS
...there just isn't time to do them all justice...
...alas, we must move on...
...Ah, time: It passes too quickly.
...don't worry, I'm almost done...

Appealing to Your Audience's Emotions

Successful special-occasion speeches often evoke emotional responses such as laughter, tears, joy, and pride. Since many special occasions are intimately connected with important human events, your audience will likely be predisposed to experiencing a particular feeling during the occasion. Your job in giving the speech will be to signal when it's time for that emotion to come to the surface.

For example, suppose you're about to deliver a eulogy at a graveside service for your grandmother—a loving family woman, accomplished artist, and dedicated supporter of important causes. Family members and friends are gathered around the headstone under a canopy of maple and oak trees. Everyone present is reflecting on your grandmother's life and feeling the sorrow of saying good-bye begin to settle around their hearts. The moment arrives for you to walk to the headstone and deliver the eulogy. You begin speaking. As you recall your grandmother's special qualities and achievements and talk about how much she meant to you, your eyes fill and your voice breaks at times. The combination of your words and the expression of your grief gives the others gathered around the gravesite permission to let their own feelings well up. By enabling your family and friends to begin experiencing and expressing their grief, you help them embark on the mourning process—something we all must do when we have lost a loved one.

Matching Your Delivery to the Mood of the Occasion

Whether joyous or solemn, lighthearted or serious, your demeanor and words should match the overall mood of the special occasion for which you're giving a speech. As the saying goes, there's a time and a place for everything: a time to be serious, and a time to be joyful; a time to tell stories, a time to show respect, and a time to share your own sadness. By ensuring that what you say and how you say it is appropriate for the occasion, you will enhance your effectiveness and impact.

For example, a eulogy calls for primarily a somber, sad tone, though an occasional lovingly humorous recollection about the deceased may also be appropriate and appreciated. At the graveside service for your grandmother, for instance, family members and friends smile through their tears and nod their heads knowingly when you help them recall her famous midnight excursions into the kitchen for some chocolate ice cream.

If you're the best man at your older brother's wedding and you're giving a toast at the reception, you'll of course evoke a different overall mood. You'll want to express your happiness that your brother has found a loving spouse as well as give voice to everyone's wish that the new couple will share a long and joyous life together. And depending on the traditions of your culture, you might introduce a bit of humor by hinting at the wild escapades your brother had in his younger years and expressing your satisfaction that he's finally settling down with a wonderful partner. You decidedly would not go on and on about any hard and painful times the couple experienced while dating. Nor would you be critical in any way of their relationship.

Adapting to Your Audience's Expectations

Listeners' cultural background, age, values, and other characteristics all affect how they perceive a special occasion and what they expect from a speech delivered during that occasion. For example, a community of Christian Arab immigrants living in Chicago would likely want to attend a church funeral service after one of their community members died. Moreover, they would probably expect a mostly religious service with brief discussion of the deceased, including comments focused particularly on how he or she cared about the community and shared its traditions. (Fuller discussion of the person might come at a community dinner in honor of the deceased, later in the day.)

On the other hand, some audiences expect a fun and lighthearted presentation, for example at a roast for a comedian or dignitary during which the audience expects funny stories about the individual being roasted. At this kind of event, it would run against audience expectations to bring up painful events from the person's childhood and thus bring an overly serious turn to the proceedings.

The lesson? Before giving any special-occasion speech, be sure you're familiar with your audience's expectations regarding what should be said during the speech and how it should be said.

Evoking Shared Values

Many effective special-occasion speeches appeal to values shared by members of the audience and the speaker. For instance, suppose you're presenting a plaque to Olivia, a fellow member of PeopleAid, an organization that helps homeless members of your community. The award is for Olivia's steady dedication to PeopleAid's mission: she has recruited an unusual number of volunteers to serve boxed lunches to the homeless at shelters throughout the community and led other valuable projects for the organization. Before handing the plaque to Olivia, you deliver a speech extolling her ability to embody PeopleAid's values, which include compassion for those in need and a strong work ethic. Your speech about Olivia reaffirms your listeners' own dedication to these values and inspires them to strive for the same high standards she has set.

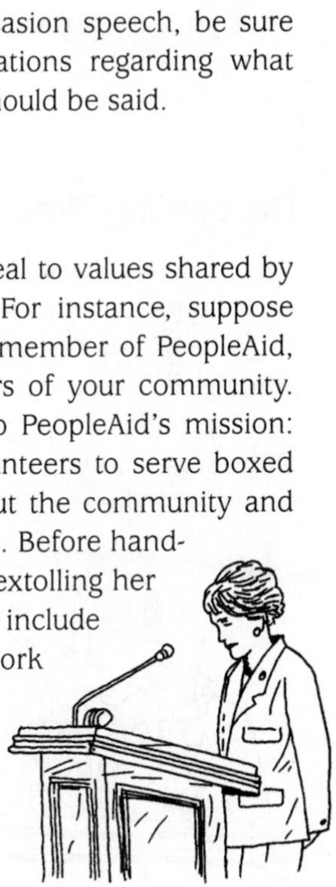

Other special-occasion speeches may touch on values such as patriotism, fairness, shared sacrifice, and religious belief. To illustrate, let's say you're giving a speech at a ceremony recognizing the first anniversary of the death of Frank, a close friend who lost his life while serving in the U.S. Army in Afghanistan after the September 11 attacks. The ceremony is held at the town hall near where you and Frank grew up. Neighbors and family members have gathered to remember Frank and honor the one-year anniversary of his death. In your speech, you note that "Frank felt the same love for his country that everyone in this room feels. We have all made sacrifices for that love. Frank lost his life, and we lost him all too soon. We will never forget our lost friend, brother, son, and neighbor." Through these words, you tap into the patriotism in your listeners' hearts and their sense of shared sacrifice—reminding them that you are all connected in a close community.

Respecting Time Constraints

Most special occasions are carefully planned affairs. Recall a wedding, christening, or retirement dinner you've recently attended. The occasion likely had a program featuring certain events occurring at specific times. The program for a retirement dinner, for example, might look something like: "Cocktails at 4:00. Award ceremony at 5:00. Dinner at 6:00." The occasion may also have featured several speeches. Whenever refreshments, meal service, and multiple speakers are involved, skillful management of the overall program schedule becomes that much more important. If a specific event listed in the program gets off to a late start or if one of the speakers uses up more time than the program has allotted, then the entire event can quickly go off the rails. For this reason, if you're giving a speech at such an occasion, make sure you know beforehand when you're scheduled to speak and what your time allotment is. Then be certain to stick to these logistics while you're delivering the presentation.

STRATEGIES FOR EACH TYPE OF SPECIAL-OCCASION SPEECH

While the general guidelines described in the preceding section can help you deliver an effective special-occasion speech, you'll also want to master strategies tailored to each of the six types of speeches. Pair these specific practices with the general suggestions, and you'll increase the odds of delivering a top-notch speech—no matter what the occasion.

Strategies for Speeches of Introduction

When you're giving a speech to introduce another speaker, a performer, or an event, you have three goals:

- Shift your listeners' focus from interacting with each other to paying attention to the upcoming event.
- Build anticipation and excitement in the audience for the upcoming topic and speaker or presentation.
- Introduce the person, performance, or event that's coming next.

When making an introduction, remember that you are not the main entertainment. Your primary goal is to facilitate what's coming next, and there is nothing more disastrous than an introductory speaker who goes on too long, or tries too hard. So, take care not to upstage the speaker or event you're introducing. In particular, resist any urge to talk at length about yourself. And be sure to express some

THE ART OF INTRODUCTION

of your own appreciation for and anticipation of the upcoming event. The following tips can further help you keep your audience focused on the main event and effectively achieve your three-part goal in giving a speech of introduction.

Be Patient. When the time comes for you to start your introduction, many listeners may still be settling into their seats, finishing a meal, or simply chatting with each other. To help them gradually shift their attention to you, stand up and begin talking above the background noise and voices in the room. But be patient: it takes time for people to transition away from what they're doing at the moment.

Use Attention-Getters. To further focus your listeners on the upcoming speaker or event, use attention-getters to cut through any noise or conversation in the room, while making sure that you remain appropriate for the setting. Consider one of the attention-getters mentioned in Chapter 10, and especially consider incorporating a striking statement or a little bit of humor, or taking the opportunity to let listeners know that you're one of them.

Modulate Your Volume. Even if you are working with a microphone, you may need to speak loudly at first to overcome the prevailing noise in the room and grab listeners' attention. But after your speech is under way, be sure to lower your voice as the room quiets down. If conversation stirs again later during your speech, you can always raise your voice once more to an appropriate level.

Be Focused and Brief. Remember that your job is to prepare the audience to pay attention to the speaker or performance that will follow you. To that end, keep your comments focused on that next event. And make sure your introduction is concise. Otherwise, audience members may start seeing you as the main entertainment, or they may lose interest in the next part of the program.

Strategies for Speeches of Presentation

Like a speech of introduction, the presentation of an award or commendation precedes and facilitates what comes next for the audience. But unlike a speech of introduction, a presentation speech usually *celebrates* the person, organization, or cause being honored—whether it's a service commendation for a teacher at a local PTA meeting, an award at a sports team banquet, or even an Oscar or Emmy.

Thus, in a presentation speech, your role will be more fundamental than in a speech of introduction; you must provide your listeners with background and context for the honor to follow. This might seem unnecessary, as listeners probably already know what the honor is and why they are there to observe it. Yet your job is to highlight the significance of the award and to build excitement and even reverence for it. You can do this by describing in detail the importance of the award itself and the background and contributions of the recipient.

Handled skillfully, a presentation speech can inspire intense emotion in listeners and even move them to dedicate themselves to the

THE ART OF PRESENTING

award recipient's work. Strong and enthusiastic applause after you've presented the award or commendation is another sure sign that you've nailed the speech. The tips below can help you achieve this kind of impact.

Adopt the Persona of a Presenter. In this type of speech, you're not just announcing the conferring of an award or honor; you're also presenting it. To demonstrate your authority as a presenter, be sure to speak respectfully and knowledgeably about your subject.

Explain the Significance and Background of the Award or Honor. Most people in your audience will understand that they are there for the presentation of an award. But they may not know why the honor or award really matters. What is its significance? Does it have an interesting history you could share? In a nutshell, a major goal of your presentation speech is to make clear why your listeners should care about the award about to be bestowed.

Connect the Recipient's Background to the Award's Criteria. Every award has qualifications or criteria that a potential recipient must meet and perhaps exceed. But these may not be obvious for the audience. In your speech, be sure to explain the criteria—and then point out how and why the recipient has met or surpassed them. Consider using stories and examples of the recipient's achievements to dramatically (and perhaps humorously) show why he or she deserves this honor.

Use Appropriate Audiovisual Aids. A video or a slide presentation, perhaps with a light music or audio accompaniment, can complement your speech. Consider using audiovisual aids both to explain the criteria for an award and how the

RICHARD FEYNMAN
1965 NOBEL PRIZE IN PHYSICS

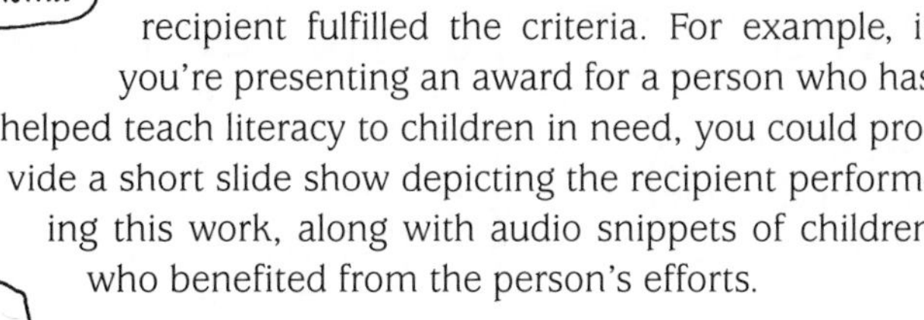

recipient fulfilled the criteria. For example, if you're presenting an award for a person who has helped teach literacy to children in need, you could provide a short slide show depicting the recipient performing this work, along with audio snippets of children who benefited from the person's efforts.

KANYE WEST
2005 GRAMMY AWARDS

Strategies for Speeches of Acceptance

Now imagine that you're the beneficiary of an award and the presenter has just handed it to you. What do you say now?

A high-quality acceptance speech is less about what you're saying ("Thank you; I couldn't have done this without the rest of the team") and more about how you're behaving while accepting the honor. By being there, you transform the presentation into a kind of public spectacle. The audience will expect you to show both humility and responsibility. You can fulfill those expectations by giving a brief, gracious, and heartfelt speech that expresses your gratitude while also recognizing others' efforts that contributed to your achievement. The following tips can help you attain this blend of important qualities.

Use Appropriate Volume and Articulation. Accepting an award can stir intense emotions within you, causing your voice to drop or break—and if you are using a microphone, such lapses will only be amplified. To overcome this challenge, anticipate the impact of strong feelings, and feel free to gather yourself for a moment or two before you start talking. Strive to speak with sufficient volume and clarity throughout, especially when thanking others during your acceptance.

SPENCER LYNN WILKISON
2007 EL PASO COUNTY FAIR QUEEN

Show Genuine Humility. Listeners can easily spot the difference between someone who's genuinely modest and humbled by an honor and one who's just acting humble. Think about it: on at least several occasions, you've probably seen a person stand at a podium and gush about how this award has "caught me off guard" and "left me speechless"—but then he or she pulls out a sheet of paper and gives a canned speech. Irritating, isn't it? To avoid making this mistake, don't act surprised if you knew you would be receiving the award. But definitely express your genuine gratitude for the honor and for the people who helped you achieve it.

Remember That Less Is More. Going on too long while accepting an award can give the impression that you always talk about yourself and rarely exhibit interest in others. To avoid conveying this impression, aim for brevity in your acceptance speech. Say enough to demonstrate your humility (perhaps through a bit of self-deprecating

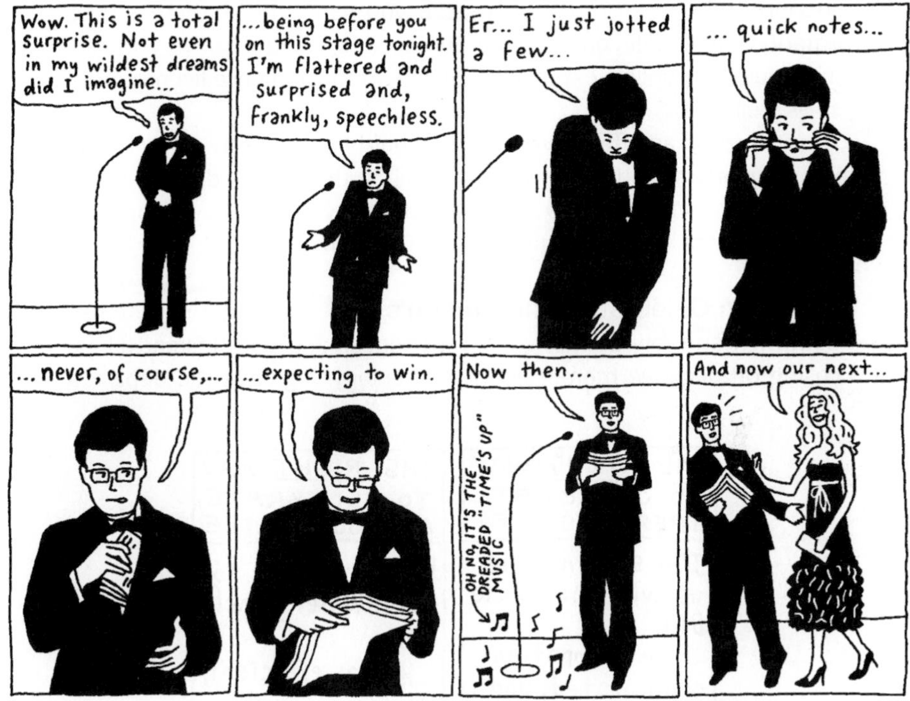

humor) and to acknowledge your deep appreciation for the award or honor. Briefly thank those to whom you are indebted. And then sit down. Otherwise, the music may start playing, and your presenter may take you by the elbow and start ushering you offstage.

Strategies for Speeches to Memorialize or Eulogize

Because death is a part of life, at some point you will inevitably lose a beloved family member or friend. You may be asked to deliver a eulogy about the person at a memorial service after his or her passing. Your purpose during this type of speech is to review and celebrate the life of your loved one and to console your listeners while simultaneously helping them to grieve publicly. It may seem that the two goals (consoling and facilitating grief) are in conflict, but consolation actually supports grieving—primarily because you can express these strong emotions as you encourage your audience to feel the same. Witnessing a eulogist publicly expressing grief gives the audience license to do so as well.

Delivering an effective eulogy is about helping the living by showing your own emotion as well as extolling the departed loved one's virtues and achievements. The following tips can help you provide this assistance while giving this kind of speech.

Focus on Celebrating the Person's Life. Each person's life has both high and low points, good experiences and bad. Instead of focusing on negative memories in your eulogy, highlight the departed

loved one's accomplishments, important relationships, and unique qualities, citing examples and stories familiar to your listeners. You'll establish common ground with your audience members and help them collectively celebrate the best of the person they've lost.

Use Humor Judiciously. At most memorial services, several people will stand up and say something about the deceased. If each of a series of speakers focuses unrelentingly on the profound sorrow of the occasion, the collective heaviness may become too much for the audience to bear. For this reason, consider providing a humorous (but appropriate) anecdote about the deceased at some point during your remarks to relieve the tension. Listeners may feel profound relief when they can laugh through their tears.

Don't Be Afraid to Show Your Own Emotions. The best way to give the audience permission to grieve openly during a memorial service is to show your own emotions. A display of feeling can set loose a flood of feelings in your listeners, which can provide just as healthy and productive a release as laughter after your lovingly humorous story about the deceased.

Strategies for Speeches to Celebrate

Life is as much about joy and celebration as it is about tragedy and loss. The birth of a child, a couple's decision to spend their lives together, a graduation, a rite of passage from youth to adulthood—these and other major milestones in our lives are all cause for happiness. And they're all marked by special occasions at which people deliver speeches to help celebrate the joyous event.

If you're delivering a speech of celebration at such an occasion, your role is to explain the significance of the occasion, acknowledge the joy everyone is feeling, and inspire the audience to take part in the celebration. The following tips can help you achieve this goal.

Aim for Brevity. Take enough time to remind your audience why the gathering is so important and joyful—but not so much time as to tire, bore, or distract the audience from the subject of the celebration.

Use Humor Appropriately. Different cultures define "appropriate" humor in different ways. Use audience analysis to determine whether humor is OK for the particular celebration, or whether listeners would find it distracting or offensive. Never use humor to hurt; instead, use it to highlight endearing qualities of the people being celebrated. Tell stories about the celebrant that he or she knows are funny, and avoid making jokes about matters the person is embarrassed about or considers sensitive. Consider using humor in a self-deprecating way, so the story you're sharing becomes funny instead of hurtful.

Strategies for After-Dinner Speeches

After-dinner speeches have a long and storied tradition in the United States, emerging in an age before television and other mass media had developed and when speaking was therefore a major form of entertainment. This tradition produced literary giants including Mark Twain, who gave several hundred of these kinds of addresses, always after a meal. Like others who delivered these types of presentations, Twain usually salted his after-dinner speeches with entertaining stories, personal references, and a great deal of wit.

While after-dinner speeches in the United States have developed a unique flavor, other cultures also have their own after-dinner speaking traditions. Some scholars argue that the North American style of toasting arose from a long-standing tradition from Great Britain, centered in formal affairs and especially in traditional British men's clubs. And Russia has a tradition of sharing many toasts—studded with anecdotes and stories for each drink—at formal occasions and especially at group meals.

Effective after-dinner speakers assume the role of entertainers and have a talent for amusing and delighting their audiences, while occasionally making a more serious point. Indeed, many after-dinner speeches are given at gatherings designed to raise funds for a particular cause, such as a charitable organization or a politician's election campaign. These speeches are longer and more involved than simple toasts, and they require the ability to thrill and captivate an audience, often after listeners have consumed a full meal and perhaps a few glasses of wine. To overcome these challenges, apply the following strategies for delivering an effective after-dinner talk.

Focus on Humorous Anecdotes and Narrative Delivery, Not Jokes. In after-dinner speeches, the tradition has always been to employ witty stories and anecdotes as opposed to a series of one-liners or jokes with punchlines. Remember that your after-dinner speech should be a combination of anecdotal references and storytelling wrapped around a larger theme, not a stand-up comedy routine.

Practice Your Storytelling and Narrative Delivery. The success of your after-dinner speech hinges just as much on how you tell a story as it does on what you say in the story itself. Rehearse your narrative enough so you can feel comfortable and relaxed sharing it during the actual speech. Think of your after-dinner speech as a kind of performance, and understand that—like all performances—this one will benefit from lots of practice and polish.

Link Your Speech to the Occasion's Theme. If the dinner gathering has a serious theme—for example, the importance of raising funds to support cancer research—consider linking a lighter narrative

to that weightier theme. You'll help the audience adopt a relaxed and receptive frame of mind while still accepting the urgency of the topic.

Adapt Your Delivery to Your Audience and the Occasion. Be prepared to make spontaneous adjustments to your structure and content based on what's happening around you. Look for opportunities to focus your wit or good-natured satire on something that another speaker or a member of the audience has said. For example, by commenting on a point that a previous speaker made or a question that an audience member has asked, you show that you're delivering an original rather than a canned or prepackaged speech. You thus let your audience know that you consider them worthy of a fresh presentation tailored specifically for them.

SAMPLE SPECIAL-OCCASION SPEECH

2002 MT. HOLYOKE COLLEGE COMMENCEMENT ADDRESS

Her Majesty Queen Noor

Her Majesty Queen Noor of Jordan is an international humanitarian activist and an outspoken voice on issues of world peace and justice. She chairs the Noor Al Hussein Foundation (NHF), the King Hussein Foundation, and the King Hussein Foundation International (KHFI). In this commencement speech, excerpted from the original version presented on May 26, 2002, at the women's college Mt. Holyoke in South Hadley, Massachusetts—Queen Noor connects with her audience and uses a modified problem-solution pattern; she describes current challenges to peoples around the world, outlines reasons why women are uniquely poised to help address these challenges, and then encourages the graduates to take an active role in tackling them.

Honored Guests, Faculty, Ladies and Gentlemen, and of course, the Graduates of 2002:

Thank you very, very much. It's an enormous privilege to be here on this truly magnificent campus, in the company of such distinguished fellow honorary degree recipients, of course the faculty of such an exceptional institution, family and friends of the graduates of the Class of 2002. •

• Queen Noor offers an appropriate opening to a commencement speech by complimenting the campus and acknowledging various groups attending the occasion.

. . .

Mt. Holyoke is certainly rich in good things. You have courses here I wish fervently had been available to me when I began my rather unusual career: your Speaking, Arguing, and Writing program would undoubtedly have helped diminish some of my agony over my early speeches and interviews; and your Center for Environmental Literacy could have provided excellent preparation for my extensive international work in the field of conservation. •

• Queen Noor connects with her audience by showing knowledge of courses offered at Mt. Holyoke.

My own university education, Princeton, did however offer some uncommon experiences that helped prepare me surprisingly well. One was the pioneering challenge of membership in the first class of women to enter Princeton. Quite the opposite from the supportive environment you have enjoyed here. When I arrived the male to female ratio was more than 22 to 1—a situation which, as you might imagine, required the quick development of diplomacy and survival skills, and as it turned out excellent preparation for my work in more traditional societies in the Middle East. •

• Queen Noor builds credibility by contrasting her own challenges as a member of the first class at Princeton that allowed women and shows how the experience helped her develop skills for her current work.

. . .

Holyoke is also rich in a long history of women's leadership. It is a place where you all can draw on the past to support your efforts to change the future. From your experience, here, and that of the distinguished Holyoke women who have gone before you into the wider world, you know that women can be leaders in any areas they choose.

Mt. Holyoke's position as a college dedicated to women's advancement in a region rich with history resonates especially with me, for I am a woman dedicated to progress in a region where the past and present are alive, and interact daily. • If you think Mt. Holyoke is old at 165, imagine, in Jordan, with every step we take forward into the future, we are reminded that we are treading pathways marked out over millennia, from the founding of the first human cities ten thousand years ago, through the flowering of the three great Abrahamic faiths, through the crossroads of trade and tumult over centuries. •

• Queen Noor continues with her theme of empowered women, a theme that will continue throughout the address.

• Transition between a focus on campus and a focus on Queen Noor's work in Jordan.

We do not let that slow our steps towards progress, especially where women are concerned . . . but on such ancient paths we tread carefully.

True progress, while it solves problems, must grow out of history and tradition; it cannot be dictated by fiat. It must respect and work with the culture of those expected to embrace it; it cannot be externally imposed. •

• Queen Noor's claim is based on her experience and may resonate with conservative listeners.

This has been a primary focus of my work over the past twenty-five years, combined with my efforts to bridge our cultures by addressing widespread misconceptions concerning Arabs and Muslims—particularly women. Few westerners realize that in the seventh century, Islam liberated attitudes towards women and granted them specific social, political, and economic rights long before Western societies did, such as the equal right to education, to conduct business, to own and inherit property, and not to be coerced into a marriage, instead introducing a marriage contract, a kind of early prenuptial agreement, to assure the rights of the woman in particular.

According to the Quran, God or Allah said, "I waste not the labor of any that labors among you, be you male or female—the one of you is as the other." And, the Prophet Mohammed said, "All people are equal. They are as equal as the teeth on a comb." •

• The claim—perhaps surprising to some listeners—that Islam has held progressive views toward women since the seventh century is bolstered by a quote from the Quran.

Women the world over, including in the Muslim world, have had to struggle with the limitations placed upon them by less enlightened members of their societies. Islam fought against this from the beginning, and today, conservative, intolerant, and restrictive interpretations of tradition and scripture clearly do not reflect the beliefs of the majority of Muslims nor the intentions of the Prophet himself.

But rather than dwell on the aberrant and oppressive beliefs of those who would twist the teachings of Islam—important as it is to correct the dangerous and false perceptions they have engendered—I would like to focus on the inseparable issues of women, leadership, and peace in our time •—vitally linked themes which I believe more accurately reflect the true message of Islam and the teachings and life of the Prophet Mohammed—a man who surrounded himself with strong women such as his first wife, once his employer, who later supported his mission . . . and his last wife who led troops into battle to defend the faith after his death. Even beyond the religious consideration, I think these are subjects of interest and crucial import to us all.

• Thesis statement.

Unfortunately, since the first time I was invited here [in 1996], circumstances have changed—for all of us. . . . Today, uncertainty reigns. And after the tragedy of September 11th, for many of you, it is an uncertainty darker and deeper than what seems like the simpler worries of only last year—

worries about jobs, the economy, and what to do after graduation. •

• Queen Noor begins outlining problems that face the world.

This new dimension of anxiety and uncertainty for many Americans and others after September 11th is nothing new in many other parts of the world. Just as many friends and relatives of the World Trade Center victims remain in wretched suspense about the precise fate of their loved ones, the women of Srebrenica in Bosnia have been waiting for almost seven years for news of theirs, since 8,000 Muslim men and boys were marched away and never seen again.

Just as many Americans now face anxiety over terrorism, citizens in both Israel and the West Bank live in a constant state of alert for attacks, whether by belt bomb or tank, and women, children, and men cannot walk freely in Afghanistan and in many other places in the world without fearing the very ground under their feet may explode from those insidious, deadly leftovers from yesterday's wars—landmines.

While Americans may worry about anthrax and even smallpox attacks, mothers in Africa worry about protecting their children from a whole range of much more common diseases ranging from dysentery to AIDS. •

• Queen Noor expands on world challenges by paralleling the situation in the United States with those in Bosnia, Israel, the West Bank, Afghanistan, and Africa.

Recent events have highlighted for some in the U.S., although perhaps not yet enough for others, that they share the problems of the rest of the world, whether they want to or not. The continuing terrorist threats have jolted many into the realization that there is no security in isolation. Now, rather than going on the offensive, it's time to assess the role of the U.S. in the community of nations and cultures, to look together for positive ways to solve these problems, and to pursue peace.

And here at Holyoke, you know that women can lead that process. •

• Queen Noor directly addresses the graduates as part of the solution.

In the long history of a world full of war, women have always at least been paid lip service as the guardians of peace. From Aristophanes' comedic heroine Lysistrata, . . . to Emily Greene Balch, who helped found the Women's

International League for Peace and Freedom and shared the Nobel Peace Prize in 1946, to another Nobel Laureate, Aung San Suu Kyi, recently released once again from house arrest in Burma, women have acted as symbols in the intermittent human battle against military oppression.

However, far too often, women have been commended in public for their commitment to peace, just before the doors to the negotiating room slammed shut in their faces.

And when they did get a foot in the door, they needed exceptional courage and resolve to introduce reform. I recall a story of the first woman on the staff of a large institution, who inquired about a particularly unjust labor practice. "Madam," she was told, "we have done it that way for one hundred years." "Sir," she replied, "your hundred years are up!" •

• An inspiring quote is likely to connect with the graduates and their loved ones.

This kind of initiative can make vital and lasting contributions to the search for peace in our world. Tapping the unique talents of women peace-builders can, I believe, ultimately end global conflict.

And we desperately need new perspectives, for women's sake, and for humanity's. Women are vital to the peace-building process, and peace is vital to the advancement of women.

Women know better than anyone else that peace is not merely the absence of hostilities, but must grow from a positive human security founded in equity, tolerance, and understanding. . . .

Women bear the brunt of war, but they have almost never been included in the process that launches or resolves conflict. And this is not only unjust, but also unwise.

On the most basic level, peace begins in the community, and women hold together the community. • To exclude them undermines the very foundation of peace. For quite some time now, the glittering prize of the global marketplace has been held out as the incentive for peace-building. But women on the ground in war zones know only too well how much cleaning up needs to be done before a society

• Queen Noor outlines why women are particularly well suited to address the current challenges.

recovering from conflict can even begin to contemplate international commerce.

The two edges of the sword that most seriously threatens the world's women are violence and poverty. Conflict destroys infrastructure and diverts funds from development in areas women desperately need, increasing the poverty from which they already suffer disproportionately. And poverty is most often the underlying cause of conflict.

When given training, resources, and opportunity, women will most often invest in their families. And as they become genuine economic players they also become active decision-makers in social and economic affairs, improving their own status and influence, as well as the overall quality of life and stability of their communities.

. . .

In this way, we are making progress at the community level. But it is time to incorporate women, their voices, opinions, and ideas at the highest political levels. This process has begun, both through the example of highly visible women and through an increasing feminization of politics, as women bring their issues to the forefront of national and global consciousness. Politicians the world over are beginning to realize that women vote. A record number of women are running for governor in U.S. states this year. Women's movements are gaining momentum and visibility. Never before have so many women held so much power. •

• Examples of women who have made recent strides on the national and world stages.

It is no accident that NGOs have emerged as a major force for world change as women's issues are coming to the center of the world stage. . . . New networks are linking grassroots women's organizations to the political process, to make women's voices heard in the corridors of power.

Those of you who attended the "Afghanistan and Beyond" forum in the Gamble Auditorium in March heard some of those voices, such as the Revolutionary Association of the Women of Afghanistan, and Women Waging Peace, groups that use networking, political influence, NGO and private sector partnerships, and especially new technology to bring about change.

Women, for the best and the worst reasons, have extensive experience with reconciliation. Opposed to violence, whether by tradition, temperament, or training, they have always relied on creative strategies and an intuitive pragmatism to stop war.

. . .

Women leaders from Israeli and Palestinian territories have formed such coalitions as the Jerusalem Link to forge a common language for peace in the Middle East. Similar examples abound from Azerbaijan to the Andes. True, alliances may be born out of necessity, but in the long run such joint ventures encourage the development of peace-oriented leadership.

After all, it is not only physical infrastructure that must be restored after decades of betrayal and violence. Trust must be carefully interwoven into the fabric of society, threading together the views and needs of the citizenry. Agreements among official leaders are not enough. Acceptance and reconciliation must begin in the streets of war-torn communities. Women working for peace often find the middle ground that eludes political leaders—that ground on which peace is built in the daily lives of the people.

Let me add this, even though I realize this is long, but for the grandfathers, fathers, brothers, and sons in this audience, of course, I would never want to imply that it is only women who pursue peace. •

• Queen Noor adds an inclusive note by noting that men have also made vital contributions to peace-building.

. . .

Now, especially now, when peace seems more elusive than ever, it's time for all of us, governments, businesses, and private individuals alike, to commit ourselves to the bold and often dangerous work of peace-builders, especially women. Women have long enough been the symbols of peace—the Goddess Pax, perched on a pediment above the parliament buildings of the world, often the first to be knocked down when the rockets flare.

Now it is time they took their rightful place as the makers of peace, in the negotiating and legislative chambers, using their all too intimate experience with war and their expertise in coalition-building to create a new world community. To the men—or anyone—who says we must continue as we always have, it is time to say, "Sir, your hundred—or thousand, or ten thousand—years are up!"

You can and must add your voice to the many other women's voices around the world calling for peace, justice, and tolerance. • Thanks to the power of technology in the service of democratic principles, never before in human history have ordinary people had so much opportunity to do good.

• A direct call to action directed toward the graduates.

Given the intense commercialism of Western culture and the current anxiety about job prospects, it is easy to assume that college graduates are dyed-in-the-wool materialists, interested solely in personal gain and career advancement. But there is heartening evidence to the contrary. According to a UCLA study last year, more students are speaking out and acting against injustice than [at] any time since 1966. Most important, the survey also marks a record number of students volunteering their time, talents, and effort to help others. •

• Data from a study supports the claim that young people do volunteer and can make a difference.

. . .

With your energy, your education, and your intelligence, you have so much more to offer not only to the world of work, but to the world at large. Those qualities are needed now more desperately than ever before.

I was impressed and heartened when I read about the graduation pledge that many of you have signed since February. I won't ask for a show of hands, or even try to do a mental tally of green ribbons, because such a pledge is a thoughtful, internal commitment. But I do congratulate you—any of you—who are trying to work out how to make a living while making a difference in the world. •

• As she nears her conclusion, Queen Noor reminds students of a pledge they have already made to volunteer work.

In the face of uncertainty, the essence of humanity is hope. You, the new graduates of Mt. Holyoke College, the next generation of women leaders, can nurture that hope. And you can build a future for us all.

God bless you and many, many, many congratulations. •

• The speech concludes with a final call to action and a warm offer of congratulations.

SAMPLE SPECIAL-OCCASION SPEECH

REMARKS AT THE FUNERAL OF CIVIL RIGHTS LEADER ROSA PARKS

Governor Jennifer Granholm

Michigan Governor Jennifer Granholm was one of the speakers who honored Rosa Parks's life at her memorial service on November 2, 2005, in Detroit.

Governor Granholm's message demonstrates the style that is a hallmark of special-occasion speeches. She uses metaphors that exemplify Rosa Parks's leadership and strength, along with repetition, to emphasize key themes. Granholm's speech appeals to the broader audience that is celebrating Rosa Parks's life, not just the dignitaries who are attending the service. She challenges the audience to honor Ms. Parks by carrying on her quest for civil rights.

To Judge Keith and all of the members of the clergy; to all of the members of Congress who are here and our state legislators; to our heads of corporations and honored guests—I'm so glad you're here. •

• Granholm begins in a way typical for formal occasions: she acknowledges dignitaries attending the funeral.

But today, I want to address my comments not to you, the "titled" people. Instead, I'd like to talk, for a moment, with everyone out there who doesn't have a title—those who aren't credentialed. I want to use my time to speak to everyone who's never been elected. I want to speak not to the CEOs, but to the secretaries of the company; not to the senators, but to the janitors; not to those who were lucky enough to be ushered into this beautiful space today, but to those who stood in line for hours waiting to get in. And to those of you who are outside who did not get in—this is your day. •

• Granholm extends the range of her address beyond the dignitaries. She hopes to connect with everyone who is celebrating Rosa Parks's life.

Rosa Parks was lain in honor in our nation's capitol, in the great Rotunda that's reserved only for war heroes and for presidents. But she was not a president. She was, though, a war hero. She was a heroic warrior for equality, and that alone, my God, surely is enough for a nation to celebrate.

But Rosa Parks was also a warrior for the everyman and the everywoman. She was a warrior with the soft armor of a seamstress; a warrior with the powerful weapon of the Sunday school teacher; a warrior wearing a warrior's helmet made of a crown of perfectly coiled braids; a soldier whose tank in this battle was a city bus; an improbable warrior leading an unlikely army of waitresses, and street sweepers, and shopkeepers, and auto mechanics; a warrior protected in this army by the piercing weapons of love and nonviolence, more powerful than any weapons or any army before or since. •

• Style—warrior metaphors and effective use of repetition.

And so, perhaps what we are celebrating today—in addition to the fight, the noble fight—is how it was fought. Rosa Parks stands for every one of us improbable warriors, in every seemingly small moment where truth and justice are at risk. She offered every one of us this example of a splendid paradox—the paradox of quiet strength. No more quiet than strong; certainly no more strong than quiet, each reinforcing the other. •

• Language amplifies Rosa Parks's quiet strength.

Rosa Parks was powerful, because she was improbable. She was unexpected. She was untitled. And what was true of Gandhi was certainly true of Rosa Parks: that her greatness lay in what everybody could do, but doesn't. We will all say today that the greatest tribute we could pay to our improbable warrior is to continue battling and to do so in a way that honors her life. • I, like you, imagine the day when the war will be won. The day when a brilliant eight-year-old chess player has the same chances in life, whether she lives in Livonia or off Livernois. We know that this war will be won when the son of a barber on Grand River receives from each of us the same looks of hope and words of encouragement as the son of a doctor in Grand Rapids. We know that the war will be won when the city of Bloomfield Hills and the city of Detroit have the same college graduation rates—and the same low prison incarceration rates as well. •

• Appeal to audience to carry on Rosa Parks's legacy.

• Effective use of examples and repetition.

We know that we will be winning Mrs. Parks's war—our war—when it's yesterday's news when a newly elected governor, senator, or president is a woman or person of color—yesterday's news. We know we will be winning the war when people in the state of Michigan do not have to vote on whether diversity in our university classrooms is a good thing. We know we will see signs that we are winning this war when love overwhelms fear and acts of quiet strength become our daily bread.

So—good night, Mrs. Parks, from the state of Michigan, to our own gently powerful hero. Because by your actions, you have given us our final marching orders. We are enlisted in this war.

On behalf of the state of Michigan, ma'am, we are reporting for duty. •

• Granholm concludes her speech by celebrating Rosa Parks and pledging that the state of Michigan will continue Parks's war for equality.

SAMPLE SPECIAL-OCCASION SPEECH

SPEECH TO ACCEPT THE 1949 NOBEL PRIZE IN LITERATURE

William Faulkner

Speeches to accept awards often demand of their speakers a mix of gratitude and humility, rejoicing and respect. Award winners in our culture should also be modest, though not falsely apologetic, and they should show wit and good nature where possible. There are few prizes better globally recognized than the Nobel Prize, and in this speech accepting the Nobel Prize in Literature, delivered in Stockholm in 1950, the great author William Faulkner speaks from the heart in words that remind the audience why he was a good speaker—and a great wordsmith.

I feel that this award was not made to me as a man, but to my work—a life's work in the agony and sweat of the human spirit, not for glory and least of all for profit, but to create out of the materials of the human spirit something which did not exist before. So this award is only mine in trust. • It will not be difficult to find a dedication for the money part of it commensurate with the purpose and significance of its origin. But I would like to do the same with the acclaim too, by using this moment as a pinnacle from which I might be listened to by the young men and women already dedicated to the same anguish and travail, among whom is already that one who will some day stand here where I am standing. •

• Faulkner acknowledges the importance of the award, but notes that it is less for him and more for his literary output.

• Although Faulkner addresses a crowd of dignitaries, he makes it clear that he speaks to a younger generation of artists. The words that follow will be for them.

Our tragedy today is a general and universal physical fear so long sustained by now that we can even bear it. There are no longer problems of the spirit. There is only the question: when will I be blown up? Because of this, the young man or woman writing today has forgotten the problems of the human heart in conflict with itself which alone can make good writing because only that is worth writing about, worth the agony and the sweat. •

• By asking "When will I be blown up?" Faulkner emphasizes that public fears of nuclear holocaust in the 1940s had replaced meditations on the essential internal conflicts we all feel as humans.

He must learn them again. He must teach himself that the basest of all things is to be afraid; and, teaching himself that, forget it forever, leaving no room in his workshop for anything but the old verities and truths of the heart, the old universal truths lacking which any story is ephemeral and doomed—love and honor and pity and pride and compassion and sacrifice. • Until he does so, he labors under a curse. He writes not of love but of lust, of defeats in which nobody loses anything of value, of victories without hope and, worst of all, without pity or compassion. His griefs grieve on no universal bones, leaving no scars. He writes not of the heart but of the glands.

• Faulkner urges future writers and poets not to ignore the essential human conflicts.

Until he relearns these things, he will write as though he stood among and watched the end of man. I decline to accept the end of man. • It is easy enough to say that man is immortal simply because he will endure: that when the last ding-dong of doom has clanged and faded from the last worthless rock hanging tideless in the last red and dying evening, that even then there will still be one more sound: that of his puny inexhaustible voice, still talking. I refuse to

• A bold, life-affirming statement made in the face of fears about nuclear Armageddon.

accept this. • I believe that man will not merely endure: he will prevail. He is immortal, not because he alone among creatures has an inexhaustible voice, but because he has a soul, a spirit capable of compassion and sacrifice and endurance.

• Effective repetition: "I refuse to accept this."

The poet's, the writer's, duty is to write about these things. It is his privilege to help man endure by lifting his heart, by reminding him of the courage and honor and hope and pride and compassion and pity and sacrifice which have been the glory of his past. The poet's voice need not merely be the record of man, it can be one of the props, the pillars to help him endure and prevail. •

• Careful word choice: Faulkner labels the necessity to write about the human condition a "duty" and a "privilege." These words elevate the calling of future artists to a responsibility and an obligation.

SUMMARY

> "Whether to mark a celebration, a milestone, or a passing, we all participate in special-occasion speaking as speakers or listeners."

At some point in your life, you will almost certainly be asked to deliver a special-occasion speech, whether it's to mark a joyous or sorrowful event, present or accept an award, introduce another speaker or performer, or give a witty but evocative talk after a formal dinner. By applying the general guidelines described in this chapter as well as the strategies tailored specifically to each of the six types of special-occasion speeches, you can lay the groundwork for a successful presentation that will have your listeners remembering the event for many years to come. If you are asked to deliver a speech on such an occasion, be aware of the type of speech your audience will expect and follow specific strategies designed to tailor your special-occasion speech for both the occasion *and* the audience.

Key Term

epideictic

Wow, we did it! I think that went really well. Turns out we can work as a group after all.
You're right, Jenny. Even Yolanda and I managed to get along without stepping on each other's toes...
Amazing, eh? I'm surprised to admit it, but I enjoyed working with you all.
What do you think Ashley?
I think URP rocks!
URP
UNIQUE REALISTIC
URP
UNIQUE REALISTI PEOPL
URP
URP
URP

19

GROUP COMMUNICATION

"Several heads are better than one."

Jenny, Sam, Juan, Ashley, and Yolanda were all taking a course called Community Service 101, in which students receive credit for performing volunteer work. The instructor had organized the students into groups and charged each group with deciding on a volunteer project and contributing at least thirty hours of service per person. At the end of the term, each group would deliver a thirty-minute multimedia presentation informing the class about its project. Jenny, Sam, Juan, Ashley, and Yolanda were placed in a group, one of five in the class.

Throughout the term, Jenny, Sam, Juan, Ashley, and Yolanda experienced firsthand the challenges and benefits of working in a group. For example, they argued over what to call themselves, eventually settling on URP ("Unique, Realistic People")—though only after intense and uncomfortable debate. During their first few meetings, Sam and Yolanda kept interrupting each other, while Ashley tried to

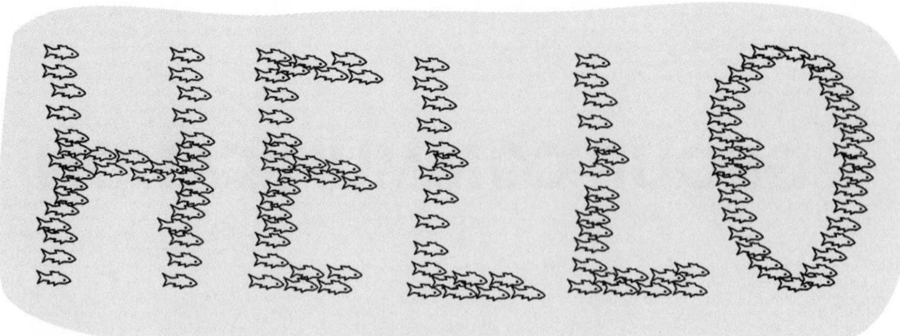

dominate the discussion. Eventually, Juan stepped in to bring things under control. He reminded the others that they needed to quickly select a project and work out a plan for implementing the project in order to fulfill the requirements of the service project. Jenny, realizing that smoother cooperation would help them achieve this goal, also suggested that the group agree on rules for communicating and making decisions. They settled on several rules, including "No interrupting when someone is speaking, everyone gets a chance to contribute ideas, and all decisions must be unanimous."

As the project unfolded, URP's attention to effective leadership and productive participation enabled the group's members to select and carry out a worthy project—supporting an after-school program at a nearby elementary school. Through spirited but respectful discussions, each member was able to offer unique and valuable ideas for carrying out the project.

Despite the rocky start, the group's commitment to the mission and to each other paid big dividends. By the time URP was scheduled to deliver its presentation on the project to the rest of the class, Jenny, Sam, Juan, Ashley, and Yolanda had mastered the challenges of managing group dynamics. Their speech was a resounding success, as each member described a different aspect of how URP had carried out its project and what results the group had achieved.

Through their URP project, these students had discovered both the difficulties and advantages of working in a **small group**—a limited number of people gathered for a specific purpose. This classroom experience showed them that **group dynamics**—the ways in which members relate to one another and view their functions—can determine whether a group achieves its mission.

Learning how to master group dynamics, work well with others in pursuit of a common goal, and communicate your group's achievement to others are valuable life skills. Although group interactions can sometimes be frustrating, you will inevitably be asked or decide to participate in a group at some point in your educational and professional lives—whether in the classroom, in your community, or at work.[1]

Why is working effectively in a group so important? Small groups offer important advantages over individual efforts. Often, people can achieve a better outcome by collaborating on a task than by working alone. Each group member has unique experiences and perspectives to offer. By sharing their ideas, each member has the chance to spot potential problems or improvements in a plan that a lone individual might miss. And each person in a group has different strengths and interests. The group can divide up a project so that each member takes responsibility for the portions of the job he or she is best suited for.

But as we've seen with URP's story, to gain the benefits of collaboration, group members must interact productively. This chapter provides suggestions for managing key elements of group dynamics—including how to lead a group, how to participate in one, how to make decisions as a group, and how to present your findings or decisions to an audience.

EFFECTIVE GROUP LEADERSHIP

When the coach of a gold-medal–winning Olympic team, the leader of a Nobel Prize–winning medical research team, or the director of a successful play is interviewed, that person is garnering recognition for being a successful leader; successful groups depend on capable participation by each group member, but the leader's actions are critical.

Why? Because it's difficult for any group to function without an effective leader. Somebody needs to organize group meetings, keep the group focused, encourage participation by all members, mediate conflict, and facilitate decision making. The leader need not have total control, but he or she must help the members reach a decision and achieve goals as a group. How do groups acquire leaders? Through several means, as we'll discover in this section.

NO LEADER

WITH A LEADER

Selecting a Leader

Groups gain leaders in various ways. Sometimes an external authority selects a **designated leader** to help the group quickly move forward with its mission. For example, a mayor may appoint a blue-ribbon committee to investigate ways to improve mass transit and designate a leader to guide the inquiry, or an army lieutenant leading a mission who needs to send soldiers on reconnaissance may designate a leader from the group of troops selected.

In other situations, there may be an **implied leader**, someone with preexisting authority or skills particularly well suited to the task at hand. For instance, Tova, a marketing manager, forms a task force to evaluate her company's advertising strategies. At the task force's first meeting, she's the implied leader because she formed the group.

In still other situations, a group may have an **emergent leader**, one who comes to be recognized as a leader by the group's members

Which one of these group members is the implied leader?

over time. While not officially elected or even named as such, an emergent leader usually comes to assume the role because he or she has the most time to commit to the group, demonstrates exceptional competence and goodwill, or simply takes the initiative and starts leading. Juan and Jenny did this for URP.

Leading Meetings

Effective group leaders conduct meetings in ways that enable members to work together productively, contribute their ideas, and make well-informed decisions. If you're the leader of a group, consider these tips for facilitating group meetings.

Address Procedural Needs. Where and when will meetings take place? Who will start meetings and record notes? And how will notes be circulated to members who could not attend a particular meeting?

Model the Behavior You Expect. Avoid interrupting others or dismissing their questions or comments. Make group members feel they can interact comfortably with you. And resist any urge to dominate discussions or decisions.

Facilitate Discussion. Ensure that all members of your group have the opportunity to participate in each discussion. If some group members are not speaking during a meeting, strive to bring them into the discussion ("Anil, what do you think?" or "That's a good point, Sarah—you've clearly researched this carefully. But let's also give Tyler a chance to share his ideas.") While it's important to contribute when you have an idea that nobody else has raised, try to let other members speak first. If you make your position known early, members may hesitate to contradict you.

Keep Members on Task. If the discussion begins to stray from the item under consideration, keep members on task in a friendly manner. For example, "I agree with Harry that our department's holiday party is going to be a blast. But let's talk about how we're going to tackle reserving the space for the event."

Help Members Avoid Groupthink. **Groupthink** is members' tendency to accept ideas and information uncritically because of strong feelings of loyalty or single-mindedness within the group.[2] Groupthink erodes the lively and open exchange of ideas necessary for informed decisions. If one person advocates a course of action in your group and everybody else nods in agreement, try to broaden the discussion before moving the group toward making a final decision. For instance, ask a particularly insightful participant if he or she can think of any potential risks to the proposed course of action. If nobody is willing to offer any reservations, consider raising some concerns yourself: "I like Sangeeta's idea, but let me play devil's advocate for a minute. . . . " Be sure that the group has considered the pros *and* cons of the proposed options before selecting one.

Facilitate Decisions. When it seems that members of your group have thoroughly discussed the issue at hand, help them come to a decision. As a leader, you will participate in the final decision, but your leadership role does not entitle you to make the decision for the group—never use your power to manipulate the group. Once the decision has been made, ensure that it is recorded and then move the group on to the next issue. Revisit decisions only when new circumstances make the original decision unfeasible.

Help Organize the Group's Presentation. Does your group need to present its conclusions? If so, who will serve as the speakers or speaker? How will the presentation be framed to best meet the audience's needs? As the leader, you don't necessarily need to make all the decisions yourself, but you do need to coordinate the decisions on these topics.

Managing Conflict

No matter the situation or setting, disagreements inevitably crop up as a group works together on a project. Some conflict is helpful. For example, when members express honest disagreement about proposed plans of action, they can help minimize the risk of groupthink. But interpersonal conflicts that have nothing to do with the group's mission only create distraction. Whenever conflict arises in your group, strive to either minimize it or channel it in a productive direction. The following guidelines can help.

Refer to Ideas by Topic, Not by Person. Focus on the content of specific suggestions, rather than attributing those suggestions to individual members. For example, suppose you're part of a group that's trying to get a candidate elected as head of the town council. Monique advocates a mass e-mail to build support for the candidate, but Tim thinks that leafleting would be better. Refer to these ideas as "the e-mail plan" and "the leafleting plan" rather than "Monique's idea" and "Tim's suggestion." When ideas get associated with an individual, that person may develop a feeling of personal investment in that option. He or she may thus become defensive if the proposal is criticized—even if it has real shortcomings.

Resolve Conflicts Quickly. If a conflict between group members becomes distracting, try to resolve it rather than allowing it to continue or repressing it. Give the members who disagree an equal opportunity to explain their perspective; let each person speak without interruption, and then ask other members for their views. If both people's ideas have merit, perhaps you can help the group find a solution that draws the best from each perspective. As leader, you may ultimately need to offer your opinion or vote in order to break a deadlock on an issue, but try to give the members an opportunity to speak before injecting your opinion.

Focus on Tasks, Not Disagreements. To help members concentrate on the task at hand and not interpersonal tensions that may be simmering, articulate desired changes in behavior rather than criticizing individuals: "Let's get back to discussing our project," not "Sally, your answers to Noah's questions are always so sarcastic."

A personality clash may better be solved by discussing the problem in private with the members who disagree, rather than airing the conflict in front of the entire group. If there is a member who gets along well with the people experiencing conflict, he or she may be able to help them find a way to manage their disagreement.

Manage Disruptive Emotions. Conflicts can spark intense and disruptive emotions within a group. Even after a conflict has been resolved, members may still feel angry, upset, or embarrassed and may withdraw from the discussion. If this happens, bring reluctant members back into the discussion by inviting their input on important issues.

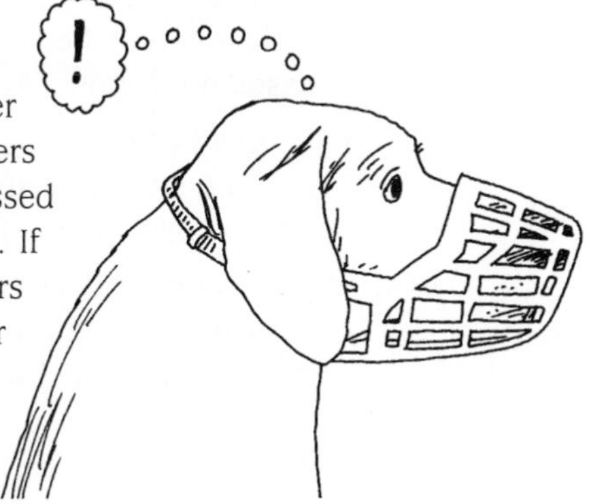

EFFECTIVE GROUP MEMBERSHIP

While strong leadership is essential to effective group communication, productive participation by members is equally vital. To contribute your best to a group as a member, start by understanding the types of roles you can take on to support your group's success.

Three Types of Member Roles

We've identified three types of roles group members can fill.[3] Two of them—task-oriented and maintenance-oriented roles—are helpful. The third type—self-oriented—is not productive and should be avoided.

Task-Oriented Roles. These roles contribute to the group's ability to accomplish its goals through enhancing members' participation and the free flow of information within the group. In a group in which members are fulfilling these roles, you'll likely see people asking good questions and making constructive comments. There are eight task-oriented roles:

- *Initiators* suggest the group's goals and offer new ideas or propose new solutions.
- *Information providers* offer facts relevant to the issue under discussion. These facts might include researched evidence or examples based on personal experience.
- *Information gatherers* ask other members to share facts they know, or they seek out needed information from other sources.
- *Elaborators* add supporting facts, examples, or ideas to a point that someone else has made during the discussion.

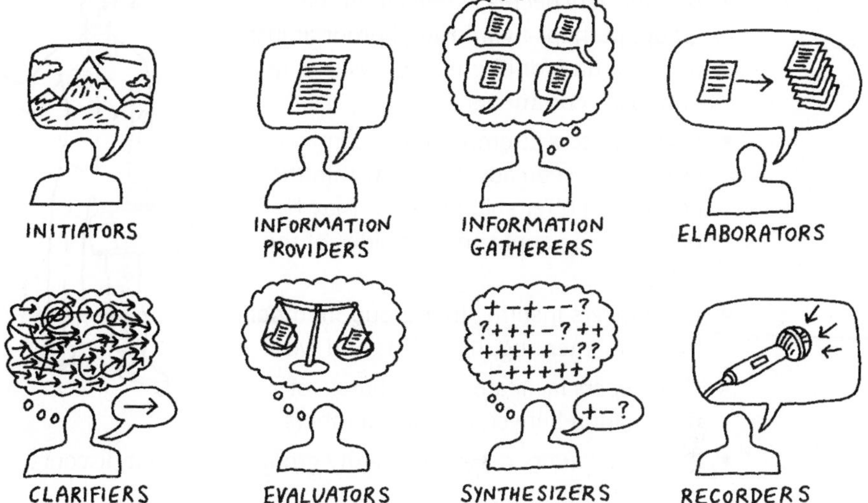

- *Clarifiers* attempt to make the meaning of another member's statement more precise.
- *Evaluators* offer their own judgments about the ideas put forward during a discussion.
- *Synthesizers* identify emerging agreements and disagreements among the group as a whole.
- *Recorders* take notes during the meeting, tracking major decisions and plans made by the group. They may send memos or e-mails to group members summarizing previous meetings, providing agendas for future meetings, or reminding people of tasks they agreed to work on between meetings.

Maintenance-Oriented Roles. These roles help sustain and strengthen efficient and effective interpersonal relations in a group. When members perform maintenance roles effectively, groups are more likely to work together comfortably as a team, support one another, and present findings or recommendations that reflect group consensus. There are five maintenance-oriented roles:

- *Harmonizers* decrease tension in the group, perhaps by infusing humor at just the right time or by making positive and optimistic comments.
- *Compromisers* attempt to find common ground between adversaries within the group, and offer solutions that may be palatable to people on both sides of the conflict.
- *Encouragers* inspire other group members by complimenting their ideas and work.
- *Gatekeepers* facilitate the exchange of information between group members.
- *Norm facilitators* reinforce healthy group norms and discourage unproductive ones.

Self-Oriented Roles. These roles accomplish little for a group and are motivated by the selfish ends of individual members. Groups with a heavy emphasis on these roles may experience incomplete findings, infighting, and dissension. There are four self-oriented roles:

- *Blockers* stop the group from moving toward its objective—by refusing to accept decisions the group has made or by arbitrarily rejecting other group members' ideas or opinions.
- *Withdrawers* refuse to make any contribution or to participate in the discussion. They may feel out of their element in the group or may be having difficulty following other members' comments and ideas.

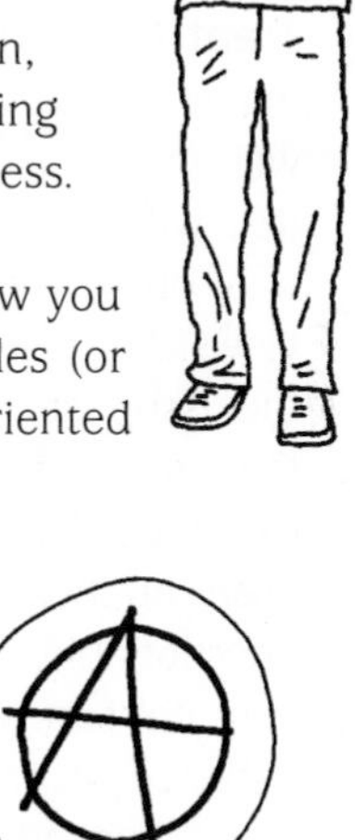

- *Dominators* monopolize group interactions, interrupting others, arguing for the sake of arguing, and insisting on having the last word. This behavior may stem from feelings of insecurity, an aggressive personality, or some other factor.
- *Distracters*—the exact opposite of *harmonizers*—send the group in irrelevant directions with off-topic comments or extraneous conversation, perhaps because they have trouble concentrating on a topic or focusing on completion of a process.

When you're participating in a group, focus on how you can fulfill task-oriented and maintenance-oriented roles (or encourage others to do so) and avoid playing self-oriented roles and discourage these roles in others.

DOMINATORS

Tips for Participating in a Small Group

In addition to fulfilling task- and maintenance-oriented roles, you can improve your effectiveness at group participation by applying the following practices.

Prepare for Group Meetings. If an agenda has been distributed for an upcoming meeting, think about the topics under consideration *before* you gather with other group members. Keep track

of any necessary commitments you make for the meeting (such as researching the answer to a question or bringing your laptop) and be sure to fulfill them.

Treat Other Members Courteously. Courtesy begins with arriving at a group meeting on time (or at least informing the group if you will be late). Turn off your cell phone unless you are expecting a call that will help the group conduct its business. During the discussion, treat other members with respect, even when you disagree with their views. And if you do disagree with other members, be sure to focus on the issue at hand, rather than on personalities. For example, if someone proposes an idea that you find questionable, don't say, "I'm not sure you have the patience to carry out this idea." Instead, try to learn more, perhaps by asking, "What's your experience in doing this sort of thing? Can you tell us more about the kinds of challenges we can expect?"

Listen Interactively. Inattention between members can cause tension in a group. Someone who doesn't feel heard may turn a deaf ear to another person's comments at later meetings. To avoid this problem, practice interactive listening (see Chapter 4). As other members of your group share their ideas and comments, try to understand their viewpoints and show that you're listening. Ask for clarification if you need it, and make sure you understand a point before you challenge it.

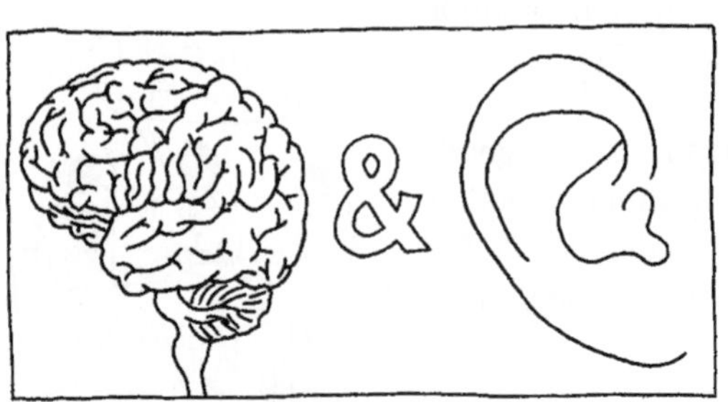

Participate, Don't Dominate. To gain the benefit of diverse perspectives, a group needs contributions from each member. When you have a relevant point to make, share your idea. Your participation is particularly important when you have experience with a topic or when you have a unique viewpoint that no one else has expressed yet.

At the same time, avoid monopolizing the discussion. If you find yourself speaking a disproportionate amount of the time, take a break and let other members contribute. You may even ask another member to chime in if it seems that he or she has an idea but is reluctant to speak.

Participate Authentically. A group functions at its best when members put diverse ideas and perspectives on the table. Therefore, be guided by honesty, not popularity, when considering problems and solutions. If you have an idea that you believe is important, don't be afraid to mention it, even if you're worried about how others might perceive it. And if you have concerns about another member's suggestion, explain your reservations to the group.

But balance candor with tact when questioning or challenging a colleague's idea. Critique the idea, not the person, in a manner that makes your concern clear. For example: "I'm not sure our group can afford to rent that facility for our project," not "Where in the world do you think we're going to get the money for this?"

And if others disagree with an idea you have presented, avoid overreacting. Instead, let others explain their position. If you disagree with what you're hearing, explain your position calmly and rationally. Conversely, if you think the other members' criticism is well taken, be honest and acknowledge that you agree.

Fulfill Your Commitments. For a group to achieve its goals, it's vital that members accept responsibility for performing certain tasks, both the ones assigned to them individually and the ones required of all participating group members. For example, you may promise to research the cost of an item that your group needs to purchase, or perhaps you've agreed to distribute notes from the last meeting to the group.

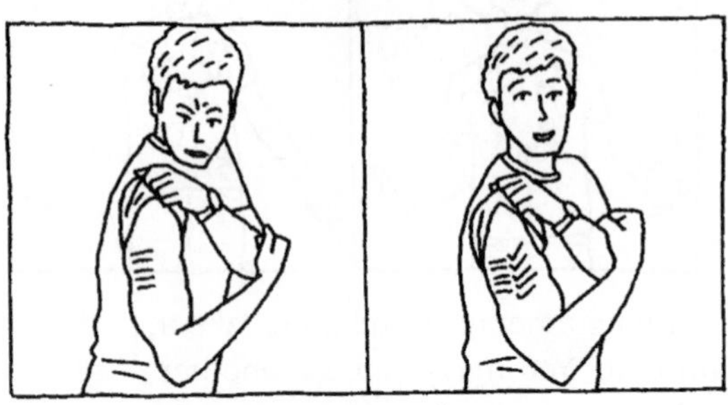

When you make commitments, the rest of your group will rely on you to fulfill them—if people drop the ball enough times, the group as a whole will find it more and more difficult to carry out its work. Moreover, in most situations, work assigned to another group member will hinge on work you've been assigned, so failing to follow up on your commitment will hurt not just you, but also the other member.

GROUP DECISION MAKING AND THE REFLECTIVE-THINKING PROCESS

Although there is no single method that a group *must* use to make decisions, research has shown that the **reflective-thinking process** is a particularly effective approach.[4] The reflective-thinking process has five steps:

1. Define the problem.
2. Analyze the problem.
3. Establish criteria for solutions.
4. Generate possible solutions.
5. Select the best solution.

In this section, we take a closer look at each of these steps.

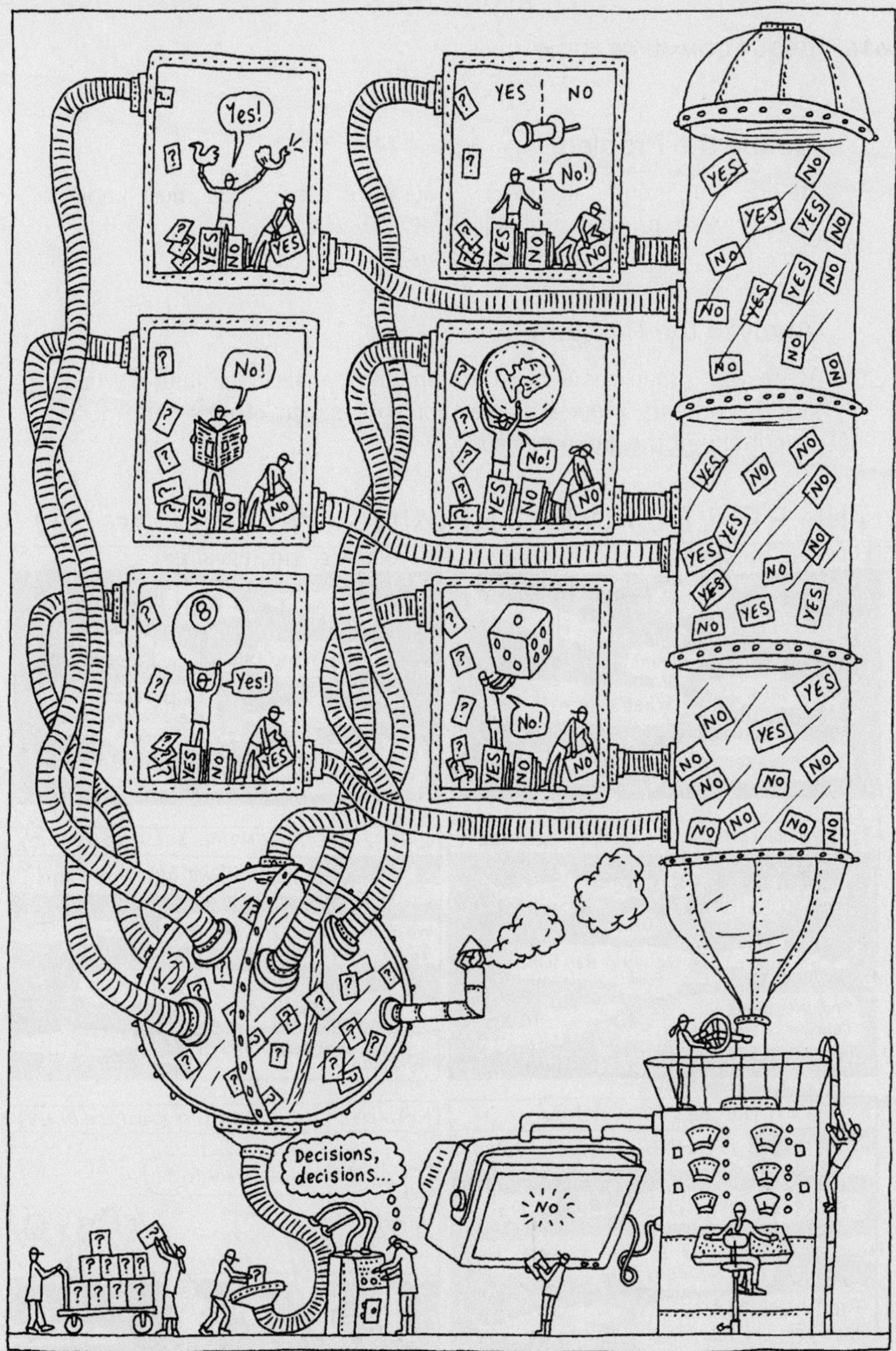

Yes!
YES
NO
No!
No!
No!
Yes!
No!
Decisions, decisions...
NO

Define the Problem

Before your group can select a course of action, you must know exactly what problem (or objective) you will address. As a group, work to define the problem or goal as precisely as possible.

Analyze the Problem

Once your group has defined the problem, analyze its nature. What are the primary aspects of the problem? Which of these are most important for the group to focus on?

THE REFLECTIVE-THINKING PROCESS (FOR FISH)

THE REFLECTIVE-THINKING PROCESS (FOR HUMANS)
Boo!
DEFINE THE PROBLEM
This is Connecticut. There aren't meant to be TUMBLEWEEDS in Connecticut.
He's right, and it's our job as ENVIRONMENTAL PROTECTION COMMITTEE members to decide what to do about them.
?
EXHIBIT A
Grrr!
ANALYZE THE PROBLEM
Clearly GLOBAL WARMING is to blame, but that's too big a subject for this meeting. We must just FOCUS on the TUMBLEWEEDS.
Here, here!
Stupid rolling things are all over the golf course. It's an outrage!
ESTABLISH CRITERIA FOR SOLVING THE PROBLEM
What solution removes TUMBLEWEEDS the fastest?
And most affordably?
We need to keep them off the golf course.
It must be tidy!
GENERATE POTENTIAL SOLUTIONS
So, here are our options:
1. BUILD A FENCE TO STOP THEM ROLLING THIS WAY.
2. ROUND THEM UP AND SELL THEM TO COWBOY MOVIE PRODUCERS.
3. BURN THEM.
4. GENETICALLY ALTER THEM SO THEY GROW CUBE-SHAPED (RATHER THAN SPHERICAL) AND THEREFORE CAN'T ROLL.
5. LEARN TO LOVE THEM.
6. WAR AGAINST THEM!
SELECT THE BEST SOLUTION
OK. Who thinks WAR is the way to go?
No WAR!
Give WAR a chance!
Let's roll!
Oh no, another war!
WAR!
WAR!
Burn them!
Surely a fence makes more sense.
But WAR doesn't MEET OUR CRITERIA, does it?
Defend our course!
WAR!
WAR!
Love them!

Establish Criteria for Solutions

Decide which factors will be most important when weighing possible solutions to the problem your group will be addressing. Each proposed solution will have strengths and weaknesses, and establishing criteria will help you select the best overall solution.

Generate Possible Solutions

Create a list of potential solutions to the problem your group is addressing. Brainstorming (see Chapter 6) is an effective technique for building this list. Remember that during brainstorming, the goal is to generate as many ideas as possible without judging them. Research can also be a good way to find out how other individuals or groups may have handled similar problems.

Select the Best Solution

Once your group has developed a number of potential solutions, evaluate the advantages and disadvantages of each based on the criteria you've defined.

After a group has reached a consensus, it often needs to communicate its findings to others. In the following section, we explain how to plan and deliver effective group presentations.

DELIVERING GROUP PRESENTATIONS

To share its ideas with an audience, a group may select from several common approaches: a **symposium**, where several or all group members speak to the audience in turn; a **panel discussion**, in which members engage in discourse with each other, observed by the audience; and a presentation by one member representing the group. In this section, we offer tips for using each of these three approaches.

Symposium

During a symposium, each group member takes responsibility for delivering a different part of the presentation, depending on his or her expertise or interest, or the needs of the group. For example, when a product team at a computer company proposes a design for a new handheld device to its research and development department, one member might describe the competing handheld designs the team used as reference points for its own design. Then, another member could present the technical resources that will be required to manufacture the device. A third member might then present the group's thoughts about how to minimize the costs of producing the design.

If your group has decided to use this presentation format, plan your symposium carefully. Make sure everyone in the group agrees on the topic that each speaker will address and the time he or she will take. Be sure that all members know what will go into each presentation, so no one unwittingly repeats points made by someone else (or forgets to mention important ideas).

When you participate in a symposium, avoid speaking longer than your allotted time. Otherwise, subsequent speakers may have insufficient time to deliver their parts of the presentation. Also treat other speakers' ideas with respect. If you need to mention points on which group members disagree, present others' ideas in a professional manner, without judging the individuals advocating those ideas.

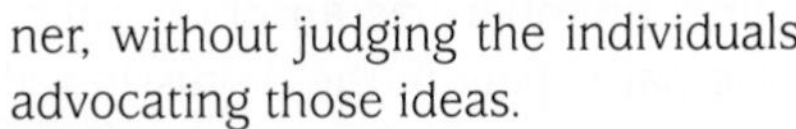

As you close your part of the presentation, make sure to briefly introduce the next speaker. Make use of any connection between topics in your transition, and as a courtesy to both the next speaker and the audience, introduce the speaker by name.

Like a speech by an individual, an effective symposium has an introduction, a body, and a conclusion. In addition to presenting his or her ideas, the first speaker should begin with an introduction that gains the audience's attention, reveals the topic of the presentation, establishes credibility, connects with the audience, and previews the main idea that each subsequent speaker will develop. The final speaker should conclude by summarizing each presenter's main idea and leaving the audience with a memorable clincher.

Panel Discussion

In a panel discussion, group members sit at a table and speak as if conversing among themselves, while the audience watches and listens. There may be time for audience questions after the discussion, but the panel members' primary role is to speak, and the audience's primary role is to listen. For example, a professor might ask a team of students to come back the following semester and conduct a panel discussion for a new class about a research project they had conducted the previous year.

A panel discussion usually requires a **moderator**, who introduces the **panelists** (the other group members) and facilitates the discussion. The moderator's role is similar to that of a leader in a group discussion. He or she monitors the time, asks questions that keep the discussion moving, and ensures that each panel member has an opportunity to participate. A moderator may also participate in the discussion, though he or she should not dominate the presentation.

Panel members, too, should contribute to the discussion without monopolizing the presentation. It is particularly important to participate if you have special experience or expertise with the point being made. If you have less information on a given issue, or you have been speaking more than other members, give other panelists the opportunity to talk. And be tactful and professional when disagreeing with another member's point.

The atmosphere in a panel discussion is usually more casual than in a symposium. Panelists may interact with the speaker and make comments or ask questions. Talk about the panel discussion in advance with your group, so you know which questions or topics you want to bring up. That way, the group will be well prepared and can prioritize the most important issues to be covered.

Single Group Representative

Sometimes, one person will be responsible for presenting on behalf of the entire group. If your group has selected this format, keep the following considerations in mind.

First, check that your group has discussed and decided on the best approach for the presentation. Which person is most qualified to present the group's opinions? Who would have the most effective delivery? Is this a topic that requires the ethos or authority of a group leader or a group member with particular expertise? Select the member who best meets these criteria.

Second, if you're the person chosen to give the presentation, be sure that your group has carefully thought through all aspects of the speech. There's an important difference between a speech that you prepare, research, and deliver yourself and one that emerges from a group: in the latter instance, the group contributes substantially to the invention process. Get input from all group members before you start preparing the presentation, and solicit their feedback after you outline your speech.

Third, as you are delivering the talk, take care to distinguish whether you are representing your own views, the views of some members of the group, or a consensus of all group members. Be fair and accurate when summarizing other members' viewpoints. Acknowledge other members' good ideas rather than presenting them as your own.

SUMMARY

"Several heads are better than one."

The adage that opens this chapter and this section reflects the fact that people tend to make the best decisions when they share and discuss their ideas. In school, the workplace, and your community, you will inevitably find yourself participating in group discussions and presenting your group's conclusions.

An effective group discussion requires skillful leadership and constructive participation. The leader must manage key elements of group dynamics, including the flow of the discussion. He or she has to ensure that all perspectives receive consideration, encourage participation, keep the group on task, and minimize interpersonal conflict. Effective members focus on task- and maintenance-oriented roles and avoid self-oriented ones. They actively share their ideas, consider one another's viewpoints, constructively participate, and help the group reach a sound decision—perhaps through the five-step reflective-thinking process. These steps include defining and analyzing a problem, establishing criteria for solving the problem, generating multiple potential solutions, and choosing the best solution from the list.

Groups may present their findings in a symposium, during which each individual member presents part of the group's message. At other times, the group may use a panel discussion format, where there is less formal structure and more give-and-take among members. In either case, thorough preparation will enable each member to know who will present which topics.

If you're called on to deliver a presentation for your entire group, preparation will again help you ensure that you're accurately reflecting the group's decision, opinion, or findings.

Key Terms

small group
group dynamics

EFFECTIVE GROUP LEADERSHIP

designated leader
implied leader
emergent leader
groupthink

GROUP DECISION MAKING AND THE REFLECTIVE-THINKING PROCESS

reflective-thinking process

DELIVERING GROUP PRESENTATIONS

symposium
panel discussion
moderator
panelists

APPENDIX
Additional Sample Speeches

SAMPLE INFORMATIVE SPEECH

INVISIBILITY: SCIENCE FICTION NO MORE!

Josh Betancur
Santiago Canyon College

In this speech about the concept of invisibility and the processes by which objects might become invisible, student Josh Betancur demonstrates how ideas once in the realm of science fiction are now coming closer to reality. Josh uses evidence from a variety of scientific sources, supplemented by analogies and definitions, to support his clearly organized main points.

When the space shuttle *Copernicus* was exposed to tremendous amounts of radiation, scientists feared the crew would not survive. The battered craft made it back to earth. Astronaut Susan Storm was amazed she was alive, but even more amazed with her newfound ability to become the invisible woman. By creating a force field, she was able to bend the light waves around her, so as not to be seen. Now this may sound like the fantastic stuff of comic books, which it is; however, this ability may someday become reality, for scientists at Duke and the University College London have just created an invisibility cloak. •

• Attention-getter presents a short fictional anecdote and a striking fact: invisibility may become scientifically possible.

Heralded by the December 2006 *Science* magazine as the fifth most influential discovery of 2006, it will affect every aspect of our lives from aesthetics, architecture, and entertainment, to [the] military, telecommunications, and transportation. •

• Josh connects with the audience by showing diverse benefits.

To understand this exciting new use of technology, it is necessary first to consider the physical science of invisibility, second to review experiments attempting to render objects invisible, and finally have a better look, so to speak, at the tremendous potential impacts of this technology on our lives in the future. •

• Preview of three main points, organized topically.

Let's begin by considering what it takes to make an object invisible.

Prior to J. K. Rowling, H. G. Wells had everyone convinced that invisibility could be achieved by drinking a magic elixir. Unfortunately, scientists could never concoct a potion to make a person transparent to light.

Rather than focusing on science fiction, researchers have focused on scientific principles. In a personal interview on February 10, 2007, Professor Craig Rutan, the Physics Chair at Santiago Canyon College, explained that in order to make something invisible two hurdles must be overcome. First, you must find a way to transport light around the object. For example, for this blackboard to be visible, light must travel toward it. If something blocks that light, the board will become invisible. So you must find a way to transport light around the object without interference. Second, you must never illuminate the object. •

• Evidence based on interview research.

Now that we know what is required for invisibility, we'll take a look at scientific efforts to make objects invisible. •

• Transition between main points I and II.

A demonstration of one technique was documented by Inami, Sekiguchi, and Tachi of the University of Tokyo, in a *Brochure of Demonstration at Laval (France) Virtual 2003*. These professors . . . created a technology known as optical camouflage. In order to overcome the first hurdle, this technology manipulates light so that an object blends in with its surroundings. The team takes a picture of what lies behind the individual and projects it onto him, giving him the necessary camouflage.

In order to overcome the second hurdle, that the object cannot be illuminated, the team used a computer to enhance the image before projecting it onto a special material known as retroreflective material. Now you've seen this used on bright road signs. According to Federal Highway Administration Publication 03-082, *Minimum Retroreflectivity Levels,* retroreflective materials use microsized glass beads, or prisms, to redirect the light from a car's headlights back to the driver. •

• Supporting material: analogy to road signs.

If light is neither absorbed nor refracted, then in theory, the object should disappear. However, work remains to be done before this can be feasible. As any highway traveler can attest, bright road signs can still be seen. This is because the surface projected upon is not perfectly flat. Folds in the material absorb and disperse the light, thus making the object visible. Other limitations include the fact that with current optical camouflage, onlookers must stand in one specific spot and look through a peephole in order for the invisibility effect to occur. Moreover, this technology is neither cheap nor easy to transport.

Optical camouflage is not the only process that scientists are analyzing. Another promising technology is an "invisibility cloak," created by scientists from Duke University and University College London. The January 2007 issue of *Discover* calls the cloak one of the top discoveries in physics for the year 2006.

Discover, November 2006, reports that Duke physicists David Smith and Dave Schurig used specially created "metamaterials" to cloak a small cylindrical object, shielding it from microwaves. Microwaves have a longer wavelength than visible light does, hence it is easier to shield an object from them. What are metamaterials? According to the Duke Web site of Professor Smith's research group, June 10,

2006, they are "artificial structures that display properties beyond those available in naturally occurring material." • On the Duke University Web site, May 25, 2006, Smith notes that the cloak acts "like a hole you've opened up in space." All electromagnetic waves are directed around the cloaked object, and they come out on the other side, much as water in a river "flows virtually undisturbed around a smooth rock."

• Supporting material: definition of *metamaterials*.

In the November 2006 *Discover*, the Duke physicists compare this process to a mirage on a hot summer road. "When light rays from the sky hit the hot, thin air just above the surface of the asphalt, they bend. . . . Light travels faster in the hot, thin air close to the road than it does in the cold, dense air above, and that difference in speed is what causes it to shift direction as it crosses the boundary between the two." The rays that were moving from the sky to the road get redirected to your eye, the road "shimmers like water," and the mirage cloaks "the now invisible road behind an image of the blue sky." •

• Supporting material: analogies to a mirage and river water flowing around a rock.

The invisibility cloak is an exciting first step, but it will be a challenge to improve the technology to shield objects from visible light. As the Duke researchers explain in *Discover*, tiny metal shapes are stamped on the metamaterials. These shapes must be smaller than the wavelength that is directed at them. Microwaves are about three centimeters (or one inch) long—60,000 times the 500 nanometer wavelength of green light waves! The researchers state that it would be theoretically possible to make such tiny shapes for the metamaterials, but they would be difficult to mass-produce. Ulf Leonhardt, a theoretical physicist at the University of St. Andrews in Scotland, also notes that the current materials are rigid—more like a suit of armor than a cloak. •

• Supporting material: explanation of why the invisibility cloak faces challenges.

Although more work needs to be done, invisibility technology offers many potential benefits to society. •

• In the following paragraphs, Josh uses diverse sources to document benefits.

There are already some practical applications of optical camouflage. BBCnews.com explains on January 4, 2007, that the underside of a plane can be cloaked to allow pilots to see the ground as they land, that it could make windows where there are none, and doctors could quite literally see through their hands. For these reasons, the August 2003 *TIME* magazine deemed it to be the coolest invention of the year.

The invisibility cloak could impact our lives in ways that we can now only imagine. *News View Researcher* on November 14, 2006, asks us to imagine a forty-story building that would block a picturesque view of Central Park. Cover the building with the invisibility cloak and it only appears three stories tall. Could you imagine covering eyesores like air conditioners, power lines, or dumpsters?

Ker Than, staff writer for LiveScience.com, writes on October 19, 2006, that "a cloak that deflects radio waves could render an object invisible to radar or improve cell phone reflections by rerouting signals around an obstruction."

These materials could also find their way into healthcare. Costas Soukoulis, a senior physicist at Ames Laboratory, explains in the January 9, 2007, *Science Daily* that metamaterials may lead to the development of a superlens that can capture "details much smaller than one wavelength of light to vastly improve imaging for materials or biomedical applications, such as giving researchers the power to see inside a human cell or diagnose disease in a baby still in the womb." The previously cited LiveScience.com article notes that cloaking materials "might also be used to protect people from penetrating and harmful radiation. 'If you knew that you had radiation of a certain bandwidth frequency, you could have it skirt around some region that you wanted shielded,'" says Duke physicist David Smith.

And of course, the military is anxious to get their hands on this technology. MSNBC.com explains on December 5, 2006, that "a cloaked ship would be impervious to radar detection. A bunker could be rendered invisible, and soldiers could be turned into superspies." The obvious danger here is that hostile groups could acquire the technology. Moreover, how will people know where invisible things are so as not to run into them?

Today, we have ventured into the unseen world of invisibility by first examining the science of invisibility. Second, we looked at the process of optical camouflage and the physics behind the new invisibility cloak. Finally, we looked at the tremendous impacts that this new technology could have on all of our lives. Now you may not be able to run out tomorrow and purchase a cloak, but in the not-too-distant future, our military will be stronger, cell phone reception clearer, and characters like Susan Storm and the invisible woman may no longer just be comic book characters. •

• Summary of main points and clincher tied to the introduction.

SAMPLE PERSUASIVE SPEECH

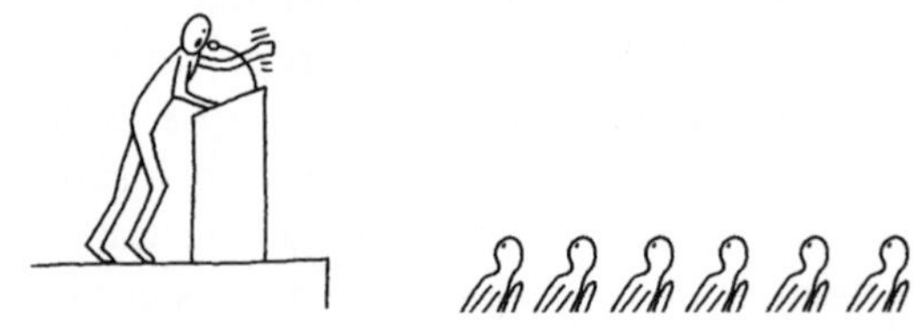

CHILD SLAVERY AND THE PRODUCTION OF CHOCOLATE

David Kruckenberg
Santiago Canyon College

Student David Kruckenberg presented this speech in the finals of the Phi Rho Pi national championship tournament in 2007.

David uses a problem-cause-solution format to address the compelling issue of child labor in the production of chocolate. He uses diverse reasoning strategies and consistently documents his claims with evidence. David's speech is well organized, with a clear preview and transitions between each main point. His audience-centered solution demonstrates how each of us can be personally involved in addressing the problem.

I was forced to stay in a large room with other children from a neighboring plantation. I tried to run

> away, but I was caught. As punishment they cut my feet; I had to work for weeks while my wounds healed.

This moving testimony may sound like past history, when slavery was prevalent. But these words are not a reminder of the past; they're found in the April 24, 2006, *Forbes* magazine. These are the words of an enslaved boy working in the cocoa fields of the country of Côte d'Ivoire, also known as the Ivory Coast. And he is not alone. UNICEF reports in February 2006 that child trafficking is on the rise in this African region. •

• Attention-getter: a shocking first-person quotation plus evidence the problem is growing.

It may surprise you to learn that the last chocolate you ate may well have been tainted with child slavery. Despite the promises and agreements made in recent years by chocolate companies, they continue to use child labor in the production of their chocolate. We as consumers must communicate that this is unacceptable. •

• David connects with the audience and presents his thesis.

To do so, we will first reveal the connection between chocolate and child slavery, second examine why the problem continues, and finally discover just how much power we have in bringing child slavery to an end.

How are chocolate and child slavery connected? •

• Preview statement and transition to first main point.

Cocoa bean production is limited to areas near the equator, such as Central America, Indonesia, and the Ivory Coast. The International Cocoa Initiative Web site, last updated February 8, 2007, explains that with almost a million acres devoted to growing cocoa, the Ivory Coast accounts for more than 40 percent of world cocoa production. Because growing cocoa is labor-intensive and labor is a significant part of the cost of production, the *Vancouver Sun* on November 10, 2006, reports that many farmers in the Ivory Coast have turned to using forced child labor to cut costs.

The conditions of these children are beyond comprehension. The International Cocoa Initiative details the hazards they face each day: they must work long hours in the fields in brutal conditions. They clear fields with machetes and apply pesticides without protective gear. After harvesting the cocoa pods, they must split them open with heavy knives. Once the beans are dried and bagged, they must carry these large loads long distances on their young backs.

Even more alarming is just how many children are forced to live this life. The *New York Times* of October 26, 2006, reports that more than 200,000 children in the Ivory Coast are forced to work in the cocoa fields. The *Chicago Tribune* of May 5, 2006, reports that in contrast to the rest of the world, this region of Africa has the highest rate of child laborers of all children five to fourteen years old; more than one in four are forced to work. Earth Save International, last updated February 14, 2007, says that these children are either enticed with promises of good wages and easy work or outright kidnapped. One example is a boy named Molique, who came to the Ivory Coast at the age of fourteen; despite the promises he was never paid. When he asked to be paid, he was beaten. He had to scavenge for food and at night was locked up with the other kids. The *New York Times* of October 29, 2006, says that almost 12,000 children in the Ivory Coast have been trafficked far from their families' homes and into slavery. •

• Combination of examples to build pathos and statistics to document the extent of the problem.

The growing use of child slavery is reprehensible, but why is it allowed to continue? The answer is our widespread and growing demand for chocolate. •

• Transition to main point II.

Unfortunately, child slavery continues because our demand for chocolate continues, enabling the Ivory Coast and the chocolate companies to ignore the problem. Farmers in the Ivory Coast invest in cocoa for its large profits. In order to maximize their gain, they cut costs by using the forced labor of children. These 600,000 farmers then turn to large export companies in the Ivory Coast to buy their cocoa. The *New York Times* of October 26, 2006, reports that these export companies are able to keep the price that they pay for cocoa low because they have so many farmers to choose from. The exporters then sell their cocoa to large chocolate companies such as Hershey's, Nestle, M&M/Mars, and Cadbury. •

• Causal reasoning.

The *Calgary Herald* of November 17, 2006, tells us that in 2001, almost all of the big chocolate companies signed the Harkin-Engel Protocol, agreeing that by 2005 they would certify that their chocolate was not tainted with child slavery; however, this deadline passed two years ago with the companies making excuses saying they need more time. But the September 20, 2006, *Seattle Post-Intelligencer* suggests that they're more concerned about the civil war in the Ivory Coast interfering with their supply of cocoa. Clearly the civil war is also the top priority with Ivory Coast government. The Associated Press on June 15, 2006, explains that the government doesn't want to interfere with the supply of cocoa because export taxes are their primary source of revenue. The government uses this money to buy military arms and equipment. The Ivory Coast may not have blood diamonds, but [the nation] certainly possesses blood chocolate. •

• Blood chocolate—compelling analogy to blood diamonds.

Ultimately, the blame rests on us, because consumer demand for chocolate keeps the industry insulated from pressure. The World Cocoa Foundation, last updated February 14, 2007, tells us that North America and Europe consume nearly two-thirds of all cocoa products and that demand for confectionary products containing chocolate rises 4 to 5 percent each year. The sad truth is most consumers are not aware of chocolate's connection to child slavery. Because we continue to buy their chocolate, the industry feels no urgency to change. •

• Evidence shows that the speaker and audience members are part of the problem.

Now that we understand the problem and why it continues, we must ask what we can do, and the answer is simple. We must stop buying slave-produced chocolate.

But don't worry, I'm not suggesting that we stop buying chocolate altogether. There is an alternative, and it's called fair trade chocolate. TransFair USA, a nonprofit organization, is the only independent third-party certifier of fair trade products in the U.S. It allows companies to display the fair trade certified label on products that meet strict standards. Some of these standards found on their Web site, last updated November 16, 2006, include a prohibition [on] forced child labor, safe working conditions, living wages, environmentally safe farming methods, a guaranteed minimum price, and direct trade between the farmers and chocolate companies, thus eliminating the manipulative exporters. •

• How the audience can be personally involved in the solution.

If we as consumers change how we buy chocolate, the industry will have to respond. Currently, they're trying to distance themselves from the bad press associated with slave labor, and as a result the Ontario *Guelph Mercury*, February 3, 2007, reports that some have begun to buy into the fair trade market. For example, Business Wire, October 11, 2006, reports that Ben and Jerry's is expanding its fair trade–certified ice cream flavors. *Forbes* magazine, previously cited, says that fair trade has even made inroads into the Ivory Coast but still accounts for only about 1 percent of cocoa exports. •

• David explains how one solution can reduce the problem.

Economics teaches us that demand controls supply; they can only sell what we buy. A perfect example of this is the industry's response to the rise in demand for organic food products. The *Boston Herald* on October 16, 2006, reports that organic food sales have risen more than 15 percent in the last two years. With a multibillion-dollar market, the September 20, 2006, *Sacramento Bee* says that big companies like Wal-Mart and Frito-Lay have made organic food mainstream. If we demand more fair trade chocolate, the industry will have to supply it, and when the chocolate companies start buying more slave-free cocoa, farmers in the Ivory Coast will have to abandon slavery to keep their buyers. •

• Analogy to consumer-generated demand for organic products.

Today we have exposed the connection between chocolate and child slavery, examined why the problem continues, and finally discovered how we can bring it to an end. The next time you go to buy chocolate, remember the words of a child, quoted in the November 10, 2006, *Toronto Star*: "When the rest of the world eats chocolate, they're eating my flesh." The Ivory Coast may be 7,000 miles away, but we have a responsibility to protect all children. Fair trade chocolate may cost us a little more money, but that's a small price to pay to free thousands of children from slavery. •

• Clincher includes another compelling quotation that connects to the introduction.

SAMPLE PERSUASIVE SPEECH

KEYNOTE SPEECH AT THE 2004 DEMOCRATIC PARTY NATIONAL CONVENTION

Senator Barack Obama

Today, Barack Obama is well-known to most Americans as a prominent leader of the Democratic Party. In 2004, he was well-known in Illinois and within smaller groups of influential politicians as a young state senator with a bright future. This speech, presented on July 27 at Boston's Fleet Center, was designed to persuade voters to support John Kerry in the upcoming presidential election. Yet here, because of his charisma and his powerful message of unity that resonated with a deeply divided electorate, Obama is arguably more successful in persuading voters that he himself might one day become an important leader of his party.

Thank you so much . . .

On behalf of the great state of Illinois, crossroads of a nation, "Land of Lincoln," let me express my deepest gratitude for the privilege of addressing this convention.

Tonight is a particular honor for me because, let's face it, my presence on this stage is pretty unlikely. • My father was a foreign student, born and raised in a small village in Kenya. He grew up herding goats, went to school in a tin-roof shack. His father—my grandfather—was a cook, a domestic servant to the British. But my grandfather had larger dreams for his son. Through hard work and perseverance my father got a scholarship to study in a magical place, America, that shone as a beacon of freedom and opportunity to so many who had come before.

• Stirring opening cleverly echoes another great speaker—the late Barbara Jordan—who made a similar statement at the 1976 national convention.

While studying here, my father met my mother. She was born in a town on the other side of the world, in Kansas. Her father worked on oil rigs and farms through most of the Depression. The day after Pearl Harbor, my grandfather signed up for duty, joined Patton's army, marched across Europe. •

• Vivid language compares Obama's grandfathers. These men shared humble origins and both took chances to make a better life.

Back home, my grandmother raised a baby and went to work on a bomber assembly line. After the war, they studied on the GI Bill, bought a house through FHA, and later moved west all the way to Hawaii in search of opportunity.

And they, too, had big dreams for their daughter. A common dream, born of two continents. My parents shared not only an improbable love; they shared an abiding faith in the possibilities of this nation. They would give me an African name, Barack, or "blessed," believing that in a tolerant America your name is no barrier to success. They imagined—they imagined me going to the best schools in the land, even though they weren't rich, because in a generous America you don't have to be rich to achieve your potential. •

• Obama simultaneously describes his own parents' dreams and establishes common ground with listeners who believe America offers opportunity to all.

They're both passed away now. And yet, I know that on this night they look down on me with great pride.

They stand here—and I stand here today, grateful for the diversity of my heritage, aware that my parents' dreams live on in my two precious daughters. I stand here knowing that my story is part of the larger American story, that I owe a debt to all of those who came before me, and that, in no other country on earth, is my story even possible.

Tonight, we gather to affirm the greatness of our nation—not because of the height of our skyscrapers, or the power of our military, or the size of our economy. Our pride is based on a very simple premise, summed up in a declaration made over two hundred years ago: "We hold these truths to be self-evident, that all men are created equal, that they are endowed by their Creator with certain [un]alienable rights, that among these are life, liberty, and the pursuit of happiness." •

• Quotation from the Declaration of Independence.

That is the true genius of America, a faith—a faith in simple dreams, an insistence on small miracles; that we can tuck in our children at night and know that they are fed and clothed and safe from harm; that we can say what we think, write what we think, without hearing a sudden knock on the door; that we can have an idea and start our own business without paying a bribe; that we can participate in the political process without fear of retribution; and that our votes will be counted—at least most of the time. •

• Examples of the "genius of America." The thought ends with a political jab about the contested 2000 U.S. presidential election.

This year, in this election, we are called to reaffirm our values and our commitments, to hold them against a hard reality and see how we're measuring up to the legacy of our forbearers and the promise of future generations.

And fellow Americans, Democrats, Republicans, Independents, I say to you tonight: we have more work to do • — more work to do for the workers I met in Galesburg, Illinois, who are losing their union jobs at the Maytag plant that's moving to Mexico and now are having to compete with their own children for jobs that pay seven bucks an hour; more to do for the father that I met who was losing his job and choking back the tears, wondering how he would pay $4,500 a month for the drugs his son needs without the health benefits that he counted on; more to do for the young woman in East St. Louis, and thousands more like her, who has the grades, has the drive, has the will, but doesn't have the money to go to college. Now, don't get me wrong. The people I meet—in small towns and big cities, in diners and office parks—they don't expect government to solve all their problems. They know they have to work hard to get ahead, and they want to. Go into the collar counties around Chicago, and people will tell you they don't want their tax money wasted, by a welfare agency or by the Pentagon. Go in—go into any inner city neighborhood, and folks will tell you that government alone can't teach our kids to learn; they know that parents have to teach, that children can't achieve unless we raise their expectations and turn off the television sets and eradicate the slander that says a black youth with a book is acting white. They know those things.

• Obama speaks to a live audience of Democrats, but his larger television audience includes Republicans and Independents.

People don't expect—people don't expect government to solve all their problems. But they sense, deep in their bones, that with just a slight change in priorities, we can make sure that every child in America has a decent shot at life, and that the doors of opportunity remain open to all. •

They know we can do better. And they want that choice.

• Theme of a unified America—traditional conservative concerns about big government combined with government's positive role in helping people.

In this election, we offer that choice. Our party has chosen a man to lead us who embodies the best this country has to offer. And that man is John Kerry.

John Kerry understands the ideals of community, faith, and service because they've defined his life. From his heroic service to Vietnam, to his years as a prosecutor and lieutenant governor, through two decades in the United States Senate, he's devoted himself to this country. Again and again, we've seen him make tough choices when easier ones were available. •

• Fulfilling the role of the keynote speaker by supporting his party's nominee.

His values and his record affirm what is best in us. John Kerry believes in an America where hard work is rewarded; so instead of offering tax breaks to companies shipping jobs overseas, he offers them to companies creating jobs here at home.

John Kerry believes in an America where all Americans can afford the same health coverage our politicians in Washington have for themselves.

John Kerry believes in energy independence, so we aren't held hostage to the profits of oil companies or the sabotage of foreign oil fields.

John Kerry believes in the constitutional freedoms that have made our country the envy of the world, and he will never sacrifice our basic liberties, nor use faith as a wedge to divide us. And John Kerry believes that in a dangerous world, war must be an option sometimes, but it should never be the first option.

You know, a while back—a while back I met a young man named Shamus in a VFW Hall in East Moline, Illinois. He was a good-looking kid—six-two, six-three, clear-eyed, with an easy smile. • He told me he'd joined the Marines and was heading to Iraq the following week. And as I listened to him explain why he'd enlisted, the absolute faith he had in our country and its leaders, his devotion to duty and service, I thought this young man was all that any of us might ever hope for in a child.

• Word choice balances formal language used elsewhere with the conversational "kid."

But then I asked myself, "Are we serving Shamus as well as he is serving us?"

I thought of the 900 men and women—sons and daughters, husbands and wives, friends and neighbors, who won't be returning to their own hometowns. I thought of the families I've met who were struggling to get by without a loved one's full income, or whose loved ones had returned with a limb missing or nerves shattered, but still lacked long-term health benefits because they were reservists.

When we send our young men and women into harm's way, we have a solemn obligation not to fudge the numbers or shade the truth about why they're going, to care for their families while they're gone, to tend to the soldiers upon their return, and to never, ever go to war without enough troops to win the war, secure the peace, and earn the respect of the world.

Now—now let me be clear. Let me be clear. • We have real enemies in the world. These enemies must be found. They must be pursued. And they must be defeated. John Kerry knows this. And just as Lieutenant Kerry did not hesitate to risk his life to protect the men who served with him in Vietnam, President Kerry will not hesitate one moment to use our military might to keep America safe and secure.

• Emphasizing an introductory phrase by repeating it, perhaps to deal with applause from a previous point.

John Kerry believes in America. And he knows that it's not enough for just some of us to prosper—for alongside our famous individualism, there's another ingredient in the American saga, a belief that we're all connected as one people. If there is a child on the south side of Chicago who can't read, that matters to me, even if it's not my child. If there is a senior citizen somewhere who can't pay for her prescription drugs, and having to choose between medicine and the rent, that makes my life poorer, even if it's not my grandparent. If there's an Arab American family being rounded up without benefit of an attorney or due process, that threatens my civil liberties.

It is that fundamental belief—it is that fundamental belief—I am my brother's keeper, I am my sister's keeper—that makes this country work. It's what allows us to pursue our individual dreams and yet still come together as one American family. *E pluribus unum*: "Out of many, one."

Now even as we speak, there are those who are preparing to divide us—the spin masters, the negative ad peddlers who embrace the politics of "anything goes." Well, I say to them tonight, there is not a liberal America and a conservative America—there is the United States of America. There is not a Black America and a White America and Latino America and Asian America—there's the United States of America. •

• Returning to the theme of a unified nation.

The pundits, the pundits like to slice and dice our country into Red States and Blue States: Red States for Republicans, Blue States for Democrats. But I've got news for them, too. We worship an "awesome God" in the Blue States, and we don't like federal agents poking around in our libraries in the Red States. We coach Little League in the Blue States, and yes, we've got some gay friends in the Red States. There are patriots who opposed the war in Iraq, and there are patriots who supported the war in Iraq. We are one people, all of us pledging allegiance to the stars and stripes, all of us defending the United States of America. •

• Juxtaposition shows U.S. unity: paired examples ascribe experiences traditionally thought of as liberal to Red States and vice versa.

In the end—in the end—in the end, that's what this election is about. • Do we participate in a politics of cynicism, or do we participate in a politics of hope?

• Another repeated introductory phrase.

John Kerry calls on us to hope. John Edwards calls on us to hope.

I'm not talking about blind optimism here—the almost willful ignorance that thinks unemployment will go away if we just don't think about it, or the healthcare crisis will solve itself if we just ignore it. That's not what I'm talking about. I'm talking about something more substantial. It's the hope of slaves sitting around a fire singing freedom songs; the hope of immigrants setting out for distant shores; the hope of a young naval lieutenant bravely patrolling the

Mekong Delta; the hope of a millworker's son who dares to defy the odds; the hope of a skinny kid with a funny name who believes that America has a place for him, too. • Hope—hope in the face of difficulty. Hope in the face of uncertainty. The audacity of hope! In the end, that is God's greatest gift to us, the bedrock of this nation. A belief in things not seen. A belief that there are better days ahead.

• Obama connects himself (the skinny kid with the funny name) and his own fate to his vision of America.

I believe that we can give our middle class relief and provide working families with a road to opportunity.

I believe we can provide jobs to the jobless, homes to the homeless, and reclaim young people in cities across America from violence and despair.

I believe that we have a righteous wind at our backs, and that as we stand on the crossroads of history, we can make the right choices and meet the challenges that face us.

America! Tonight, if you feel the same energy that I do, if you feel the same urgency that I do, if you feel the same passion that I do, if you feel the same hopefulness that I do—if we do what we must do, then I have no doubt that all across the country, from Florida to Oregon, from Washington to Maine, the people will rise up in November, and John Kerry will be sworn in as president, and John Edwards will be sworn in as vice president, and this country will reclaim its promise, and out of this long political darkness a brighter day will come. •

• Conclusion: a sweeping vision for the United States that supports the Kerry/Edwards ticket.

Thank you very much, everybody. God bless you. Thank you.

SAMPLE SPECIAL-OCCASION SPEECH

1962 SYLVANUS THAYER AWARD ACCEPTANCE SPEECH

General Douglas MacArthur

General MacArthur delivered an acceptance speech when he was honored with the Thayer Award at the U.S. Military Academy in 1962. This award is given annually to a U.S. citizen whose service and accomplishments in the national interest exemplify personal devotion to the ideals expressed in the West Point motto: duty, honor, country. The version below excerpts the first two-thirds of the original speech text.

General MacArthur builds his speech around the motto of "duty, honor, country." He explains what these ideas mean to him, and he uses repetition to emphasize the motto. The general uses stylistic devices such as description, metaphor, and simile to express his message. MacArthur presents an inspirational message to his West Point audience, encouraging them to live up to the USMA motto.

General MacArthur's speech refers to the military service and heroism of "men." In 1962, women were not allowed to serve in combat, nor were women accepted as cadets at West Point until 1976. Nevertheless, women also performed heroic service in wars; for example, many women worked as "Rosie the Riveters" in war production industries during World War II. Any contemporary speaker should not make gendered references to war heroes, nor to the accomplishments of cadets currently at West Point.

General Westmoreland, General Grove, distinguished guests, and gentlemen of the Corps!

As I was leaving the hotel this morning, a doorman asked me, "Where are you bound for, General?" And when I replied, "West Point," he remarked, "Beautiful place. Have you ever been there before?" •

• Attention-getter: an ironic anecdote—clearly, he's been to West Point before!

No human being could fail to be deeply moved by such a tribute as this [Thayer Award]. Coming from a profession I have served so long, and a people I have loved so well, it fills me with an emotion I cannot express. But this award is not intended primarily to honor a personality, but to symbolize a great moral code—the code of conduct and chivalry of those who guard this beloved land of culture and ancient descent. That is the animation of this medallion. For all eyes and for all time, it is an expression of the ethics of the American soldier. That I should be integrated in this way with so noble an ideal arouses a sense of pride and yet of humility which will be with me always. •

• MacArthur connects with his audience.

Duty, Honor, Country: those three hallowed words reverently dictate what you ought to be, what you can be, what you will be. They are your rallying points: to build courage when courage seems to fail; to regain faith when there seems to be little cause for faith; to create hope when hope becomes forlorn. •

• The theme of MacArthur's speech is identical to the Academy's motto: "Duty, Honor, Country."

Unhappily, I possess neither that eloquence of diction, that poetry of imagination, nor that brilliance of metaphor to tell you all that they mean.

The unbelievers will say they are but words, but a slogan, but a flamboyant phrase. Every pedant, every demagogue, every cynic, every hypocrite, every troublemaker, and I am sorry to say, some others of an entirely different character, will try to downgrade them even to the extent of mockery and ridicule.

But these are some of the things they do. • They build your basic character. They mold you for your future roles as the custodians of the nation's defense. They make you strong enough to know when you are weak, and brave enough to face yourself when you are afraid. They teach you to be proud and unbending in honest failure, but humble and gentle in success; not to substitute words for actions; not to seek the path of comfort, but to face the stress and spur of difficulty

• Functional definition of "Duty, Honor, Country" is made through a long series of examples.

and challenge; to learn to stand up in the storm, but to have compassion on those who fall; to master yourself before you seek to master others; to have a heart that is clean, a goal that is high; to learn to laugh, yet never forget how to weep; to reach into the future, yet never neglect the past; to be serious, yet never to take yourself too seriously; to be modest so that you will remember the simplicity of true greatness, the open mind of true wisdom, the meekness of true strength. They give you a temper of the will, a quality of the imagination, a vigor of the emotions, a freshness of the deep springs of life, a temperamental predominance of courage over timidity, of an appetite for adventure over love of ease. They create in your heart the sense of wonder, the unfailing hope of what next, and the joy and inspiration of life. They teach you in this way to be an officer and a gentleman.

And what sort of soldiers are those you are to lead? Are they reliable? Are they brave? Are they capable of victory? Their story is known to all of you. It is the story of the American man-at-arms. • My estimate of him was formed on the battlefield many, many years ago and has never changed. I regarded him then as I regard him now—as one of the world's noblest figures, not only as one of the finest military characters, but also as one of the most stainless. His name and fame are the birthright of every American citizen. In his youth and strength, his love and loyalty, he gave all that mortality can give.

• At the time of this speech, women were not allowed in combat. If the speech were given today, the men *and* women who serve must be recognized.

He needs no eulogy from me or from any other man. He has written his own history and written it in red on his enemy's breast. But when I think of his patience under adversity, of his courage under fire, and of his modesty in victory, I am filled with an emotion of admiration I cannot put into words. He belongs to history as furnishing one of the greatest examples of successful patriotism. He belongs to posterity as the instructor of future generations in the principles of liberty and freedom. He belongs to the present, to us, by his virtues and by his achievements. In twenty campaigns, on a hundred battlefields, around a thousand campfires, I have witnessed that enduring fortitude, that patriotic self-abnegation, and that invincible determination which have carved his statue in the hearts of his people. From one end of the world to the other, he has drained deep the chalice of courage. •

As I listened to those songs [of the glee club], in memory's eye I could see those staggering columns of the First World War, bending under soggy packs, on many a weary march from dripping dusk to drizzling dawn, slogging ankle-deep through the mire of shell-pocked roads, to form grimly for the attack, blue-lipped, covered with sludge and mud, chilled by the wind and rain, driving home to their objective, and for many, to the judgment seat of God. •

I do not know the dignity of their birth, but I do know the glory of their death. They died unquestioning, uncomplaining, with faith in their hearts, and on their lips the hope that we would go on to victory. Always, for them: *Duty, Honor, Country*; • always their blood and sweat and tears, as we sought the way and the light and the truth.

And twenty years after, on the other side of the globe, again the filth of murky foxholes, the stench of ghostly trenches, the slime of dripping dugouts; those boiling suns of relentless heat, those torrential rains of devastating storms; the loneliness and utter desolation of jungle trails; the bitterness of long separation from those they loved and cherished; the deadly pestilence of tropical disease; the horror of stricken areas of war; their resolute and determined defense, their swift and sure attack, their indomitable purpose, their complete and decisive victory—always victory. • Always through the bloody haze of their last reverberating shot, the vision of gaunt, ghastly men reverently following your password of *Duty, Honor, Country*.

The code which those words perpetuate embraces the highest moral laws and will stand the test of any ethics or philosophies ever promulgated for the uplift of mankind. Its requirements are for the things that are right, and its restraints are from the things that are wrong.

• MacArthur honors the Thayer Award and his audience by expressing his admiration for all U.S. soldiers.

• MacArthur employs strong style and reinforces his credibility: descriptive language and personal remembrance.

• Repetition of theme throughout speech.

• A long descriptive sentence filled with alliteration and vivid language evokes the harrowing conditions in Asia during World War II.

The soldier, above all other men, is required to practice the greatest act of religious training—sacrifice. •

• Allusions to religion can be effective, but should also be made with care and with audience analysis in mind. Otherwise, speakers might connect poorly with listeners who do not share their beliefs.

In battle and in the face of danger and death, he discloses those divine attributes which his Maker gave when he created man in his own image. No physical courage and no brute instinct can take the place of the Divine help which alone can sustain him.

However horrible the incidents of war may be, the soldier who is called upon to offer and to give his life for his country is the noblest development of mankind. •

• MacArthur once again praises the commitment and devotion of soldiers.

. . .

SAMPLE SPECIAL-OCCASION SPEECH

SPEECH AT THE TAHP RECEPTION ON CESAR CHAVEZ DAY

Arturo V. Ramirez

Speeches that commemorate special occasions—like the birthday of a prominent leader—occupy a regular space in the tradition of public speaking in the United States. In words eloquent for their simplicity, Arturo Ramirez remembers labor leader and social activist Cesar Chavez on April 1, 2000, in Houston, Texas—the day after what would have been Chavez's seventy-third birthday. Ramirez's speech precedes a parade and a street renaming in Chavez's honor.

Muchas gracias. Antes que todo, un brindis (saludo) al cumpleaños de César Chávez. First and foremost, a toast (salute) to the birthday of Cesar Chavez. • Yesterday, March 31, was Cesar Chavez's birthday. He would have been seventy-three years old. We should not only remember March 31 as the day Selena died, but just as importantly—if not more—we should remember it as the day Cesar Chavez was born. •

• Opening line establishes common ground with Spanish speakers. Ramirez quickly translates for non-Spanish speakers.

• Juxtaposition contrasts the death of pop singer Selena with the birth of Chavez.

Thank you for inviting me to the Cesar Chavez parade and street naming celebration. I want to first extend my congratulations to Benny Martinez and all the members, supporters, and volunteers of the Tejano Association for Historical Preservation for their tireless efforts and dedication to this project and the excellent preparations for today's festivities that made this long-overdue tribute to Cesar Chavez a resounding success. •

• Acknowledging individuals and groups central to the event.

I am honored to have been selected as one out of the so many you could have chosen to say a few words on this historic occasion. I stand humbly before you as just one common person—out of millions—who was profoundly and eternally touched by Cesar Chavez and who was forever changed and influenced by his mighty spirit, so deeply influenced that to this day I still boycott grapes!

What can I say about Cesar Chavez that has not already been said about him, especially by people with higher rank than I have, and perhaps with a lot more eloquence than I could deliver. All I can do is share with you what you already know—or should know—of his incomparable legacy, his lasting achievements, and his bold vision, through the prism of my own experiences in life and my perceptions of what Cesar Chavez represents to us.

As an organizer of "la raza," *nosotros, la plebe, los de abajo, el pueblo hispano*, in this country, Cesar Chavez has no equal.

As a man of commitment to *la causa*, Chavez has no equal. As a man of sacrifice, a man of absolute unselfishness, Chavez has no equal.

As a Hispanic/Latino leader in this country, Chavez has no equal. •

• List of Chavez's achievements plus repetition ("has no equal") to emphasize Chavez's importance.

Let it be written that Cesar Chavez was the greatest Hispanic/Latino leader—without exception—this country has ever had.

Let it be known, let it be etched in stone that Cesar Chavez is unequivocally among the greatest "American" leaders of the twentieth century. •

• Another repetition: "Let it be known . . ."

We look up to him as a hero. Yet he never sought to be one, or saw himself as a hero. A soldier, a warrior, in both war and civil strife, yes, but not a hero. "We" see him as a hero because we respect the unparalleled valor we witnessed in the actions he undertook, the marches he led, and the fasting he endured, all for the victory in the struggle for social justice. Yet, he saw himself as a humble person, no better than his fellow man, and doing nothing more than what any one of us could do. While this may be the plain truth, it is not the reality. What made him special and above the rest of us was his courage. He had more *ganas* and courage than all of us put together. Cesar Chavez is uniquely an American paradox. •

• Following this statement, four examples of the "paradox."

He had immense knowledge and wisdom—yet quit school after the eighth grade to become a migrant farmworker and help his family.

His life was incredibly valuable; his worth was beyond any economic measure—yet during his lifetime he never earned more than $5,000 a year.

He took an act of weakness—fasting—and turned it into his strongest weapon to achieve national recognition and support for the struggle and victory for the farmworkers.

He redefined the word *macho*. While mostly everyone had a negative view of being macho, and stereotyped Latino males as being male chauvinists, Cesar put it in a positive context. He was once asked by a reporter what being macho meant to him. He answered, "to be a man is to suffer for others." It sounds better in Spanish, "*ser macho es saber sufrir por otros.*" •

• Additional bilingual address connects with all listeners.

Esto, mis hermanos y hermanas, I believe, was Cesar's greatest gift—and the legacy he left us. He knew how to give of himself to others—and he did it unconditionally every day. He was a man who suffered for others who were in greater need—to us that makes him a hero. • To him, it was just being human.

• Functional definitions of "macho" and "hero" used to define Chavez himself.

I would like to close with a prayer Cesar Chavez wrote and leave you with his actual voice as he tells us, "*sí se puede*," and hope that not only will we celebrate his birthday every year, but also, in his honor, continue the struggle every day! *Hasta la victoria!* •

• Alternating between English and Spanish maintains common ground with Spanish speakers, while remaining inclusive for all.

> Show me the suffering of the most miserable, so I may know my people's plight. Free me to pray for others, for you are present in every person. Help me to take responsibility for my own life, so that I can be free at last. Grant me courage to serve others, for in service there is true life. Give me honesty and patience, so that I can work with other workers. Bring forth song and celebration, so that the Spirit will be alive among us. Let the Spirit flourish and grow, so that we will never tire of the struggle. Let us remember those who have died for justice, for they have given us life. Help us love even those who hate us, so we can change the world. •

• The United Farm Workers' Prayer.

Que viva César Chávez!

NOTES

Chapter 1

1. NACE, "Employers Cite Communication Skills as Key, but Say Many Job Seekers Lack Them," *NACEWeb*, April 26, 2006, http://www.naceweb.org/press/display.Asp?year+&prid+235.
2. R. H. Whitworth, and C. Cochran, "Evaluation of Integrated versus Unitary Treatments for Reducing Public Speaking Anxiety," *Communication Education* 45 (1996): 306.
3. D. J. DeNoon, "Help for Public Speaking Anxiety," *CBS News Healthwatch*, April 20, 2006, http://www.cbsnews.com/stories/2006/04/20/health/webmd/main1523045.shtml.
4. J. Gatz, "What You Need to Succeed in the Workplace," *Job Web*, http://www.jobweb.com/resources/library/Workplace_Culture/What_you_need_to_18_01.htm (accessed June 15, 2006).
5. NACE, April 26, 2006.
6. Heldrich Center for Workforce Development, *Are America's Schools and Skills Making the Grade?* June 14, 2000, http://www.heldrich.rutgers.edu/publications/WTV/release614.000.doc (accessed November 11, 2001).
7. L. Feldmann, "Now Running for Office: An Army of Iraq Veterans," *Christian Science Monitor*, February 22, 2006, http://www.csmonitor.com/2006/0222/p01S03-upso.htm.
8. M. I. Finley, *Politics in the Ancient World* (New York: Cambridge University Press, 1983), 59, 73.
9. D. Bodde, *China's First Unifier* (Hong Kong: Hong Kong University Press, 1967), 181.
10. A. A. Boahen, "Kingdoms of West Africa," in *From Freedom to Freedom*, ed. M. Bain and E. Lewis (New York: Random House, 1977), 69.
11. G. Welch, "The Authors Who Talked," in *From Freedom to Freedom*, ed. M. Bain and E. Lewis (New York: Random House, 1977), 39.
12. C. Brooks, R. W. B. Lewis, and R. P. Warren, *American Literature: The Makers and the Making*, vol. 1 (New York: St. Martin's Press, 1973), 1179.
13. A. Brinkley, *American History: A Survey*, 10th ed., vol. 1 (Burr Ridge, Ill.: McGraw-Hill, 1999), 103–4.
14. N. Gabler, "A Victim of the Third Great Awakening," *Los Angeles Times*, January 14, 2001, M1.

15. Brooks, Lewis, and Warren, *American Literature,* 84.
16. C. A. Brekus, *Strangers and Pilgrims: Female Preaching in America, 1740–1845* (Chapel Hill: University of North Carolina Press, 1998), 3.
17. Lincoln-Douglas Debates of 1858, *Illinois in the Civil War*, 2000, http://www.illinoiscivilwar.org/debates.html.
18. E. C. DuBois, *The Elizabeth Cady Stanton–Susan B. Anthony Reader* (Boston: Northeastern University Press, 1992), 8.
19. B. Harris, "Texans Take Bush Fight on the Road," *Los Angeles Times*, July 28, 2000, A16.
20. A. Ayres, ed., *The Wisdom of Martin Luther King, Jr.* (New York: Penguin Books, 1993).
21. M. Z. Muhammad, "Students Are the Vanguard of Million Woman March," *Black Collegian* 28 (February 1998): 10; "Million Man March Draws More Than 1 Million Black Men to Nation's Capital," *Jet*, October 30, 1995, 4.
22. R. M. Berko, A. D. Wolvin, and D. R. Wolvin, *Communicating: A Social and Career Focus*, 3rd ed. (Boston: Houghton Mifflin, 1985), 42.
23. J. Stewart, *Bridges, Not Walls*, 7th ed. (New York: McGraw-Hill, 1999), 16.
24. M. W. Lustig, and J. Koester, *Intercultural Competence: Interpersonal Communication across Cultures* (New York: HarperCollins, 1993), 31.
25. J. H. Bodley, "An Anthropological Perspective," *What Is Culture?* 1994, http://www.wsu.edu:8001/vcwsh/commons/topics/culture/culture-definitions/bodley-text.html.
26. U.S. Senate, *Hearing to Receive Testimony on S. 1367, S. 1617, S. 1670, S. 2020, S. 2478, and S. 2485: Before the Subcommittee on National Parks, Historic Preservation, and Recreation of the Senate Energy Committee*, testimony of Arnoldo Ramos, 106th Cong., 2nd Sess., May 11, 2000, http://energy.senate.gov/hearings/national_parks/5_11Cats&Dogs/Ramos.htm (accessed June 28, 2000).
27. Forum on Child and Family Statistics, *America's Children: Key Indicators of Well-Being*, 2005, http://www.childstats.gov/americaschildren/2002spe1.asp.
28. "The Myth of the Melting Pot," Washingtonpost.com, 1998, http://www.washingtonpost.com/wp-srv/national/longterm/meltingpot/maps.htm (accessed July 12, 2000).
29. H. El Nasser, "Hispanics Move up List of Nation's Home Buyers," *USA Today*, May 11, 2006, http://www.usatoday.com/news/nation/2006-05-10-hispanic-homeowners_x.htm?POE = NEWISVA.
30. Lustig and Koester, *Intercultural Competence*, 11.
31. "More Marches, a Growing Backlash," *Economist*, May 6, 2006, 30.

32. H. Maurer, "A Fracas over Immigration," *Business Week*, April 10, 2006, 28.
33. Letters to the Editor. "Immigration Divides the Nation," *Time*, May 1, 2006, 8.
34. Comtex News Network, "National Press Conference Held: No Human Being Is Illegal; AFSC Calls for Substantive Immigration Policy Solutions." *US Newswire*, May 24, 2006.
35. J. Bell, *Evaluating Psychological Information: Sharpening Your Critical Thinking Skills*, 2nd ed., 72, cited in *Critical Thinking as Described by Psychologists*, J. Bell, December 15, 1996, http://academic.pg.cc.md.us/~wpeirce/MCCCTR/bell1.html (accessed June 12, 2006).
36. C. Morris, *Psychology*, 1993, xv–xvi, cited in *Critical Thinking as Described by Psychologists*, J. Bell, December 15, 1996, http://academic.pg.cc.md.us/~wpeirce/MCCCTR/bell1.html (accessed June 12, 2006).
37. P. Bizzell, and B. Herzberg, *The Rhetorical Tradition* (Boston: Bedford/St. Martin's, 1990), 35.
38. Gallup Poll, November 17–20, 2005, www.pollingreport.com/values.htm.

Chapter 2

1. L. G. Davis, *I Have a Dream . . . The Life and Times of Martin Luther King, Jr.* (Westport, Ct.: Greenwood Press, 1973).
2. A. Ayres, ed., *The Wisdom of Martin Luther King, Jr.* (New York: Penguin Books, 1993).
3. Davis, *I Have a Dream*, 137.
4. K. D. Miller, and E. M. Lewis, "Touchstones, Authorities, and Marian Anderson: The Making of 'I Have a Dream,'" in *The Making of Martin Luther King and the Civil Rights Movement*, ed. B. Ward and T. Badger (New York: New York University Press, 1996), 151.
5. Ayres, *The Wisdom of Martin Luther King, Jr.*, 62–63.
6. E. Rothstein, "A Resonance That Shaped a Vision of Freedom," *New York Times*, June 29, 2006, B7.
7. J. F. Wilson, and C. C. Arnold, *Public Speaking as a Liberal Art*, 3rd ed. (Boston: Allyn and Bacon, 1974), 337.
8. P. Bizzell, and B. Herzberg, *The Rhetorical Tradition* (Boston: Bedford/St. Martin's, 1990), 32, 310.
9. N. H. Rogers, "Good Public Speaking," June 13, 2006, http://www.eep.com/merchant/newsite/samples/pe/pe1201.htm.
10. J. Ayres, "Comparing Self-Constructed Visualization Scripts with Guided Visualization," *Communication Reports* 8 (1995): 193–99.

11. C. R. Sawyer, and R. R. Behnke, "State Anxiety Patterns for Public Speaking and the Behavior Inhibition System," *Communication Reports* 12 (1999): 34.

Chapter 3

1. United States National Park Service, "History Continued," *Statue of Liberty National Monument*, August 14, 2006, http://www.nps.gov/stli/historyculture/history-continued.htm (accessed March 14, 2007).

Chapter 4

1. J. Stewart, *Bridges, Not Walls*, 4th ed. (New York: Random House, 1986), 181.
2. Study by TCC Consulting (San Francisco, Calif.), undertaken between 1987 and 1997.

Chapter 5

1. For research that supports Minh's claim, see "Women See Fuel Economy as Major Factor in Car Buying Decision," *United Business Media Newswire*, November 15, 2005, http://www.prnewswire.com/news/index_mail.shtml?ACCT=104&STORY=/www/story/11-15-2005/0004216674&EDATE (accessed March 15, 2007).
2. This statistic first emerged from two of Alfred Kinsey's studies: *Sexual Behavior in the Human Male* (1948) and *Sexual Behavior in the Human Female* (1953). Although there has been some controversy over Kinsey's methodology, subsequent studies have indicated that a significant proportion of the population self-identifies as GLBT or as having participated in homosexual activity. See, for example, Australian Research Centre in Sex, Health and Society, *Sex in Australia: The Australian Study of Health and Relationships*, published as the *Australian and New Zealand Journal of Public Health* 27.2 (April 2003); and C. F. Turner, L. Ku, S. M. Rogers, L. D. Lindberg, J. H. Pleck, and F. L. Sonenstein, "Adolescent Sexual Behavior, Drug Use, and Violence: Increased Reporting with Computer Survey Technology," *Science* 280 (1998): 867–73.
3. There is a wide range of literature on the complicated and controversial subject of the relationship between Pope Pius XII, the Catholic Church, and the Holocaust. For an overview of the subject, see Jose M. Sanchez, *Pius XII and the Holocaust: Understanding the Controversy* (Washington, D.C.: Catholic University Press, 2002).

4. For more on this speech, go to http://www.americanrhetoric.com/speeches/tedkennedytruth&tolerance.htm.

Chapter 6

1. P. Russell, *How to Mind Map*, http://www.peterussell.com/Mindmaps/HowTo.html (accessed April 28, 2006).
2. S. Boyley, *Mind Mapping*, 1998, http://www.nlpmind.com/mind_mapping.htm.
3. J. F. Wilson, and C. C. Arnold, *Public Speaking as a Liberal Art*, 3rd ed. (Boston: Allyn and Bacon, 1974), 70–71.

Chapter 7

1. R. D. Rieke, and M. O. Sillars, *Argumentation and Critical Decision Making*, 5th ed. (New York: Addison Wesley Longman, 2001), 136.
2. J. C. Reinard, *Foundations of Argument* (Dubuque, Ia.: Wm. C. Brown, 1991), 113.
3. Reinard, *Foundations of Argument*, 115.
4. N. Pastore, and M. W. Horowitz, "The Influence of Attributed Motive on the Acceptance of a Statement," *Journal of Abnormal and Social Psychology* 51 (1955): 331–32.
5. Pew Internet and American Life Project, *The Internet Goes to College: How Students Are Living in the Future with Today's Technology*, September 15, 2002, http://www.pewinternet.org/PPF/r/71/report_display.asp, 2–3.
6. P. Lyman, and H. Varian, "How Much Information?" 2003, http://www.sims.berkeley.edu:8000/research/projects/how-much-info-2003/.
7. M. J. Metzger, A. J. Flanagin, and L. Zwarun, "College Student Web Use, Perceptions of Information Credibility, and Verification Behavior," *Computers and Education* 41.3 (November 2003): 271–90.
8. ICANN, "Top Level Domains," December 16, 2003, http://www.icann.org/+lds.
9. R. Berkman, "Internet Searching Is Not Always What It Seems," *Chronicle of Higher Education* 46 (July 28, 2000): B9.
10. The Virtual Chase, "How to Evaluate Information—Checklist," March 6, 2006, http://www.virtualchase.com/quality/checklist.
11. D. Sullivan, "How Search Engines Work," *Search Engine Watch*, October 14, 2002, http://searchenginewatch.com/webmasters/article.php/2168031.

12. D. Sullivan, "How Search Engines Rank Web Pages," *Search Engine Watch*, July 31, 2003, http://searchenginewatch.com/webmasters/article.php/2167961.
13. University of California, Berkeley, Library, "Meta-Search Engines," *Finding Information on the Internet: A Tutorial*, August 23, 2005, http://www.lib.berkeley.edu/TeachingLib/Guides/Internet/MetaSearch.html.
14. J. Tanaka, "The Perfect Search: The Web Is Growing by Millions of Pages Every Year," *Newsweek*, September 27, 1999, 71.
15. University of California, Berkeley, "How Much Information?" 2000, http://www2.sims.berkeley.edu/research/projects/.
16. A. Clyde, "The Invisible Web," *Teacher Librarian* 29 (April 2002): 47.
17. R. Lackie, "The Evolving 'Invisible Web': Tried-and-True Methods and New Developments for Locating the Web's Hidden Content," *College and Undergraduate Libraries* 10.2 (2003): 65, 69.

Chapter 8

1. Cambridge University Press, *Cambridge Dictionaries Online*, 2006, http://dictionary.cambridge.org (accessed January 31, 2007).
2. M. Boyce, *Zoroastrians: Their Religious Beliefs and Practices* (London: Routledge, 1979), 2.
3. Boyce, *Zoroastrians*, 2.
4. Ontario Consultants on Religious Tolerance, *Zoroastrianism*, March 24, 2005, http://www.religioustolerance.org/zoroastr.htm.
5. National Association of College Stores, *FAQ on College Textbooks*, April 2006, http://www.nacs.org/common/research/faq_textbooks.pdf.
6. J. Reinard, *Foundations of Argument* (Dubuque, Ia.: Brown, 1991), 111.
7. W. R. Fisher, *Human Communication as Narration: Toward a Philosophy of Reason, Value, and Action* (Columbia: University of South Carolina Press, 1987).
8. S. Hymon, "About Goldfishcam," March 15, 2006, http://www.latimes.com/news/local/la-031506fishcam_lat,0.1619074.
9. J. Barrett, "Campaigning for a Healthier America," May 10, 2005, http://www.msnbc.msn.comid/7752179/site/newsweek; M. Tanneeru, "Obesity: A Looming National Threat?" March 24, 2006, http://www.cnn.com/2006/HEALTH/DIET.FITNESS/03/24/hb.obesity.epidemic/index.html.
10. K. E. Rowan, "A New Pedagogy for Explanatory Public Speaking: Why Arrangement Should Not Substitute for Invention," *Communication Education* 44 (July 1995): 245.

11. M. Walton, "Jellyfish Lures Dinner with Flashing Red Light," *Science & Space*, CNN.com, July 7, 2005, http://www.cnn.com/2005/TECH/science/07/07/redlightlure/index.html.
12. R. M. Felder, and B. A. Soloman, "Learning Styles and Strategies," http://www.ncsu.edu/felder-public/ILSdir/styles.htm (accessed April 17, 2006).
13. Felder and Soloman, "Learning Styles and Strategies."
14. R. M. Felder, and L. K. Silverman, "Learning and Teaching Styles in Engineering Education," *Engineering Education* 78.7 (1988): 677.

Chapter 9

1. J. C. McCroskey, *An Introduction to Rhetorical Communication*, 5th ed. (Englewood Cliffs, N.J.: Prentice-Hall, 1986), 185.
2. J. C. McCroskey, "The Effects of Disorganization and Nonfluency on Attitude Change and Source Credibility," *Speech Monographs* 36 (March 1969): 13–21; H. Sharp, Jr., and T. McClung, "Effect of Organization on the Speaker's Ethos," *Speech Monographs* 33 (June 1966): 182–83.
3. L. M. Simons, "Inside Bollywood," *Smithsonian* 31 (January 2001): 50.
4. L. M. Simons, "Inside Bollywood," 55.
5. L. M. Simons, "Inside Bollywood," 49.
6. L. M. Simons, "Inside Bollywood," 52.

Chapter 10

1. P. Bizzell, and B. Herzberg, *The Rhetorical Tradition* (New York: St. Martin's Press, 1990), 429.
2. K. Kohrs Campbell, *The Rhetorical Act,* 2nd ed. (Belmont, Calif.: Wadsworth, 1996), 264–65.
3. V. Havel, "Playwright-Dissident Vaclav Havel Assumes the Presidency of Czechoslovakia," in *Lend Me Your Ears: Great Speeches in History*, ed. W. Safire (New York: Norton, 1992), 629–34.
4. A. Richards, "Keynote Address to the Democratic National Convention," in *Great Speeches for Criticism and Analysis*, ed. R. Cook and L. Rohler (Greenwood, Ind.: Educational Video Group, 2001), 79.
5. J. Stewart, *BrainyQuote*, 2007, http://www.brainyquote.com/quotes/authors/j/jon_stewart.html.
6. J. Byrne, L. Kurdgalashvili, D. Poponi, and A. Barnett, "The Potential of Solar Electric Power for Meeting Future US Energy Needs: A Comparison

of Projections of Solar Electric Energy Generation and Arctic National Wildlife Refuge Oil Production," *Energy Policy* 32 (2004): 289, 295.

7. R. Clark, *Einstein: The Life and Times* (London: Hodder and Stoughton, 1973), 26.

Chapter 12

1. G. Lakoff, and M. Johnson, *Metaphors We Live By* (Chicago: University of Chicago Press, 1980), 5.
2. C. R. Jorgensen-Earp, and A. Q. Staton, "Student Metaphors for the College Freshman Experience," *Communication Education* 42 (1993): 125.
3. J. L. Stringer, and R. Hopper, "Generic *He* in Conversation?" *Quarterly Journal of Speech* 84 (1998): 209–21.
4. D. Cameron, *Feminism and Linguistic Theory* (New York: St. Martin's Press, 1985), 68.

Chapter 13

1. K. Menzell, and L. Carrell, "The Relationship between Preparation and Performance in Public Speaking," *Communication Education* 43 (1994): 19–26.
2. J. S. Tuman, and Reverend Paul Levine, Personal Communication, St. Francis Episcopalian Church, Turlock, Calif., in 1976.
3. V. Manusov, "Perceiving Nonverbal Messages: Effects of Immediacy and Encoded Intent on Receiver Judgments," *Western Journal of Speech Communication* 55 (1991): 236.
4. J. K. Burgoon, and B. A. LePoire, "Nonverbal Cues and Interpersonal Judgments: Participant and Observer Perceptions of Intimacy, Dominance, Composure, and Formality," *Communication Monographs* 66 (1999): 107.
5. Much of the original research on proxemics was pioneered by anthropologist Edward T. Hall: E. T. Hall, *The Hidden Dimensions* (New York: Doubleday, 1966). See also M. L. Patterson, "Spatial Factors in Social Interactions," *Human Relations* 21 (1968): 351–61.
6. Patterson, "Spatial Factors in Social Interactions," 351–61.
7. J. K. Burgoon, D. Buller, and M. deTurck, "Relational Messages Associated with Nonverbal Behaviors," *Human Communication Research* 10.3 (1984): 351–78.

8. E. T. Hall, *Hidden Differences: Doing Business with the Japanese* (New York: Doubleday, 1987).
9. L. J. Smith, and L. Malandro, "Personal Appearance Factors Which Influence Perceptions of Credibility and Approachability of Men and Women," in *The Nonverbal Communication Reader*, ed. J. A. Devito and M. L. Hecht (Prospect Heights, Ill.: Waveland Press, 1990), 163.

Chapter 14

1. E. Bohn, and D. Jabusch, "The Effect of Four Methods of Instruction on the Use of Visual Aids in Speeches," *Western Journal of Communication* 42.3 (1982): 253–65.
2. H. E. Nelson, and A. W. Vandermeer, "Varied Sound Tracks on Animated Film," *Speech Monographs* 20 (1953): 261–67.
3. S. Jobs, Keynote (address presented at the annual Macworld Conference and Expo, San Francisco, January 9, 2007). Jobs spoke to a friendly audience of Apple enthusiasts and a neutral but receptive audience of industry analysts and media representatives at this conference.

Chapter 15

1. D. Russakoff, "Building a Career Path Where There Was Just a Dead End," *Washington Post*, February 26, 2007, A1.
2. D. M. Fraleigh, and J. S. Tuman, *Freedom of Speech in the Marketplace of Ideas* (New York: St. Martin's Press, 1997).
3. J. S. Tuman, *Communicating Terror: The Rhetorical Dimensions of Terrorism* (Los Angeles: Sage Publishing, 2004).
4. K. E. Rowan, "A New Pedagogy for Explanatory Public Speaking: Why Arrangement Should Not Substitute for Invention," *Communication Education* 44 (July 1995): 236–50.

Chapter 16

1. Aristotle, *On Rhetoric*, trans. G. A. Kennedy (New York: Oxford University Press, 1991), 1355.
2. M. Sherif, and C. I. Hovland, *Social Judgment, Assimilation, and Contrast Effects in Communication and Attitude Change* (New Haven: Yale University Press, 1961), 195–96.
3. Sherif and Hovland, *Social Judgment*, 195–96.

4. D. K. O'Keefe, *Persuasion: Theory and Research* (Newbury, Park, Calif.: Sage, 1990), 36–37.
5. R. E. Petty, and J. T. Cacioppo, *Communication and Persuasion: Central and Peripheral Routes to Attitude Change* (New York: Springer-Verlag, 1986).
6. A. H. Maslow, "A Theory of Human Motivation," *Psychological Review* 50 (1943): 370–96.
7. V. Packard, *The Hidden Persuaders* (New York: Pocket Books, 1964).
8. M. Rokeach, *Understanding Human Values* (New York: Free Press, 1979), 2.
9. J. S. Tuman, "Getting to First Base: Prima Facie Arguments for Propositions of Value," *Journal of the American Forensic Association* 24 (Fall 1987): 86.
10. M. Rokeach, *Beliefs, Attitudes, and Values: A Theory of Organization and Change* (San Francisco: Jossey-Bass, 1968).
11. R. D. Rieke, and M. O. Sillars, *Argumentation and Critical Decision Making*, 5th ed. (New York: Addison Wesley Longman, 2001), 207.
12. For an analysis of how this argument and other strategies may influence a change in audience values, see N. Rescher, "The Study of Value Change," *Journal of Value Inquiry* 1 (1967): 12–23.
13. M. Fishbein, and I. Ajzen, *Belief, Attitude, Intention, and Behavior: An Introduction to Theory and Research* (Reading, Mass.: Addison-Wesley, 1975).
14. K. K. Reardon, *Persuasion in Practice* (Newbury Park, Calif.: Sage, 1991).
15. M. Allen, "Comparing the Persuasive Effectiveness: One- and Two-Sided Message," in *Persuasion: Advances through Meta-Analysis*, ed. M. Allen and R. W. Preiss (Cresskill, N.J.: Hampton Press, 1998), 96.
16. M. Rokeach, *Beliefs, Attitudes, and Values*, 3.
17. R. Hamill, T. Wilson, and R. Nesbit, "Insensitivity to Sample Bias: Generalizing from Atypical Cases," *Journal of Personality and Social Psychology* 39 (1980): 578–89.
18. A. Monroe, *Principles and Types of Speech* (New York: Scott, Foresman, 1935).
19. R. E. McKerrow, et. al., *Principles and Types of Public Speaking*, 16th ed. (Boston: Pearson Education, Inc., 2007), 168.

Chapter 17

1. J. C. Reinard, *Foundations of Argument* (Dubuque, Ia.: William C. Brown, 1991), 353–54.
2. Aristotle, *On Rhetoric*, trans. G. A. Kennedy (New York: Oxford University Press, 1991), 1378a.

3. J. C. McCroskey, and J. J. Teven, "Goodwill: A Reexamination of the Construct and Its Measurement," *Communication Monographs* 66.1 (1999): 92.
4. Cable News Network, "Vice President Gore on CNN's *Late Edition*," (transcript), March 9, 1999, http://www.cnn.com/ALLPOLITICS/stories/1999/03/09/president.2000/transcript.gore.
5. T. Craig, and M. D. Shear, "Allen Quip Provokes Outrage, Apology," *Washington Post*, August 15, 2006, A1.
6. Craig and Shear, "Allen Quip Provokes Outrage, Apology," A1.
7. K. Parker, "Allen's 'Macaca' Moment," *Louisville Courier Journal*, August 23, 2006, http://www.courierjournal.com/apps/pbcs.dll/article?AID = /20060823/OPINION04/60822040.
8. H. Flesher, J. Ilardo, and J. Demoretcky, "The Influence of Field Dependence, Speaker Credibility Set, and Message Documentation on Evaluations of Speaker and Message Credibility," *Southern Communication Speech Journal* 34 (Summer 1974): 400.
9. J. C. McCroskey, "A Summary of Experimental Research on the Effects of Evidence in Persuasive Communication," *Quarterly Journal of Speech* 55 (April 1969): 172.
10. McCroskey, "A Summary of Experimental Research," 175.
11. D. J. DeNoon, "Drink More Diet Soda, Gain More Weight?" June 13, 2005, http://www.webmd.com/content/article/107/108476.htm#.
12. R. E. Nisbett, and L. Ross, *Human Interference: Strategies and Shortcomings of Social Judgment* (Englewood Cliffs, N.J.: Prentice-Hall, 1980).
13. Canadian Broadcasting Corporation, "Caribou Comeback," November 30, 2002, http://archives.cbc.ca/IDC-1-75-1391-8983/science_technology/endangered_species/.
14. J. Doyle, "Extraordinary Comeback of the Peregrine Falcon: Predators to Come off Endangered List," June 10, 1998, http://www.sfgate.com/cgi-bin/article.cgi?file = /chronicle/archive/1998/06/10/MN75129.DTL.
15. J. L. Eliot, "Our Majestic National Bird Is Flying High over Much of Its Former Range and May Soon Be off the Endangered List," *National Geographic*, June 2002, http://magma.nationalgeographic.com/ngm/0207/feature2/.
16. C. Rice, "Remarks at the 104th National Convention of the VFW," August 25, 2003, http://www.whitehouse.gov/news/releases/2003/08/20030825-1.html.
17. Associated Press, "Hagel Says Iraq War Looking More Like Vietnam," August 21, 2005, http://www.usatoday.com/news/washington/2005-08-21-hageliraq_x.htm.

18. S. Callahan, "The Role of Emotion in Ethical Decision Making," *Hastings Center Report* 18.3 (1988): 9.
19. G. Anders, *Health against Wealth: HMOs and the Breakdown of Medical Trust* (Boston: Houghton Mifflin, 1996), 108–9.
20. K. Witte, and K. Morrison, "Examining the Influence of Trait Anxiety/Repression-Sensitization on Individuals' Reactions to Fear Appeals," *Western Journal of Communication* 64 (Winter 2000): 1.
21. P. A. Mongeau, "Another Look at Fear-Arousing Persuasive Appeals," in *Persuasion: Advances through Meta-Analysis*, ed. M. Allen and R. W. Preiss (Cresskill, N.J.: Hampton Press, 1998), 66.
22. Mongeau, "Another Look at Fear-Arousing Persuasive Appeals," 66.

Chapter 18

1. Aristotle, *On Rhetoric*, trans. G. A. Kennedy (New York: Oxford University Press, 1991), 1358a-b.
2. Aristotle, *On Rhetoric*, 7, 47.

Chapter 19

1. B. R. Patton, and K. Giffen, *Decision-Making Group Interaction*, 2nd ed. (New York: Harper & Row, 1978), 2.
2. I. Janis, *Victims of Groupthink* (Boston: Houghton Mifflin, 1972).
3. K. D. Benne, and P. Sheats, "Functional Roles of Group Members," *Journal of Social Issues* 1.4 (1948): 41, 49.
4. The reflective-thinking method was developed from the ideas of John Dewey, an American philosopher who was interested in problem solving.

GLOSSARY

abstract A summary of an article's contents, often included in indexes.

abstract words Generic terms that can be ambiguous or confusing for an audience. To say "I have a pet" is less informative than saying "I have a gray tabby cat."

ad populum fallacy (bandwagoning) Often found in advertising and marketing, a misuse of logic that deceives an audience by implying that, because a large number of people are engaging in an activity, everyone should engage in the activity. Bandwagoning is unethical if speakers fail to give support for their proclamations.

age A demographic consideration that affects an audience's response to and understanding of a speaker's message. For example, avoiding popular culture references that are too old or too young for an audience is a good way to take age into consideration.

agenda-driven listening The failure of a speaker to adequately entertain an audience's questions or comments for fear of straying too far from his or her speech points.

analogy A comparison based on similarities between two phenomena—one that is familiar to an audience and one that is less familiar—that helps listeners use their existing knowledge to absorb new information.

appeal to tradition fallacy Arguing that a practice or policy is good because people have followed it for a long time.

argumentative listening The act of listening to only part of a question or comment. Usually done out of anger or defensiveness.

arrangement One of the five classical canons of rhetoric, arrangement is the effective organization of ideas to present them to an audience. Arrangement is dictated by topic, purpose, and audience analysis.

articulation Speaking with crispness or clarity so that listeners can distinguish separate words as well as separate syllables and vowel or consonant sounds within words.

atlas A reference work that provides maps, charts, and tables relating to different geographic regions.

attention-getter Material intended to capture an audience's interest in the introduction of a speech. Techniques a speaker can use to get an audience's attention include telling a story or anecdote, offering a provocative statement, building suspense, letting listeners know the speaker is one of them, using humor, asking a rhetorical question, or providing a quotation.

audience analysis The process of learning about an audience's interests and background in order to create and/or adapt a speech to their wants and needs.

audience size The number of people who will be present for a speech.

audiovisual aid Something that an audience can see or hear that helps them better understand a speaker's message by supporting the speaker's main points or subpoints. Examples include drawings, photographs, charts, maps, sound recordings, video, and PowerPoint or slide presentations.

bandwagon fallacy See **ad populum fallacy (bandwagoning)**.

bar graph A type of graph consisting of parallel bars of varying height or length that compares several pieces of information.

biased language Word choice that suggests prejudice or preconceptions about other people, usually referring to their race, ethnicity, gender, sexuality, religion, or mental or physical ability.

bibliographic information Details about a researched source, including the title, author, publication date, and page numbers or URL.

bibliography An alphabetized list of the sources a speaker cited in his or her speech; usually written in accordance with a particular style of documentation, such as the American Psychological Association (APA) style or the Modern Language Association (MLA) style.

body (of speech) The section of a speech that falls between the introduction and conclusion and contains the main part of the speech. This includes all major and supporting points.

body clock (chronemics) The time of day or day of the week when an audience will be listening to a presentation. An audience is more prone to distraction at certain times of the day, such as lunchtime, and certain days of the week, such as Friday.

boomerang effect The act of pushing an audience more firmly into their previously held beliefs as a result of the speaker choosing a position that falls on the extreme end of an audience's latitude of rejection (see **latitude of rejection**).

brainstorming A strategy for generating topic ideas in which a potential speaker lists every idea that comes to mind—without evaluating its merits—in order to develop a sizable list of ideas quickly.

brief examples Single-sentence or otherwise short points of different instances that support or illustrate a more general claim.

categorical pattern (topical pattern) An all-purpose speech organization pattern in which each main point emphasizes one of the most important aspects of the speaker's topic; often used if a speaker's topic doesn't easily conform to a spatial, temporal, causal, comparison, problem-cause-solution, criteria-application, or narrative pattern.

causal pattern A speech organization pattern that explains cause-and-effect relationships in which each main point is either an event that leads to a situation or a link in a chain of events between a catalyst and a final outcome.

causal reasoning Arguing that one event has caused another.

channel The medium through which a source delivers a message, such as projecting one's voice, using a microphone, broadcasting on the airwaves, or streaming on the Internet.

chart A graphic representation that summarizes information and ideas. Common types of charts include verbal charts, pie charts, and flowcharts.

clincher Something that leaves a lasting impression of a speech in the listeners' minds, usually used as the second element in a speech conclusion. To go out with a bang, a speaker can extend a story or anecdote he or she used at the start of the speech, relay a new story or anecdote, end with a striking phrase or sentence, or conclude with an emotional message.

common ground Beliefs, values, and experiences a speaker shares with an audience. A speaker seeks to establish common ground with an audience, whether verbally or nonverbally, so that listeners will be more receptive to his or her message.

common knowledge Widely known information that can be found in many sources and that does not require citation.

comparison pattern A speech organization pattern that discusses the similarities and differences between two events, objects, or situations; especially useful when comparing a new subject to one that the audience is familiar with.

comparison reasoning Arguing that two instances are similar enough that what is true for one is likely to be true for the other. If a speaker argues that U.S. residents will eventually accept mandatory health insurance because they accepted mandatory car insurance, the speaker would be using comparison reasoning.

competence Knowledge and experience in a subject.

conclusion The final part of a speech in which the speaker summarizes the main points and leaves the audience with a clincher, such as a vivid quote, image, or call to action.

concrete words Specific words or phrases that suggest exactly what a speaker means. For example, to say a man was wearing a "dark blue suit" is more specific than saying he was wearing "clothes."

connotative meaning An association that comes to mind when a person hears a word. For example, saying "he tackled the project" brings to mind competitive sports and is a more vivid way to convey competence and enthusiasm than saying "he was excited to start the project and knew he could do a good job."

constructive criticism Thoughtful and tactful suggestions for improvement that take into account what a speaker is trying to accomplish. These kinds of suggestions allow speakers to build upon their feedback and make improvements for future presentations.

context The occasion, surrounding environment, and situation in which a speaker gives a presentation.

coordination A feature of a well-organized speech in which certain points share the same level of significance. For example, each main point is coordinate with the other main points, each subpoint with the other subpoints, and each sub-subpoint with the other sub-subpoints.

core beliefs Long- and closely held viewpoints that are particularly immune to persuasion.

credibility An audience's perception that a speaker is well prepared and qualified to speak on his or her topic. Trustworthiness, dynamism, and goodwill are also elements of a speaker's credibility. (See also **ethos**.)

criteria-application pattern A speech organization pattern that proposes standards for making a judgment about a topic, then applies those standards to a related topic. For example, if a speaker were arguing that a city should budget money to renovate a specific crumbling, historic neighborhood, the speaker would first define the criteria for a "historic neighborhood," then would discuss how his or her city's specific neighborhood is historic and, thus, worth renovating.

critical thinking The analysis and evaluation of others' ideas, as well as one's own assumptions, based on reliability, truth, and accuracy.

culturally relative The recognition that ideas about ethical behavior sometimes differ from society to society.

culture The values, traditions, and rules for living that are passed from generation to generation. Culture is learned, not innate, and pervades all aspects of a person's life.

decode To interpret a message by making sense of a source's verbal and nonverbal symbols. Decoding is performed by a receiver.

defeated listening Pretending to understand a message while actually being overwhelmed by or uninterested in the subject matter.

definition A technique used in informative speeches that explains the essence, meaning, purpose, or identity of something.

delivery The speaker's varied and appropriate use of vocal and nonverbal elements such as voice, eye contact, and gestures while presenting a speech.

delivery reminders Special instructions speakers include within a speaking outline to remind themselves about such things as body language, pauses, and stressing key points.

demographics Audience members' characteristics, including, but not limited to, age, gender, sexual orientation, race, ethnicity, religious orientation, educational background, and political affiliation.

demonstration A technique used in informative speeches involving both physical modeling and verbal elements with the goal of teaching an audience how a process or set of guidelines works.

denotative meaning The exact, literal dictionary definition of a word.

description A technique of informative speeches that uses words to paint a mental picture for audience members so that they can close their eyes and imagine what the speaker is saying.

designated leader A person chosen by an authority figure to help a group quickly move forward with its mission.

diction See **word choice (diction)**.

dictionary A reference work that offers definitions, pronunciation guides, and sometimes etymologies for words.

dictionary definition A type of support that provides the meaning of a term as presented in a general or specialized dictionary.

digital projector A specialized machine that enables a speaker to show an electronic presentation on a screen or blank wall.

disposition An audience's likely attitude toward a subject. In most cases, an audience can be divided into three groups: hostile, sympathetic, and neutral.

drawing A visual depiction that enables a speaker to emphasize or de-emphasize certain details about a topic through techniques such as labeling parts of the main picture.

educational (and informational) background An audience's level of formal schooling or life experience that determines what they're likely to know and not know.

emergent leader One who comes to be recognized as a leader by a group's members over time.

encode To choose verbal or nonverbal symbols to organize and deliver one's message.

encyclopedia A reference work that offers relatively brief entries providing background information on a wide range of alphabetized topics.

epideictic Speaking that praises or blames.

ethical absolutism The adoption of a code of behavior to which a person adheres in all circumstances.

ethical audience An audience that exhibits courtesy, open-mindedness, and a willingness to hold the speaker accountable for his or her statements.

ethical speech Speech that incorporates ethical decision making, follows guidelines to tell the truth, and avoids misleading the audience.

ethics A set of beliefs shared by a group about what behaviors are correct or incorrect.

ethnicity Cultural background that is usually associated with shared religion, national origin, and language.

ethos (credibility) Inspiring belief in an audience by conveying a sense of the speaker's knowledge, honesty, trustworthiness, experience, authority, and/or wisdom.

etymological definition A type of support that explains the linguistic origin of a term or word—useful when the origin is interesting or will help the audience understand the word.

evidence Information gathered from credible research sources that helps a speaker support his or her claims.

example reasoning Presenting specific instances to support a general claim in the hope that the cited instances will be sufficient to convince listeners that the claim is reasonable or true.

examples Samples or instances that support or illustrate a general claim.

expert definition A type of support that provides the meaning of a term as presented by a person who is a credible source of information on a particular topic.

expertise The possession of knowledge necessary to offer reliable facts or opinions about the topic in question.

expert testimony A type of support consisting of statements made by credible sources who have professional or other in-depth knowledge of a topic.

explanation A technique used in informative speeches that provides an analysis of something for the purposes of clarity and specificity by tracing a line of reasoning or a series of causal connections between events.

extemporaneous delivery The ability, enabled by practice, to deliver a speech smoothly and confidently from a speaking outline without reading from it.

extended examples Detailed narratives that serve as samples or instances that support or illustrate a general claim.

eye contact The act of a speaker and the audience members of looking directly into each other's eyes as they are speaking or listening.

fact claim A statement asserting that something is true or false, such as "Animal experimentation is necessary for human survival."

fallacious reasoning A type of faulty, and thus unsound, reasoning in which the link between a claim and its supporting material is weak.

false dilemma fallacy A speaker incorrectly claiming that there are only two possible choices to solve a problem, that one of them is wrong, and that the audience should therefore support the speaker's solution. You can usually detect this fallacy if you know there are more than two choices.

false inference Deceiving an audience by presenting information that leads them to assume an incorrect conclusion.

fear appeal A form of pathos in which an argument arouses fear in the minds of audience members.

feedback An audience's verbal and nonverbal responses to a source's message.

fixed-response questions Survey questions that give a respondent a set of specific answers to choose from. Examples include true/false, multiple choice, or select-all-that-apply questions.

flowchart A type of chart that demonstrates the direction of information, processes, and ideas.

forum See **location (forum)**.

full text sources The complete text of an article linked within an online periodical index.

functional definition A type of support that explains how something is used or what it does.

gender composition A demographic characteristic that considers how many men versus how many women will be in an audience.

gender-neutral terms Words that do not suggest a particular gender. For example, *stewardess* is gender-biased, but *flight attendant* is gender-neutral; likewise, *waiter* or *waitress* is gender-biased, but *server* is gender-neutral.

gender stereotype An oversimplified, often distorted view of what it means to be male or female.

gesture A hand movement used as a part of delivery that points, pantomimes, demonstrates, or calls attention to something.

goodwill Speakers wanting what is best for their audience rather than what would most benefit themselves.

graph A visual representation of the relationship between different numbers, measurements, or quantities. The two main types of graphs are line graphs and bar graphs.

groupthink The tendency of the members of a group to accept ideas and information uncritically because of strong feelings of loyalty or single-mindedness within the group.

half-truth A statement that deceives an audience by revealing part of the truth, but mixing the truth with a lie.

hasty generalization Misusing logic and deceiving an audience by asserting that a piece of evidence—one that applies to a limited number of cases—applies to all cases.

hearing Passively receiving messages without trying to interpret or understand them.

hostile audience A type of audience that opposes a speaker's message, or the speaker personally, and will probably be reluctant to accept the message.

hybrid search engine A specialized online program combining a search engine and Web directory. (See also **search engine** and **Web directory**.)

hypothetical example An imagined example or scenario that a speaker invites his or her audience to consider in order to help them follow a complicated point presented immediately afterward.

imagery Mental pictures or impressions painted with vivid language.

implied leader A person with preexisting authority or skills that make him or her likely to be recognized as a leader by a group, even if leadership has not been formally assigned.

inductive reasoning Generalizing from facts, instances, or examples and then making a claim based on that generalization. If a couple has two bad experiences in a row at the same restaurant, they might conclude that they will always have bad experiences at that restaurant.

informative purpose The rhetorical purpose that aims to educate and increase an audience's understanding and awareness of a topic.

interactive listening The process of a receiver filtering out distractions, focusing on what others have said, and communicating that he or she has paid attention.

interference (noise) External or internal phenomena that disrupt communication between a sender and a receiver. External sources include nearby loud noises, while internal sources might include wandering thoughts of the sender or receiver.

internal noise (internal distractions) Thoughts that distract a sender or receiver from processing and retaining a message.

internal preview A short list of ideas before a main point or subpoint that quickly summarizes points that will follow. Using an internal preview is akin to giving the audience an advance warning of what is to come.

internal summary A quick review of what a speaker has just said in a main point or subpoint, used to help an audience remember a particularly detailed point.

Internet A popular research tool connecting computers around the world and containing millions of Web sites and other resources of varying quality maintained by individuals, businesses, and organizations.

interruptive listening The act of interjecting questions or comments before a sender is finished speaking. Both audience members and speakers can be guilty of interruptive listening.

interview A means of gathering information—used for research or audience analysis—in which a speaker has a conversation with experts or select members of a future audience and records their responses. The interview can be conducted in many ways; for example, in person, by e-mail, or by instant messaging.

introduction Occurs at the beginning of a speech and serves several purposes, including gaining the audience's attention, establishing speaker credibility, building common ground with the audience, presenting the thesis statement, and previewing the speech's main points.

invention One of the five classical canons of rhetoric, this refers to using a variety of techniques and sources to gather and choose ideas for a speech.

invisible Web Online information, sometimes password-protected, that cannot be easily accessed using typical search engines. Search tools that specialize in finding information on the invisible Web include Complete Planet (www.aip.completeplanet.com), GoshMe (www.goshme.com), Library Spot (www.libraryspot.com), and OAIster (www.oaister.org).

jargon Specialized or technical words or phrases familiar only to people in a specific field or group.

keywords Words or terms related to a topic, including synonyms of those words. Keywords are often used in online or database searches.

latitude of acceptance The range of positions on a given issue that are acceptable to an audience.

latitude of rejection The range of positions on a given issue that are unacceptable to an audience.

lay testimony A type of support consisting of statements made by persons with no special expertise in the subject they are discussing.

legally protected speech Telling the truth or withholding information based on whether the law allows unethical speech. If you (unethically) use legal protection as your guiding principle for speaking, you can technically stay within the bounds of what is lawful but still speak unethically.

line graph A type of graph that plots lines on a pair of axes to show relationships between two elements.

listening Actively receiving and processing messages to understand their meaning and remember their content.

location (forum) The setting where a speaker delivers, and an audience listens to, a speech.

logos The sound reasoning that supports a speaker's claims and makes the argument more persuasive to an audience.

main points Key ideas that support a thesis and help an audience understand and remember what is most important about a speaker's topic; main points are supported by subpoints (see **subpoints**).

map A visual representation of geography.

marking a special occasion A rhetorical purpose that seeks to honor a person or event by entertaining, inspiring, or emotionally moving an audience.

memory (preparation) One of the five classical canons of rhetoric, memory is the process of preparing and practicing a speech to ensure confident and effective delivery. Originally, the canon memory referred to learning a speech by heart; however, in the twenty-first century, using notes and other memory aids is usually preferred.

message Verbal or nonverbal ideas that a source conveys through the communication process.

metaphors Implicit comparisons of unlike objects by identifying one object with another. For example: "Her advisor was *a fount of knowledge.*"

metasearch engine A type of search engine that searches with several different search engines at once. (See also **search engine**.)

mind mapping A strategy for generating topic ideas in which a person writes down an initial word or phrase and then surrounds it with additional words, pictures, and symbols to create an interconnected map of ideas.

mobile audience An audience that is not bound to sit or stand for the duration of a speech. Mobile audiences might be found at an exhibitor's booth or on a city sidewalk.

moderator In a panel discussion, the person who introduces the panelists and leads the discussion.

motivated sequence A persuasive organizational pattern that is structured around five main points: attention, need, satisfaction, visualization, and action.

narrative A story a speaker tells to share information and capture an audience's attention. As used in informative speeches, the story can be a personal remembrance, a humorous anecdote, or a serious account of an event that happened in someone else's life.

narrative pattern A speech organization pattern that uses a story, including characters and a plot, to support the speaker's thesis.

needs The objects an audience desires and the feelings that must be satisfied.

negative stereotypes Critical generalizations about the characteristics of a person or group that rest on the false assumption that characteristics shared by some members of the group are shared by all members of the group. For example: "If the homeless weren't a bunch of lazy drunks, they could find jobs and get off the streets."

nervous listening Talking through silences during lapses in conversation.

neutral audience A type of audience that has neither negative nor positive opinions about a speaker or message.

nonlistening Failing to pay attention to what one is hearing, and thus failing to process, understand, and retain the message.

nonverbal delivery skills Use of gestures, eye contact, and other techniques—such as physical movement, proxemics, and personal appearance—to deliver a speech.

nonverbal symbols Means of communication without using words. Examples include gestures, facial expressions, eye contact, and images.

objectivity A quality of credible sources by which they avoid bias; that is, prejudice or partisanship.

observational capacity A source's ability to witness a situation for himself or herself, thus increasing the source's reliability.

omission A form of false inference that deceives an audience by withholding important information.

open-ended questions Survey questions that invite respondents to give answers of their own choosing, rather than offering them a limited set of responses.

outline A written means of organizing a speech using sentences, phrases, or keywords. An outline includes the main ideas of a speech's introduction, body, and conclusion.

outlining Organizing the points of a speech into a structured form that lays out the sequence and hierarchy of a speaker's ideas.

panel discussion A form of group presentation in which group members engage in discourse with one another, observed by the audience.

panelists The participants in a panel discussion.

panning A form of nonverbal delivery in which a speaker looks out and surveys all audience members. As the speaker looks back and forth across the audience, he or she pauses and makes extended eye contact with an individual listener for a few moments before moving on to do the same with another.

paraphrasing Putting someone else's ideas into one's own words and giving appropriate credit to the original source.

pathos Appealing to an audience's emotions.

pausing Leaving strategic gaps of silence between the words and sentences of one's speech.

peer review The act of subjecting articles submitted to a scholarly journal to critical readings by other experts in a particular field.

periodicals Weekly, monthly, quarterly, or annual publications, including newspapers, magazines, and scholarly journals.

peripheral beliefs Viewpoints that people do not hold closely as core beliefs and that they may not have had for a long time; thus, they may be open to persuasion. (For contrast, see also **core beliefs**.)

personal appearance The impression a speaker makes on an audience through his or her clothing, jewelry, hairstyle, grooming, and other elements influencing how the speaker looks.

personal attacks (*ad hominem* attacks) Persuading an audience to dislike someone by targeting his or her character rather than the relevant issues.

persuasive purpose A rhetorical purpose that seeks to strengthen listeners' commitment, weaken listeners' commitment, or promote a particular action.

persuasive speech A speech that aims to influence audience members' beliefs, attitudes, or actions; to which end, it employs strategic discourse and calls for the audience to accept fact, value, and/or policy claims.

photograph A visual representation that is an exact depiction of a person, place, object, or event.

physical movement How much or how little a speaker moves around while giving a presentation.

pie chart Information arranged to resemble a sliced pie that helps a speaker clarify how proportions and percentages relate to one another and add up to a whole.

plagiarism Presenting another person's words or ideas as one's own.

policy claim A statement that advocates action by organizations, institutions, or members of the audience. For example: "Anyone opposed to animal experimentation should join an activist organization, such as the Humane Society, to help put a stop to this cruel and unnecessary practice."

political affiliation A person's political beliefs and positions.

post hoc fallacy Incorrectly naming the cause of one event as the event that immediately preceded it.

power wording The unethical practice of paraphrasing evidence in a way that better supports one's own claim but misrepresents a source's point of view.

precise evidence Supporting materials consisting of specific dates, places, numbers, and other facts.

presentation time The length of time a speaker has to deliver his or her speech.

preview A brief statement of the main points a speaker will be presenting in his or her speech; tells an audience what to expect and helps them visualize the structure of a speech. Sometimes also referred to as a "road map" for the speech.

prior exposure The extent to which an audience has already heard a speaker's message, which will affect an audience's interest or belief in what the speaker is saying.

problem-cause-solution pattern A speech organizational pattern that identifies a problem, explains the problem's causes, and proposes one or more solutions, which often includes asking an audience to support a policy or to take specific action.

processing Actively thinking about the meaning of the verbal and nonverbal components of a message. Processing is the first step in effective listening.

projection The act of "booming" one's voice across a speaking forum in order to reach all audience members.

pronunciation Correctness in the way one says words.

proxemics The use of space and distance between a speaker and an audience.

quotation book Reference work offering famous or notable quotations on a variety of subjects.

race Common heritage based on genetically shared physical characteristics of people in a group.

rate of delivery How quickly or slowly a person speaks while giving a presentation.

reasoning The line of thought that connects the facts a speaker presents and the conclusions he or she draws from the facts.

receiver One who processes a message to perceive its meaning.

recency A quality of credible sources that holds that, because of our rapidly changing world, newer evidence is generally more reliable than older evidence.

reference work A compilation of background information on major topic areas useful for doing introductory research or discovering a specific fact.

reflective thinking A five-step strategy for group decision making: 1) Define the problem; 2) Analyze the problem; 3) Establish the criteria for solving the problem; 4) Generate potential solutions; 5) Select the best solution.

relaxation strategies Techniques to be performed before giving a speech that help relieve muscle tension and banish negative thoughts. These strategies include deep breathing, tensing and releasing one's shoulder muscles, or engaging in an enjoyable, unrelated activity, such as watching a movie or listening to music.

religious orientation A person's set of religious beliefs that can shape his or her response to a speech.

representative examples Instances that are typical of the class they represent. For example, if a speaker is arguing that Americans are getting tired of corrupt politicians, providing representative examples would mean citing instances from across the country, rather than examples from one or two states or regions.

research The process of gathering and recording information from libraries, the Internet, and interviews to increase a speaker's credibility and understanding of a topic.

research plan A strategy for finding and keeping track of information in books, periodicals, Web sites, and other sources a speaker might use to prepare a presentation.

retention The ability to remember what one has heard. The second step in effective listening, retention is directly related to how much attention one pays during an event; the more attentive one is, the more one will remember.

reversed causality Missing the fact that the effect is actually the cause.

rhetorical purpose One of three goals of a presentation, either to inform, to persuade, or to mark a special occasion. The rhetorical purpose answers the question "why" a speaker is giving a particular speech.

rhetorical question A question that a speaker expects listeners to answer in their heads; used to capture an audience's attention and get them thinking about a speaker's topic.

scaled questions Survey questions that measure a respondent's feelings on an issue by offering a range of fixed responses, such as numbers one (lowest) to ten (highest) or a list of options including "strongly agree," "agree," "neutral," "disagree," or "strongly disagree."

search engine A specialized online program that allows users to conduct keyword searches and then provides links to relevant Web pages. Examples include Google (www.google.com), Yahoo! (www.yahoo.com), MSN (www.msn.com), and Ask (www.ask.com). Also referred to as a "spider" or "crawler."

sexist language Language with a bias for or against a given gender.

sexual orientation A demographic characteristic that considers whether audience members may be straight, gay, lesbian, bisexual, or transgendered.

shared meaning A common understanding with little confusion and few misinterpretations. Achieving shared meaning is a priority of the transactional model of communication.

signposts Words or phrases within sentences that identify the section of the speech or indicate organizational features of the speech.

sign reasoning Arguing that a fact is true because indirect indicators are consistent with that fact. For example, a speaker might argue that the United States is in a recession, supporting that claim with evidence that people are making greater use of payday loan businesses.

simile An explicit comparison of objects using the words *like* or *as*. For example: "My grandmother's lap was *as soft as a pillow*."

situational audience analysis Quick audience analysis just before or during a speech, to be conducted if the makeup or responses of an audience were unknown before the speech or are different from what the speaker expected.

situational characteristics Factors in a specific speech setting that a speaker can observe or discover before giving the speech. Examples include audience size, time, location, forum, and audience mobility.

situational ethics The belief that proper ethical behavior can be informed by a person's circumstances, especially if those circumstances are extreme or unusual.

slippery slope fallacy Arguing against a policy because one assumes (without proof) that the policy will inevitably lead to another outcome that is undesirable. For example: "If we legalize marijuana, that will be the first step toward legalization of all drugs, which would create a public health catastrophe."

small group A limited number of people (three or more) gathered for a specific purpose.

source In models of communication, a person who creates and sends a message to receivers.

spatial pattern A speech organization pattern in which each main point discusses a topic's different aspects of location or geography. If a speaker were explaining how the three largest cities within a state contribute to that state's economy, the speaker might use a spatial pattern of organization.

speaking outline A type of outline containing words or short phrases representing the speaker's key ideas and giving reminders of delivery guidelines. Also referred to as an "extemporaneous outline" or a "delivery outline."

specific purpose A concise phrase consisting of the rhetorical purpose followed by the objective of a speech. For example, the specific purpose of a speech on traveling in the Yucatan Peninsula might be "to inform my audience of the educational and recreational opportunities in addition to the health and safety hazards of traveling in the Yucatan Peninsula."

speech anxiety (stage fright) Nervousness before a speech, resulting in a variety of symptoms such as sweaty palms, dry mouth, or even nausea or hyperventilation. A speaker can manage anxiety by being prepared, practicing, being well rested, and by performing visualization and relaxation exercises.

speech critique Written or oral feedback for a presentation that identifies the presentation's main points and objectives, thoughtfully discusses strengths and weaknesses, and offers suggestions for improvement.

stationary audience An audience that will be relatively motionless while listening to a speech. Classrooms, lecture halls, and conference rooms often contain stationary audiences.

statistics Numerical data that help a speaker quantify points and help an audience understand how often a given situation occurs.

strategic discourse The process of selecting arguments that will best achieve a speaker's rhetorical purpose in an ethical manner.

straw person fallacy Substituting a real claim with a weaker claim that a speaker can more easily refute. If a mayor proposes that bike lanes be added to a city's main thoroughfares, but the city council argues that it would be prohibitively expensive to add bike lanes to every street in the city, the city council would be committing this fallacy.

style A speaker's word choice, sentence structure, and clarity.

subordination A principle of speech outlining that dictates the hierarchy in the relationship of main points and supporting materials. Each subpoint must support its corresponding main point, and each sub-subpoint must support its corresponding subpoint. On an outline, supporting points are written below and to the right of the point they support. (See also **subpoints** and **sub-subpoints**.)

subpoints Ideas gathered from brainstorming and research that explain, prove, and expand upon a speech's main points.

sub-subpoints Ideas gathered from brainstorming or research that explain, prove, and expand upon a speech's subpoints.

summary A brief review of the speech's main points; used in the conclusion of a speech to help an audience remember what they've heard.

superficial listening Pretending to pay attention while actually succumbing to internal or external distractions, such as wandering thoughts or conversation.

supporting materials (supporting points) Examples, definitions, testimony, and statistics that support or illustrate a speaker's main points.

survey A series of written questions a speaker asks others to answer in advance of the speaker's presentation.

sympathetic audience A type of audience that is already inclined to believe a speaker's message or holds the speaker in high esteem, and that will probably respond favorably to the speech.

symposium A method of group presentation in which group members take turns speaking.

taking evidence out of context A form of false inference that deceives an audience by selectively choosing from a source's data or statements and presenting them in a manner that is inconsistent with that source's beliefs or conclusions.

temporal pattern (chronological pattern) A speech organization pattern in which the speaker presents information in chronological order, from beginning to end, with each main point addressing a particular time within the chronology.

testimony A type of support consisting of statements provided by other people, the source of these statements often being researched in a library, found online, or recorded in an interview.

thesis statement A single sentence that conveys the topic and purpose of the speech. All the different parts of a speech, such as the main points and subpoints, should tie into the thesis statement. Sometimes also referred to as a "topic statement" for informative and special-occasion speeches.

tone The high and low qualities of a person's speaking voice. Moderate tonal variety is preferable to using a single tone—known as *monotone*—which is usually either low and mumbling or high-pitched and annoying.

topic The subject of a speech. Speakers should choose a topic based on their own and their audience's interests and knowledge level, as well as their ability to cover the topic during the allotted time frame.

top-level domain The designation at the end of a Web address that indicates the site sponsor's affiliation: commercial (.com), nonprofit (.org), educational (.edu), government (.gov, .uk), or other organization (.net). Based on the top-level domain alone, it cannot be determined whether an online source is credible. The credibility of the person or organization that created the site must be assessed.

transaction A communicative exchange in which all participants continuously send and receive messages.

transition A word or phrase that smoothly connects one idea or part of a speech to another.

trustworthiness The characteristic of exhibiting honesty and fairness. Oftentimes seen as one component of a speaker's ethos.

two-sided argument An argument in which the speaker acknowledges an argument against his or her thesis, then uses evidence and reasoning to refute that argument.

unprocessed note taking Writing down a speech word for word without thinking about what is being said. Unprocessed note taking hampers retention.

value claim A statement that attaches a judgment—such as deeming something good, bad, moral, or immoral—to a subject. For example: "Animal experimentation is inhumane."

values People's "core conceptions" about what is desirable for their own lives and for society. Values guide people's judgments and actions.

verbal chart Words arranged in a certain format, such as bullet points, to explain ideas, concepts, or general information.

verbal clutter Extraneous words that make a presentation hard to follow. To say "*In spite of the fact that* you disagree with me" is more verbally cluttered than "*Although* you disagree with me."

verbal fillers Words and phrases such as *you know* and *like* that a speaker uses to fill uncomfortable silences.

verbal symbols Spoken, written, or recorded words a source uses to convey a message.

verbal tics Sounds such as *um* or *ah* that speakers use when searching for a correct word or when they have lost their train of thought.

visualization A method of easing speech anxiety in which the speaker imagines himself or herself giving a relaxed, well-received speech from start to finish.

vivid language Attention-grabbing and descriptive words and phrases that appeal to the senses.

vocal delivery skills The use of one's voice to effectively deliver a speech. A speaker should consider volume, tone, rate of delivery, projection, articulation, pronunciation, and pausing.

volume How loud or soft a speaker's voice is when delivering a speech.

Web directory A searchable index of reviewed Web sites compiled by human editors and organized into categories and subcategories. Popular Web directories include the Librarians' Internet Index (www.lii.org), Academic Info (www.academicinfo.net/table.html), and Infomine (www.infomine.ucr.edu).

Web site A group of one or more "pages" of personal, commercial, nonprofit, or other information organized within the World Wide Web and hosted on the Internet.

word association A strategy for generating topic ideas in which one idea leads to another, then another, and so on, until the speaker happens upon an appropriate topic.

word choice (diction) Taking into consideration the audience, occasion, and nature of one's message when choosing the language for a speech.

working outline A type of outline containing full sentences or detailed phrases of all the main points, subpoints, and sub-subpoints in a speech. Also referred to as a "detailed outline" or "preparation outline."

worldview The "lens" through which a person sees and interprets reality. Listeners' worldviews will affect how they respond to a source's message.

World Wide Web An electronic, easily navigable global collection of text, graphics, audio, and video accessed through the Internet. A substantially more extensive source of information than any library print collection, but the credibility of the sources you find must be carefully assessed.

yearbook A reference work that is updated annually and contains statistics and other facts about social, political, and economic topics.

Credits

William Faulkner. "Speech to Accept the 1949 Nobel Prize in Literature." Excerpt from "Address upon Receiving the Nobel Prize for Literature," from *Essays, Speeches, and Public Letters*. Copyright © 1950 by The Nobel Foundation. Reprinted by permission.

Jennifer Granholm. "Remarks at the Funeral of Civil Rights Leader Rosa Parks." November 2, 2005. Reprinted with the permission of the Communications Office, Governor Jennifer Granholm.

Douglas MacArthur. "1962 Sylvanus Thayer Award Acceptance Speech." West Point, 1962. Reprinted with permission of the General Douglas MacArthur Foundation.

Her Majesty Queen Noor. "2002 Mt. Holyoke College Commencement Address." Copyright © 2002. Reprinted with permission.

Barack Obama. "Keynote Speech at the 2004 Democratic Party National Convention." Reprinted with permission.

Sue Suter. "Women with Disabilities: How to Become a Boat Rocker in Life." August 16, 1993. Reprinted with the permission of the author. This speech contains an excerpt from Stuart Wilde, "'Come to the cliff,' he said." From *The Quickening*. Copyright © 1988 by Stuart Wilde. Reprinted with the permission of Hay House, Inc., Carlsbad, CA.

INDEX